The New European Private Law

Private Law in European Context Series

VOLUME 3

Series Editors:

Martijn Hesselink
Ugo Mattei
Horatia Muir Watt

1. M. Bussani and U. Mattei (eds.): *The Common Core of European Private Law*. Essays on the Project. 2002 ISBN 90-411-1852-7
2. S. Grundmann and J. Stuyck (eds.): *An Academic Green Paper to European Contract Law*. 2002 ISBN 90-411-1853-5
3. M. W. Hesselink: *The New European Private Law*. Essays on the Future of Private Law in Europe. 2002 ISBN 90-411-1962-0

Private Law in European Context Series

The New European Private Law

Essays on the Future of Private Law in Europe

Martijn W. Hesselink

Kluwer Law International
The Hague / London / New York

A C.I.P. Catalogue record for this book is available from the Library of Congress.

ISBN 90-411-1962-0

Published by Kluwer Law International,
P.O. Box 85889, 2508 CN The Hague, The Netherlands.

Sold and distributed in North, Central and South America
by Kluwer Law International,
101 Philip Drive, Norwell, MA 02061, U.S.A.
kluwerlaw@wkap.com

In all other countries, sold and distributed
by Kluwer Law International, Distribution Centre,
P.O. Box 322, 3300 AH Dordrecht, The Netherlands.

Printed on acid-free paper

Contents

Preface

This book contains a selection of the papers which I have presented and the essays which I have published during the last five years on the new European private law. Although most of the chapters have previously been published, it makes sense to publish them together in this book. This because, first, because many of the publications have either been published by a local national publisher or in a foreign language or, alternatively, in a journal which is not readily available in most European libraries. Therefore, many of these publications have not been readily accessible for all the participants in the European private law debate and I hope that this book will render them so. Secondly, and more importantly, bringing these essays together into one publication will emphasise the unity (or at least the similarity) they share as regards the themes, ideas and approach. I will come back to this aspect in the Introduction.

I have not attempted to completely rewrite the essays and to turn them into a coherent book. Therefore, although these essays share a clear unity as regards method, themes and views (which I will further explain in the Introduction) the book also has certain characteristics (the fragmentary and the overlapping) which are typical for a collection of essays. Nevertheless, I have edited all the chapters, updated them when and where necessary, adapted them in a few cases where my views have changed, and added cross-references and an index.

The Introduction (Chapter 1) was obviously written specifically for this book. Chapter 2 is based on my inaugural lecture at the *Universiteit van Amsterdam* which I delivered on June 27th, 2001 and which was published in Dutch ('De nieuwe Europese rechtscultuur', in: M.W. Hesselink, C.E. du Perron, A.F. Salomons, *Uitgesproken Teksten*, Vossiuspers UvA, Amsterdam 2002, pp. 17-30). The present elaborated version was published in the Netherlands by Kluwer in 2001. I partly wrote this chapter as a visiting scholar at Boalt Hall, School of Law, UC Berkeley, and as a Visiting Professor at the *Université René Descartes (Paris V)*. I would like to thank John Cartwright, Edgar du Perron, Jan Jans, Peter Morris, Jacobien Rutgers, Arthur Salomons and Theo Veen for their comments. Chapter 3 was prepared as a *preadvies* for the annual meeting of the Dutch Society for Private Law (*Vereniging voor Burgerlijk Recht*) which was held in The Hague on April 26th, 2001. It was published in the Netherlands ('The Principles of European Contract Law: Some Choices Made by the Lando Commission', in: Martijn W. Hesselink, Gerard de Vries, *Principles of European Contract Law*, Deventer 2001, pp. 5-95) and on the Internet (*Global Jurist Frontiers*: Vol. 1:

No. 1, Article 4). I partly wrote it as a visiting scholar at Boalt Hall, School of Law, UC Berkeley. I would like to thank James Gordley for his inspiring conversations on the subject and Maurits Barendrecht, Hugh Beale, Arthur Hartkamp and Edgar du Perron for their comments on the paper. Chapter 4 is based on a paper which I presented in Italian at the conference *Le riforme dei codici civili europei e l'armonizzazione delle regole di diritto privato (Il codice civile Europeo, III° giornata di studio)* organised by Guido Alpa in Rome on July 14th, 2001. That paper was published in Italian ('Il codice civile olandese del 1992 - un esempio per un codice civile Europeo?', in Guido Alpa and Emilio Nicola Buccico (eds.), *La riforma dei codici in Europa e il progetto di codice civile europeo; Materiali dei seminari 2001*, Milan 2002, pp. 71-82). Chapter 5 is based on paper which I presented at the conference entitled *Communication from the Commission on European Contract Law* organised by the Society of European Contract Law on November 30th and December 1st, 2001 in Leuven, Belgium. It was published on the Internet in *Global Jurist Frontiers*: Vol. 2: No. 1, Article 3. Chapter 6 is based on a paper which I presented at the conference entitled *Diritti fondamentali e formazione del diritto privato europeo* organised by Vincenzo Zeno-Zencovich at the *Università degli studi 'Roma Tre'* on June 28th, 2002. Chapter 7 is based on my doctoral thesis entitled *De redelijkheid en billijkheid in het Europese Privaatrecht*, Deventer 1999. The main conclusions were published as 'Good Faith', in: Hartkamp et al. (eds.), *Towards a European Civil Code*, 2nd. ed., Nijmegen and The Hague, London, Boston 1998, pp. 285-310. The present text is a revised and updated version of that article. Chapter 8 is based on a paper which I prepared for the *XVI Congress of the International Academy of Comparative Law*, held on July 14th-20th, 2002, in Brisbane, Australia, in reply to the questionnaire on *La structure des systèmes juridiques* by Professor Jacques VanderLinden. It was published in Ewoud Hondius and Carla Joustra (eds.), *Netherlands Reports to the Sixteenth International Congress of Comparative Law*, Antwerp, Oxford, New York, 2002, pp. 7-23.

I would like to thank my research assistant Julia van Ooststroom for her assistance in editing this volume and Peter Morris for revising the English.

Amsterdam, July 2002

1
Introduction

I. Culture, Principles, Models, Politics, Rights, Concepts, and Structure

HUNDREDS OF legal scholars across Europe are currently involved in the academic debate on the future of European private law. Some of the main issues in that debate relate to culture, principles, politics, models, rights, concepts and structure. In this book I will address each of these subjects, usually by focusing on a more specific question but sometimes by addressing the particular subject in general.

Chapter 2 describes the major shift that is currently taking place, as a result of the Europeanisation of private law, from a rather formal, dogmatic and positivistic stance to a more substance-oriented and pragmatic approach to private law. It argues that European legal culture is undergoing a radical change: the instrumentalist and impressionist approach of directives, the pragmatic style of the European Court of Justice, the subversive role of comparative law with its functional method, the external economic, cultural and political perspectives given by academics, the success of soft law which is based on substantive authority rather than on formal enactment, and the depositivisation of legal education as a result of the implementation of the Bologna Declaration together contribute to a new European legal culture that is significantly less formal, dogmatic and positivistic than national legal cultures in Europe have been.

In 2000 the Lando Commission published its 'Principles of European Contract Law'. Chapter 3 discusses some of the choices which the Lando Commission has made when drafting its Principles. In particular, it examines the choices which have been made with regard to the purpose of the PECL, the authors and their working methods, the format and style, the subject matter, politics, culture, economics, and progress v. tradition. By assessing these choices this Chapter provides a deconstruction of the PECL as a restatement of the common core of European contract law.

In 1992 the Netherlands enacted the central part of its new Civil Code, the *Burgerlijk Wetboek*. Chapter 4 examines whether this Civil Code - the most recent in the European Union - could serve as a model for a European Civil

Code. The recent Dutch codification experience also raises some more general considerations regarding codification today.

Chapter 5 explores the political stakes in the debate on the future of European contract law which was launched by the European Commission in July 2001. It focuses on the question: 'who has an interest in what kind of European contract law?' By doing so, it demonstrates that the European contract law debate - and the European private law debate in general - is not merely technical, but deeply political. Three political dimensions of the European contract law debate are addressed: empowerment, national traditions, and ideology. An obvious consequence of the conclusions is that the debate should not remain limited to the community of legal academics, heterogeneous as it may be.

Chapter 6 examines the constitutionalisation of European private law, in particular the effect of fundamental rights on contractual relationships. It is especially concerned with the need to guarantee the constitutional protection of social rights, including a 'general social clause', which is indispensable in order to avoid that ideological battles (autonomy v. solidarity) being fought once again on a different level of governance, and on an unequal footing.

Chapter 7 deals with the concept of good faith. It is generally thought that the concept of good faith may provide a major obstacle to the unification of private law in Europe, since it is, on the one hand, a central concept in the civil law tradition, whereas, on the other, it is traditionally unknown to the common law and is even rejected by it. However, a closer examination of the way in which good faith operates in practice demonstrates that this concept need not, in itself, keep the civil law and common law traditions divided. The reason is that good faith, as it has developed in many civil law countries, cannot (or at least cannot any longer) be regarded as a distinct normative concept: in reality it has developed into a completely open norm, which is not a norm at all, but rather a cover for the creation of new rules by the courts. This conclusion, however, raises another more fundamental problem which is common to both the civil law and common law traditions: where does judge-made law come from? The Chapter argues that the creation of new legal rules ultimately depends on the choices made by judges.

Chapter 8, the final chapter, brings together some of the ideas which were developed in the previous chapters. Assuming that at least a certain part of private law could and should be common in the future, the question arises what structure this future common European private law should have. For most participants in the debate on the future of European private law, both partisans and adversaries, the default model for such a structure would be a European civil code. This chapter discusses some aspects of the structure of European private law which cast some doubt on the desirability of a civil code in the classical sense today.

II. The New European Private Law

The title of this book has, of course, been deliberately chosen. I will now briefly explain it by discussing each of its elements and I will do so in the reverse order: 'law', 'private', 'European', 'new'.

First, this book is based on a specific conception of the law. It does not approach private law in the traditional dogmatic and positivistic way. Rather, it goes beyond legal rules, doctrines, concepts and dogma, and approaches the law in its context, in this case the European context. It especially focuses on the political, economic and cultural dimensions of the European private law enterprise. It emphasises that making law necessarily means making choices, and that people with different views, from different backgrounds et cetera will make these choices differently. This approach to the law is by no means original or unique. On the contrary, not only is it inspired by the traditions of European and American legal realism, critical legal studies, and all sorts of 'law &' movements, but this book is also merely one exponent of a much broader development which is currently taking place in Europe, the development of a new European legal culture, which is less dogmatic and formal than national legal cultures in Europe used to be.

What does private law mean today? Is private law still to be regarded as a largely neutral branch of the law, quite distinct from public law which is instrumental to social and political aims? Throughout this book I argue that the answer must be no. Private law is not neutral. On the contrary, it has an important function in ordering society. Indeed, most citizens in their daily lives will usually have at least as much to do with private law rules as with public law. The same applies to enterprises, especially in this age of deregulation and privatisation. However, people have different views on how society should be ordered. These views are often inspired by ideology. Two ideologies which have dominated the political debate throughout Europe for most of the last century are the liberal/conservative on the one (right) hand, and social-democrat/progressive on the other (left) hand. These ideologies have their pendants in private law, in the ideals of party autonomy and solidarity. In this book I demonstrate that many private law rules in Europe can (however, by no means exclusively) be explained in these terms. Moreover, I argue that a common European private law should be sufficiently social, based not only on the idea of party autonomy but also on the equally fundamental European value of solidarity.

This book is based on the conviction that our private law should, at least in part, be European. This conviction is inspired by European idealism, i.e. by the idea that it is desirable to do some things together in Europe because we share a common identity and common ideals. However, an important aspect of our common European identity is pluralism. Not only does every European have many identities at the same time (or one fragmented identity) - e.g. as a European, a Dutchman and as an Amsterdammer - in addition many Europeans share strong regional identities, which are sometimes even stronger than their national identity -, but Europe is also a multi-cultural society which prides itself on traditions emanating from all over the world. Moreover, doing things together should not, of course, at the same time mean excluding others. A fortress Europe is not a part of the European dream. Therefore, the Europeanisation of private law will occur on many different levels of governance (including universities, legal practice et cetera) and on each of them at various speeds. As a result, the Europeanisation of private law will inevitably be complex and will frequently be troublesome, no different, in this respect, from the process of European integration in general. Ready-made solutions like a common European Civil Code in the classical sense, elegant as they may seem to some because of their simplicity, are probably unrealistic because they are too simplistic. Therefore, this book will not (and cannot) propose a blueprint for some sort of 'end result' for the Europeanisation of private law. Rather, it will make some observations on the process which has no doubt only just started.

Finally, this book argues for a new European private law. Interesting as the *ius commune* may be from the perspective of a historian, it definitely belongs to the past. Our future belongs to a new European private law which certainly must be deeply-rooted in our present law (and sometimes even in the law of the past) but would not be worth the effort if it were not 'better' than the private law we have had so far, and if it did not mean some sort of progress. Now, of course, one could argue, as a European idealist, that the mere fact of having a common European private law means progress, independent of what its content may be. However, I think we should be more ambitious. We should not be satisfied when we have found the greatest common denominator, the 'common core'. Instead, we should try to find solutions to problems which have not yet been solved, or not in a satisfactory way (and people will differ on what that means), on a national level. With 'problems' I mean, of course, not in the first place conceptual problems, but rather social problems. It is in this sense that we should strive for a truly *new European private law.*

Culture

2
The New European Legal Culture

I. Classical European Legal Culture

A. General

IN EUROPE throughout the 20th century the method in legal practice, scholarship and education has been largely dogmatic and positivistic. With 'positivistic' I mean the approach to the law whose main concern is to find out what the law *is* on a certain issue in a certain place, typically one's own country. In this approach written documents which are issued, in a formal way, by the state authorities, such as the legislator (codes, statutes) or courts (decisions), usually play a central role. With 'dogmatic' I mean the approach to the law which is based on the (largely implicit) assumption that the law is a coherent (though not necessarily comprehensive, and therefore: open) system of rules (integrity), and it is possible to derive answers to specific questions and solutions for specific cases from abstract rules and concepts (and the values 'contained' in them) in a more or less objective way, and that the system contains only one 'right answer' to each question.

Thus, in classical European legal culture formal arguments play an important role. With a formal argument I mean an argument which, in order to find answers to questions of law, refers to a source of law which has been previously established by the public authorities, such as statutes and case law. Substantive arguments, which refer to the relative merits of one possible solution or the other, play only a secondary role.

Some important characteristics of European legal culture include the following: its national character, its internal perspective, its systematic thinking (*Systemdenken*), its use of abstract rules and concepts, its deductive thinking, its striving for objectivity, and its text orientation. These characteristics of a dogmatic and positivistic (formal) approach to the law are found in most legal actors and most legal actions, be it by the legislator, in the courts, in academic debate or in legal education.

B. *The Legislator*

In most European countries the democratically elected legislator is the primary source of law and its main product in private law is the civil code. Not only did most European countries, on the waves of Enlightenment and nationalism, adopt a code in the 19th century, many European countries even embarked on a recodification in the course of the 20th century. One important reason to do so was in order to codify case law, thereby confirming the legislator's primacy[1]. This second wave of codes - Italy (1942), Portugal (1966), the Netherlands (1992[2]) – is much more systematic, abstract and comprehensive than the former[3]. In the Netherlands the systematic and abstract approach to the law has recently spread to administrative law, the 'general part' of which has now been codified[4]. Some legislators, especially the French, are still very active today in adapting and modernising their civil codes, and in adopting new, functional codes[5]. Today, Germany is embarking on a major reform of the law of obligations in the *BGB*[6]. Also most Eastern European countries have recently adopted codes, and in Scotland, as a result of devolution, there is a project for a national civil code[7]. Even in England a (commercial) code was recently proposed by Roy Goode[8]. More generally, in England the legislator is very active in private law, with the help of the Law Commission, issuing a variety of statutory reforms of the common law[9].

Thus in most European legal systems the point of departure for legal reasoning is the Civil Code. The code is presumed to be comprehensive and coherent. Comprehensive in the sense that, as a result of abstraction, in principle it deals with all matters of private law (is applicable to all conflicts

---

[1] See E.M. MEIJERS, 'Wijzigingen en aanvullingen van het Burgerlijk wetboek na 1838', in: Paul Scholten, E.M. Meijers (eds.), *Gedenkboek Burgerlijk Wetboek 1838-1938*, Zwolle 1938, p. 33 ff.

[2] The new Dutch Civil Code has still not been completely enacted. Although Meijers was appointed as the drafter of a new code as early as in 1947 the first of the nine Books that were planned was only enacted in 1970 ((Book 1: Family law) and the three most important Books (3, 5, 6, on patrimonial law) in 1992. See on the various troubles during the recodification process E.O.H.P. FLORIJN, *Ontstaan en ontwikkeling van het nieuwe Burgerlijk Wetboek*, Maastricht 1995 and T.J. VEEN, *''En voor berisping is hier ruime stof''. Over codificatie van het burgerlijk recht, legistische rechtsbeschouwing en herziening van het Nederlands privaatrecht in de 19de en 20ste eeuw*, Amsterdam 2001.

[3] In the Dutch Civil Code, one has to 'collect' the law relating to a consumer sales contract from 6 different places in the code, each dealing with a different degree or type of abstraction: juristic acts, obligations, contracts, synallagmatic contracts, sales contracts, consumer sales contracts. The Portuguese code even contains further layers of abstraction.

[4] *Algemene Wet Bestuursrecht.*

[5] See also Atias' plea for a renewal of private law, naturally in the shape of a new civil code (CHRISTIAN ATIAS,'Le code civil nouveau', *D. 1999*).

[6] I will come back to this below.

[7] See HECTOR MACQUEEN, *'Scots Law and the Road to the New Ius Commune', Ius Commune Lectures on European Private Law*, 1, Maastricht 2000.

[8] Compare EWAN MCKENDRICK, 'Traditional Concepts and Contemporary Values', 10 *ERPL* 2001, pp. 95 ff.

[9] See, as a recent example, the Contracts (Rights of Third Parties) Act 1999. For an update on the law reform projects see www.lawcom.gov.uk/misc/common.htm.

between private parties)[10], not in the sense of exclusivity: the legislator (or the courts) may come up with specific rules outside the code (e.g. in separate statutes). The code is presumed to be coherent in the sense that there is no contradiction between the rules contained in it, that each rule has one true meaning, and that it provides only one right answer to each legal question[11].

C. The Courts

After the enactment of the codes in the 19th century, at first the task of the courts was thought to be merely to apply the rules contained in the code (doctrine of separation of powers). Judges were thought to be *'la bouche qui prononce les paroles de la loi; des êtres inanimés qui n'en peuvent modérer ni la force, ni la rigueur.'*[12]. However, in the course of the last century it became clear in all European countries that such an extreme separation is neither tenable nor desirable. It became obvious that courts effectively do and must create new law. Thus it became normal to speak of a change in the courts' direction or policy (*'revirement de la jurisprudence'*, *'de HR gaat om'*), and courts do now frequently formulate general rules or principles (*'attendu de principe'*, *'massima giudiziaria'*, *'principeoverweging'*). Moreover, it is now widely accepted that *jurisprudence* should be regarded as a source of law (sometimes in less straightforward language referred to as 'unwritten law', as opposed to the written law in the codes, which is 'found' by the courts). Finally, in most European countries we now speak openly of

---

[10] Compare art. 4 French *Cc*: 'Le juge, qui refusera de juger, sous prétexte du silence, de l'obscurité ou de l'insuffisance de la loi, pourra être poursuivi comme coupable de déni de justice.' and art 13 Dutch *Wet Algemene Bepalingen*. Contrast art. 1 Swiss *ZGB/CC* (1907): 'Das Gesetz findet auf allen Rechtsfragen Anwendung, für die es nach Wortlaut oder Auslegung eine Bestimmung enthält. Kann dem Gesetze keinen Vorschrift entnommen werden, so soll der Richter nach Gewohnheitsrecht und, wo auch ein solches fehlt, nach der Regel entscheiden, die er als Gesetzgeber aufstellen würde. Er folgt dabei bewährter Lehre und Überlieferung.'

[11] Sacco considers 'the principle of non-contradiction' to be 'the fetish of municipal lawyers' (RODOLFO SACCO, 'Legal Formants: A Dynamic Approach To Comparative Law', 39 *AJCL* (1991), pp. 1-34, pp. 343-401, p. 24). Compare RODOLFO SACCO, *Introduzione al diritto comparato*, 5th ed. Torino 1997, p. 44: 'Nella nostra attività di giuristi "territoriali" noi rendiamo onore a questo principio di unità. Il nostro massimo sforzo di civilisti è quello di scoprire *il* modello giuridico all'interno di un determinato ordinamento giuridico. Posto un determinato quesito giuridico, noi facciamo ogni ragionevole sforzo per trovare la risposta (al singolare!) al quesito; vogliamo trovare la norma (al singolare!) che regola quel determinato fenomeno.' (emphasis in original) See also SACCO, *Introduzione al diritto comparato*, p. 45: 'noi siamo pronti ad ammettere che ci possono essere divergenze fra le diverse risposte ad un quesito giuridico, a condizione di poter dire che una sola di esse è giusta, e le altre sono sbagliate.' Sacco himself distinguishes various legal formants which may contradict each other. See further *infra*. Compare also DANIELA CARUSO, 'The Missing View of the Cathedral: The Private Law Paradigm of European Legal Integration', 3 *European Law Journal* (1997), pp. 3-32, p. 6: codes are conceived as 'self-contained systems, internally coherent and self-referential.'

[12] MONTESQUIEU, *De l'esprit des lois*, Paris 1979 (first edition 1748), XI, 6. Contrast PORTALIS, 'Discours préliminaire', in: P.A. FENET, *Recueil complet des travaux préparatoires du Code civil, discussions, motifs, rapports et discours*, livre troisième, titre troisième, Paris 1836, Part I, pp. 466 and 469 ('Un code, quelque complet qu'il puisse paraître, n'est pas plutôt achevé, que mille questions inattendues viennent s'offrir au magistrat.').

our (highest) courts' task as a creator of law (*'rechtsvormende taak van de rechter'*).

However, in spite of the general recognition that the courts are not merely 'les bouches de la loi', the role of our courts today is still far from clearly articulated[13]. The present situation in most European countries is rather indeterminate and not without confusion. On the one hand, courts play a major (frequently dominant) role in the development of private law, but, on the other, not only do the separation of powers and the primacy of the democratically elected legislator still exist (at least as an ideal), but most of the dogmas and institutional arrangements related to it are also still in force. For example, most European legal systems still make a distinction between questions of law and questions of fact. As a consequence, some of the questions which are most relevant to practice (e.g. the interpretation of contracts, the measure of damages) are not dealt with by the highest court because they remain at the discretion of the lower courts[14]. Moreover, contrary to Parliament, the other law maker, courts still speak through one single mouth. The absence of dissenting opinions is just another reminiscence of the idea that the courts say what the law is and always has been; there is only one right answer to each question of law and the courts tell us what it is. For the same reason the grounds given in support of decisions by the courts are sometimes very brief, especially in France[15], and in any case are rather formal. The style is usually one of necessity: the decision is said to follow more or less logically from a specific rule, or from the system as a whole, or from the values contained in it. In particular, most courts provide few substantive arguments: why this new rule and not another, what interests were at stake, why should one prevail and not the other? Similarly, in our cassation system, the style is not one of substantive argumentation; when an appeal is upheld the idea is rather that the lower court was wrong: it did not properly apply or understand the law. As a result, in most European countries there is

[13] See MARTIJN W. HESSELINK, '"Wat is recht etc.?"; Antwoorden op vragen van Tilburgers over rechtsregels, rechtspraak en rechtsvorming', *NJB* 2000, p. 2032 ff.

[14] The distinction seems to be stronger in France than in Germany.

[15] See for France HORATIA MUIR WATT, 'La fonction subversive du droit comparé', *RIDC* 3-2000, p. 503 ff, p. 508: '[le] caractère opaque des décisions judiciaires peu motivées, notamment celles de la Cour de cassation'. See also the classical ADOLPHE TOUFFAIT & ANDRE TUNC, 'Pour une motivation plus explicite des décisions de justice notamment de celles de la Cour de cassation', *R.T.D. civ.*1974, p. 487 ff, on p. 489: 'La décision française se veut aussi brève que possible. A la Cour de cassation, notamment, le modèle de la décision est le syllogisme le plus simple. Une affirmation de principe forme la majeure, une constatation de fait, la mineure: une conclusion en résulte, incontestable en apparence.'; p. 507 : 'le style actuel des décisions, notamment de la Cour de cassation, est un peu la messe en latin. C'est le prolongement d'une tradition infiniment respectable. Mais c'est aussi la répétition de formules que beaucoup ne comprennent pas et qui permettent à l'esprit de s'orienter où il veut. C'est une garantie contre toute manifestation d'hérésie, mais un piétinement qui ralentit le progrès collectif. La motivation explicite, c'est la possibilité d'erreurs et de maladresses, mais aussi celle de cérémonies qui transforment les «cœurs de pierre » en « cœurs de chair ». C'est l'autorité qui ne résulte plus de l'emploi d'une langue ésotérique et d'un refus de toute discussion, mais qui s'appuie sur la force d'idées, de sentiments, sur la vie elle-même.'

not much political attention devoted to the nomination of judges in the highest courts. Although these judges will play an important role in the development of the law, neither Parliament nor the press actually scrutinise the candidate's political preferences, because the courts are thought to be objective experts rather than political actors.

D. Scholars

In the introduction to his classical *Methodenlehre der Rechtswissenschaft*[16] Karl Larenz defines 'legal science' as follows[17]: 'Unter "Rechtswissenschaft" wird in diesem Buche diejenige Wissenschaft verstanden, die sich mit der *Lösung von Rechtsfragen im Rahmen und auf der Grundlage einer bestimmten, historisch erwachsenen Rechtsordnung* befaßt, also die herkömmlicherweise so genannte Jurisprudenz'. Therefore, in Larenz' definition, legal science is concerned with solving questions of law within the framework of a certain legal order. He distinguishes legal science from e.g. legal sociology[18]. Larenz explicitly takes the internal perspective. And indeed this may be regarded as typical of European legal scholars. The object of study for most legal scholars in Europe is their own positive national law. They study how, within their system, a certain case must be resolved (what the law is with regard to certain facts), how a new decision by the highest court can be best placed in the system (*einordnen*), and how the legal system can be best 'thought further' (*weiterdenken*)[19].

Therefore, in many European countries for a scholar in private law the most typical and prestigious activity is to write a commentary (or a manual) on a certain part of the law (of the code). Thus a scholar becomes an authority, who may enter into a more or less explicit dialogue with the (supreme) court[20]. The more he is followed by the courts, the greater his success as a

---

[16] The book has been translated into several languages including Italian, Spanish, Portuguese, and Japanese.

[17] KARL LARENZ, *Methodenlehre der Rechtswissenschaft*, 5th ed., Berlin, Heidelberg, New York, Tokyo 1991, p. 5 (emphasis added).

[18] KARL LARENZ, *Methodenlehre der Rechtswissenschaft*, p. 6: 'Mit dem Recht befassen sich auch *andere Wissenschaften*, so die Rechtshistorie und die Rechtssoziologie.' (Emphasis added).

[19] Compare PHILIPPE JESTAZ & CHRISTOPH JAMIN, 'L'entité doctrinale française', *D.* 1997, p. 167 ff, p. 175, on *la doctrine* in France: 'Elle s'est donné pour mission d'édifier une dogmatique au sens fort, c'est-à-dire un véritable système de pensée, et de là vient, en profondeur, la solidarité'.

[20] This is especially true for Germany. In the Netherlands the dialogue is more indirect, via the conclusions of the Advocate-General (which are published). In France, dialogue is less explicit but some authors (e.g. Ghestin) have clearly inspired the *Cour de cassation*. In Great Britain the House of Lords pays more and more explicit attention to scholarly writing. See e.g. Lord Goff's famous speech in *White* v *Jones* [1995] 2 WLR 187. See on this case BASIL MARKESINIS, *Five Days in the House of Lords: Some Comparative Reflections on White v. Jones*, in: Centro di studi e ricerche di diritto comparato e straniero (directed by M.J. Bonell), *Saggi, conferenze e seminari*, no. 16, Roma 1995. In Italy, see as an example *Cass.*, 18 July 1989, no. 3362, *Foro it.* 1989, I, 2750, notes di Majo and Mariconda, which literally follows a passage in C. MASSIMO BIANCA, 'La nozione di buona fede quale regola di comportamento contrattuale', *Riv. dir. civ.* XXIX (1983), I, pp. 205-216, p. 210 (see now C. MASSIMO BIANCA, *Diritto Civile, III Il contratto*, Milano 1987 (reprinted in 1992),

commentator[21]. Of course, this is not an incentive for originality and criticism. If success is measured by how much one is followed by the courts the best strategy is to try to predict what the courts would probably decide rather than proposing an alternative solution.

A scientific product on a smaller scale, and of varying prestige among European legal systems, but equally classical, are notes under (or comments to) court decisions. In such a note a scholar explains the implications of the decision and establishes the place of the decision (the new rule) within the system. Another typical activity is writing doctrinal articles or monographs[22], for example an article which establishes the specific implications of a certain (new) abstract rule, concept or institution (typically contained in the code)[23], or how the law would deal with certain imaginary or actual new situations or problems (e.g. e-commerce or wrongful life). More generally, many scholars wish to write what is 'useful for practice'[24]. Thus many scholars are also involved in writing and editing newsletters, overviews, and chronicles which aim to inform practising lawyers of new developments in the law and to explain such developments and put them into perspective.

In a code system the courts and the scholars together master the gap between the abstract rules and the specific cases (concretisation) that the legislator has left. The legislator (necessarily) provides abstract rules, the scholars are the experts on what their specific implications are, and the courts (inspired by these scholars) decide what they mean in specific cases[25].

All this does not mean that there are no debates in the legal academia. On the contrary, in most European countries there are many lively doctrinal debates among individual scholars and among schools of thought. However, in these debates underlying normative, political and economic preferences are

---

no. 224), on good faith.

[21] In turn, the commentator may exploit his authority by acting as a consultant to law firms, which is normal practice in most civil law countries.

[22] In a thesis or monograph some originality is frequently appreciated (especially in France), although departing too much from the mainstream (from 'positive law') may endanger a successful academic career; the balance is rather delicate.

[23] See for a typical example MARTIJN HESSELINK, 'Vragen bij de toepassing van art. 6:230 BW', *WPNR* 6191-6192 (1995), pp. 541-545, 563-567.

[24] See for France CHRISTOPHE JAMIN, 'Henri Capitant et René Demogue: notation sur l'actualité d'un dialogue doctrinal', in: *Mélanges François Terré*, Paris, 1999, p. 125 ff, p. 135, who speaks of: 'cette constante volonté de la doctrine française, qui se veut héritière des *prudents*, d'être un guide pour les praticiens plus qu'un observateur extérieur'. See, in the Netherlands, the first line of Meijers's inaugural lecture (E.M. MEIJERS, *De taak der rechtswetenschap ten aanzien der vrije rechtspraak*, Haarlem 1910, p. 5): 'De rechtswetenschap heeft in de eerste plaats tot opgave de rechtspractijk voor te lichten.'

[25] Compare RODOLFO SACCO, *Introduzione al diritto comparato*, p. 45: 'C'è una sola verità giuridica, la quale ha la sua fonte nella legge e viene fedelmente ricostruita dalla dottrina, e applicata dalla giurisprudenza. (...) È evidente che la legge potrebbe subire più di una interpretazione; ma proprio questa circostanza rinforza il principio dell'unicità della regola di diritto. Se più interpretazioni sono astrattamente possibili, si dirà che *una di esse è esatta*. La dottrina si imporrà come fine quello di identificarla, e di indicarla.' (Emphasis added.)

rarely articulated[26]. The stake in the academic debate is rather merely thought to be reputation: who is able to provide a proper account of the law relating to a certain issue (the right interpretation)[27]. Also, the language which is used conceals underlying conflicts of interest and stakes or (political) preferences in those conflicts. For example, a phrase frequently used is that 'practice' needs this rule or another (e.g. more extensive security facilities) or that a rule proposed by others would 'not work in practice', whereas in reality (in practice) the proposed rule or interpretation frequently only serves the needs of one party in a conflict (frequently the stronger one) and would indeed not work for the other party.

Many doctrinal debates are highly conceptual[28]. A classical example is the way in which the horizontal effect (i.e. between citizens) of human rights should be conceived (direct or indirect, via general clauses). A classical Dutch debate centres on the way the concept of good faith operates: *normatieve uitleg* (interpretation) versus *beperkende werking* (limitation)[29]. In Germany there are more than 50 theories of *Wegfall der Geschäftsgrundlage*[30] and in France there may be as many *cause* theories (the concept is there in the code; scholars debate as to what it means)[31]. Frequently, both alternatives would lead to pretty much the same result in most cases[32]. But not always!

---

[26] For example, in several countries (e.g. France, Belgium, the Netherlands) many professors of insurance law have important links with insurance companies (e.g. because their chairs are sponsored by them) but they are usually regarded as experts rather than as partisans. See, generally, for the Netherlands, O.A. HAAZEN, *Algemeen deel van het rechterlijk overgangsrecht; Een verhandeling over de terugwerkende kracht van rechtspraak, de rechtsdwaling en de democratische rechtsvindingsleer*, 2001, p.150: 'In Nederland is het nog steeds gebruikelijk politieke aspecten te onderdrukken, te bagatelliseren of te ontkennen.'

[27] See RODOLFO SACCO, *Introduzione al diritto comparato*, p. 45: 'È vero che i dottrinari - e in genere, gli interpreti - sono più di uno e non sempre le loro opinioni concordano; ma l'idea che portiamo con noi è che esista una sola risposta al quesito giuridico; quando ci sono più risposte ciò significa che c'è una soggettiva incertezza che si spera provvisoria, in attesa del momento in cui verrà resa definitivamente e felicemente nota la risposta giuridica.'

[28] See for France HORATIA MUIR WATT, 'La fonction subversive du droit comparé', p. 508: 'La doctrine est perçue comme monolithique, peu encline à s'interroger sur sa propre démarche scientifique, et mobilisée essentiellement par des querelles de texte à intérêt exclusivement local.'

[29] See especially J.M. VAN DUNNÉ, *Normatieve uitleg van rechtshandelingen; Een onderzoek naar de grondslagen van het geldende verbintenissenrecht*, Deventer 1971, P. ABAS, *Beperkende werking van de goede trouw*, Deventer 1972; H.C.F. SCHOORDIJK, *Het algemeen gedeelte van het verbintenissenrecht naar het Nieuw Burgerlijk Wetboek*, Deventer 1979; P. VAN SCHILFGAARDE, 'Uitleg van rechtshandelingen', *WPNR* 6282-6283 (1997), pp. 587-592, pp. 611-615.

[30] See HELMUT HEINRICHS, in: *Palandt Bürgerliches Gesetzbuch*, 61st ed., München 2002, § 242, no. 113.

[31] See on the *cause* debate PHILIPPE MALAURIE & LAURENT AYNÈS, *Cours de droit civil*, part IV, *Les obligations*, 10th ed., Paris 1999, nos. 492-510; JACQUES GHESTIN, *La formation du contrat*, in: *Traité de droit civil*, 3rd ed., Paris 1993, no. 818-838; F. TERRE, PH. SIMLER, Y. LEQUETTE, *Les obligations*, 5th ed., Paris 1996, no. 312-316.

[32] For *normatieve uitleg* v *beperkende werking* see MARTIJN HESSELINK, BERT OOSTING, EDGAR DU PERRON, 'Verandering van omstandigheden en de uitleg van overeenkomsten, naar aanleiding van "Rebus sic stantibus" door prof. mr. P. Abas,' *AA* 39 (1990) 9, 563-570. In the same sense A.S. HARTKAMP, *Mr. C. Asser's handleiding tot de beoefening van het Nederlands burgerlijk recht; Verbintenissenrecht;* Vol. II, *Algemene leer der overeenkomsten*, 11th ed., Deventer 2001,

Sometimes the result would actually be different, but this fact frequently remains implicit. It is not concrete consequences that are usually at the core of the debate, but rather concepts and whether they fit within the system. Thus, frequently the substantive arguments are there but they remain in the background, not articulated, hidden as it were, in conceptual debates[33].

E. Education

Legal education in Europe is largely positivistic. We mainly teach our students what the law is here and now[34]. This mode of teaching presumes that there is something like 'the law', and that we can know it and tell our students what it is. Legal education in Europe is predominantly dogmatic. What students typically first learn of private law is its system: the structure of the code; its basic concepts and distinctions[35]. All this is not presented as just one of many possible ways of framing reality. No, it is *the law* and students should know it[36]. Therefore examinations frequently resemble tests in taxonomy. How do you call this? What does this concept mean? At best, alternatives (e.g. comparative law) are presented during a later stage in their studies; first, students should know their own system properly.

Case law is taught in a similar way to the code. What the student should look for is the abstract rule which the courts formulate (*attendu de principe, massima*), quite similar to a rule in the code. And even if in the particular case the court of first instance, the court of appeal, the Advocate-General and the annotator have said something different, what the highest court has said is the law. Frequently students are told that they do not have to know the facts of the case. They rather have to learn what place the case has in the system. Each case is presumed to fit within the system; the question is only how. Clearly, what the highest court says is the law to the extent that it is most likely that in a new similar conflict the same side would win. But that is not really the point. The point is that students do not usually learn to consider the law as

---

no. 281.

[33] I will come back to this below.

[34] See for criticism from students, the members of DIS (many of whom are law students), who complain that education in university is today not sufficiently 'academic'. See *Folia*, February18th, 2000, and *NRC Handelsblad*, March, 25th, 2000. See recently explicitly in favour of positivism in legal education J.W. ZWEMMER, 'De bachelor-masterstructuur', 50 *AA* (2001), p. 240 ff.

[35] For the Netherlands see H.C.F. SCHOORDIJK, *Redelijkheid en billijkheid aan de vooravond van een nieuw millennium*, Zwolle 1996, p. 69: 'Verbazing wekt bij mij steeds, hoe deductief veel juristen nog denken (…) Hier dient zich het gevolg aan van ons juridisch onderwijssysteem, dat zich teveel aan abstracties te buiten gaat en nog steeds naadloos aansluit bij een rechtspraak die zich in de 19e eeuw steeds meer als 'la bouche de la loi' ontwikkelde.'

[36] However, see H.C.F. SCHOORDIJK, 'Een en ander over dogmatiek, constructie en (hun betekenis voor het) onderwijs', in: *J.L.P. Cahen bundel*, Deventer 1997, p. 379 ('Omdat alle juristen - al is het maar miniem - hun eigen ervaringen en waardeoordelen hebben, kennen wij even zovele rechtssystemen als er geschoolde juristen zijn') and MAURITS BARENDRECHT, 'Naar een echte visie op het onderwijs', *NJB* 2001, pp. 164-165, p. 164 ('niet het leren van een systeem, maar het construeren of kiezen van een eigen persoonlijk systeem').

being problematic[37]. The confrontation between the law in the books and the law in action is rarely sought[38].

Thus, students are given an impression of the law as a coherent and, above all, rational system which provides right answers to legal questions. This impression is reinforced by the way in which we examine. In the Netherlands we test the students' understanding and knowledge of private law by asking them to resolve a number of 'practical cases'. However, these cases do not at all resemble the cases as a lawyer or a court would typically hear them, because they are stripped of all 'irrelevant' facts. Therefore these cases are highly abstract. As a matter of fact they can best be described as personalised legal rules. In addition, after the examination we provide our students with right answers to these questions. Indeed, our students are entitled to receive these 'standard answers' in order to check where they have got the law wrong

---

[37] Moreover, the picture is incomplete. What if the parties had not appealed to the *Hoge Raad* or had not gone to court but to a mediator or had resolved the conflict amongst themselves. Was there then no law between these parties? Moreover, it may be interesting to study why the court has decided in such a way. Was the decision fair? (what is fair?) Was it efficient? What were the alternatives? What was at stake? Are these questions less relevant to students? It does not seem so. They rather seem to be more relevant. Not just for those who want to become militant demonstrators against the system (people from Seattle), but also for those (who seem to be the majority today) who want to be successful lawyers in one of the major law firms. In order to advise their clients properly all these aspects may be relevant. A perfect knowledge of the concepts and the system of the code is only of limited importance. A friend of mine, when she had just become a trainee in a major law firm in The Hague, was shocked when she found out that some of the most successful lawyers did not know the difference between avoidance for mistake and termination for non-performance or between *bezit* (possession) and *houderschap* (possession). And that another even more successful lawyer did not demonstrate any real awareness of the enactment (3 years previously) of the new civil code. 'They do not know the law!', she exclaimed. But the same lawyers have lists in their office which say which judge is employer-friendly and which is not. A Dutch 'lawyer of the week' (F.H.A.M. Thunnissen) recently said that at most 5% of his work had to do with the application of legal rules: 'Welk stokpaardje berijdt u? Dat juristerij niet bestaat en het juridisch vak veelal niet meer is dan logisch analyseren van feiten in een maatschappelijk of commercieel kader. De rechtspraktijk bestaat voor 95% uit feitenonderzoek en logica en voor ten hoogste 5% uit toepassing van rechtsregels of regeltjes.' (*Mrweb-nieuwsbrief*, week 14 - 2001) This idea might be expressed more appropriately by redefining what the law is. Does the law really only consist of abstract rules which are enacted by the state? Law is context, battle, and manifold.

[38] When dealing with actual real-life cases, e.g. taken from the lives of their relatives ('Can I sue my landlord?'), our students are lost. They do not know the answer. They know that a contract may be annulled for mistake when the other party has violated its duty to inform. But *was* there a duty to inform in this case? Or: was there a duty of care, and if so, was it violated? Our students simply do not know. But, of course, we do not know either! Because in real-life concrete cases there is no standard right answer. For one thing, this is because 'the facts' as they objectively occurred do not exist. In each case there are always two sides of the story. The judge hears them and then he decides; he chooses the position of one party or the other. Of course, one can have a (normative) view that the court should assess the facts and apply the law objectively and rationally (*Methodenlehre*), but that does not *make it* objective and rational. Neither does it imply that what is irrational is not the law. We should stop giving a simplistic account of the law and start teaching our students the law with all its aspects, most of which are highly complex and problematic. Therefore one may be entitled to ask to what extent that abstract system of concepts *is* actually the law.

and whether we were objective in evaluating their account of the law[39]. In many European universities, particularly in France, Italy, Spain and Portugal, even practical cases are a rare form of examination. Obviously, the impression of the rationality and coherence of our law is most easily upheld on a high degree of abstraction.

As for teaching materials, textbooks frequently resemble (or actually are) commentaries on the code. Sometimes a book, which was meant in the first place as a textbook for teaching purposes, obtains an authority which is equivalent to a commentary[40]. This shows how positivistic these teaching materials are: they (claim to) tell the students what the law is.

F. Some Qualifications

Before I move on to my next point, I have to make some qualifications. Of course, my general statements (by definition) do not fully appreciate the rich variety of the subject under discussion, in this case European legal cultures. First, in order to avoid the charge of caricature, it should be emphasised that today in most of Europe the days of extreme formalism are long gone. In the 19th century most European legal systems went through what may be regarded with hindsight as an extremely formalist period. Since then very much has changed. It is, of course, difficult to say where we stand today; things are constantly moving and we are in the middle. I will come back to this later. Secondly, there are, of course, great differences between the various European countries, and within them. For example, the style of the French *Cour de cassation* is far more formalistic than that of the German *Bundesgerichtshof*; in the Netherlands legal doctrine is much more pragmatic and less dogmatic than in Germany; and within one country there is a great difference between one judge or scholar and another. Thirdly, although the national focus, internal perspective, systematic thinking (*Systemdenken*), use of abstract rules and concepts, deductive thinking, striving for objectivity, and text orientation characterise the dogmatic (formalist) and positivistic approach to private law which is dominant in Europe, there is no necessary link between these elements. Not only do they not coincide, but it is also very well possible to think of one without the others[41]. Finally, and most importantly, there is a fallacy, which is not always fully appreciated by foreign (especially

[39] See e.g. art. 23, *Onderwijs- en examenregeling 1998* (Faculty of Law, *Universiteit van Amsterdam*).

[40] See in Germany e.g. KARL LARENZ, *Lehrbuch des Schuldrechts*, I Band *Allgemeiner Teil*, 14th ed., München 1987 and DIETER MEDICUS, *Bürgerliches Recht*, 18th ed., Köln, Berlin, Bonn, München 1999. See in the Netherlands e.g. the *Asser*-series, *Van der Pot/Donner, Hazewinkel/Suringa*.

[41] However, NORBERTO BOBBIO, *Il positivismo giuridico*, Torino 1996, especially 249 ff., regards 'la teoria della coerenza dell'ordinamento giuridico', 'la teoria della completezza dell'ordinamento giuridico' and 'la teoria dell'interpretazione logica o meccanistica del diritto' as essential to the theory of legal positivism (in a strict sense).

American) observers[42]. European jurists do not believe as much in concepts and system as their language suggests. To a large extent European legal actors do something different from what they say[43]. Their language is much more formalist than their actions. It would, in turn, be formalist for an observer to stop at that language. Frequently, scholars and courts use the language of right answers but actually (consciously) express value judgements. A scholar, for example, will say that his colleague or the court has not properly understood 'what the law *is*', where he could also have said 'what, in his view, the law *should* be'. Thus an important (and regrettable) characteristic of the European methodology is that its substantive approach is not articulated: there is a lack of transparency. I will come back to this later.

G. Common Law

On the other hand, however, I think that most of what I have said above applies not only to the legal systems on the European continent (civil law systems), but also to the so-called common law systems of England and Wales and Ireland, and the 'mixed' system of Scotland. Obviously, formalism is different in England. First of all, English law has no civil code and is therefore much less deductive and makes much less use of abstractions. However, the English approach to the law is also highly conceptual and positivistic. The national focus, the internal perspective, the extensive use of concepts and doctrines, the central role of texts are all equally characteristic of English legal culture. This becomes apparent when the English legal culture is compared with the legal culture in another country with a so-called common law system, the United States. In their famous study *Form and Substance in Anglo-American Law*, which was published in 1987, Atiyah and Summers concluded that 'the American and the English legal systems, for all their superficial similarities, differ profoundly: the English legal system is highly "formal" and the American highly "substantive". First, substantive *reasoning* is used far more widely than formal reasoning in the American system when decisions have to be made or other legal actions taken, while in the English system, the reverse is true. Secondly, this difference in methods of reasoning reflects a deep difference in legal style, legal culture and, more generally, the *visions* of law which prevail in the two countries.'[44] As explained above, more or less the same can be said of most other European countries[45]. Indeed, it

[42] See, however, MITCHEL DE S.-O.-I'E. LASSER, 'Judicial (Self-) Portraits: Judicial Discourse in the French Legal System', 104 *Yale L.J.* (1995), p. 1325 ff, who paints 'the unofficial French portrait of the civil judge'.

[43] Compare for France MITCHEL DE S.-O.-I'E. LASSER, 'Judicial (Self-) Portraits', p. 1325 ff.

[44] P.S ATIYAH & R.S. SUMMERS, *Form And Substance in Anglo-American Law; A Comparative Study of Legal Reasoning, Legal Theory, and Legal Institutions*, London 1987 (emphasis in the original).

[45] See also DUNCAN KENNEDY, *A Critique of Adjudication {fin de siècle}*, Cambridge Massachusetts 1997, p. 107: 'your ordinary American lawyer is likely to find European solutions to classic legal problems blatantly formalist, in the sense of overestimating the power of

may very well be that, in this respect, English law has more in common with civil law systems on the European Continent than with American law. Or, to put it differently, the unity of European legal culture may be stronger than the unity of the common law[46]. I will come back to this later.

II. American Legal Culture

Let me first turn to the American legal culture. Most of the characteristics I have described as being dominant in European legal culture do not seem to have the same importance in American legal culture. Indeed, the way American legislators, courts, scholars and law teachers deal with the law looks distinctly different from their equivalents in Europe. An important explanation for the striking difference between European and American legal cultures seems to lie in the success which legal realism has had in the U.S.[47] Many of the characteristics of American legal culture today, including many of its main academic schools of thought, would not have been possible without the ground-breaking work which was done by the realist movement.

A. American Legal Realism

In the 1920s and 1930s the American legal realists embarked upon what is frequently referred to as 'the revolt against formalism'[48]. They attacked the prevailing conception of the law (classical legal thought) according to which answers to questions of law could largely be obtained by objective, deductive reasoning, and according to which law was regarded as a science (see especially the legendary Harvard dean Langdell). The realists denounced this approach as 'formalist'.

Although the realists were nothing like as coherent as a school of thought[49], they may be regarded as a movement that shared some

---

deduction, and to find European legal culture in general formalist in the same sense.'

[46] In the same sense REINHARD ZIMMERMANN, '"Common law" und "civil law", Amerika und Europa', in Reinhard Zimmermann (ed.), *Amerikanische Rechtskultur und europäisches Privatrecht*, Tübingen 1995, p. 9, who questions the existence of an 'Anglo-American legal culture': 'Pointiert gesagt: das englische Recht ist europäisch, Amerika ist anders.'

[47] In the same sense UGO MATTEI, 'Why The Wind Changed: Intellectual Leadership In Western Law', 42 *AJCL* (1994) 195, HORATIA MUIR WATT, 'La fonction subversive du droit comparé', p. 512, MATHIAS REIMANN, *Einführung in das US-amerikanische Privatrecht*, München 1997, p. 11; CHRISTOPHE JAMIN, 'Henri Capitant et René Demogue: notation sur l'actualité d'un dialogue doctrinal'; H.C.F. SCHOORDIJK, *De Nederlandse rechtscultuur vergeleken met de Anglo-Amerikaanse*, Antwerpen, Zwolle 1989, p. 29. Compare DUNCAN KENNEDY, *A Critique of Adjudication {fin de siècle}*, p. 108.

[48] MORTON WHITE, *Social Thought in America: the Revolt Against Formalism*, Boston 1957. See on American legal realism WILLIAM TWINING, *Karl Llewellyn and the Realist Movement*, London 1973, MORTON J HORWITZ, *The Transformation of American Law 1870-1960; The Crisis of Legal Orthodoxy*, New York/Oxford 1992, M.D.A. FREEMAN, *Lloyd's Introduction to Jurisprudence*, 6th ed., London 1994, NEIL DUXBURY, *Patterns of American Jurisprudence*, Oxford 1995, DUNCAN KENNEDY, *A Critique of Adjudication {fin de siècle}*; O.A. HAAZEN, *Algemeen deel van het rechterlijk overgangsrecht*, 2001, p. 141.

[49] See for a famous (but also contested, see MORTON J HORWITZ, *The Transformation of*

characteristics[50]. One of the most important was their rule scepticism (impossibility to reason in a neutral way from rules to specific cases[51]), which inspired their distrust of abstractions ('general propositions do not decide concrete cases'[52]) and their attacks on deductive legal reasoning and on legal classifications and categories[53]. Other characteristics were their fact scepticism (facts from the past cannot be established and selected objectively[54]); their pragmatic functional approach[55]; their emphasis on the connection between law and other social sciences; their attack on the private/public law dichotomy ('all law is public law'); their interest in law in action rather than in law in the books[56]; their scepticism concerning (the need for) legal certainty[57]; their focus on those who make the law ('men-of-law'[58]); and their interest in practice, especially in conflict resolution.

American Law 1870-1960; The Crisis of Legal Orthodoxy, p. 171) list of realists KARL N. LLEWELLYN, 'Some Realism about Realism', (1931) 44 *Harv. L. Rev.* 1222 (reprinted, with adaptations, in KARL N. LLEWELLYN, *Jurisprudence; Realism in Theory and Practice*, Chicago and London 1962, pp. 42, where quotes are take from).

[50] See KARL N. LLEWELLYN, 'Some Realism about Realism', M.D.A. FREEMAN, *Lloyd's Introduction to Jurisprudence*, p. 655 ff; WILLIAM TWINING, *Karl Llewellyn and the Realist Movement*; MORTON J HORWITZ, *The Transformation of American Law 1870-1960; The Crisis of Legal Orthodoxy*, p. 169 ff, all with further references.

[51] See KARL N. LLEWELLYN, 'Some Realism about Realism', p. 56: 'a distrust of the theory that traditional prescriptive rule-formulations are *the* heavily operative factor in producing court decisions.'; and J. FRANK, *Law and the Modern Mind*, 1930, 264 ff on 'rule-fetichism' and J. FRANK, *Courts on Trial*, 1949, p. 53 ('legal rule magic').

[52] Holmes in Lochner v. New York, 198 U.S. 45 (1905) (dissenting). See KARL N. LLEWELLYN, 'Some Realism about Realism', p. 60: 'distrust of, instead of search for, the widest sweep of generalisation words permit'. In the same sense JOHN DEWEY, 'Logical Method and Law', 10 *Cornell Law Quarterly* (1924), 17, p. 18: 'No concrete proposition, that is to say one with material dated in time and placed in space, follows from any general statements or from any connection between them.'

[53] KARL N. LLEWELLYN, 'Some Realism about Realism', p. 70: 'deduction does not solve cases, but only shows the effect of a given premise'. See also OLIVER WENDELL HOLMES JR., *The Common Law*, Boston 1881, p. 5: 'The life of the law has not been logic: it has been experience.'

[54] See J. FRANK, *Courts on Trial*, p. vii ff: who argues that the extent of legal certainty is generally 'grossly exaggerated': 'in truth, the major cause of legal uncertainty is fact-uncertainty - the unknowability, before the decision, of what the trial court will "find" as the facts, and the unknowability after the decision of the way in which it "found" those facts.'

[55] See KARL N. LLEWELLYN, 'Some Realism about Realism', p. 57: 'an insistence on evaluation of any part of law in terms of its effects, and an insistence on the worthwhileness of trying to find these effects'. See for Llewellyn's 'law jobs' KARL N. LLEWELLYN, 'The Normative, The Legal and The Law-Jobs: The Problem of Juristic Method', 49 *Yale L.J.* 1355.

[56] See ROSCOE POUND, 'Law in Books and Law in Action' (1910) 44 *Am. L. Rev.*, 12. On the (troublesome) relationship between Pound and the realists, especially after his attack in 1931 (ROSCOE POUND, 'The Call for a Realist Jurisprudence', (1931) 44 *Harv. L. Rev*, 697) and Llewellyn's reply (KARL N. LLEWELLYN, 'Some Realism about Realism', (1931) 44 Harv. L. Rev. 1222), see *Karl Llewellyn and the Realist Movement*, pp. 22f, 72f, and MORTON J HORWITZ, *The Transformation of American Law 1870-1960; The Crisis of Legal Orthodoxy*, p. 172.

[57] KARL N. LLEWELLYN, 'Some Realism about Realism', p. 60: 'there is less possibility of accurate prediction of what courts will do than the traditional rules would lead us to suppose (and what possibility there is must be found in good measure outside these same traditional rules). The particular kind of certainty that men have thus far thought to find in law is in good measure an illusion.' See also J. FRANK, *Law and the Modern Mind*, p. 11-12 on 'the basic legal myth' that

The revolt against legal formalism was not an isolated event in the law. Rather, it was 'an important part of the general intellectual climate' in the United States that fostered their approach[59], more specifically the realists were closely connected to philosophical pragmatism (John Dewey, William James and Charles Sanders Pierce), which attempted to link truth with practical success in solving problems[60]. Moreover, according to Horwitz[61], the realist attack on formalism is best regarded as the continuation of the Progressive attack (by Roscoe Pound's sociological jurisprudence and others) on late-nineteenth century Classical Legal Thought, which started after the *Lochner* case[62], and which included attacks on the neutral, natural and apolitical character of freedom of contract, absolute property, fault liability and other institutions of the *laissez-faire* free market economy[63]. However, this latter view is denounced by Posner as 'the left-wing history of American legal thought'[64].

Although most central figures in the realist movement were professors at law schools, especially Yale and Columbia, this does not mean that the revolt against formalism was limited to university classrooms and law journals. On the contrary, it also had a major impact on practice[65]. An important example is the Uniform Commercial Code, whose chief reporter was Karl Llewellyn, and

---

the law is certain: 'Which is to say that the widespread notion that law either is or can be made approximately stationary and certain is irrational and should be classed as an illusion or a myth.'

[58] KARL N. LLEWELLYN, 'Some Realism about Realism', p. 62: 'All that has become clear is that our government is not a government of laws, but one of law through men.' See Jerome Frank's 'assertion that a judge's decision could be traced back to what he ate for breakfast.' (see MORTON J HORWITZ, *The Transformation of American Law 1870-1960; The Crisis of Legal Orthodoxy*, p. 176). See also BENJAMIN N. CARDOZO, *The Nature of the Judicial Process*, New Haven and London 1921, p. 115: 'The law which is the resulting product is not found, but made.' and p. 119: 'Everywhere there is growing emphasis on the analogy between the function of the judge and the function of the legislator'.

[59] See MORTON WHITE, *Social Thought in America: the Revolt Against Formalism*; *Karl Llewellyn and the Realist Movement*, p. 9; MORTON J HORWITZ, *The Transformation of American Law 1870-1960; The Crisis of Legal Orthodoxy*, p. 188.

[60] See M.D.A. FREEMAN, *Lloyd's Introduction to Jurisprudence*, p. 655.

[61] MORTON J HORWITZ, The *Transformation of American Law 1870-1960; The Crisis of Legal Orthodoxy*. In the same sense DUNCAN KENNEDY, 'Form and Substance in Private Law Adjudication', 89 *Harv. L. Rev.* (1976), p. 1685 ff, on p. 1713-24; M.D.A. FREEMAN, *Lloyd's Introduction to Jurisprudence*, p 654.

[62] In Lochner v. New York (1905) the US Supreme Court overturned a maximum-hours law for bakers and thus, effectively, constitutionalised freedom of contract. See MORTON J HORWITZ, *The Transformation of American Law 1870-1960; The Crisis of Legal Orthodoxy*, p. 5. For a parallel with the four freedoms in Europe today see CHRISTIAN JOERGES, 'The Impact of European Integration on Private Law: Reductionist Perceptions, True Conflicts and a New Constitutional Perspective', *ELJ* 1997, pp. 378-406.

[63] MORTON J HORWITZ, *The Transformation of American Law 1870-1960; The Crisis of Legal Orthodoxy*, p. 170.

[64] RICHARD A. POSNER, *Overcoming Law*, Cambridge (Massachusetts) and London 1995, pp. 271-286.

[65] See e.g. RICHARD A. POSNER (ED.), *The Essential Holmes; Selections from the Letters, Speeches, Judicial Opinions, and Other Writings of Oliver Wendell Holmes, Jr*, 1992 Chicago and London, p. xi.

which, for its functional approach and its lack of abstractions, may be regarded as a typical product of realism[66]. Another example is Jerome Frank, who was a New York attorney and later became a senior judge. And, of course, the most eminent example was the proto-realist Oliver Wendell Holmes. It is important to note that Holmes was not merely a scholar with interesting theoretical ideas. Although he was a professor at Harvard for a few years, for most of his career he was a highly influential judge. He served for more than 20 years at the US Supreme Court, and became America's most admired judge.

B. Legacy

The revolt against formalism has decisively marked American legal culture. It has given American legal culture its own distinct character and has moved it away from the legal culture in England (and the rest of Europe). Since the realist revolution the American approach to the law has been far from dogmatic. Recently Richard Rorty remarked: 'everybody seems now to be a legal realist'[67]; the battle against formalism seems to have been won. Today, in American legal discourse, policy issues are at the heart of legal debate[68]. The pragmatic focus is on consequences of legal decisions. Although it is very much disputed what exactly the significance and success of the realist movement has been[69], and what their legacy is[70], their anti-formalist (in European terms: anti-dogmatic) approach, their pragmatic focus on consequences of rules, their external and critical perspective of the law and their removal of artificial boundaries between the social sciences, paved the

[66] See WILLIAM TWINING, *Karl Llewellyn and the Realist Movement*, Ch. 11 and 12. Another example is the Chicago Arbitration Project. See M.D.A. FREEMAN, *Lloyd's Introduction to Jurisprudence*, p. 662; WILLIAM TWINING, *Karl Llewellyn and the Realist Movement*, p. 181.

[67] RICHARD RORTY, *Philosophy and Social Hope*, London 1999, p. 93. He continues: 'Nobody wants to talk about a 'science of law' any longer. Nobody doubts that (...) 'the revolt against formalism' was a real advance, both in legal theory and in American intellectual life generally.'; p. 94: 'it seems plausible to claim that the battles that the legal realists fought in alliance with Dewey have essentially been won'. However, in recent years a movement of new formalism has emerged. See further *infra*.

[68] Compare JAN SMITS, *The Good Samaritan in European Private Law; On the Perils of Principles without a Programme and a Programme for the Future*, Deventer 2000, p. 26: 'In my mind, there is no legal system in the world that allows so much place for policy issues in the private law debate as the American legal system'.

[69] RICHARD A. POSNER (ED.), *The Essential Holmes*, p. xi regards 'the legal-realist movement (more accurately, the legal-pragmatist movement)' as 'the most influential school of twentieth-century American legal thought and practice'.

[70] See M.D.A. FREEMAN, *Lloyd's Introduction to Jurisprudence*, p. 667 ff; WILLIAM TWINING, *Karl Llewellyn and the Realist Movement*, p. 375 ff; MORTON J HORWITZ, *The Transformation of American Law 1870-1960; The Crisis of Legal Orthodoxy*, p. 193 ff, RICHARD A. POSNER, *Overcoming Law*, p. 271 ff; NEIL DUXBURY, *Patterns of American Jurisprudence, passim.* Compare NEIL DUXBURY, *Patterns of American Jurisprudence*, p. 64: 'American legal realism is one of the great paradoxes of modern jurisprudence. No other jurisprudential tendency of the twentieth century has exerted such a powerful influence on legal thinking while remaining so ambiguous, unsettled and undefined.'

way for such varied disciplines and movements as law & economics, law & society, law & literature, critical legal studies (cls), law & gender and law & race et cetera. The typical first reaction of the European who opens an American law journal is that it contains hardly any articles on 'law'. Indeed, these journals are dominated by economic, political, sociologic, behavioural and other analyses of specific problems rather than by articles on the relationship between concepts. Moreover, since the realist revolution American legal culture never seems to have lost its dynamic: new movements contesting prevailing opinion keep stirring up the process[71].

III. Realism in Europe

As we saw above, European legal culture (especially as far as private law is concerned) is still largely formal, dogmatic and positivistic. This is surprising because Europe also had a Realist movement. Realism even started here.

A. Realism

Nearly a century ago, on 31 October 1910, Henri Hijmans delivered his inaugural lecture at the University of Amsterdam. In this lecture, which was entitled 'Het recht der werkelijkheid' (the law of reality), Hijmans called for a new approach to the law by courts, scholars, and the legislator[72]. Hijmans' lecture was a forceful plea against the then prevailing dogmatic approach to the law: against sophisticated legal reasoning ('scherpzinnige redeneerkunst'), against legal constructions ('juridische constructies'), for liberation from statute ('vrijmaking van de wet') and from language's coercion ('vrijmaking van de dwang der taal') and for a new, realistic approach to what he called the 'real living law'[73]. Hijmans was far from isolated; on the contrary.

In Germany, Eugen Ehrlich, Hermann Kantorowicz and other leaders of the *Freirechtbewegung* had made similar pleas[74]. The main characteristic of the *Freirechtslehre* of Ehrlich, Kantorowicz and others was their loss of faith in rationality: in their view the decision of a judge was determined in the first place by his subjective will to decide in a certain way[75]. In particular they

---

[71] Compare HORATIA MUIR WATT, 'La fonction subversive du droit comparé', p. 407: 'En effet, le prestige dont jouit actuellement le droit américain tient en grande partie, me semble-t-il, à sa capacité d'adaptation, à son dynamisme, à sa flexibilité, bref à des qualités qui s'expliquent par un facteur culturel très important : c'est un système juridique où l'ordre établi des choses est constamment remis en question par des tendances contestataires, dont la présence évite la sclérose ou, en tout cas, en réduit le risque.'.

[72] I. HENRI HIJMANS, *Het recht der werkelijkheid*, Haarlem 1910.

[73] I. HENRI HIJMANS, *Het recht der werkelijkheid*, p. 4: 'Het is mij er slechts om te doen U aan te toonen wanneer, en hoe, onafhankelijk van de wet de beslissing van privaatrechtelijke geschillen kan worden gezocht in het leven zelf: m.a.w. ik wensch U te laten zien hoe naast het recht der wet ook het recht der werkelijkheid, en wel als hooger in rang, zijn plaats in de wetenschap, zijn gelding in de rechtspraak opeischt.'

[74] See KARL LARENZ, *Methodenlehre der Rechtswissenschaft*, p. 59 ff.

[75] The same applies, of course, to scholars. See GNAEUS FLAVIUS (HERMANN KANTOROWICZ), 'Der Kampf um die Rechtswissenschaft', Heidelberg 1906 (reprinted in: THOMAS

were sceptical about the rationality and objectivity of analogies, extensive interpretation, legal fictions, *ratio legis*, the spirit of the code or statute, system, abstraction and deduction, and legal certainty[76]. Kantorowicz was particularly critical of the 'dogmas' of integrity and comprehensiveness which he rejected as 'juristic megalomania' ('juristischen Größenwahn'): no other science claims to be able to have an answer (and the correct one) to all its own questions[77]. Earlier, in the last decades of the 19th century Rudolph von Jhering, after first having been a devoted system-builder himself, had turned against the *Begriffsjurisprudenz* of his day, with biting irony[78]. Jhering defended a pragmatic view of the law[79]. What counted was the purpose of rules, given to them by society. He said[80]: 'Unsere juristische Methode legt

---

WÜRTENBERGER (ed.), *Rechtswissenschaft und Soziologie; Ausgewählte Schriften zur Wissenschaftslehre von Hermann Kantorowicz*, Karlsruhe 1962, pp. 13-39), pp. 27-28: 'So entstehen denn jene großen, in Lehrbüchern niedergelegte *Systeme* individuelles Rechtes, die in dem Maße vollständig und widerspruchslos sein können, als es die Individualitäten ihrer Urheber sind, und in dem Maße einander widersprechen müssen, als die Individualitäten ihrer Urheber sich widersprechen. (...) Allen diesen Lehrbüchern und Systemen aber ist gemeinsam, daß sie die Persönlichkeiten ihrer Schöpfer in all ihren sittlichen, politischen, rechtlichen Fühlen mit Scharfe zum Ausdruck bringen, was ganz unmöglich wäre wenn sie wirklich staatliches Recht darstellten, wie ihre Titel angeben.'

[76] GNAEUS FLAVIUS (HERMANN KANTOROWICZ), 'Der Kampf um die Rechtswissenschaft', p. 43: 'Ein schönes Ideal gewiß, - aber in Ewigkeit unerfüllbar. Wenn das Urteil voraussehbar wäre, gäbe es ja keine Prozesse und also keine Urteile, denn wer würde einen Prozeß anstrengen, in dem er, wie sich voraussehen läßt, - unterliegt?'

[77] GNAEUS FLAVIUS (HERMANN KANTOROWICZ), 'Der Kampf um die Rechtswissenschaft', p. 17-18: 'In keiner theoretischen, in keiner praktischen Wissenschaft besteht die Ansicht, daß sie je imstande sein könne, geschweige denn schon jetzt imstande wäre, jedes erdenkliches Problem lösen zu können. (...) Nur ganz allein die Jurisprudenz traut sich infolge ihrer angeblich systematischen Vollkommenheit zu, jedes denkbare Problem lösen zu können, und verlangt diese Fähigkeit sogar von dem letzten ihrer Jünger.'

[78] His most famous work in this respect is 'Im juristischen Begriffshimmel', published in RUDOLPH VON JHERING, *Scherz und Ernst in der Jurisprudenz; Eine Weihnachtsgabe für das juristische Publikum*, 12th ed., Leipzig 1921 (first published in 1884). As a Roman lawyer, after his death Jhering is entitled to go to the heaven of legal concepts (where practitioners are not admitted): 'Da Du Romanist bist, so kommst Du in den juristischen Begriffshimmel. In ihm findest Du alle die juristischen Begriffe, mit denen Du Dich auf Erden so viel beschäftigt hast, wieder. Aber nicht in ihrer unvollkommenen Gestalt, in ihrer Verunstaltung, die sie auf Erden durch die Gesetzgeber und Praktiker erfahren haben, sondern in ihrer vollendeten fleckenlosen Reinheit und idealen Schönheit.' However, before being admitted, like Puchta, Savigny and others have been before, Jhering has to undergo an examination of intellectual exercises where various interesting machines are involved ('Haarspaltemaschine', 'Fiktionsapparat', 'Konstruktionsapparat', 'dialektisch-hydraulische Interpretationspresse', 'Schwindelwand').

[79] See the title of one of his main works after his 'conversion', *Der Zweck im Recht* (1877).

[80] RUDOLPH VON JHERING, *Geist des Römischen Rechts auf den verschiedenen Stufen seiner Entwicklung*, Part I, 6tth ed, Leipzig 1907, p. 50, note 19; see also, p. 48: 'Nichts ist verkehrter, als ein Recht gleich einem philosophischen System bloß von seiten seines geistigen Gehaltes, seiner logischen Gliederung und Einheit zu beurteilen. Möge es unter diesem Gesichtspunkt immerhin ein Meisterstück erscheinen, so ist doch damit über seinen wahren Wert noch in keiner Weise entschieden; letzterer liegt in seinen Funktionen, d.h. in seiner praktischen Brauchbarkeit. Was nützt es, daß einen Maschine untauglich ist?'; p. 49: 'Ja, es kann der Darstellende sich leicht der Täuschung hingeben, es sei etwas Hohes und Großes, den Stoff so zu verarbeiten, als sei derselbe eine Emanation des Begriffes, der Begriff also das Ursprüngliche, seiner selbst wegen Daseiende,

leider ein gar zu großes Gewicht auf die anatomische Struktur der Institute, und ein zu geringes auf die Funktionen.' And in France scholars like Raymond Saleilles (comparative law) and (especially) François Gény with his method of '*libre recherche scientifique*' had undermined many of the assumptions of the *École des exégètes*, especially *'le postulat de la plénitude de la loi écrite'*, and had denounced the artificial character of logical construction[81]. Moreover, just like in the United States, the social and economic conditions for radical change were there.

B. Reconstruction

However, although in all European countries the 19th century's extreme formalism (*Begriffsjurisprudenz, École des exégètes, legisme*) was defeated[82], and although from the beginning of the 20th century social change had a forceful impact on the law, realism was never victorious in Europe (with the exception of Scandinavia). The movement even sometimes met with very sharp criticism. Whereas today in the United States realists are celebrated as heroes[83], in Europe most of their counterparts have been long forgotten or are at best remembered as eccentrics[84].

What happened? In Europe, the dogmatic-systematic approach to the law was not set aside by a realist revolution. The desire for change was rather internalised within the system and into the prevailing method. The main institutions of the 19th century private law construction, like freedom of

---

während doch in der Tat die ganze logische Gliederung des Rechts, und sei sie noch so vollendet, nur das Sekundäre, das Produkt der Zwecke ist, denen sie dienen soll.'; p. 49: 'Die Funktion des Rechts im allgemeinen besteht nun darin sich zu verwirklichen. Was sich nicht realisiert, ist kein Recht, und umgekehrt was diese Funktion ausübt, ist Recht, auch wenn es noch nicht als solches anerkannt ist (Gewohnheitsrecht).'

[81] See FRANÇOIS GENY, *Méthode d'interprétation et sources en droit privé positif : Essai critique*, 1899. Compare JACQUES GHESTIN & GILLES GOUBEAUX, *Traité de droit civil, Introduction générale*, 3rd ed., Paris 1990, nos. 147 ff; JEAN CARBONNIER, *Droit Civil; Introduction*, 25th ed., Paris 1997, no. 152.

[82] See KARL LARENZ, *Methodenlehre der Rechtswissenschaft*, 1991, pp. 11 ff; JACQUES GHESTIN & GILLES GOUBEAUX, *Introduction générale*, nos. 140 ff; P.C. KOP, *Legisme en Privaatrechtswetenschap*, Deventer 1982, G.G.J.J. VAN DEN BERGH, *Geleerd recht*, 4th ed., Deventer 2000, p. 105 ff.

[83] The number of biographies and other books on realists and realism is overwhelming.

[84] An anthology of the University of Amsterdam around 1900 (J.C.H. BLOM, P.H.D. LEUPEN, P. DE ROOY, T.J. VEEN, L. KOOIJMANS (eds.), *Een brandpunt van geleerdheid in de hoofdstad; De Universiteit van Amsterdam rond 1900 in vijftien portretten*, Hilversum/Amsterdam 1992) contains portraits of three law professors, T.M.C. Asser, A.A.H. Struycken and P. Scholten, but not of Hijmans, and neither does a collection of portraits of 60 significant Dutch jurists (T.J. VEEN, P.C. KOP (eds.), *Zestig juristen; Bijdragen tot een beeld van de geschiedenis der Nederlandse rechtswetenschap*, Zwolle 1987) contain any mention of Hijmans. However, see TH.M. DE BOER ET AL., *De werkelijkheid van I. Henri Hijmans; symposium gehouden op 23 oktober 1987*, Deventer 1988, especially Van Schellen's contribution (J. VAN SCHELLEN, 'Het recht der Werkelijkheid', p. 57 ff), (who regards Hijmans as a 'een miskend genie' (p. 58)). And see recently H.C.F. SCHOORDIJK, 'Het einde van het recht der werkelijkheid?', *WPNR* 6444 (2001), p. 449, p. 451: 'Op weer naar het recht der werkelijkheid!'

contract, absolute property and fault liability were not set aside. Instead, new institutions were added in order to moderate their effect. Abuse of right, good faith, strict liability, and unjust enrichment operated as safety valves that removed the pressure on the system. Similarly, the teleological method of interpretation was added to the grammatical and systematic methods[85]. The leading scholars did not step out of the system into reality, like Kantorowicz, Hijmans and other realists did. No, they faithfully remained inside the system but opened windows towards reality, thus creating an 'open system' which communicated with society and which adapted to its changes.

In the Netherlands Meijers and Scholten played an important part in the reconstruction of the systematic approach to the law[86]. In France Capitant seems to have played a crucial role[87]. See Jamin[88]: 'à la méthode classique ou encore exégétique succède et triomphe peut-être avec lui ce que je serais tenté de qualifier de méthode *doctrinaliste.* Prenant appui sur la jurisprudence, censée exprimer la vie du droit, plus sûrement que sur la loi, celle-ci ne se contente pas de la décrire dans sa complexité et de laisser ouvertes plusieurs voies, elle la sélectionne, la trie, en tire des principes qu'elle systématise pour les confronter à d'autres principes, à des cadres et des classifications traditionnelles qu'il ne s'agit pas de briser, afin de donner à l'ensemble sa cohérence, ou du moins ce qui paraît être sa cohérence; bref, elle en fait la *théorie générale.* Ce faisant, elle ne renie nullement le formalisme juridique pas plus que l'autonomie du droit.' And in Germany the *Interessenjurisprudenz* (Philipp Heck and others) was victorious in theory and in practice (it won the *Methodenstreit*)[89]. The *Interessenjurisprudenz* was a reaction against the *Begriffsjurisprudenz* (a term branded by Heck) and was experienced as a liberation (similar to Gény's impact in France and Scholten's impact in the Netherlands): courts were now allowed to take the needs and desires of society into account. They replaced their method of mechanical

[85] See e.g. PAUL SCHOLTEN, *Mr. C. Asser's handleiding tot de beoefening van het Nederlands burgerlijk recht; Algemeen Deel*, Zwolle 1974 (first edition 1931), p. 35. For France compare JEAN CARBONNIER, *Droit Civil; Introduction*, 25th ed., Paris 1997, no. 155.

[86] See PAUL SCHOLTEN, *Algemeen Deel*, p. 76: 'Toch vormt het recht ongetwijfeld een systeem, een geheel van logisch passende regelingen. Maar een systeem dat niet, omdat het gebrekkig mensenwerk is, hier en daar hiaten vertoont, maar dat uit zijn aard niet af is en niet af kan zijn, omdat het grondslag is van beslissingen, die aan het systeem zelf iets toevoegen. Ik meen, dat dit het beste uitkomt, indien we van een open systeem spreken.' Meijers' most significant contribution to reconstruction has been his plea for (see E.M. MEIJERS, 'Wijzigingen en aanvullingen van het Burgerlijk wetboek na 1838') and his design of the new civil code. Compare P.C. KOP, *Legisme en Privaatrechtswetenschap*, p. 65.

[87] Moreover, Gény's method itself was not all that revolutionary. Gény regarded the cases where the law was silent (which allowed for *'libre recherche scientifique'*) as exceptional, and did not regard *'libre recherche'* as arbitrary; it was *'scientifique'*.

[88] CHRISTOPHE JAMIN, 'Henri Capitant et René Demogue: notation sur l'actualité d'un dialogue doctrinal', p. 133 (emphasis in the original).

[89] See KARL LARENZ, *Methodenlehre der Rechtswissenschaft*, p. 49. See also WOLFGANG FIKENTSCHER, *Methoden des Rechts in vergleichender Darstellung*, Band III *Mitteleuropäischer Rechtskreis*, Tübingen 1976, p. 380: 'Das Entscheidende an der Interessenjurisprudenz ist (...) ihr Sieg in der Praxis'.

formal-logical subsumption with an evaluation of the interests at stake in a certain conflict[90]. However, they never actually broke with positivism (they added new facts that were causal for positive law: values and interests[91]) and with systematism[92], and they explicitly and forcefully rejected the *Freirechtslehre*[93]. In other European countries there were similar developments[94]. Instead of a realist revolution, more moderate attacks on legal formalism, which did not abandon their faith in rationality and system, won the day.[95]

Thus, instead of a revolt there was gradual transformation[96]. Legislators and courts accepted exceptions to freedom (e.g. labour legislation) and the binding force (good faith) of contract, to absolute property (abuse of right), and to fault liability (strict liability). All this happened relatively peacefully and without any revolt. Rather, new social developments were accommodated within the system, frequently within the code. There were no fundamental attacks on the private law pillars of contract, tort and property, or on the private/public divide which was exemplified by the civil codes. Rather, there was gradual adaptation by the legislator and (especially) by the courts[97]. The new important role of the courts themselves was also easily accommodated: they were simply integrated into the system as a source of law (unwritten in addition to written law)[98]. This transformation led to the situation which I described above as the current European legal culture[99].

---

[90] See KARL LARENZ, *Methodenlehre der Rechtswissenschaft*, p. 58.

[91] Compare KARL LARENZ, *Methodenlehre der Rechtswissenschaft*, p. 53: 'Dadurch, daß sie den Richter anwies, die im Gesetz enthaltenen Werturteile im Hinblick auf den zu beurteilenden Fall denkend nachzuvollziehen, hat die Interessenjurisprudenz auf eine im formalen Denken und im strengen Gesetzespositivismus erzogenen Juristengeneration – ohne doch die Schranken des Positivismus wirklich zu durchbrechen – befreiend und befruchtend gewirkt'.

[92] They simply added an inner system (*inneres System*) to the outer system (*außeres System*).

[93] Compare KARL LARENZ, *Methodenlehre der Rechtswissenschaft*, p. 62: 'Mit Recht haben die Vertreter der Interessenjurisprudenz wiederholt und mit Nachdruck betont, daß sich ihre Lehre von der der "Freirechtsbewegung" wesentlich unterscheide. Denn, von wenigen Ausnahmefällen abgesehen, sehen sie die richterliche Rechtsfindung als durch rationale Erwägungen geleitet an. (...) Die Rechtspraxis ist daher auch ganz überwiegend der Interessenjurisprudenz, nicht aber der Freirechtslehre gefolgt.'

[94] For Italy see RODOLFO SACCO, *Introduzione al diritto comparato*, p. 256 ff. ('L'Italia paese imitatore').

[95] In 1933 Hijmans made another attempt (I. HENRI HIJMANS, *De tweesprong der rechtswetenschap*, Zwolle 1933), but again failed to force a radical change.

[96] See on transformation in France HORATIA MUIR WATT, 'La fonction subversive du droit comparé', p. 516: 'l'attachement du droit français à la rationalité normative, qui s'est avérée en réalité suffisamment sophistiquée pour s'assouplir de façon très adéquate, sans emprunter la voie de la révolution méthodologique «copernicienne» proclamée aux États-Unis'.

[97] With new statutes and recodifications even an interest in 'the legislator's intention' returned, which scholars and courts hoped to find in the *travaux préparatoires*. See for France (after the reform of family law) JACQUES GHESTIN & GILLES GOUBEAUX, *Introduction générale*, no. 160.

[98] Compare CHRISTOPHE JAMIN, 'Henri Capitant et René Demogue: notation sur l'actualité d'un dialogue doctrinal', p. 134: 'Au fond, [la méthode inaugurée par Capitant] ne rompt pas profondément avec celle de ses prédécesseurs. Au lieu de prendre la loi ou le code pour point de départ, elle s'attache à la jurisprudence, afin de payer son tribut à la sociologie ambiante, mais elle lui applique un type de raisonnement, emprunt en définitive d'un même formalisme, au

C. Some Suggested Explanations

How is this difference in the success of realism in Europe and the United States explained? Why has Europe not embraced anti-formalism? Especially American scholars have asked this question.

For the difference between the United States and England Atiyah and Summers offer a rational explanation in terms of trust in the proper functioning of other institutions[100]: 'To make a decision by reference to formal reasons, after all, is to refuse to consider reasons of substance arising in the circumstances of the case which bear on the issue[101]. This requires a degree of confidence in the decision-maker that the rest of the system is working properly, so that he can exercise some self-discipline and refuse to deal with it himself, here and now. But if these reasons of substance are never to be considered at all, still more, if there never has been any opportunity to consider them, then to make the decision by purely formal reasoning shuts out the possibility of that decision ever being based on the factors most directly relevant to it.' According to Atiyah and Summers the assumptions which are made in the two countries about the working of the rest of the legal and political system are fundamentally different: English judges generally have a high degree of confidence in the proper functioning of the rest of the machinery of government and of its officials, whereas in America, this degree of confidence is often lacking[102]. This observation with regard to England

service de constructions harmonieuses réputés scientifiques. En construisant un système assis non plus sur la loi mais sur la jurisprudence, Capitant diversifiait certes les sources du droit mais il ne se montrait guère plus *réaliste* que ses prédécesseurs, au point que l'on pourrait presque parler, du moins sous cet angle, de *permanence de l'exégèse*.' (Emphasis in the original.)

[99] As said, in some European countries reconstruction efforts even led to the adoption of a new civil code. In the Netherlands it was generally expected that the 1992 code would not introduce neo-formalism (*legisme*). See A.S. HARTKAMP, *Wetsuitleg en rechtstoepassing na de invoering van het nieuwe Burgerlijk Wetboek*, Deventer 1992 and P.C. KOP, *Legisme en Privaatrechtswetenschap*, p. 65. However, since the enactment of the new code (and even somewhat before) the focus, especially in education, has been very much on the structure and the concepts of the new code. An extreme example is the *Studiereeks Burgerlijk Recht*, which is the main teaching material in most Dutch universities. Nevertheless, admittedly there is no neo-*legisme* in the strong 19th century sense of exclusive and strict exegesis of the text of the code. Compare T.J. VEEN, *''En voor berisping is hier ruime stof''*, p. 87. But see the *Hoge Raad*'s position on 'the right to terminate' discussed below.

[100] P.S ATIYAH & R.S. SUMMERS, *Form And Substance in Anglo-American Law*, p. 36-37.

[101] Compare the Dutch *Hoge Raad* which gives a very formal interpretation of art. 6:265 *BW* (on the termination of synallagmatic contracts) because it holds the view that the 1992 legislator made this rule on purpose after properly balancing the interests of the parties to a contract, and therefore refuses to go into the substantive reasons put forward by a considerable part of legal doctrine (F.B. BAKELS, *Ontbinding van wederkerige overeenkomsten, Deventer 1993*, TON HARTLIEF, *Ontbinding: over ongedaanmaking, bevrijding en rechterlijke bevoegdheden bij ontbinding wegens wanprestatie*, Deventer 1994 and others), whereas it feels free to do so with regard to the (related) question of the limits to the right of specific performance. See on this issue further M.M. STOLP, 'De bevoegdheid tot ontbinding ex art. 6:265 lid 1 BW in het licht van subsidiariteit en proportionaliteit', *NTBR* 2000, p. 352 ff, MURIEL VELDMAN, 'Grenzen aan het recht op nakoming', *WPNR* 6455 (2001), pp. 727-738, and *infra*, Chapter 3, Section VI, B, 9.

[102] On the other hand, according to Atiyah and Summers, English judges are much less inclined

may equally apply to many other European countries. If this latter observation is true, Europeans may become less formalist when they distrust other institutions, for example those of the European Union[103]. I will come back to this below.

Another interesting explanation was suggested by Duncan Kennedy. He thinks that the continuous threat of totalitarianism in Europe in the 20th century may be at the root of the difference, and that this fear of instability aborted realist movements[104]: 'In Europe, until recently, the stakes in general ideological conflict have been higher than in the United States. Liberals (social democrats) and conservatives have defended the center against a communist left and a fascist authoritarian right that have actually held and have continuously threatened to take power. (...) The center has affirmed the rule of law as the heart of its program, along with human rights and representative democracy based on free elections. It has developed the legislation/adjudication dichotomy, through the politics/law, objective/subjective, and democratic/professional accountability distinctions, as a powerful normative position. (...) Confronted with the American cls critique of the rule of law, Europeans tend to explain it by reference to the historical innocence of Americans. Because we haven't experienced either fascism or actually existing socialism, we crits are naively willing to play with fire by questioning a central pillar of humane politics in the modern age of barbarism.' In the same sense Guido Calabresi, who argues that in the 1920s it was hoped that a formal approach to rights protected by the code and by the constitution would be a safeguard against the arbitrariness of the fascist regime in Italy[105]. Thus, in Europe things might have gone differently if the Russian Revolution, the First World War, fascism, nazism, the Second World

---

than American judges to trust the people at large or their representative, the jury. According to Atiyah and Summers there are strong elitist traditions in England which influence the way in which formal and substantive reasoning is used. P.S ATIYAH & R.S. SUMMERS, *Form And Substance in Anglo-American Law*, p. 38: 'The public, in other words, must not be given grounds to believe that the law will take account of substantive reasons arising in the particular circumstances of the case: formal rules ought to be observed by the populace without question, but the elite may sometimes stretch out the hand of mercy. The mercy will not lead to the incorporation of these substantive reasons in the rules themselves, but may be available by way of discretion in sentencing, or by extensive use of the power of pardon, or in other ways.' Compare, on the continent, the separate doctrines of good faith, abuse of right, and strict liability (freedom and binding force of contract, absolute property and fault liability remain intact). According to Atiyah and Summers the American tradition rejects such elitist assumptions: 'Law, to the American, is not something imposed or laid down from above, by a sovereign; it comes from the people'.

[103] An extreme example of trust is provided by the Netherlands: we trust that the legislator will not make unconstitutional laws. Therefore, our courts are not entitled to check the constitutionality of Acts of Parliament, nor do we have a Constitutional Court.

[104] DUNCAN KENNEDY, *A Critique of Adjudication {fin de siècle}*, pp. 73-74.

[105] GUIDO CALABRESI, 'Two Functions of Formalism', 67 *U Chi L Rev* (2000), 479, p. 482: 'To the scholars opposing Fascism, the nineteenth-century self-contained formalistic system became a great weapon. Well, a formal, self-contained, uncriticizable system of law is conservative. It can't be changed.'

War and the Cold War had not taken place. This is an interesting thesis[106]. If it holds true it may now be time for some change.

A third explanation is a pragmatic one: our European method *works* in the sense that, generally, we are quite satisfied with the substantive results it has brought us. It should not be forgotten that this was different both for the American realist and the cls movements. The Realists fought for the socialisation of law and attacked the formalist defence of classical private law which was based on free contract, absolute property and fault liability[107]. Equally, most 'crits' wanted a radically different American society. They all had their (sometimes quite radical) substantive agendas: Marxism, 'left mpm', feminism, racial equality, to name but a few. The revolts against formalism were not politically neutral debates on methodology[108]. Realists and (especially) crits accused their adversaries of defending their substantive (political) positions by way of a formal approach to the law. The defenders of classical legal thought defended what they had by simply saying 'you may not like it but this is the law'; they sat on their rights as it were. The anti-formalists tried to undermine their adversaries' advantage in the political debate and to force them into discussing the substantive issues on equal terms. Crits attacked what was presented as 'positive law' by saying that in fact it was just one side of the story, the story as told by the dominant establishment. Most Europeans think that we have obtained the same substantive results without a realist revolution. Indeed, most Europeans seem to be quite satisfied with most of our private law, and on many points may find it preferable in substance to the law of most American States[109]. Moreover, many Europeans are quite satisfied with the role which dogmatic-positivistic legal doctrine plays in the development of the law. A sceptic may say that this role (which I described above) is more beneficial to the status of scholars than to the quality of our law, but at least the courts take a variety of views into account. Under these circumstances anti-formalism itself risks becoming formalist. If one wishes to change the legal methodology adopted by legislators, the courts, scholars and students without envisaging any substantive changes in the law one is actually only addressing the form of the law. So, all is well on the Old Continent? No, not quite. As a matter of fact there is an important substantive

[106] MORTON J HORWITZ, *The Transformation of American Law 1870-1960; The Crisis of Legal Orthodoxy*, p. 187, says of the American Realists: 'They were lucky to have been present at a particular moment in history when the Great Depression and the early New Deal swept away the legitimating premises of the old order and made things seem possible that just a short time before seemed impossible, if not illegitimate. Rebellion could be tolerated for a time.'

[107] See MORTON J HORWITZ, *The Transformation of American Law 1870-1960; The Crisis of Legal Orthodoxy*, New York/Oxford 1992.

[108] Compare G.G.J.J. VAN DEN BERGH, *Geleerd recht*, 4th ed., Deventer 2000, p. 90: 'Legisme en anti-legisme blijven juristenmythen, zolang men niet wil zien wat er achter steekt.'

[109] For example, the Americans have interesting and intense debates on constitutional rights, but as regards their discrimination, poverty, state killing (the death penalty) and the treatment of those labelled by the government as 'terrorists' most Europeans would not envy them.

concern in Europe, and that is a lack of transparency[110]. In our judgements, scholarly articles and teaching the stakes in a conflict, the economic and social effects of a solution, the pros and cons of alternative solutions, the agendas of those involved in the debate are usually not at the forefront of the debate. Our method which presumes rationality, unity, system, one right answer et cetera hides the plurality of possible solutions, stakes, aspects and the need to make a choice between them. Many of the substantive issues are there but are put less straightforwardly.

A final, related, possible explanation is that maybe formalism is not all that wrong. There may be something good in formalism as well. I will come to that later[111].

IV. European Private Law: Shift From Form To Substance

However, European legal history is not my main concern here. My topic is rather its future. In the rest of this chapter I will argue that as a result of European integration, our legal culture is undergoing a radical change. I will show that as a result of the emerging new European private law a new European legal culture is developing which is much less formal-dogmatic and much more substantive-pragmatic than the national legal cultures have been in Europe[112]. I will first present some of the most significant developments in legislation, adjudication, academic debate and legal education which all have in common a shift in emphasis from a more formal deductive way of reasoning to a more substantive approach. Subsequently I will assess the new European legal culture and its implications for national legal cultures.

A. Disruptive Directives

Directives are the instrument of European harmonisation which has had by far the greatest impact on private law in Europe, especially in recent years[113]. Because of their specific characteristics EC Directives introduce an approach to private law which is new in Europe in a number of ways.

1. Instrumental and Functional Approach

[110] In the same sense JAN SMITS, *The Good Samaritan in European Private Law*, p. 25: 'That [value] judgements often do not come to the surface (...) is a danger from the viewpoint of transparent and consistent national private law.'

[111] There is another explanation: on the whole American culture is more pragmatic than European cultures. Compare RICHARD RORTY, *Philosophy and Social Hope*, p. 95: 'Pragmatism was reasonably shocking 70 years ago, but in the ensuing decades it has gradually been absorbed into American common sense.' The same does not seem to apply to all European countries.

[112] See also CHRISTIAN JOERGES, 'Editorial and Acknowledgements', *ERPL* 2000, p. vii, who speaks of a 'new realism'.

[113] See for an inventory PETER CHRISTIAN MÜLLER-GRAFF, 'EC Directives as a Means of Private Law Unification', in : A.S. Hartkamp et al. (eds.), *Towards a European Civil Code.*, 2nd ed., Nijmegen and The Hague, London, Boston 1998, pp. 71 ff., on p. 83.

First, this legislative device of directives is based on an instrumental approach to the law, which is alien to the traditional conception of private law. Traditionally, private law is regarded as being relatively apolitical[114]. However, with the help of directives private law is explicitly made instrumental in achieving political, social, economic and other aims. With the presence of directives we have to face the fact that also private law is an instrument for private ordering (regulation). Private law may be used by the legislator to achieve certain aims.

Many scholars are still used to thinking of private law, or at least its general part (especially contract, tort and property) as having its own internal logic and as being based essentially on 'fairness' or morality[115]. However, this position has become increasingly untenable[116]. The legislator uses private law in order to achieve certain aims. It has done so for more than a century with specific statutes or other specific rules. It has been attempted to accommodate this development by regarding these new rules enacted by the legislator as 'specific parts' so that the general private law (or in England and Wales the common law) would remain politically neutral. However, as a result of this strategy 'general private law' risks becoming increasingly abstract and irrelevant: most of the relevant parts are in the specific rules (consumer law, labour law, competition law etc). In the United States it has long been understood (since realism) that private law is also instrumental to policies, not only by left-wing interventionists, but also by more market-oriented scholars. Indeed, scholars in law & economics study the economic effects of different rules of general private law (common law) and uphold one rule because it is more efficient than another. It is time that we fully face this reality in Europe. In any case the presence of directives will force us to do so. This is what we are facing now that directives are also interfering with the general law of obligations. Therefore we need to adopt a new approach to private law. We should no longer adopt the perspective of the internal logic of our system of private law which has to be established after the transposition of a directive. We should rather concentrate on what the purpose of the directive is and we should interpret it in the light of that substantive purpose rather than to concentrate on the formal concepts used to implement it.

---

[114] Compare DANIELA CARUSO, 'The Missing View of the Cathedral: The Private Law Paradigm of European Legal Integration', p. 28: 'centuries of legal formalism across the entire spectrum of European jurisprudential thought have bestowed upon private law a patina of technical neutrality'.

[115] See explicitly JAN SMITS, *The Good Samaritan in European Private Law*. Compare DANIELA CARUSO, 'The Missing View of the Cathedral: The Private Law Paradigm of European Legal Integration', p. 28: 'codes are meant to be entirely self-referential machines, finite sets of rules and doctrines capable of yielding exhaustive answers to any legal question.'

[116] See CHRISTIAN JOERGES, 'The Impact of European Integration on Private Law: Reductionist Perceptions, True Conflicts and a New Constitutional Perspective', p. 394: '[O]ne must take care not to remain bogged down in out-dated and "pre-Community" versions of the public private distinction. The regulatory state's intrusion into the economic sphere by means of all manner of mandatory, paternalistic or distributive legal provisions and the recognition of fundamental rights even within private relationships, are simple facts, omnipresent in all our systems of private law.'

A (related) second characteristic of directives, and probably the most important one, is their functional approach to the law. Directives are not directly binding upon citizens (they have no direct horizontal effect[117]); they only bind the Member States. These States are only bound to achieve a certain substantive result; in principle, each state is free to determine in which form that result will be achieved (art. 249 (3) (= *ex* 189(3)) EC Treaty)[118]. Therefore directives, in principle, do not impose the introduction of specific legal concepts[119]. They have a substantive aim, for example to remove market impediments or to provide consumer protection. Thus the legislative device of EU Directives is based on the idea of functional equivalents: the EU is concerned with a certain substantive result and leaves it to the national legislators to decide in which form they prefer to implement it. Thus, directives do not adopt a formal-dogmatic but a functional approach to the law[120].

2. Impressionistic Harmonisation

Another (related) characteristic of harmonisation by directives is that it is rather impressionistic. Directives deal with specific subjects which in most legal systems are just one part of a broader subject, which in turn may be

[117] Case C-91/92 (Faccini Dori *v* Recreb). On the differences between regulations and directives see PAUL CRAIG & GRÁINNE DE BÚRCA, *EU Law; Text, Cases, and Materials*, 2nd ed., Oxford 1998, p. 108. Critical: PETER CHRISTIAN MÜLLER-GRAFF, 'EC Directives as a Means of Private Law Unification', p. 75. In the light of recent cases like Case C-194/94 (CIA Security International SA *v* Signalson SA & Securitel SPRL), and Case C-443/98 (Unilever Italia *v* Central Food) it is questioned whether the ECJ's rejection of a horizontal effect of directives will remain tenable. See e.g. J.H. JANS & R. DE LANGE & S. PRECHAL & R.J.G.M. WIDDERSHOVEN, *Inleiding tot het Europees bestuursrecht*, Nijmegen 1999, p. 74. Compare PAUL CRAIG & GRÁINNE DE BÚRCA, *EU Law; Text, Cases, and Materials*, p. 208, who speak of 'incidental horizontal direct effect' and remark: 'The question for us is whether this can realistically be distinguished from horizontal direct effect.' On the obligation for national courts to interpret their law in conformity with directives see *infra*.

[118] Art. 249, para 3 (= *ex* 189(3)) EC Treaty: 'A directive shall be binding, as to the result to be achieved, upon each Member State to which it is addressed, but shall leave to the national authorities the choice of form and methods.' Compare W. VAN GERVEN, 'L'harmonisation du droit des contrats en Europe; Rapport introductif', in : Christophe Jamin, Denis Mazeaud (eds.), *L'harmonisation du droit des contrats en Europe*, Paris 2001, p. 3: 'Harmonisation doit être distinguée d'unification. Alors que des règlements de droit communautaire qui sont obligatoires dans tous leurs éléments et directement applicables dans tout État membre, produisent du droit unifié dans l'ordre national des États membres, les directives ne lient les États membres destinataires quant au résultat à atteindre et mènent donc seulement à une harmonisation de règles nationales (art. 189, devenu 249, CE).'

[119] See on the meaning of 'the choice of form and methods' in art. 189 (3) EC, SACHA PRECHAL, *Directives in European Community Law; A Study on EC Directives and their Enforcement by National Courts*, Ph. D. thesis Amsterdam 1995, 86 f.

[120] See PETER CHRISTIAN MÜLLER-GRAFF, 'EC Directives as a Means of Private Law Unification', p. 77: 'This method implies the opportunity (...) to respect national sovereignty as far as the form and methods of implementation are concerned. In short, approximation by directives seems to be a way of combining the necessities for uniform Community standards on the one hand and the possibility to tolerate national individualities on the other.'

systematically connected with other subjects. This patchwork character of harmonisation by directives is a direct result of the instrumental approach to the law[121]. The EU is concerned with certain specific changes in the law which it regards as economically, socially or politically desirable, and is not concerned with the rest of the national legal system in which the directive must be implemented[122]. Frequently, the European Union seems to possess a very narrow-minded view (the view of its Brussels Directorate-General) and does not seem to care about the broader picture[123]. Moreover, even if it wished to do so in many cases it may very well be that it simply cannot. The EU is not free to enact directives as it pleases. It needs specific authority from the EC Treaty for each directive it enacts[124].

This functional and impressionistic approach to private law leads to frictions within the national legal systems, especially the civil law systems with their codes, abstractions, and general ideas. Thus, whereas directives aim at unity on a European level, they cause disunity on a national level. They lead to national 'disintegration'[125]. The disruptive effect of directives is a direct result of the impressionistic approach. As said, directives deal with specific subjects which in most legal systems are merely one part of a broader subject, which in turn may be systematically connected with other subjects

[121] See also L.A.D. KEUS, 'Europees privaatrecht - Een bonte lappendeken', in: *Preadviezen, uitgebracht voor de Vereniging voor Burgerlijk Recht en de Nederlandse Vereniging voor Europees Recht*, Lelystad 1993.

[122] See PETER CHRISTIAN MÜLLER-GRAFF, 'EC Directives as a Means of Private Law Unification', p. 81: 'A last problem to be mentioned is the rather scattered appearance of the measures taken, both in regard to the areas covered and to the rules created. Coming from an institution that is composed of members of national governments, the directives show a feeling for actualities, but no coherent concept of legislation in private law (except company law) so far.'

[123] Some scholars openly express their doubts concerning the legal skills of the civil servants in Brussels who are involved in drafting the directives. See VINCENZO ZENO-ZENCOVICH, 'The "European Civil Code", European Legal Traditions and Neo-positivism', in Guido Alpa, Emilio Nicola Buccico (eds.), *Il codice civile europeo; Materiali dei seminari 1999-2000*, Milano 2001, pp. 375 ff., on p. 377-378: 'Legrand's doubts, expressed in a manner that could be even more forthright, as to the legal skills of the EU bureaucracy should be entirely supported. (...) with obvious exceptions, this group does not have at its disposal great legal skills. This is because of its background, its methods of recruitment, the cultural differences amongst its members, and the lack of a profound knowledge of the legal traditions of member states. (...) It is therefore perfectly justifiable to be severely critical of the EU legislation, both as regards its content and the mentality it expresses.' See also OLIVIER REMIEN, 'Einheit, Mehrstufigheit und Flexibilität im europäischen Privat- und Wirtschaftsrecht', 62 *RabelsZ* (1998), p. 627 ff, p. 646: 'Unvollkommenheit der redaktionellen Qualität mancher Richtlinien'.

[124] See W. VAN GERVEN, 'L'harmonisation du droit des contrats en Europe; Rapport introductif', p. 3: 'L'exigence de base légale est souvent responsable du caractère limité et ponctuel des directives ou règlements communautaires, ce qui a pour conséquence qu'ils ne couvrent qu'une partie seulement du secteur du droit national concerné et qu'ils sont à l'origine d'une nouvelle disparité (ou 'dé-harmonisation') dans l'ordre juridique de chaque État membre à savoir entre règles (couvrant des matières similaires) dont les unes sont affectées et les autres non affectées par la directive ou le règlement concerné.'

[125] CHRISTIAN JOERGES, 'The Impact of European Integration on Private Law: Reductionist Perceptions, True Conflicts and a New Constitutional Perspective', p. 385.

(national integrity)[126]. From a national systematic perspective it does not make sense to change the law on just the specific subject. Thus, the implementation of directives on unfair terms, consumer guarantees, and, most recently, on late payment of money debts, have raised some very difficult systematic questions in various legal systems in Europe. How should product liability relate to the existing tort and contractual (*action directe*) liabilities?[127] Should the protection against unfair terms (e.g. controlling their content or the *contra proferentem* rule) be extended to persons other than consumers?[128] Should the hierarchy of remedies, the unitary concept of non-conformity, the rejection of the concept of *aliud* be extended to other sales contracts or to other consumer contracts or to all contracts?[129] Should the rules on interest in case of late payment in commercial contracts be extended to other commercial or non-commercial contracts or to non-contractual monetary debts?[130] Should the formation rules on contracts concluded via the Internet (e-commerce) be extended to other contracts?[131]

Therefore, in many European countries the obligation to implement a specific directive has raised the question whether or not broader parts of the law should be changed accordingly. Indeed, it took France over a decade to transpose the directive on product liability because it tried to broaden it into a major reform of the law of contractual and delictual liability and the law of hidden defects. Eventually, this reform partly failed (as a result of a producers' lobby), but nevertheless the French legislator felt that it could not change the producer's liability without bringing the seller's (provider's) liability into line[132]. And at this moment in time the German legislator is

[126] CHRISTIAN JOERGES, 'The Impact of European Integration on Private Law: Reductionist Perceptions, True Conflicts and a New Constitutional Perspective', p. 396: 'European regulatory initiatives never address the legal-institutional environment of a social field in its entirety, but always concern only one particular aspect. Their innovative potential and their disintegrative effects in fact derive from this selectivity.'

[127] Directive 85/374/EEC on liability for defective products.

[128] Directive 1993/13/EEC on unfair terms in consumer contracts.

[129] Directive 1999/44/EC of 25 May 1999 on certain aspects of the sale of consumer goods and associated guarantees. Compare EWOUD HONDIUS & CHRISTOPH JELOSCHEK, 'Towards a European Sales Law - Legal Challenges posed by the Directive on the Sale of Consumer Goods and Associated Guarantees, 9 *ERPL* 2001, p. 3 ff., p. 5: 'Reducing the amendment to a reception of the Directive only could result in an unstable and confusing set of rules since pure consumer provisions have to be inserted in a general system.'

[130] Directive 2000/35/EC on combating late payment in commercial transactions.

[131] Directive 2000/31/EC on certain legal aspects of information society services, in particular electronic commerce, in the Internal Market. See A.F. SALOMONS, 'Inpassen of aanpassen? Vermogensrecht voor het digitale tijdperk', *WPNR* 6427 (2000), p. 901 ff and CHRISTINA H. RAMBERG, 'The E-Commerce Directive and Formation of Contract in a Comparative Perspective', *Global Jurist Advances*: Vol. 1: No. 2, Article 3 (www.bepress.com/gj/advances/vol1/iss2/art3), both of whom are critical.

[132] See JACQUES GHESTIN, 'Le nouveau titre IV bis du Livre III du Code civil "De la responsabilité du fait des produits défectueux"; L'application en France de la directive dur la responsabilité du fait des produits défectueux après l'adoption de la loi n° 98-389 du 19 mai 1998', *JCP*, 1998, no. 27, pp. 1201 ff.

working on a reform of the law of obligations[133], especially the law of non-performance, as a result of its obligation to transpose the directives on consumer sales and guarantees[134], on late payment of money debts[135] and on e-commerce[136]. This reform takes up the major *Schuldrechtreform*[137] which reached a standstill due to a lack of political interest at the beginning of the 1990s[138]. Other countries leave the systematic questions for the courts to resolve by simply transposing the directive into a separate statute. Italy is adopting this strategy for the consumer guarantees directive[139], and this has been the current practice in Great Britain for a number of years[140].

The most general and fundamental question of national normative coherence is raised by the EU's development of consumer law. The EU has issued a great variety of directives which are meant to give consumers better protection. However, it is not unimaginable, to say the least, that similar protection should be given to small or even all businesses. Indeed, the limitation to consumers was frequently not inspired by normative considerations but by the way in which European Union bureaucracy is organised in Brussels. Different Directorates-General are responsible for the Common Market and for Consumer Protection, which has significantly

---

[133] See the federal government's draft of 9 May 2001*: Entwurf eines Gesetzes zur Modernisierung des Schuldrechts*, p. 169-170. 'Dabei ist zu berücksichtigen dass die durch die Richtlinie geforderten Umsetzungsmaßnahmen eng mit weiteren, von ihr nicht unmittelbar erfassten Bereichen des Schuld- und Verjährungsrecht verwoben sind (...) Die Diskussion hat auch gezeigt, dass es auch im Schuldrecht an der Zeit ist, die das Bürgerliche Gesetzbuch immer mehr überwuchernden (schuldrechtlichen) Sondergesetze zu sichten und ihren dauerhaften Bestand in das Bürgerliche Gesetzbuch zu integrieren. Dies führt zu einer übersichtlicheren Schuldrechtsordnung. Die Zurückführung der schuldrechtlichen Sondergesetze stärkt nicht nur das Bürgerliche Gesetzbuch als zentrale Zivilrechtskodifikation. Sie nutzt die integrative kraft des Bürgerlichen Gesetzbuchs, um die Einheit des Schuldrechts zu gewährleisten und zu stärken. Sie droht verloren zu gehen, weil sich die einzelnen Sondermaterien immer mehr verselbständigen und weil das Schuldvertragsrecht des Bürgerlichen Gesetzbuchs für die Massengeschäften des täglichen Lebens immer mehr durch Sondergesetze verdrängt wird.' See further STEFAN GRUNDMANN, 'European sales law - reform and adoption of international models in German sales law', 9 *ERPL* 2001, p. 85 ff. and www.stephan-lorenz.de/schumod (in German) by Prof. Stephan Lorenz, with many documents and references to more than 50 doctrinal articles.

[134] 1999/44/EC (25 May 1999).

[135] 2000/35/EC (29 June 2000).

[136] Arts. 10, 11, 18 directive 2000/31/EC (8 June 2000).

[137] See *Regierungsentwurf*, p. 170.

[138] See 'Abschlußbericht der Kommission zur Überarbeitung des Schuldrechts, herausgegeben vom Bundesminister der Justiz', *Bundesanzeiger, Köln 1992.*

[139] In contrast, previous directives like the one on unfair terms were incorporated into the code. See for criticism MANOLA SCOTTON, 'Directive 99/44/EC on certain aspects of the sale consumer goods and associated guarantees', 9 *ERPL* 2001, pp 143-153.

[140] However see now the *Unfair Terms in Contracts; A Joint Consultation Paper* (Law Commission Consultation Paper No 166 and Scottish Law Commission Discussion Paper No 119), London 2002, which provisionally proposes replacing the Unfair Contract Terms Act 1997 and the Unfair Terms in Consumer Contracts Regulations 1999 with a single piece of legislation; rationalising the controls over non-negotiated terms in business-to-business contracts; and re-writing the legislation in a way that is clearer and more accessible to consumer and business advisers.

increased the tendency to enact separate rules for consumers and commercial parties. However, many European countries have been familiar with normative coherence in contract law, and do not (or no longer) distinguish between contract rules on account of the status of the contracting parties[141]. The schizophrenic contract law as introduced by the EU directives has therefore led to perplexity in many European countries[142]. For, if normative coherence in contract law is to be maintained the only viable solution for national legislators would be to adopt the same solutions that the directives impose for consumers, for other contracting parties as well[143].

Moreover, directives are also frequently incoherent among themselves (EU integrity). See Müller-Graff[144]: 'The development of the EC directives which contain rules for the conduct between individuals has not so far been guided by a coherent concept of private law codification. This can be explained as a consequence of the functional orientation of the specific empowerments laid down in the EC-Treaty and their piece-by-piece use by the Community. The adoption of a directive is usually inspired and spurred by single problem areas like, for example, the consumer credit contracts or product liability.' Incoherence is also frequently due to a lack of collaboration (and sometimes outright competition) between Directorates-General in Brussels who are responsible for drafting the directives[145].

This impressionistic approach to private law is much lamented by national private law scholars[146], and it has been one of the main reasons for pleas for a systematic unification in the form of a European civil code[147].

---

[141] But see R.P.J.L. TJITTES, *De hoedanigheid van contractspartijen*, Deventer 1994.

[142] Very critical of schizophrenic contract law, on efficiency grounds, is UGO MATTEI, 'Efficiency and Equal Protection In The New European Contract Law: Mandatory, Default and Enforcement Rules', 39 *Va. J. Int'l L.* (1999), p. 537.

[143] Compare art 4:110 PECL where the unfair terms directive's consumer rule is adopted for all contracting parties.

[144] PETER CHRISTIAN MÜLLER-GRAFF, 'EC Directives as a Means of Private Law Unification', p. 77; see also CHRISTIAN JOERGES, 'The Impact of European Integration on Private Law: Reductionist Perceptions, True Conflicts and a New Constitutional Perspective'.

[145] See UGO MATTEI, 'The Issue of Civil Codification and Legal Scholarship: Biases, Strategies and Developments', 21 *Hastings Int'l & Comp. L. Rev.* (1998), p. 883, UGO MATTEI, 'Efficiency and Equal Protection In The New European Contract Law: Mandatory, Default and Enforcement Rules'; EWOUD HONDIUS, *Consumer Guarantees: Towards a European Sale of Goods Act*, in: Centro di studi e ricerche di diritto comparato e straniero (directed by M.J. Bonell), *Saggi, conferenze e seminari*, no. 18, Rome 1996.

[146] See e.g. OLE LANDO & HUGH BEALE (eds.), *Principles of European Contract Law, Parts I and II, Prepared by The Commission on European Contract Law*, The Hague 2000, p. xxii, and HEIN KÖTZ, 'Comparative Law in Germany Today', *RIDC* 1999, p. 753 ff. See further PETER CHRISTIAN MÜLLER-GRAFF, 'EC Directives as a Means of Private Law Unification', p. 82, CHRISTIAN JOERGES, 'The Impact of European Integration on Private Law: Reductionist Perceptions, True Conflicts and a New Constitutional Perspective', DANIELA CARUSO, 'The Missing View of the Cathedral: The Private Law Paradigm of European Legal Integration', p. 14, OLIVIER REMIEN, 'Einheit, Mehrstufigheit und Flexibilität im europäischen Privat- und Wirtschaftsrecht', p. 639, VINCENZO ZENO-ZENCOVICH, 'The "European Civil Code", European Legal Traditions and Neo-positivism', p. 378, MARTIJN W. HESSELINK, *De redelijkheid en billijkheid in het Europese privaatrecht*, Deventer 1999, p. 20, with references. See further *infra*.

3. Legal Irritants

Although, as said, directives in principle only require a certain substantive result, in practice many directives are actually quite detailed and leave the national legislator little choice in drafting[148]. Moreover, they frequently contain specific legal concepts[149]. These concepts do not always fit very well into all the European legal systems. For example, until recently English law did not know of the concept of good faith. It had even been explicitly rejected on several occasions. However, as a result of the transposition of the unfair terms directive the concept was introduced into English law. This raised the question what its scope should be. Should it become a general clause like it is on the European Continent which operates not only in all branches of contract law, the law of obligations or private law, but in some countries even outside private law? Or should its field of application be limited to controlling the content of standard terms in consumer contracts? In this respect Gunther Teubner quite rightly speaks of *legal irritants*[150]. These irritants have yet another disruptive effect on the coherence of national legal systems.

4. Continued Friction

It would be an illusion to think that the disturbing effect of directives is a temporary nuisance which ends with their successful incorporation into the national legal system (*einordnen*) by means of careful transposition. Not only will there always be new directives to disturb our national legal order - the

---

[147] Compare See VINCENZO ZENO-ZENCOVICH, 'The "European Civil Code", European Legal Traditions and Neo-positivism', p. 378: 'it may reasonably be argued that the idea of a European civil code is one reply to growing dissatisfaction at the piecemeal and theoretically-inconsistent nature of the ordinary legislation promoted by the EU bureaucracies.' Contrast PETER CHRISTIAN MÜLLER-GRAFF, 'EC Directives as a Means of Private Law Unification', p. 73: 'At present directives of the EC seem to constitute the most realistic and preferred way of achieving a higher degree of common private law elements in the Member States of the European Community.'

[148] See PETER CHRISTIAN MÜLLER-GRAFF, 'EC Directives as a Means of Private Law Unification', p. 73, SACHA PRECHAL, *Directives in European Community Law*, p. 16. Thus the effective difference between directives and regulations has considerably diminished. See Mattei 1999. See PETER CHRISTIAN MÜLLER-GRAFF, 'EC Directives as a Means of Private Law Unification', p. 81: 'in all cases in which the purpose of private law approximation is to overcome restrictions of trade or distortions of competition in consequence of differences in precise private law rules (e.g., requirements for the validity of consumer credit contracts) (...) even the 'result to be achieved' (e.g. the abolition of certain restrictions or distortions as a result of specific legal differences) requires precise definition. Therefore detailed rules nearly inevitably become part of the result to be achieved in the sense of Article 189 paragraph 3 EC-Treaty. In fact, directives for the approximation of private law contain loosely knit provisions which can be seen, for example, in the directives concerning product liability or consumer credit contracts. Directives may then partially approach the linguistic structure of regulations in the sense of Article 189 paragraph 2 EC-Treaty.'

[149] Or, sometimes states decide themselves to literally transpose the directive into a statute thus introducing new concepts into their system.

[150] GUNTHER TEUBNER, 'Legal Irritants: Good Faith in British Law or How Unifying Law Ends Up in New Divergences', *MLR* 1998, p. 11 ff.

late payment and e-commerce directives are already awaiting transposition -, but it would also be an illusion to think that after transposition the problems have vanished. The disturbing effect of directives on the equilibrium of the national legal systems will continue after their transposition. The reason for this is that the new rules do not become purely national by their transposition. They remain connected with the directives which are European law[151]. They therefore continue to be disturbing factors, especially as a result of the obligation for the courts to interpret national law in conformity with directives[152]: 'When applying national law, whether adopted before or after the directive, the national court called upon to interpret that law must do so, as far as possible, in the light of the wording and purpose of the directive so as to achieve the result pursued by the directive'[153]. The court which oversees consistent interpretation in the last instance is the European Court of Justice. And even if it wishes to do so the ECJ would simply be unable to maintain the internal coherence of 15 national legal systems at the same time. Thus, there will be continuing friction between national and European aspirations, a dynamic tension between concerns with national and European systematic and normative coherence.

5. Hope for Integrity?

Thus directives, which are meant to harmonise the law in Europe, form a threat to the normative (substantive) and conceptual (formal) coherence of national legal systems in several ways. First, each new directive undermines national integrity whenever it introduces new normative solutions and new concepts in a part of the law that has normative and conceptual connections

---

[151] Compare SACHA PRECHAL, *Directives in European Community Law*, p. 122: 'As an instrument of Community intervention, the directive imposes upon the Member States the obligation to implement it. This obligation exists primarily vis-à-vis the Community and other Member States. However, (...), from their entry into force directives form part of the law in the Member States and thus constitute a source of law within the national legal system.' See for administrative law J.H. JANS & R. DE LANGE & S. PRECHAL & R.J.G.M. WIDDERSHOVEN, *Inleiding tot het Europees bestuursrecht*, esp. 367 ff.

[152] Two other mechanisms which are of assistance in enforcing directives are the doctrines of (vertical) direct effect and State liability (*Francovich*). See SACHA PRECHAL, *Directives in European Community Law*, p. 115 ff.; M.W. WISSINK, *Richtlijnconforme interpretatie van burgerlijk recht*, Deventer 2001, nos. 29 ff.

[153] Settled case-law: Case C-106/89 (Marleasing *v* La Comercial Internacional de Alimentación), Case C-334/92 (Wagner Miret *v* Fondo de Garantía Salarial), and Case C-91/92 (Faccini Dori *v* Recreb). See on the relevance of this obligation for private law GERRIT BETLEM, 'Een vierde type van rechtsvinding; Richtlijnconforme interpretatie van de onrechtmatige daad', *NJB* 1991, p. 1363 and M.W. WISSINK, *Richtlijnconforme interpretatie van burgerlijk recht.* The latter author seems rather optimistic with regard to the resolution of conflicts between aspirations of European and national laws ('Het samenspel tussen Europees recht en nationaal recht bij de grensbepaling verloopt vrij moeiteloos'). He argues (no. 483) that in case of uncertainty regarding the 'right interpretation' of a directive national courts should look at what their foreign colleagues do and adopt a 'Europe-friendly' (which means, in case of tension with national aspirations: 'own national law unfriendly') interpretation.

with other parts of the law. Secondly, when directives lack coherence between themselves as a result of their varying political and institutional origins, the national legislator is nevertheless under an obligation to transpose them (and with them their incoherence) into its system. Thirdly, even if at some given point in time all directives were in perfect harmony with each other and all the parts of the law which are related to a harmonised part were brought into accordance with that harmonised part, national coherence will still be under a continuous threat because the final authority is with the ECJ which will by definition be unable to guarantee the national integrity of 15 different legal systems.

In Europe we are faced with competing normative aspirations and logics. It is important to note that in this competition the European aspirations are favoured. Not only are most European rules mandatory, they are also of a higher level (hierarchy). This not only holds true for directives but also (and more directly) for those provisions in the EC Treaty which have so-called 'direct effect', like the rules on competition law and on the four freedoms[154]. The EU has, as it were, 'constitutionalised' these freedoms and competition law[155]. As a result, internal substantive concerns (e.g. contractual fairness) may have to be abandoned in favour of constitutionalised European substantive concerns (competition), as was shown in the famous Pronuptia case[156].

[154] The impact of the four freedoms on national private law should not be underestimated. See on the 'unexpected *renaissance* in private law' CHRISTIAN JOERGES, 'The Impact of European Integration on Private Law: Reductionist Perceptions, True Conflicts and a New Constitutional Perspective', p. 378: 'while there have been very few European interventions into the core areas of civil codes or the common law, the integration process has impacted forcefully upon deeper structures of national legal systems. Challenging the institutional embeddedness of national private law, European primary and regulatory law has remodelled (public) concepts of private autonomy, the realm of private governance and the social responsibility of private actors.' See also JACOBIEN W. RUTGERS, *International Reservation of Title Clauses; A study of Dutch, French and German Private International Law in the Light of European Law*, The Hague 1999, p. 169, with further references.

[155] CHRISTIAN JOERGES, 'The Impact of European Integration on Private Law: Reductionist Perceptions, True Conflicts and a New Constitutional Perspective', p. 405: 'To assert that European freedoms 'trump' national restrictions of 'natural' liberties is to regard these possibly separable and individual rights as a comprehensive legal body, and to assign to this body of law constitutional validity and supremacy over national law.'; and p. 383: 'Private law in this respect *is* constitutional law.'

[156] Case 161/84 (Pronuptia de Paris GmbH *v* Pronuptia de Paris Irmgard Schillgallis). See on this case CHRISTIAN JOERGES, 'The Impact of European Integration on Private Law: Reductionist Perceptions, True Conflicts and a New Constitutional Perspective', p. 398: 'How does the competition policy driven approach to franchising as a means of efficiently organising distribution interact with a private legal logic which seeks to assess the fairness of such arrangements under contract law? From the perspective of antitrust's new economic rationale, any protection of the franchisee's interest through mandatory rules of contract law will seem to be misguided in principle. All legal orders must deal with substantive conflicts of this kind. Within the European system, however, these tensions have an additional 'constitutional' dimension. European competition law claims 'supremacy' over national law.'

How should we deal with these competing aspirations? This raises the issue of the relationship between national legal orders of private law and EU private law (in legislation, adjudication, legal education and scholarship). Joerges[157], sketching a general framework for an understanding of the Europeanisation of private law, referring to analyses of the European Union as a multi-level system of governance[158], suggests that: 'the much criticised patchwork character of European private law initiatives reflects the lack of a hierarchical order, and that Europe's legal pluralism will inevitably result in disintegrative effects within formerly national systems.' Accordingly, he argues that 'legal scholarship should try to imagine and conceptualise a "law of Europeanisation" rather than some pan-European system that might be codified or compiled out of Europe's common legal heritage.' Rather than creating new static coherent structures or rigid institutional arrangements we should find a dynamic solution for the interplay between EU law and 15 national legal systems of private law. See again Joerges[159]: 'The complex and contingent nature of both the current and future state of private law within the EU appears to be decisive, determining that lawyers should *not* at the outset attempt to develop or promote comprehensive and systematic responses to the integration challenge. European integration forces us to re-evaluate the societal links of our legal systems in general, and to reconsider the normative task of private law in particular. Since this is an extraordinarily complex task and because future European evolution is contingent in so many ways, the design of new ready-made systems does not seem feasible, and it would instead appear to me more constructive to restrict oneself to the analysis of patterns of exemplary importance and to generalise only in relation to methodological considerations.' In the process we will inevitably have to give up some of our hopes for national normative coherence[160]. In the words of Duncan Kennedy[161]: 'the experience of unresolvable conflict among our own values and ways of understanding the world is here to stay.'

---

[157] CHRISTIAN JOERGES, 'Interactive Adjudication in the Europeanisation Process? A Demanding Perspective and a Modest Example', 8 *ERPL* 2000, pp. 1-16, on p. 1.

[158] See also OLIVIER REMIEN, 'Einheit, Mehrstufigheit und Flexibilität im europäischen Privat- und Wirtschaftsrecht', 62 *RabelsZ* (1998), p. 627 ff.

[159] CHRISTIAN JOERGES, 'The Impact of European Integration on Private Law: Reductionist Perceptions, True Conflicts and a New Constitutional Perspective', p. 396. Joerges' approach seems to be inspired by Brainerd Currie's famous 'governmental interest analysis' of conflict of laws. See CHRISTIAN JOERGES, 'The Impact of European Integration on Private Law: Reductionist Perceptions, True Conflicts and a New Constitutional Perspective', p. 399.

[160] The problems would not be minor in this respect if the EU decided to enact a European code of general contract law (the Commission recently instigated the debate by publishing its *Communication on European Contract Law*; see http://europa.eu.int/comm/off/green/index_en.htm): this would inevitably raise many questions with regard to the connection with the rest of the law of obligations, the law of specific contracts (especially protective regulation), CISG, contracts concluded by the State (administrative law), and property law (transfer of property).

[161] DUNCAN KENNEDY, 'Form and Substance in Private Law Adjudication', p. 1712.

B. The ECJ's Pragmatic Style

As said the European Court of Justice watches over the (direct and indirect) effect of European law on the national private laws of the EU Member States. It mainly does so by way of preliminary rulings. The ECJ has a rather pragmatic and undogmatic style[162]. This pragmatic style is reflected, for example, in the adoption of state liability for the late transposition of directives (*Francovich*)[163]. However, until recently the role of the ECJ in the development of general private law (understood as the law dealing with conflicts between private parties) was rather limited[164]. However, with the recent sequence of directives which interfere with the traditional 'core of private law' (see above), the ECJ has obtained a pivotal role in the further development of the new European private law. A recent case shows that its impact may be enormous. And in that case the ECJ adopted a very pragmatic, result-oriented, functional approach.

In the *Océano* case a consumer had bought an encyclopaedia (a contract for purchase by way of instalments)[165]. The contract contained a clause that in case of a dispute the district court of Barcelona would have exclusive jurisdiction. When a number of instalments remained unpaid the seller brought the case before the *Juzgado de Primera Instancia* in Barcelona. Barcelona was the seller's place of business but the buyer lived somewhere else in Spain and the latter did not turn up at the hearing. The court, assuming that the jurisdiction clause was unfair in the sense of art. 3 of the Directive on unfair terms in consumer contracts, wondered whether it should declare the term to be void of its own motion or whether it had to await the invocation of the invalidity of the clause by the buyer. The wording of the directive was unclear on this point. Article 6, section 1 says: 'Member States shall lay down

---

[162] See PAUL CRAIG & GRÁINNE DE BÚRCA, *EU Law; Text, Cases, and Materials*, p. 86 ff. (p. 89: 'Its approach to interpretation is generally described as purposive or teleological, although not in the sense of seeking the purpose or aim of the authors of a text.') Many German scholars are critical of the style of the ECJ's judgements. They especially consider the grounds for the judgements to be too brief and as being apodictic. See e.g. STEFAN LEIBLE, 'Die Rolle der Rechtsprechung des Europäischen Gerichtshofes bei der europäischen Privatrechtsentwicklung', in Dieter Martiny & Normann Witzleb (eds.), *Auf dem Wege zu einem Europäischen Zivilgesetzbuch*, Berlin, Heidelberg, New York 1999, p. 79: 'Bei der Rechtsanwendung, mehr aber noch bei der Rechtsfortbildung sollten vom Gerichtshof alle apodiktischen Töne vermieden und die von ihm gewonnenen Erkenntnisse dogmatisch solide begründet werden.' (with further references). See also PAUL CRAIG & GRÁINNE DE BÚRCA, *EU Law; Text, Cases, and Materials*, p. 86.

[163] Case C-6&9/90 (Francovich & Bonifaci *v* Italy).

[164] See WALTER VAN GERVEN, 'The ECJ Case-law as a Means of Unification of Private Law?', in: *Towards a European Civil Code*, 2nd ed., Nijmegen and The Hague, London, Boston 1998, pp. 91 ff.; CHRISTIAN JOERGES, 'Editorial and Acknowledgements', 8 *ERPL* 2000, p. vii.

[165] Case C-240/98 (Océano Grupo Editorial *v* Murciano Quintero). See on this case EWOUD HONDIUS, 'Ambtshalve toepassing van algemene voorwaarden: het Europese Hof van Justitie spreekt zich uit', *WPNR* 6417 (2000), p. 651-652, N. FRENK, 'Ambtshalve toetsing van dwingend Europees consumentenrecht: gevolgen van het arrest van het Europese Hof van Justitie van 27 juni 2000 voor het Burgerlijk Wetboek', *WPNR* 6431 (2001), p. 73 ff. and MARCO B.M. LOOS, 'Europese toetsing van algemene voorwaarden', *NTBR* 2001, p. 98 ff.

that unfair terms used in a contract concluded with a consumer by a seller or supplier shall, as provided for under their national law, not be binding on the consumer and that the contract shall continue to bind the parties upon those terms if it is capable of continuing in existence without the unfair terms.' Does this mean that such a clause is void, voidable or unenforceable? The Spanish judge decided to ask the European Court of Justice. In its preliminary ruling the Court held as follows: 'The aim of Article 6 of the Directive, which requires Member States to lay down that unfair terms are not binding on the consumer, would not be achieved if the consumer were himself obliged to raise the unfair nature of such terms. In disputes where the amounts involved are often limited, the lawyers' fees may be higher than the amount at stake, which may deter the consumer from contesting the application of an unfair term. While it is the case that, in a number of Member States, procedural rules enable individuals to defend themselves in such proceedings, there is a real risk that the consumer, particularly because of ignorance of the law, will not challenge the term pleaded against him on the grounds that it is unfair. It follows that effective protection of the consumer may be attained only if the national court acknowledges that it has power to evaluate terms of this kind of its own motion.'

Thus, the ECJ examined what the aim of art. 6 was and whether this could be achieved without accepting that courts have the power to evaluate terms of this kind of their own motion. The Court did not say anything concerning the wording and structure of the directive: it did not go into sophisticated conceptual distinctions between nullity, voidability and unenforceability. Moreover, the court did not pay any attention to the remainder of the Spanish legal system where this rule forms a part, like contract law, consumer law or the law of civil procedure. The ECJ only seemed concerned with achieving the aim of the directive. For that purpose it is necessary that a court should be allowed to evaluate a jurisdiction clause in consumer contracts of its own motion. This is a clear example of an instrumental and very pragmatic approach to the law.

C. Comparative Law: Subversive Role and Functional Approach

Scholars have played an important role in the development of a new European legal culture. First, I will discuss the role of comparative law, then what may be termed the interdisciplinary turn ('law & …').

1. Subversive Role

Comparative lawyers have played a central role in the European private law movement. Moreover, the emerging European private law has turned most self-respecting private lawyers into comparative lawyers. Comparative law has proved to be a powerful weapon against a positivistic and dogmatic approach to private law. What I am hinting at is what Horatia Muir Watt has felicitously called the subversive function of comparative law[166]. Comparative law demonstrates the relativity of our own national systems, and deconstructs the myth of right answers[167]: 'L'enseignement que l'on peut tirer du regard porté sur l'autre est que si les présupposés fondamentaux de ce dernier n'ont pas de valeur universelle, ils n'ont peut-être pas, non plus, une valeur absolue, indiscutable chez soi.' This subversive effect of legal comparison is particularly powerful in Europe where most socio-economic and other circumstances are quite similar: 'if that other civilised country has adopted the opposite rule maybe we need to rethink our rule'. Comparative law makes national positivism look parochial and challenges the internal perspective and its related right answers. Does Europe really have 15 right answers to each question of law? Thus the central role of comparative law in the European private law debate contributes to a shift towards a less formal approach to our law. A dogmatic approach to the law is easier to retain when there is just one dogma, one system, like the Bible, the Digest, or the national civil code[168]. But as soon as one starts to look around it becomes difficult to maintain that the one and the whole truth is contained in one's own national system which is centred around one's own national code. This is especially true for conceptual differences[169]: 'La comparaison est ainsi de nature à libérer le raisonnement juridique de certains carcans conceptuels sclérosants en ouvrant la porte à d'autres grilles de lecture.'

Comparative law forces us, as it were, to adopt an external perspective towards our own positive law and to regard it as just one possible solution and no longer as *the* truth[170]. Muir Watt expects comparative law to have an equally subversive potential as Realism, cls and interdisciplinary schools of thought have had in the U.S.[171]: 'Car il existe un parallélisme assez

---

[166] HORATIA MUIR WATT, 'La fonction subversive du droit comparé', *RIDC* 3-2000, p. 503 ff. See earlier GEORGE P. FLETCHER, 'Comparative Law as a Subversive Discipline, 46 *AJCL* (1998), p. 683 ff., p. 695 on comparative law's 'unique opportunity to generate critical, subversive self-reflections about American law.'

[167] HORATIA MUIR WATT, 'La fonction subversive du droit comparé', p. 523.

[168] The parallel between a dogmatic approach to the law and religion has often been made. See e.g. GNAEUS FLAVIUS (HERMANN KANTOROWICZ), 'Der Kampf um die Rechtswissenschaft', J. FRANK, *Courts on Trial*, 1949, DUNCAN KENNEDY, *A Critique of Adjudication {fin de siècle}*, MARTIJN W. HESSELINK, '"Wat is recht etc.?"; Antwoorden op vragen van Tilburgers over rechtsregels, rechtspraak en rechtsvorming'.

[169] HORATIA MUIR WATT, 'La fonction subversive du droit comparé', p. 503. See also HEIN KÖTZ, 'Comparative Law in Germany Today', p. 766: 'Comparative law also provides an effective antidote to uncritical faith in legal doctrine: it teaches the student that what is often presented as pure natural law proves to be nothing of the sort as soon as one crosses a frontier, and it keeps reminding him that while doctrine and categories are essential in any system, they can sometimes become irrelevant to the functioning and efficacy of the law in action and degenerate into futile professorial games.'

[170] See on loss of faith also DUNCAN KENNEDY, *A Critique of Adjudication {fin de siècle}*.

[171] HORATIA MUIR WATT, 'La fonction subversive du droit comparé', p. 503 ff., p. 509. Interestingly Muir Watt remarks (p. 517) that legal systems that have been used to exporting their legal systems (France, England, the US) have more difficulty in admitting lessons from comparative law (importation from abroad).

remarquable entre les dires des auteurs comparatistes sur les bienfaits de la comparaison et l'entreprise de subversion menée de façon plus massive par les tendances déconstructrices internes au système américain. Selon ces dernières, pareille entreprise se réalise en deux temps. Elle consiste tout d'abord à démanteler l'illusion que projette un positivisme trop étroit, puis, dans un second temps, à démasquer la ruse. L'illusion c'est celle d'une légalité univoque et autosuffisante, d'une réponse unique et indiscutable pour chaque problème juridique qui se pose. La ruse, c'est de faire croie à la neutralité du discours officiel, qui sert pourtant à légitimer u seul point de vue en occultant d'autres. Or, la comparaison des droits est largement apte à dénoncer les deux mêmes travers. Son potentiel subversif consiste à révéler la richesse cachée d'un système juridique derrière une apparence réductrice, pour dénoncer ensuite la partialité du discours positif.'

2. Functional Approach

The subversive effect is especially strong when comparison shows, as it does in Europe, that many of the differences between the various legal systems are differences in conceptual and formal structure rather than in substance. And the functional method of comparison, which has become the dominant comparative method[172], helps us to bring these differences to light. This method is aimed at establishing which substantive solutions different legal systems reach for the same legal problem. With the help of the functional method it becomes clear that legal systems frequently reach the same substantive solutions with the help of quite different legal concepts[173]. Thus, many functional equivalents are found. Indeed, scholars involved in European private law tend to concentrate their comparative research more on functional equivalents than on conceptual, dogmatic differences[174]. The most eminent example is Hein Kötz' *European Contract Law*[175]. The functional method of comparison was also successfully adopted by the Trento Common Core project. In this project national reporters are asked to answer, for their own

---

[172] See e.g. KONRAD ZWEIGERT, HEIN KÖTZ, *Introduction to Comparative Law*, 3rd ed., Oxford 1998, RODOLFO SACCO, *Introduzione al diritto comparato*. Compare A.E. ODERKERK, *De preliminaire fase van het rechtsvergelijkend onderzoek*, Nijmegen 1999, p. 83, KLAUS-PETER BERGER, 'Auf dem Wege zu einem europäischen Gemeinrecht der Methode', *ZEuP* 2001, p. 4 ff., p. 22 ff.

[173] Compare GIL CARLOS RODRÍGUEZ IGLESIAS, 'Gedanken zum Entstehen einer Europäischen Rechtsordnung', *NJW* 1999, 1, 8 ff., p. 8: 'Für die Richter [des EuGH] sind die Gegenüberstellungen der nationalen Rechte eine außerordentlich wichtige Erfahrung. Als Ergebnis - und dies möchte ich besonders unterstreichen - stellt sich meistens heraus, daß die Unterschiede zwischen den Rechtsordnungen gar nicht einmal so groß sind. In der Regel läßt sich feststellen, daß die verschiedenen nationalen Rechte in der Substanz zu gleichen Lösungen der aufgeworfenen Fragen kommen. Dies gilt auch dann, wenn dogmatische Ansätze divergieren oder rechtstechnisch unterschiedliche Wege beschritten werden.'

[174] Critical of the functional approach is JAN SMITS, *The Good Samaritan in European Private Law*, p. 23.

[175] HEIN KÖTZ, *European Contract Law*, Part I (translated by Tony Weir), Oxford 1997.

national system, a number of questions with regard to practical cases, in order to establish what the real differences and common grounds in Europe are[176]. The first results of this international project, in which hundreds of European scholars collaborate[177], show that the substantive differences in Europe are not as great as is frequently thought[178]. This is especially true for the much emphasised difference between common law and civil law systems.

Thus, as a result of European private law our law will no longer be the same. In the words of Rodolfo Sacco[179]: 'rien n'est plus pareil après la comparaison. La science juridique tout entière est affectée par l'essor de la connaissance critique du droit comparé.' Our national law will be affected by it in two closely connected and crucial ways (functional approach and subversive effect) which have in common a shift from form to substance. This may not be a revolt against formalism, but it is a radical change in legal methodology and legal culture. 'La comparaison s'engage ainsi contre le dogmatisme, contre les stéréotypes, contre l'ethnocentrisme, c'est-à-dire, contre la conviction répandue (quel que soit le pays) selon laquelle les catégories et concepts nationaux sont les seuls envisageables. Cette conviction serait celle qui procède d'un discours "officiel" trop exclusivement légaliste et par ailleurs trop peu enclin à regarder au delà des horizons purement nationaux.'[180] European private law will ensure that we can no longer deal with our own national law in quite the same way. It is changing our way of seeing our law and therewith our law itself[181].

D. Law & ...

A second characteristic of the academic debate on European private law is that it is decisively less dogmatic and positivistic than national academic debates have been. This is, of course, not surprising, because Europe has no common civil code or other common formal conceptual structure which could serve as a framework within which an internal perspective could be taken and within which a dogmatic-deductive approach could be used. Neither would it

---

[176] See on the method MAURO BUSSANI, UGO MATTEI, 'The Common Core Approach to European Private Law', 3 *The Columbia Journal of European Law* (1997/1998), 339. See also the comments collected in MAURO BUSSANI, UGO MATTEI (eds.), *Making European Private Law; Essays on the 'Common Core' Project'*, Trento 2000.

[177] It is interesting to note that many distinguished American scholars are involved in the Trento project, and have played an important role in the methodological discussions. Thus some realism has gained entry (or rather re-entry: Europeans originally inspired American realists) through the back door.

[178] See REINHARD ZIMMERMANN & SIMON WHITTAKER (eds.), *Good Faith in European Contract Law*, Cambridge 2000, JAMES GORDLEY (ed.), *The Enforceability of Promises in European Contract Law*, Cambridge 2001.

[179] Quoted by HORATIA MUIR WATT, 'La fonction subversive du droit comparé', p. 503 ff., p. 526.

[180] HORATIA MUIR WATT, 'La fonction subversive du droit comparé', p. 503 ff., p. 506.

[181] In the same sense JAN SMITS, *The Good Samaritan in European Private Law*, p. 47.

be acceptable to choose between the various European legal systems and to adopt one as the framework for the new European private law[182].

As a result the barrier between 'legal science', which no longer has its own national, dogmatic, internal perspective, and other (social) sciences has fallen[183]: in the academic debate on European private law interdisciplinary approaches are flourishing. Indeed, many scholars in European private law reject the artificial boundaries between disciplines[184]. There is a host of 'law &...' disciplines which are clearly inspired by American scholarly work[185]. Some of them (e.g. law & economics, law & politics) share an instrumentalist approach to private law: the law, including private law, serves to achieve certain social, political, and economic aims.

Especially the link between law and culture has played an important role in the European private law debate[186]. Opponents of unification argue that law

---

[182] This has been attempted, however: the Gandolfi Project proposes to base a European Code of Contracts on Book 4 of the Italian *Codice civile* (see GIUSEPPE GANDOLFI, 'Pour un code européen des contrats', *RTD Civ.* 1991, p. 707 ff; PETER STEIN (ed.), *Incontro di studio su: Il futuro codice europeo dei contratti*, Milano 1993; and GIUSEPPE GANDOLFI (ed.), *Code Européen des contrats - Avant-projet*, Milano 2001). See also Monateri's and Mattei's attack on what they regard as Zimmermann's agenda of Germanic hegemony (P.G. MONATERI, 'Black Gaius; A Quest for the Multicultural Origins of the "Western Legal Tradition"', 51 *Hastings Law Journal* (2000), 479-555, UGO MATTEI, 'The Issue of Civil Codification and Legal Scholarship: Biases, Strategies and Developments', 21 *Hastings Int'l & Comp. L. Rev.* (1998), p. 883 ff.).

[183] Compare GNAEUS FLAVIUS (HERMANN KANTOROWICZ), 'Der Kampf um die Rechtswissenschaft', p. 33: 'Mit dieser, endgültigen, späten Einreihung der Jurisprudenz in das gemeinsame Glaubensbekenntnis aller Kulturwissenschaften fällt auch die trennende Mauer, die man zwischen ihr und den übrigen hat aufrichten wollen'. See for the interdisciplinary approach of '*sciences de l'homme*' FERNAND BRAUDEL, *Écrits sur l'histoire*, Paris 1969, p. 7.

[184] JAN SMITS, *The Good Samaritan in European Private Law*, p. 47, also welcomes an interdisciplinary approach to European private law. See also the recent conference in Nantes (May, 11-12th, 2001) on 'Law and Market: Examining the Foundations of Law in European Societies'. An interdisciplinary approach does not, however, in itself mean the end of disciplines. See JACQUES DERRIDA, *L'Université sans condition*, Paris 2001, p. 65.

[185] See J.H.H. WEILER, *The Constitution of Europe; "Do the New Clothes Have an Emperor?" and Other Essays on European Integration*, Cambridge 1999, p. 15: 'The plea for a "law and ..." approach is of course *de rigueur*, be it law and economics, law and culture, law and society, that is, in general, law in context.' Compare also the 'Aims And Scope' of Global Jurist (www.bepress.com/gj; editors Ugo Mattei and Pier Giuseppe Monateri): 'Global Jurist offers a forum for scholarly cyber-debate on issues of comparative law, law and economics, international law, law and development, and legal anthropology. Edited by an international board of leading comparative law scholars from all the continents, Global Jurist is mindful of globalization and respectful of cultural differences. We will develop a truly international community of legal scholars where linguistic and cultural barriers are overcome and legal issues are finally discussed outside of the narrow limits imposed by positivism, parochialism, ethnocentrism, imperialism and chauvinism in the law.'

[186] See PIERRE LEGRAND, 'European legal systems are not converging', 45 *International and Comparative Law Quarterly* (1996), pp. 52-81; PIERRE LEGRAND, *Fragments on Law-as-Culture*, Deventer 1999; PIERRE LEGRAND, *Que sais-je? Le droit comparé*, Paris 1999; PIERRE LEGRAND, 'On the Unbearable Localness of the Law: Academic Fallacies and Unseasonable Observations', 10 *ERPL* 2002, pp. 61-76; HUGH COLLINS, 'European Private Law and Cultural Identity of States', *ERPL* 1995, pp. 353-365; JAN SMITS, *Europees Privaatrecht in wording: naar een Ius Commune Europaeum als gemengd rechtsstelsel*, Antwerpen, Groningen 1999; JAN SMITS, *The Good Samaritan in European Private Law; On the Perils of Principles without a Programme and a*

should be regarded as culture and that differences between legal systems should not be seen as mere obstacles to the proper functioning of the common market which should be removed. Instead, in their view, these differences are related to deeper-lying cultural differences and diversity should rather be regarded as a cultural richness which should be cherished[187].

However, many advocates of unification also agree that we should not limit our attention to formal rules. There are many institutional, social, political and other factors which together determine the extent to which there is true uniformity among legal systems. Sacco has pointed out that these legal formants are just as important as formal rules[188]. And the Trento project (see above) has adopted this theory as the basis of its methodology[189].

The economic analysis of law also plays an increasingly important role in the European private law debate[190]. The main argument that is usually put forward in favour of the unification of private law in Europe is an economic argument: the diversity between systems of private law, and especially of contract law, is said to be an obstacle to the proper functioning of the Common Market[191]. However, opponents of unification 'from above' also

---

Programme for the Future, Deventer 2000; JAN SMITS, *The Making of European Private Law; Towards a Ius Commune Europaeum as a Mixed Legal System*, Antwerp, Oxford, New York 2002; TONY WEIR, 'Die Sprachen des europäischen Rechts; Eine skeptische Betrachtung', *ZeuP* 1995, p. 368 ff.

[187] See especially Legrand.

[188] RODOLFO SACCO, *Introduzione al diritto comparato*, 5th ed. Torino 1997, p. 43 ff.; RODOLFO SACCO, 'Legal Formants: A Dynamic Approach To Comparative Law', 39 *AJCL* (1991), pp. 1-34, pp. 343-401.

[189] See MAURO BUSSANI & UGO MATTEI, 'The Common Core Approach to European Private Law'.

[190] Some contributions to the debate include LUISA ANTONIOLLI DEFLORIAN, *La struttura istituzionale del nuovo diritto comune europeo: competizione e circolazione dei modelli giuridici*, Trento 1996, JÜRGEN BASEDOW, 'Un Droit Commun des contrats pour le marché commun', *RIDC* 1998, pp. 7-28, HUGH COLLINS, 'Formalism and Efficiency: Designing European Commercial Contract Law', 8 *ERPL* 2000, p. 211 ff., MICHAEL FAURE, 'Economic aspects of environmental liability: an introduction', 4 *ERPL* 1996, p. 85 ff., MICHAEL FAURE, 'Economic Analysis', in: Bernard Koch, Helmut Koziol (eds.) *Unification of Tort Law: Strict Liability*, The Hague 2001, HEIN KÖTZ, 'Vertragliche Aufklärungspflichten; Eine rechtsökonomische Studie', in: Jürgen Basedow, Klaus J. Hopt, Hein Kötz (eds.), *Festschrift für Ulrich Drobnig zum siebzigsten Geburtstag*, Tübingen 1998, p. 563 ff., UGO MATTEI, 'A Transaction Costs Approach to the European Code', *ERPL* 1997, p. 537 ff.; UGO MATTEI, *Comparative Law and Economics*, 1998; UGO MATTEI, 'The Issue of Civil Codification and Legal Scholarship: Biases, Strategies and Developments'; UGO MATTEI, 'Efficiency and Equal Protection In The New European Contract Law: Mandatory, Default and Enforcement Rules'; ANTHONY OGUS, 'Competition between National Legal Systems: A Contribution of Economic Analysis to Comparative Law', 48 *International and Comparative Law Quarterly* (1999), 405-418; ANTHONY OGUS, 'Comparative Regulatory Techniques and Cultures: First Steps for Lex Commune', keynote lecture delivered at the Ius Commune Congress, Priorij Corsendonk, 26 November 1999 (unpublished); JAN SMITS, 'Een Europees privaatrecht als gemengd rechtsstelsel', *NJB* 1998, p. 61; JAN SMITS, *The Making of European Private Law; Towards a Ius Commune Europaeum as a Mixed Legal System*, Antwerp, Oxford, New York 2002. See also many contributions to *Global Jurist* (on this journal see *supra*). See further *infra*, Chapter 3, Section VIII.

[191] See e.g. JÜRGEN BASEDOW, 'Un Droit Commun des contrats pour le marché commun'. The Lando Commission has explicitly endorsed this argument; it was one of the main reasons for

invoke the concept of the market. They argue that competition among various legal models enhances economic activity and innovation, and therefore economic growth (comparative law & economics). In that view rather than imposing (code) or suggesting (encouraging restatement) unity the European authorities should encourage competition between law firms which draft different kinds of model contracts (most of the *Principles of European Contract Law* are default rules)[192], and between national legislatures and judiciaries which adopt codes and statutes[193]. Still others propose to base the choice as to which common European private law rules should be enacted on economic analysis[194]. In their view we should enact those rules which are the most efficient. Some of the issues in European private law & economics concern the choice between unitary contract law or separate laws for merchants and consumers, and the choice between hard and fast rules and open standards. It is obvious that this debate is neither formal-dogmatic nor positivistic. See Mattei[195]: 'law and economics is again an effort to understand the forces that are at play in the law and not in any particular legal system. It is, indeed, an approach remarkably unconcerned with positive law, ready to be applied in the analysis of any local variant of a legal system.'

Finally, there are more and more European scholars who emphasise the political dimension of the enterprise[196]. More specifically, some scholars

---

drafting the PECL. See OLE LANDO & HUGH BEALE (eds.), *Principles of European Contract Law, Parts I and II*, p. xxi.

[192] Compare MARTIN SHAPIRO, 'The Common Core: Some Outside Comments', in: Mauro Bussani, Ugo Mattei (eds.), *Making European Private Law; Essays on the "Common Core' Project"*, Trento 2000.

[193] See LUISA ANTONIOLLI DEFLORIAN, *La struttura istituzionale del nuovo diritto comune europeo: competizione e circolazione dei modelli giuridici*; UGO MATTEI, 'A Transaction Costs Approach to the European Code'; UGO MATTEI, *Comparative Law and Economics*, 1998 UGO MATTEI, 'The Issue of Civil Codification and Legal Scholarship: Biases, Strategies and Developments'; UGO MATTEI, 'Efficiency and Equal Protection In The New European Contract Law: Mandatory, Default and Enforcement Rules'; JAN SMITS, 'Een Europees privaatrecht als gemengd rechtsstelsel'; JAN SMITS, *The Making of European Private Law; Towards a Ius Commune Europaeum as a Mixed Legal System.*

[194] UGO MATTEI, 'Efficiency and Equal Protection In The New European Contract Law: Mandatory, Default and Enforcement Rules', HUGH COLLINS, 'Formalism and Efficiency: Designing European Commercial Contract Law'.

[195] UGO MATTEI, 'Efficiency in Legal Transplants: An Essay in Comparative Law and Economics', *International Review of Law and Economics*, 14 (1994), p. 3 ff. See also Oliver Wendell Holmes's visionary view: 'For the rational study of the law the blackletter man may be the man of the present, but the man of the future is the man of statistics and the master of economics.' (OLIVER WENDELL HOLMES JR., 'The Path of the Law', in: Sheldon M. Novick (ed.) *The Collected Works of Justice Holmes; Complete Writings and Selected Judicial opinions of Oliver Wendell Holmes*, Vol. III, Chicago and London 1995, pp. 391 ff. (originally published in 1897 in 10 *Harvard Law Review*, 457)).

[196] See especially DANIELA CARUSO, 'The Missing View of the Cathedral: The Private Law Paradigm of European Legal Integration', 3 *European Law Journal* (1997), pp. 3-32, p. 29: 'Integrationist pressure from Brussels is increasingly shaking the presumption of the neutrality of private law. It is forcing national legislators to engage in debates and make choices on subjects that were once the prerogatives of civil courts with their piecemeal adjudication. It is pressuring national law-makers to rethink aloud, in politically accountable parliamentary arenas, the

claim that the new European private law should be sufficiently social and should not, like many of our national codes, be based on the classical 19th century conception of party autonomy[197]. Others argue that from a political perspective a European consumer code might be more desirable, urgent, and feasible than a European civil code[198].

E. The Success of Soft Law

Another important example of the shift from form to substance in the new European private law is provided by the recent success of soft law in Europe. Following the example of the American Restatements of the Law private committees have drafted various sets of principles[199]. Now there are not only *Principles of European Contract Law*[200], but also *Principles of European Trust Law*[201], *Principles of European Tort Law*[202], and principles of European patrimonial law are currently being drafted (under the somewhat misleading title of the *European Civil Code* project). These principles are not law in a formal sense; their success is entirely based on their substantive quality and authority. The drafting of such principles is largely based on the functional approach; their drafters have looked for the common core of functional equivalents[203]. Moreover, they have tried not to be very conceptual. And

underlying goals of their private law doctrines.' See also *infra*, Chapter 3, Section VI. See generally J.H.H. WEILER, *The Constitution of Europe*, p. 10 ff. Compare ANDRE-JEAN ARNAUD, *Pour une pensée juridique européenne*, Paris 1991: 'Que la politique imprègne le Droit, il n'y a que des juristes pour le nier.'

197 THOMAS WILHELMSSON, *Social Contract Law and European Integration*, Dartmouth, Aldershot 1995, THOMAS WILHELMSSON, 'Private Law in the EU: Harmonised or Fragmented Europeanisation?', 10 *ERPL* 2002, pp. 77-94; DANIELA CARUSO, 'The Missing View of the Cathedral: The Private Law Paradigm of European Legal Integration'; BRIGITTA LURGER, *Vertragliche Solidarität, Entwicklungschancen für das allgemeine Vertragsrecht in Österreich und in der Europäischen Union*, Baden-Baden 1998; BRIGITTA LURGER, *Grundfragen der Vereinheitlichung des Vertragsrechts in der Europäischen Union*, Wien, New York 2002. See also CHRISTOPHE JAMIN, 'Plaidoyer pour le solidarisme contractuel', in: Gilles Goubeaux et al. (ed.), *Études offertes à Jacques Ghestin; Le contrat au début du XXIe siècle*, Paris 2001; JAN B.M. VRANKEN, 'Over partijautonomie, contractsvrijheid en de grondslag van gebondenheid in het verbintenissenrecht' in: J.M. Barendrecht, M.A.B. Chao-Duivis and H.A.W. Vermeulen (eds.), *Beginselen van contractenrecht: Opstellen aangeboden aan B.W.M. Nieskens-Isphording*, Deventer 2000; GUIDO ALPA, *Trattato di diritto civile, I Storia, fonti, interpretazione*, Milano 2000, p. 604 ff. See further *infra*, Chapters 5 and 6.

198 See the unpublished paper presented by Staudenmayer, a senior civil servant at the European Commission, in Utrecht in December 1999.

199 See on the link between principles and restatements infra, Chapter 2, Section II.

200 OLE LANDO & HUGH BEALE (eds.), *Principles of European Contract Law, Parts I and II.*

201 D.J. HAYTON & S.C.J.J. KORTMANN & H.L.E. VERHAGEN (eds.), *Principles of European Trust Law*, The Hague, Deventer 1999.

202 JAAP SPIER (ed.), *The Limits of Expanding Liability; Eight Fundamental Cases in a Comparative Perspective*, Dordrecht 1998; JAAP SPIER (ed.), *Unification of Tort Law: Causation*, Dordrecht 2000, and U. MAGNUS (ed.), *Unification of Tort Law: Damages*, The Hague, London, Boston 2001 (in: Jaap Spier, Helmut Koziol (eds.) *Principles of European Tort Law Series*).

203 Critical of principles for this reason is JAN SMITS, *The Good Samaritan in European Private Law; On the Perils of Principles without a Programme and a Programme for the Future*, Deventer

indeed the PECL use less concepts and, especially, less abstractions than most national codes in Europe. In addition, the principles are accompanied by an extensive and highly informative commentary which contains many illustrations. Finally, the style of the PECL is rather discursive. Sometimes they do little more than provide the relevant elements for debate. Often they merely mention a set of factors which should be taken into account[204]. Obviously, this style is in stark contrast to the dogmas of coherence and right answers.

Another example of the success of soft law is the CENTRAL project which is based in Münster. In that project scholars have compiled a list of some 70 principles of international commercial law[205]. This inventory is intended, in the first place, for arbitrators who have to apply the Lex Mercatoria. Clearly the scope of this project is not limited to Europe. Neither are the Incoterms and other model contracts provided by the International Chamber of Commerce which provide a by now classical example of the success of soft law devices in international trade law.

F. Taking Bologna Seriously

In Bologna in June 1999 the European Ministers of Education made a joint declaration to create a 'European area of higher education as a key way to promote citizens' mobility and employability and the Continent's overall development'.[206] More specifically, the European ministers agreed to co-ordinate their policies in order to attain, before 2010, a number of specific objectives including the promotion of 'the most widespread students' and

---

2000, *passim*. More moderate, however, JAN SMITS, 'De Principles of European Contract Law en Common Law en Civil Law', *WPNR* 6436 (2001), p. 235 ff.

[204] See, as an example, art. 4:107 (3) (Fraud): 'In determining whether good faith and fair dealing required that a party disclose particular information, regard should be had to all the circumstances, including: (a) whether the party had special expertise; (b) the cost to it of acquiring the relevant information; (c) whether the other party could reasonably acquire the information for itself; and (d) the apparent importance of the information to the other party.' Another typical example is art. 5:102, on interpretation.

[205] See KLAUS-PETER BERGER, *Formalisierte oder "schleichende" Kodifizierung des transnationalen Wirtschaftsrechts*, Berlin, New York 1996, KLAUS-PETER BERGER, *The Creeping Codification of the Lex Mercatoria*, The Hague 1997, CENTER FOR TRANSNATIONAL LAW (ed.), *Transnational Law in Commercial Legal Practice*, Münster 1999, and www.uni-muenster.de/Jura.iwr/central. Compare KLAUS-PETER BERGER, 'Transnational Commercial Law in the Age of Globalization', in: Centro di studi e ricerche di diritto comparato e straniero (directed by M.J. Bonell), *Saggi, conferenze e seminari*, no. 42, Rome 2001, p. 8-9: 'The states' loss of their formerly dominant position in international policy- and rule-making, the decreased significance of sovereignty and the freedom of the parties in international contract law have caused a reconsideration of the traditional theory of legal sources which has moved beyond yesterday's narrow-minded positivism. (...) Today the picture has changed. A non-positivistic notion of the law is beginning to emerge.'

[206] Joint declaration by the European Ministers of Education convened in Bologna on the 19th of June 1999 (http://europa.eu.int/comm/education/socrates/erasmus/ bologna.pdf). The Bologna declaration followed the Sorbonne declaration of the 25th of May 1998. See generally on the 'Bologna process', especially on the Prague follow-up summit in May 2001: www.unige.ch/cre.

teachers' mobility by overcoming obstacles to the effective exercise of free movement' and the 'promotion of the necessary European dimensions in higher education, particularly with regard to curricular development'.

Thus, the objective of the Bologna declaration is to create a European area of higher education in which free movement of students and teachers will be possible. This may be relatively simple to attain for most other disciplines. There is no such a thing as Spanish quantum mechanics or Danish dermatology. However, as a result of legal positivism, in law this may be far from easy. Indeed, it is obvious that as long as the curriculum in most European law faculties is concerned with teaching national positive law it will be virtually impossible to realise a European area of legal education. Therefore if we take the Bologna declaration seriously, we cannot but decide to move towards a less positivistic and less provincial curriculum in Europe[207].

Some objectors might argue that a Dutch student needs to have detailed knowledge of positive Dutch law in order to be able to work in Dutch practice. At first sight this seems to be a sound argument. However, there are at least two important counter-arguments. First, if this is true it only applies to those Dutch students who actually wish to practice in the Netherlands. However, for those who wish to make their career in Brussels, Cologne or Barcelona this may be different. For them the national and positivistic character of legal education is an impediment to their freedom to circulate and work elsewhere in Europe, and for the EU it is an impediment to the proper functioning of the common market.

Secondly, and more importantly, it is simply not true that proper education for legal practice necessarily has to be national and positivistic. The best example is provided by the United States. There, in law schools of international repute, such as Harvard, Yale, or Berkeley students are taught something that is not, as such, the law anywhere[208]. These national law schools teach national American contract law as if there was one American law of contracts, whereas there is patently not; there are as many contract laws as there are American states. Nevertheless, the law schools prefer not to teach

---

[207] See my intervention at the *NJB Salon* on February 16th, 2001 in The Hague (see PAULINE HOEFER-VAN DONGEN, 'Meesters en Masters; De NJB-Salon op 16 februari 2001', *NJB* 2001, p. 528 ff.). In the same sense F. BRUINSMA, 'De ondraaglijke lichtheid van de rechtenstudie', *NJB* 2000, p. 1371 ff and TON HOL, 'Recht als ervaring; Over academische vorming in de juridische opleiding', *NJB* 2001, p. 158 ff.

[208] See MELVIN A. EISENBERG, 'The Unification of Law', in: Mauro Bussani, Ugo Mattei (eds.), *Making European Private Law; Essays on the 'Common Core' Project*, Trento 2000, p. 15 ff., p. 19: 'if you walk into almost any law school in America, or read almost any leading American treatise or law review, you will find that many of the statements that you hear or read in those forums are neither statements of federal law nor statements of local law, that is, the law of particular states. Rather, statements you will hear and read will be statements of and about law in general terms, divorced from particular federal or state jurisdictions.' See on the birth of the national law school (after the example of Harvard) LAWRENCE M. FRIEDMAN, *A History of American Law*, 2nd ed., Simon and Schuster, Touchstone, New York 1985, p. 606 ff.

the law of the state they are in, e.g. Californian law at Berkeley[209]. Obviously, they do so because they wish to prepare students to practice all over the United States. And it seems to work: students do their very best to enter these law schools, even though they have to pay a huge amount of money and even though they do not learn the positive law of the state where they intend to practice. We all saw David Boies on television explaining the details of the Florida constitutional law to the Florida Supreme Court whereas he has his law firm in New York and was educated at Yale (New Haven, Connecticut). It works because what students do learn in the United States is how the law works, what its main problems are and who are its main actors. They also learn to discuss possible solutions to substantive problems and their consequences.

Therefore, if we take the Bologna declaration seriously we will have to make our legal education less positivistic and less provincial. Should we take Bologna seriously? I think we should. A network of European law schools could educate students who are better equipped to successfully work in commercial legal practice, which is of necessity becoming more and more international (international co-operation and mergers of law firms) as a result of the further intensification of international trade. I expect that there will be an increasing need for lawyers who are not educated with merely knowledge of private law in one legal system. Of course, not all European law students will wish to circulate in Europe. Probably the vast majority will wish to stay in their own country. But even for them, in my view, it is more useful to understand how the law works than to know what exactly the law is in the Netherlands today. Therefore, I think that a common European legal education which is much less positivistic and much more problem-oriented and which teaches sociological, economic, philosophical, and historical aspects of the problem and compares solutions in the various legal systems, is not only inevitable, as a result of the Bologna declaration, but also desirable[210]. I think that the 'Bologna process' could and should lead to a major improvement in legal education in Europe[211].

---

[209] To be admitted to the bar in one of the states graduates have to pass the state bar examinations. But it is surprising to see that even in many of these examinations attention is not primarily focused on state law.

[210] In the same sense J.H. NIEUWENHUIS, 'Principles of European Contract Law; Vooraankondiging Preadviezen voor de Vereniging voor Burgerlijk Recht', *NTBR* 2001, p. 132 ff. See further the contributions to BRUNO DE WITTE, CAROLINE FORDER (eds.), *The common law of Europe and the future of legal education*, Deventer 1992, especially HEIN KÖTZ, 'A common private law for Europe: perspectives for the reform of European legal education', in: Bruno De Witte, Caroline Forder (eds.), *The common law of Europe and the future of legal education*, Deventer 1992; MARTIJN W. HESSELINK, *De redelijkheid en billijkheid in het Europese privaatrecht*, p. 17f. The *Universiteit van Amsterdam* is planning to take a first step in that direction with its new curriculum.

[211] Moreover, in most European countries statutes on *effectus civilis* should change. A much better system would be one that allows graduates (Masters) from any law school in Europe to the national bar after taking the national bar examinations.

In this respect, it is important to note that very much has already been done. For example, in many Dutch universities (e.g. in Utrecht, Amsterdam, Maastricht) there are courses in European contract law, European tort law, European consumer law et cetera; Maastricht even has a European law school. And, of course, there is the European University Institute in Florence. Other interesting initiatives include the Paris/Oxford LLM, the Bucerius Law School in Hamburg, and Warwick University which all have programmes based on a comparative and/or interdisciplinary approach to the law. Finally, specific teaching materials are being prepared: Van Gerven's *Ius commune Casebooks Series* and Kötz's *European Contract Law*[212], which is already a classic, are but two outstanding examples in a stream of new books[213].

G. Background

Of course, the European trend towards a less dogmatic and less positivistic legal culture is not limited to developments initiated by or related to European integration. There are many similar developments, both on the national and on the international level.

First, there is the deformalisation of legal procedure which is taking place or is proposed in many European countries. Both the success in many countries of alternative dispute resolution (ADR)[214] and the deformalisation of the classical procedure, which is being undertaken by the courts, and in some countries (England, the Netherlands) by the legislator, provide important examples[215].

Another important development is the disintegration of private law into functional fields of law[216]. In many countries these functional fields are the most dynamic branches of the law: labour law, medical law, environmental

---

[212] See WALTER VAN GERVEN & JEREMY LEVER & PIERRE LAROUCHE & CHRISTIAN VON BAR & GENEVIÈVE VINEY, *Cases, Materials and Text on National, Supranational Tort Law; Scope of Protection (Ius Commune Casebooks for the Common Law of Europe)*, Oxford 1998, HUGH BEALE et. al. (eds.) *Cases, Materials and Text on Contract Law (Casebooks on the common law of Europe: Contracts)*, Oxford and Portland, Oregon 2002, and HEIN KÖTZ, *European Contract Law*, Part I (translated by Tony Weir), Oxford 1997.

[213] Another interesting example is FILIPPO RANIERI, *Europäisches Obligationenrecht; Lehr- und Textbuch*, Wien, New York 1999.

[214] See e.g. W.A. JACOBS, *ADR en consument: Een rechtsvergelijkende studie naar de mogelijkheden van alternatieve geschillenoplossing*, Deventer 1998.

[215] See J.B.M. VRANKEN, 'De radicale vernieuwing van het civiele procesrecht in Engeland en Wales, *NJB* 1999, p. 1879 ff and W.D.H. ASSER, *Fair, redelijk en billijk; Over deformalisering in het burgerlijk procesrecht*, 2000, with further references (p. 12: "Ik geloof zelfs dat er geen grenzen aan deformalisering gesteld kunnen worden. Aan de orde is namelijk een wijze van wetsuitleg en rechtstoepassing, een bepaalde attitude, die een onvervreemdbaar deel is geworden van het instrumentarium van de civiele rechter en niet meer kan en ook niet meer mag worden verlaten'; p. 16: 'De stem uit het verleden spoort ons aan: geen koudwatervrees voor verdere deformalisering, integendeel met vermeerderde kracht dient te worden doorgegaan op de ingeslagen weg.').

[216] See CHRISTIAN JOERGES, 'Interactive Adjudication in the Europeanisation Process? A Demanding Perspective and a Modest Example', p. 5.

law, information law, construction law. Their main characteristics are a functional, pragmatic and non-dogmatic approach, and a mix between private and public law aspects. Some nostalgic civil law scholars will say that all these fields are in essence private law. But they essentially miss the point. First, because these fields are mixes of private and public law (the relative quantity depending on the politico-economic climate of the day: regulation/deregulation). But secondly, because the approach to the law in those functional fields is much more pragmatic and less dogmatic. They have, as it were, abandoned the 'general part' of private law.

Moreover, the shift from form to substance may be enhanced by the recent success in Europe of American legal culture. Examples include the reception of American legal concepts like the trust, franchise, factoring and leasing. Mattei has argued that the wind changed (Europe turned from an exporter of legal ideas into an importer) precisely because of the non-formal approach in American law which considerably facilitates the flow of ideas (transplants) from one tradition to another[217]: 'My main thesis is that there is an inverse relationship between leadership in Western law and the degree of positivism and localism of a given legal culture. Leading ideas which influence other systems are those which *help* to understand the law as a phenomenon of social organisation and which are not too narrowly limited to the peculiarities of one given legal system.' However, another explanation may lie in the increasing economic dominance of American law firms[218].

These developments may even be regarded as warning signs that if national general private law does not adapt then it risks becoming sterile because it will simply be abandoned in favour of more pragmatic solutions. Then the dogmatic, formal approach with its concepts, abstractions and technicalities will become the exclusive toy of law professors in their ivory tower and in their *Begriffshimmel*[219]. Even if scholars do not adapt, practice will not wait for them. There are few law firms that are divided into departments called 'Law of Obligations' or 'Property Law' (*Sachenrecht, droit des biens*), let alone 'General Part': 'Merger and Acquisition' and 'Litigation' are more likely. How will legal academia respond to these pragmatic and functional trends in practice?[220] To what extent *is* our dogmatic

[217] UGO MATTEI, 'Efficiency in Legal Transplants: An Essay in Comparative Law and Economics', p. 196; see also p. 213: 'We can see from the changes of leadership we have discussed that the more a legal culture takes a narrow positivistic approach, focusing on certain particular texts or on local issues, the less likely it is to achieve leadership within the worldwide scholarly community. In modern times in the face of orgies of statutes and statutory instruments, scholars in most countries feel bound to solve concrete problems of textual interpretation.'

[218] Compare MARTIN SHAPIRO, 'The Common Core: Some Outside Comments', p. 129 ff.

[219] In many European countries this seems to apply even more strongly to private international law (*renvoi au deuxième degré* et cetera).

[220] There are similar developments in Chemistry where industrial laboratories have abandoned departments like Organic Chemistry, which corresponded to University departments, in favour of much more pragmatic categories like 'Washing Powders', 'Ice Creams' et cetera. One could argue that universities should not follow this example because it would not be academic. But what is academic? Does it necessarily have to coincide with 'no direct relevance to society', the less

system the law? Is our account not a highly rationalised, intellectualised version of a much less coherent and less sophisticated reality? (thousands of cases a day decided by our courts and many more settled out of court)[221].

H. Some New Formalist Trends

However, in European private law there are also some examples of more formal and dogmatic trends[222].

1. European Civil Code

First, of course, the plea by some scholars for a European Civil Code (ECC) is rather formalistic to the extent that such a code is favoured quite independently from what may be its substantive content, and from whether that may be better than possible alternatives or existing national law. Moreover, the argument for the need for a European Civil Code is formal where such a code is merely proposed, especially by German scholars[223], as a solution to the disintegrative effects of the deplored directives' patchwork. Finally, the ECC effort may also be regarded as an attempt by dogmatic legal scholars to gain (or in many European countries, especially Germany, rather: regain) the initiative in shaping the law over European bureaucrats and politicians (directives) to whom they do not entrust such an important job. Compare Kötz[224]: 'Recently, however, people have begun to realise that European legal unity is too important a matter to be left entirely to legislatures.' These formal arguments for a European civil code will probably seem rather weak to European citizens and politicians. However, there may be sound substantive reasons. If a European civil code is 'better' in a substantive sense (e.g. more 'social' or more 'efficient' or more 'modern') this may be a good reason to abandon national law in favour of such a new code.

2. Neo-Pandectism

Another example of a new formalist trend is neo-pandectism: some scholars (especially Reinhard Zimmermann[225]) argue that the new common law for

---

relevant the more academic? It is not at all certain that a university should cherish this meaning of the word 'academic' and abound in 'academic discussions'.

[221] Compare HORATIA MUIR WATT, 'La fonction subversive du droit comparé', p. 512.

[222] See also DANIELA CARUSO, 'The Missing View of the Cathedral: The Private Law Paradigm of European Legal Integration', who emphasises that national States' resistance to private law integration may take the shape of formalist entrenchment: 'Entrenched in legal formalism, obstinate in the defence of the doctrinal coherence of their code and unwilling to discuss the political merits of their consolidated policies [State legal actors] manage to slow down, and even at times to halt, the process of private law integration.' On New Formalism in the U.S. see *infra*.

[223] Compare CHRISTIAN JOERGES, 'Interactive Adjudication in the Europeanisation Process? A Demanding Perspective and a Modest Example', p. 4.

[224] HEIN KÖTZ, *European Contract Law*, p. v.

[225] See e.g. REINHARD ZIMMERMANN, 'Civil Code and Civil Law- The "Europeanization" of

Europe should be based on the concepts of the old Ius Commune which in turn was based on the Roman Digest. To most others than some (but not all!) legal historians this proposition does not seem more obvious than to suggest Latin as the official language for the Internet. Clearly, most of Jhering's criticism of *Begriffsjurisprudenz* can be equally directed (and even with greater force) against neo-pandectism: 'An die Unveränderlichkeit der römischen Rechtsbegriffe zu glauben, ist eine völlig unreife Vorstellung, die von einem gänzlich unkritischen Studium der Geschichte zeugt.'[226] Compare also the practitioner Von Kirchmann's criticism of the scholarly work (i.e. *Begriffsjurisprudenz*) in his time (1847), which he reproached[227]: 'die Bildung der Gegenwart in die wohlbekannten Kategorien erstorbener Gestalten zu zwängen'. Compare also Holmes[228]: 'Every one instinctively recognizes that in these days the justification of a law cannot be found in the fact that our fathers have always followed it. It must be found in some help which the law brings towards reaching a social end which the governing power of the community has made its mind up that it wants.'

There have been some strong reactions against neo-pandectism, both by legal historians, who argue that legal history should not be instrumentalised[229], and by comparative lawyers, who reject the 'Aryan Model' of Western legal tradition[230] and their proponents' conservative

Private Law within the European Community and the Re-Emergency of a European Legal Science', *The Columbia Journal of European Law*, 1995, pp. 63 ff.; REINHARD ZIMMERMANN, '"Common law" und "civil law", Amerika und Europa', in Reinhard Zimmermann (ed.), *Amerikanische Rechtskultur und europäisches Privatrecht*, Tübingen 1995; REINHARD ZIMMERMANN, *The Law of Obligations*, Oxford 1996; REINHARD ZIMMERMANN, 'Roman Law and European Legal Unity', in: A.S. Hartkamp et al. (eds.) *Towards a European Civil Code*, 2nd ed., Nijmegen and The Hague, London, Boston 1998, pp. 21 ff.; REINHARD ZIMMERMANN, *Roman Law, Contemporary Law, European Law; The Civilian Tradition Today*, Oxford 2001; see also REINER SCHULZE, 'Gemeineuropäisches Privatrecht und Rechtsgeschichte', in Peter-Christian Müller-Graff (ed.), *Gemeinsames Privatrecht in der Europäischen Gemeinschaft*, Baden-Baden 1993.

226 RUDOLPH VON JHERING, *Geist des Römischen Rechts auf den verschiedenen Stufen seiner Entwicklung*, Part III, 3rd ed., Leipzig 1877, p. 305.

227 VON KIRCHMANN, *Wertlosigkeit der Jurisprudenz als Wissenschaft*, 1848, quoted from KARL LARENZ, *Methodenlehre der Rechtswissenschaft*, p. 43. Another famous quote from the same lecture is: 'Drei berichtigende Worte des Gesetzgebers und ganze Bibliotheken werden zu Makulatur.'

228 OLIVER WENDELL HOLMES JR. (1899), quoted in G.G.J.J. VAN DEN BERGH, *Geleerd recht*, 4th ed., p. IV. See also OLIVER WENDELL HOLMES JR., 'The Path of the Law', p. 187: 'It is revolting to have no better reason for a rule of law than that so it was laid down in the time of Henry IV. It is still more revolting if the grounds upon which it was laid down have vanished long since, and the rule simply persists from blind imitation of the past.'; and 'why should any merely historical distinction be allowed to affect the rights and obligations of business men?'.

229 See PIO CARONI, 'Der Schiffbruch der Geschichtlichkeit; Anmerkungen zum Neo-Pandektismus', *Zeitschrift für Neuere Rechtsgeschichte* (1994), pp. 85-100; J.A. ANKUM, Stenen voor brood, *AA* 42 (1993), p. 459 ff. See also PAOLO GROSSI on Zimmermann's *usus hodiernus pandectarum*: 'All of this is appalling to me' (quoted by UGO MATTEI, 'The Issue of Civil Codification and Legal Scholarship: Biases, Strategies and Developments', p. 887).

230 See Monateri's exercise in law-in-history (P.G. MONATERI, 'Black Gaius; A Quest for the Multicultural Origins of the "Western Legal Tradition"', 51 *Hastings Law Journal* (2000), 479-

agenda and who accuse them of wanting to restore German hegemony[231], or who dismiss the idea that (national) legal change in the course of the 20th century (especially statutory regulation) should merely be regarded as historical accidents that drove the European countries away from the *ius commune*, instead of celebrating these changes as social and political achievements[232].

3. Mixed Legal Systems

Thirdly, some scholars propose the so-called mixed legal systems (e.g. Scots and South African law) as a model for a common European private law because these systems have overcome differences between the civil law and the common law tradition by taking elements from both traditions[233]. See in this respect Jan Smits: 'It is my profound belief that the experience mixed legal systems already have with the mixing of the civil law and the common

555). He provides a powerful deconstruction of 'the myth of Roman Law': the theory of continuity is based on a strategy which in turn aims at 'the survival of Romanists as professionals'. See pp. 507, 515: 'Now we can perceive how feeble this approach is in fact. It is feeble because its very foundation lies in the desire to see continuity, and an unwillingness to admit change. But it is quite easy to simply reverse this approach. Since it is based on putting continuity in the foreground, and changes and breaks in the background, we can adopt the delegitimizing move to reverse the grounds. So we can contrast the evolutive model with a kind of "archeological" discontinuous approach to the dissemination of events. (...) From this viewpoint, the "renewal" of Roman law through the ages does not demonstrate a peculiar capacity in Roman Law itself, but rather the peculiar capacity of later lawyers, especially in the Civil law, to adopt newer rules and solutions and to attach them to the authority of the old Roman texts. Coptic, Ethiopian, or Chinese text would have worked as well. The "recall to Rome" does not reflect the quality of Roman products, but the strategy of legitimization that dominated in Europe.'

231 See UGO MATTEI, 'The Issue of Civil Codification and Legal Scholarship: Biases, Strategies and Developments', p. 884: 'The Savigny-Thibaut opposition in nineteenth century Germany with the former opposing codification and the latter favoring it itself had a strong political stake: Savigny's historical approach representing a thoroughly ethno-centric, conservative, class-privileged, self-serving attitude. This same attitude and conservative politics, is today reflected by Professor Reinhard Zimmermann and some of his followers who, by the use of a biased historiography, pursue a defense of the status quo in the professional-legal leadership in Europe. The only difference is that while Savigny feared the hegemony of the French codification, Professor Zimmermann seems to fear the hegemony of U.S. legal culture and the challenge of different voices within European legal culture.'

232 MARTIJN W. HESSELINK, *De redelijkheid en billijkheid in het Europese privaatrecht*, p. 15: the one thing all European countries have been in agreement on for more than a century now, is that they no longer want the *ius commune* to be their law. And it does not seem very hazardous to assume that most European citizens would regard their present law as better than the *ius commune*, which was the law before the enactment of national codifications. (On the - in his view very limited - extent to which the *ius commune* actually *was* the law, PIO CARONI, 'Der Schiffbruch der Geschichtlichkeit; Anmerkungen zum Neo-Pandektismus'.)

233 See especially JAN SMITS, *The Good Samaritan in European Private Law*; JAN SMITS, *The Making of European Private Law; Towards a Ius Commune Europaeum as a Mixed Legal System*. See also REINHARD ZIMMERMANN, *Roman Law, Contemporary Law, European Law; The Civilian Tradition Today*, p. 126 ff., and REINHARD ZIMMERMANN & DANIEL VISSER (eds.), *Southern Cross; Civil Law and Common Law in South Africa*, Oxford 1996.

law can be of great significance for the venture of establishing a European private Law.'[234]

However, the idea has led to great perplexity. How can South African law be an example for European integration if their legal tradition is so closely related to segregation? To give an example, to most South Africans today property means something completely different from what it means to us. To most of them it is simply what they do not have and for a few people (the white) it is what they fear losing. It suffices to read a few lines from Coetzee's recent novel *Disgrace* to see what I mean[235]: 'No ordinary burglary. A raiding party moving in, cleaning out the site, retreating laden with bags, boxes, suitcases. Booty; war reparations; another incident in the great campaign of redistribution. Who is at this moment wearing his shoes? Have Beethoven and Janáček found homes for themselves or have they been tossed out on the rubbish heap?'

One must be an extreme conceptualist not to take these contextual facts into account and to say that South Africa may be an example for Europe because they were able to reconcile the common law and the civil law concept of property[236]. The concept of mixed legal systems only concentrates on rules, concepts and institutions. It does not care about context at all. How can such different countries, states and provinces as South Africa, Scotland, Quebec and Louisiana provide examples for European integration? The idea of mixed legal systems as an example and as a source of inspiration for the unification of private law in Europe is an unfortunate result of an extraordinary obsession with the difference between common law and civil law (as if that was the real problem of European private law) and an excessive preoccupation with the law's form (institutions, concepts), in sum *Begriffsjurisprudenz*.

4. Culture as Cliché

The scholars who are opposed to the unification of European private law because they regard the law as an important part of national culture which should be preserved, sometimes display a very formal and conceptual view of legal culture.

Especially Legrand, in his account of the differences between common law and civil law, mainly concentrates on the formal aspects of these legal traditions. According to Legrand the common law exclusively concentrates on facts, has no system, no rules, no rights, no history et cetera, and is therefore fundamentally different from the civil law[237]. So much so, in fact, that a

[234] JAN SMITS, *The Good Samaritan in European Private Law*, p. 34.
[235] P. 176.
[236] Incidentally, it remains to be seen how important the role of both common law and civil law concepts will be in South Africa since the law is undergoing a rapid transformation as a result of the new post-apartheid Constitution.
[237] See PIERRE LEGRAND, 'European legal systems are not converging'; PIERRE LEGRAND, 'Against a European Civil Code'; PIERRE LEGRAND, *Fragments on Law-as-Culture*; PIERRE

common law lawyer and a civil law lawyer cannot even understand each other; their conceptions of the law are incommensurable (epistemology). However, if he were to concentrate on substantive aspects the picture would be completely different. If a common law lawyer were to present a civil law lawyer with a certain set of facts and were to ask him who would be the most likely to win a dispute concerning these facts in his jurisdiction[238], it would be perfectly possible for them to communicate. They would be able to understand each other: the message would be passed on. The whole idea of legal families (of René David and others[239]) that Legrand embraces concentrates very much on formal aspects of the law. Legrand does not argue, for example, that private law in Europe should not be harmonised because the French should be able to preserve their tough rule on *imprévision*[240] or because the Scandinavians should preserve their possibility to police the imbalance between obligations in a contract even (in principle) in commercial settings[241] (pluralism in a substantive sense), or that the Dutch should be able to maintain their eccentric liability for the expectation interest in the case of breaking off negotiations[242]. No, he rather regards the French, the Scandinavians, the Italians and the Dutch as people sharing the same (civil law) tradition. He can only do so because he rather concentrates on the law's form than on its substance. Moreover, an Englishman who votes Labour may very well favour a certain French or German rule whereas a conservative Spaniard may be impressed by an Irish rule: in other words, citizens may (at least in certain cases) care more about substantive results than the culturally determined form of their laws[243].

LEGRAND, *Que sais-je? Le droit comparé*; PIERRE LEGRAND, 'On the Unbearable Localness of the Law: Academic Fallacies and Unseasonable Observations'.

[238] This is the approach adopted in the Trento project. The first results demonstrate striking similarities as to results among the various European systems and show also that the differences in some results are rarely to be found along the lines of classical legal families. See *infra*.

[239] See RENE DAVID & CAMILLE JAUFFRET-SPINOSI, *Les grands systèmes de droit contemporain*, 19th ed. Paris 1988.

[240] *Civ.*, 6 March 1896, *D.* 1876, 1, 193, note Giboulot.

[241] In the Nordic countries on the basis of § 36 Contract Act any clause in any contract may in principle be policed with a view to substantive unfairness. See THOMAS WILHELMSSON, 'Standard Form Conditions', in: A.S. Hartkamp et al. (eds.) *Towards a European Civil Code*, 2nd ed., Nijmegen en The Hague, London, Boston 1998, pp. 255 ff., p. 259, RUTH NIELSEN, *Contract Law in Denmark*, The Hague, London, Boston 1997, no. 128, CHRISTINA HULTMARK, 'Obligations, Contracts and Sales', in: Michael Bogdan (ed.) *Swedish Law in the New Millennium*, Stockholm 2000, p. 278.

[242] HR, 18 June 1982, *NJ* 1983, 723, note Brunner, *AA* 32 (1983), 758, note Van Schilfgaarde (Plas/Valburg), HR, 23 October 1987, *NJ* 1988, 1017, note Brunner (VSH/Shell), HR, 14 June 1996, *NJ* 1997,481, note HJ Snijders (De Ruiterij/Ruiters). See for a (critical) comparison with other European countries MARTIJN HESSELINK, 'De schadevergoedingsplicht bij afgebroken onderhandelingen in het licht van het Europese privaatrecht', *WPNR* 6248 (pp. 879-883), 6249 (pp. 906-910).

[243] More generally, Legrand's theory does not seem to be able to accommodate pluralism within one country (especially as a result of migration – are immigrants simply supposed to assimilate to the common law or civil law tradition, or - worse - should they be held to be unable to understand the law of their new home country?) very well. In the same sense Sefton-Green 2001.

Legrand regards the difference between common law and civil law as the main cultural difference in Europe. However, it seems absurd to consider, say, Dutch culture as largely the same as Italian but as being completely different from English culture[244]. See also Joerges[245]: 'I simply fail to see in what sense the differences between German and French adjudication in its highest courts or the styles of the German Constitutional Court and the ECJ might be less significant than the differences with e.g. their American counterparts.' To me it seems obvious that other cultural differences in Europe are of more (substantive) importance than what Legrand and Smits call 'the great divide'. For example, the one between Catholics and Protestants which divides Europe more or less between north and south, and which seems to have been much more determinant of differences in *'mentalité'*[246]. Today, in Europe, the risk of cultural imperialism by the North towards the South seems much greater than the one by civil law against common law[247]. In other words, Legrand should protect Spain rather than England.

The first results of the Trento project show that most cases are resolved in much the same way in most European countries[248], and - which is relevant here - that the dividing lines far from coincide with what Legrand and Smits call 'the great divide'[249]. The problem with their claims is that they are too abstract, dogmatic, deterministic and essentialist. In short, they are too obsessed with form. A more realistic approach (which concentrates on results) would provide a very different picture. Especially with regard to such classical apples of discord as the concept of 'good faith'[250].

---

[244] See on Italian *mentalité* Antonio Gambino, *Inventario italiano; Costumi e mentalità di un Paese materno*, Torino 1998. He addresses reactions by 18th and 19th century travellers from Germany, England, and France to Italy. Goethe, Stendhal, Dickens and other Northern Europeans were astonishingly united in their view of Italians, as indeed they might still be today.

[245] CHRISTIAN JOERGES, 'The Impact of European Integration on Private Law: Reductionist Perceptions, True Conflicts and a New Constitutional Perspective', p. 385. For further criticism of Legrand's theory see JÜRGEN BASEDOW, 'Rechtskultur - zwischen nationalem Mythos und europäischem Ideal', 4 *ZEuP* 1996, pp. 379 ff.; ALAN WATSON, 'Legal Transplants and European Private Law', in: Hesselink, Hondius, Smits, Stijns eds., *Ius Commune Lectures on European Private Law*, no. 2, Maastricht 2000, Sefton-Green 2001. See also Zeno-Zencovich's very nuanced discussion (VINCENZO ZENO-ZENCOVICH, 'The "European Civil Code", European Legal Traditions and Neo-positivism').

[246] In the same sense VINCENZO ZENO-ZENCOVICH, 'The "European Civil Code", European Legal Traditions and Neo-positivism', p. 381.

[247] Most of the committees that are drafting the various sets of principles (see *supra*) are dominated by Northern Europeans.

[248] REINHARD ZIMMERMANN & SIMON WHITTAKER, *Good Faith in European Contract Law*, Cambridge 2000, JAMES GORDLEY (ed.), *The Enforceability of Promises in European Contract Law*, Cambridge 2001, RUTH SEFTON-GREEN, '*Compare and contrast*: monstre à deux têtes', *Global Jurist* Advances: Vol: No. 3, Article 1 (www.bepress.com/gj/asvances/vol1/iss3/art1).

[249] See also JAN SMITS, *The Good Samaritan in European Private Law*, p. 31: 'irreconcilable cleavage between the civil law and the common law mentality'.

[250] See MARTIJN W. HESSELINK, *De redelijkheid en billijkheid in het Europese privaatrecht*, and *infra*, Chapter 7, where I conclude that good faith, if properly understood, does not divide civil law and common law.

V. The New European Legal Culture

A. A European Revolt Against Formalism?

However, on the whole the anti-formalist trends in Europe seem to be far stronger than the formalist trends, both in their arguments and in their number. Therefore, the conclusion must be that in Europe we are facing a shift from a rather formal, dogmatic and positivistic approach to a more substance-oriented and pragmatic approach to private law. It would probably be exaggerated to speak of a European revolt against formalism or even a European realist revolution. And European integration will not bring us Hijmans' *recht der werkelijkheid* (reality's law). However, it is undeniable that as a result of Europeanisation private law is undergoing a major transformation.

Unlike a century ago, in Europe legal culture is undergoing a radical change (at least as far as private law is concerned). The instrumentalist and impressionist approach of directives, the pragmatic style of the ECJ, the subversive role of comparative law with its functional method, the external economic, cultural and political perspectives given by academics, the success of soft law which is based on substantive authority rather than on formal enactment, and the depositivisation of legal education as a result of the implementation of the Bologna Declaration together contribute to a new European legal culture that is significantly less formal, dogmatic and positivistic than national legal cultures in Europe have been. The emergence of this new European legal culture is a result of these separate but related developments, and of the Europeanisation of private law in general[251].

B. Aspects of the New European Legal Culture

The emerging new European private law and the new European legal culture are definitely less formalist than the classical method of national legal cultures in Europe. Actors in European private law seem to share a much more moderate belief in the powers of abstraction and of concepts. Moreover, they seem to be less concerned with system, and, on the whole, their approach to the law is less dogmatic and less deductive. Private law is regarded more as instrumental to political, economic, social, cultural and other aims, and there is a pervasive use of the functional approach. More generally, the approach to the law is pragmatic: there is more attention to the consequences of rules and legal decisions. There is less belief in right answers and in integrity (making law means making choices, law is politics) and in the necessity and rationality of a given legal system, which is more considered as contingent (e.g. depending on decisions made by politicians in Brussels) and therefore also uncertain. The (external) perspective is frequently more critical. Moreover,

[251] And maybe, if Kennedy and Calabresi are right (see *supra*), also of the end of the Cold War.

there is less positivism and more pluralism: we recognise the relative importance of our national positive laws. There is also less focus on texts; especially on codes, and more on other legal formants, legal institutions, legal actors (lawmakers, 'men of law') and their strategies, in other words on law in action. Finally, European law is not very respectful of traditional boundaries between disciplines (between public and private law, between law and social sciences); it is largely interdisciplinary.

'*None of the ideas set forth in this list is new.* Each can be matched from somewhere; each can be matched from recent orthodox work in law. New twists and combinations do appear here and there. What is as novel as it is vital is for a goodly number of men to pick up ideas which have been expressed and dropped, used for an hour and dropped, played with from time to time and dropped - to pick up such ideas and set about *consistently, persistently, insistently to carry them through.*'[252] The development of the new European legal culture is nothing as virulent as the American revolt against formalism. This is not a time of revolutions. Nevertheless, there are some clear parallels between the new European legal culture and American legal realism (and early 20th century European realism).

C. The Value of Anti-Formalism

The most important problem with classical European legal culture is its lack of transparency. In our present national legal cultures (in adjudication, in academic debate, in education), value judgements in legal reasoning, the pros and cons of legal decisions, their alternatives and the choice between them are not the centre of debate (to say the least). This applies at least to so-called general private law. This is the main reason why I regard the emergence of the new European legal culture, which I described above, as a positive development. Compare the classical observation by Oliver Wendell Holmes[253]: 'The danger of which I speak is (...) the notion that a given system, ours for instance, can be worked out like mathematics from some general axioms of conduct. This is the natural error of the schools, but it is not confined to them. I once heard a very eminent judge say that he never let a decision go until he was absolutely sure that it was right. So judicial dissent often is blamed, as if it meant simply that one side or the other were not doing their sums right, and if they would take more trouble, agreement inevitably would come. This mode of thinking is entirely natural. The training of lawyers is a training in logic. The processes of analogy, discrimination, and deduction are those in which they are most at home. The language of judicial decision is mainly the language of logic. And the logical method and form flatter that longing for certainty and for repose which is in every human mind. But certainty generally is illusion, and repose is not the destiny of man. Behind the logical form lies a judgment as to the relative worth and importance of

[252] KARL N. LLEWELLYN, 'Some Realism about Realism', p. 57 (emphasis in original).
[253] OLIVER WENDELL HOLMES JR., 'The Path of the Law', p. 396-397.

competing legislative grounds, often an inarticulate and unconscious judgment, it is true, and yet the very root and nerve of the whole proceeding. You always can imply a condition in a contract. But why do you imply it? It is because of some belief as to the practice of the community or of a class, or because of some opinion as to policy, or, in short, because of some attitude of yours upon a matter not capable of exact quantitative measurement, and therefore not capable of founding exact logical conclusions. Such matters really are battle grounds where the means do not exist for determinations that shall be good for all time, and where the decision can do no more than embody the preference of a given body in a given time and place.'

Of course a less formal legal culture has other advantages. First, the characteristics of the new European legal culture themselves facilitate the rise and further development of a new common legal culture[254]; they help us to overcome those differences which are merely formal (concepts, structure et cetera), and show that differences in substance by no means necessarily coincide with national borders[255]. It helps us to concentrate on (and preserve if we wish) the differences in substance that really matter.

Another advantage would be that European and American legal cultures would come together which would considerably facilitate communication, both in legal practice and in academia[256]. How exciting that may be is experienced by the participants of the annual meetings of the common core project in Trento.

---

[254] See on a common European legal culture ANDRE-JEAN ARNAUD, *Pour une pensée juridique européenne*, p. 44 (and *passim*): 'Nous autres, juristes et chercheurs en sciences sociales, souhaitons coopérer à une prise de conscience populaire du caractère inéluctable de ce grand rassemblement de forces vives (...). Plaider pour l'existence d'une pensée juridique européenne me semble important pour établir des bases intellectuelles solides communes à tous ceux qui se sentent concernés par l'Europe' ; JÜRGEN BASEDOW, 'Rechtskultur - zwischen nationalem Mythos und europäischem Ideal', p. 381 : 'Die Aussichten für die Herausbildung einer *europäischen* Rechtskultur und damit eines gemeinsamen europäischen Rechtsbewußtseins sind nicht slecht'; and KLAUS-PETER BERGER, 'Auf dem Wege zu einem europäischen Gemeinrecht der Methode', p. 6, who argues for a uniform European legal method ('Für das Gelingen der Vereinheitlichung des europäischen Privatrechts ist die Schaffung eines europäischen Gemeinrechts der Methode von entscheidender Bedeutung'). See also JAN SMITS, *Europees Privaatrecht in wording*, p. 271 ff. and REINHARD ZIMMERMANN, *Roman Law, Contemporary Law, European Law; The Civilian Tradition Today*, p. 188. Incidentally, it should be noted that there is no reason why this common European legal culture should necessarily replace national (or indeed regional or other) cultures. Today, most people have several cultural identities at one time (or one fragmented identity).

[255] See *infra*, Chapter 3, Section VI, A, 4 ('comparative law and politics'). Compare GIL CARLOS RODRÍGUEZ IGLESIAS, 'Gedanken zum Entstehen einer Europäischen Rechtsordnung', p. 8: 'Unterschiedlichen Auffassungen der Richter [des EuGH] über materiellrechtliche Fragen sind selten auf die jeweiligen Rechtstraditionen zurückzuführen.'

[256] Compare JAMES GORDLEY, 'The Common Law in the Twentieth Century: Some Unfinished Business', *California Law Review* 2000: 'coherence and good sense have little to do with national boundaries. We will have moved toward a world in which jurists everywhere recognize that the fundamental problems are the same, and can talk to each other about them in the same vocabulary.'

And of course the main value of anti-formalism is that it allows substantive reasons to prevail. They may be of any kind. But, as said above, people in Europe do not seem to have any radical substantive agendas with regard to private law. There does not seem to be widespread dissatisfaction with the substantive results which our national legal systems generally lead to. As said, there is a major difference here, with the realists at the beginning of the last century and with the crits most of whom had important political agendas. I agree with Duncan Kennedy when he says[257]: 'I argue that ideology influences adjudication, by structuring legal discourse and through strategic interpretation. I argue that the denial of the presence of ideology in adjudication leads to political results different from those that would occur in a situation of transparency.' Indeed, we need more transparency with regard to (political, economic, cultural etc.) choices made by law-makers in private law[258]. However, I think that also with complete transparency the centre would win, as usual in politics, (although I admit that the 'general part of private law' in many European countries is still more economically liberal than one would expect in view of the balance of power in Parliament).

D. The Values of Formalism

To be sure, I do not mean to say that there is nothing good in a formal approach to the law[259]. For example, efficiency, equality, democracy and culture are important values[260]. It may be more efficient if interests are balanced for a set of cases (by the legislator) than in each individual case. Likewise, concepts may help in achieving efficient communication[261]. An important reason to strive for integrity (and system) may be the wish to treat like cases alike[262]. And a court may decide to give a very strict and formal

---

[257] DUNCAN KENNEDY, *A Critique of Adjudication {fin de siècle}*, p. 19.

[258] See *infra*, Chapter 3.

[259] In the United States there is a recent development of what has been called the New Formalism. One of their leading figures is Justice Scalia, one of the most conservative justices on the Supreme Court bench. He says (ANTONIN SCALIA, *A Matter of Interpretation; Federal Courts and the Law*, Princeton 1997, p. 22): 'The text is the law, and it is the text that must be observed.' Scalia is an outspoken formalist: 'Of all the criticisms leveled against textualism, the most mindless is that it is "formalistic." The answer to that is, *of course it's formalistic*! The rule of law is *about* form. (...) Long live formalism. It is what makes a government a government of laws and not of men.' (p. 25). See further the 'Symposium: Formalism Revisited' (5-6, 1999), the contributions to which were published in *The University of Chicago Law Review* 1999, p. 527 ff. See also ROBERT S. SUMMERS, 'How Law is Formal and Why it Matters', in: Robert S. Summers, *The Jurisprudence of Law's Form and Substance*, Hampshire 2000, p. 100: 'For me form is one of the law's most important characteristics, though, of course, there is far more to law than appropriate form.'

[260] See further ROBERT S. SUMMERS, 'How Law is Formal and Why it Matters' and the contributions to the Chicago symposium.

[261] But they may also lead to confusion and to exclusion (creating elites).

[262] I.e. the wish by a legal actor to treat in the same way all cases which in its view are the same. See MARTIJN W. HESSELINK, *De redelijkheid en billijkheid in het Europese privaatrecht*, p. 400, and infra, Chapter 7, Section IV, B. Compare RICHARD A. POSNER, *Overcoming Law*, p. 282 (criticising Horwitz) : 'rules in the normative rather than descriptive sense are useful features for

interpretation to a recent statute out of respect for the democratically elected legislator. The law of criminal procedure is very formal (*lex certa*) because we do not want any substantive consideration to override the protection of citizens against the state. Even the aesthetic value of the law's form may be of some (cultural) relevance[263]. The assimilation by Philippe Malaurie of a uniform European private law with us all going to McDonald's makes it not very tempting[264]. Likewise, EU directives are often criticised as being ugly.

On the other hand, however, efficiency, equality, democracy and cultural identity (or rather diversity) are not always the most important values at stake, and these values are not always best served by formalism. Moreover, the problem with formalism in Europe is that it is usually rather mechanical and routine-like. The (substantive) value of formalism is rarely explicitly balanced against other substantive values. It is the formalist routine that we should get rid of. Moreover, it is one thing to say that our law should be a coherent system[265]. It is quite another to assume that it actually is[266]. There is nothing wrong with an ideology of integrity (e.g. on the basis of an ideology of equality). But it is naïve to think that one's dream has already come true[267].

In sum, law needs both substance and form[268]. Therefore every legal system will have to find its own balance between form and substance, between formal and substantive arguments. Thus, the question arises what is the right mix between formal and substantive elements in European private law?[269] A central issue in this respect is the importance of system today. See Joerges[270]: 'where critics of European innovations deplore the destruction of the "systematic" character of private law or all sorts of doctrinal inconsistencies, their proponents tend to praise some superior substantive merits of the imposed changes, most notably progress in the field of consumer

even a just legal system to have - they are not *only* instruments of mystification and oppression.'

[263] See recently ANNA DI ROBILANT 'The Aesthetics of Law', *Global Jurist Advances*: Vol. 1: No. 2, Article 1 (www.bepress.com/gj/advances/vol1/iss2/art1).

[264] DENIS TALLON, 'Redazione del Codice europeo e necessità di rifarsi alle più valide esperienze normative', in: Peter Stein (ed.), *Incontro di studio su: Il futuro codice europeo dei contratti*, Milano 1993, p. 148: 'Vi sono ancora delle riserve: menzionerò uno dei grandi civilisti della mia generazione, Philippe Malaurie, che dice: "Dell'unificazione del diritto io non voglio sentir parlare. Sarebbe un po' come se, invece di avere la cucina francese, italiana, spagnola, tutti andassero a mangiare da McDonald's.'

[265] In this sense RONALD DWORKIN, *Law's Empire*, London 1986, p. 96.

[266] In this sense RONALD DWORKIN, *Law's Empire*, p. 225, 412.

[267] Compare J. FRANK, *Courts on Trial*, p. 420: 'One major defect of the traditional legal assumptions is that those who use them mix up two attitudes: (a) "This is true." (b) "This should be true." The users, without knowing it, slide back and forth between saying, "This is what now happens in courts", and "This is what I would like to have happen in courts", between a description of the existent and a program for the future.'

[268] In the same sense GUIDO CALABRESI, 'Two Functions of Formalism', 67 *U Chi L Rev* (2000), 479.

[269] This does not mean right in the sense of 'objectively true' but in (pragmatic) terms of convincing and acceptable.

[270] See CHRISTIAN JOERGES, 'Interactive Adjudication in the Europeanisation Process? A Demanding Perspective and a Modest Example', p. 5.

protection.' Finding a satisfactory balance between form and substance, between formal and substantive arguments, is the challenge which European private law is now facing.

E. National Law Never the Same Again

Change will not be limited to the new common European private law. National private law will also be affected: it will never be the same again.

First, as a result of comparative law national law will never look the same again. This is the subversive effect of comparison which I described above. Once you have seen the alternatives, your own law looks different. When you have seen the structure, concepts, and solutions in other countries, you cannot but regard your own positive law and its system as less absolute. Are there really 15 right answers (in Europe) to each legal question?

Secondly, our national legal system and its logical and normative coherence will be under continuous 'attack' from EU law[271]. This influence will simply not go away. As a result of further-going European integration private law and European law are no longer separate bodies of law. As said, it is an illusion to think that order and balance in our national system will be restored for some time after the meticulous transposition of the last directive. New disruptive directives will inevitably come. And the directives that have been transposed will remain connected with European law as a result of the obligation for the courts to interpret national law, as far as possible, in the light of the wording and purpose of directives. Moreover, there is the influence of the four freedoms and of competition law, and of human rights. Finally, there does not seem to be a plan and no one seems to be in charge of the integration project[272]. Quoting Joerges: 'Quite simply, we all experience and know that the so-called Europeanisation of private law does not occur comprehensively; instead it affects private law only selectively at different levels.'[273] In particular, there is no institution which has formal authority in the last instance over the whole of our system, national and European institutions share this responsibility. Compare Joerges: 'Not only do legislative projects within the European Union require activities at different levels; the European Judiciary is equally dispersed. No level and no branch of government disposes of comprehensive powers, which is why recognition of

---

[271] Legal systems which have a very systematic code like the German, Greek, Portuguese and the Dutch, and which tend to integrate all new developments into the civil code will have more difficulty than e.g. the French system.

[272] See OLIVIER REMIEN, 'Einheit, Mehrstufigheit und Flexibilität im europäischen Privat- und Wirtschaftsrecht', p. 629: 'Ein umfassendes Programm für ein europäisches Privat- und Wirtschaftsrecht aber gibt es nicht'. Critical of this characteristic of European integration is Smits (JAN SMITS, *The Good Samaritan in European Private Law*, p. 19) who calls for a coherent European private law which, in his view, 'cannot be developed without a well-defined direction of where the law should go'.

[273] CHRISTIAN JOERGES, 'Interactive Adjudication in the Europeanisation Process? A Demanding Perspective and a Modest Example', p. 4.

the claims to supremacy of European law cannot ensure the coherence of the legal system in which we live. In a nutshell; legislative as well as judicial innovations at European level are not automatically compatible with the rest of Europe's legal system simply because the European Union does not harbour just one law.'[274] In any case, the European institutions do not seem to be wholeheartedly committed to a balanced formal structure and system, to say the least; they rather have a pragmatic and instrumental conception of private law. Moreover, it is an illusion to think that one day all problems will be solved by a comprehensive and coherent code[275]. The existing instrumental approach of EU law will simply have gone too far. If there are going to be European codes, they will be much more fragmented: a consumer code or a contracts code. Such specific codes will lead to the same kind of problems of co-ordination with the rest of (national) private law (e.g. the rest of 'the law of obligations') as the directives do now. Therefore, we will have to find a way to deal with the continuous influence of European law on our national private laws. Part of the solution will certainly lie in adopting a less formal-dogmatic and more functional-pragmatic approach to our national law.

[274] CHRISTIAN JOERGES, 'Interactive Adjudication in the Europeanisation Process? A Demanding Perspective and a Modest Example', p. 4.

[275] Compare CHRISTIAN JOERGES, 'Interactive Adjudication in the Europeanisation Process? A Demanding Perspective and a Modest Example', p. 16 : 'We should not place our hopes in comprehensive legislative solutions; not only because we know too much about codification failures within national systems, but, more importantly, because we would be unable to identify a legislator with *Kompetenz-Kompetenz* to unify the plurality of legal orders in the European system of governance.'

PRINCIPLES

3

Principles Of European Contract Law: Some Choices Made By The Lando Commission

I. Making Law Means Making Choices

MOST SCHOLARS involved in the discussion on the future of European private law agree that choices will have to be made and many see it as their task not only to present the various positions in a neutral, objective, 'scientific' mode, but also to show more *engagement* and to actually propose and defend their own choices. In December 1999, after nearly twenty years of preparation, the Lando Commission presented its Principles of European Contract Law (PECL)[1]. This was a major event in the development of European private law. In this Chapter I will discuss some of the main choices made by the Lando Commission when drafting its principles.

What choices have the Lando Commission made? Here I will concentrate on choices with regard to the purpose of the PECL (II), the authors and working method (III), the format and style (IV), the subject matter (V), politics (VI), culture (VII), economics (VIII), and progress *v.* tradition (IX). Finally, I will make some concluding remarks (X). Clearly, there are some overlapping grounds among most of my themes (as usually happens with rational distinctions), but they nevertheless seem to be sufficiently distinctive to justify separate discussion.

II. Purpose

With regard to the purpose of the PECL the Commission on European Contract Law did not make a choice for just one purpose. They rather opted for a number of purposes at the same time. They clearly wanted the PECL to be as widely used as possible.

---

[1] OLE LANDO & HUGH BEALE (eds.), *Principles of European Contract Law, Parts I and II, Prepared by The Commission on European Contract Law*, The Hague 2000. A first part had been published in 1995 (OLE LANDO & HUGH BEALE (eds.), *The Principles of European Contract Law, Part I: Performance, Non-Performance and Remedies, Prepared by the Commission on European Contract Law*, Dordrecht, Boston, London 1995).

In their Introduction the Commission on European Contract Law formulate five 'benefits' that can be derived from the PECL, and five 'purposes' for which they are designed[2]. Moreover, in art. 1:101 (Application of the Principles), the first article of the PECL, under the Section 'Scope of Principles', six situations are envisaged in which they can be used. Although these 'benefits', 'purposes' and 'uses' are not completely identical they do overlap to a great extent.

As a matter of fact, one can distil from them three aspirations of the Lando Commission. First, to state the common core of the contract laws of Europe (A). Second, to contribute to a future unification of contract law in Europe (B). Third, to provide a set of rules that can be applied as law in Europe as from today (C). A fourth, and in my view highly important, purpose of the Principles of European Contract Law is not mentioned as such among the Commission's aspirations: they may provide us with a common European language for discussions on contract law (D).

A. Restatement of the Common Core

In their Introduction and in other places the Commission on European Contract Law emphasise that the PECL should be regarded as a statement of the common core of contract law in Europe[3]. Both from their format and from their content it is clear that the PECL have been inspired by the American Restatements of the Law and the Uniform Commercial Code (UCC)[4], and by the UNIDROIT Principles. The American experience with restatements and with the UCC may help us to appreciate the Lando Commission's aim to provide a restatement of the common core of contract law in Europe.

1. The American Restatements of the Law. - The American common law has never been codified[5]. However, the United States have adopted their own unique method for making the common law more coherent and accessible: the Restatements of the Law. The Restatements are published by the American Law Institute (ALI), a private organisation which was founded in 1923 with the assistance of the Carnegie Corporation and the Rockefeller Foundation.

---

[2] PECL, Introduction, p. xxi.

[3] PECL, Introduction, p. xxii.

[4] PECL, Introduction, p. xxvi.

[5] Codes are not completely alien to the American legal system: most states have a Penal Code and a Code of Civil Procedure. There was also a codification debate in the 19th century, but, apart from California and Louisiana that have enacted civil codes, private law has never been codified. There was a fierce debate between David Dudley Field, who was impressed by Napoleon's civil code and had prepared a draft for this purpose, and James C. Carter, who was influenced by the German Historical School, and who feared that a code would prevent natural evolution. Field's Civil Code was rejected by most states including New York (on several occasions). However, it was not a complete failure since it was adopted in some Western states including California. See LAWRENCE M. FRIEDMAN, *A History of American Law*, 2nd ed., New York 1985, p. 403 ff.; MORTON J HORWITZ, *The Transformation of American Law 1780-1860*, Cambridge Massachusetts 1977, p. 265, and MORTON J HORWITZ, *The Transformation of American Law 1870-1960; The Crisis of Legal Orthodoxy*, New York and Oxford 1992, p. 117 ff.

Today the ALI has nearly three thousand members, including the most distinguished judges, practitioners and scholars. The object of the ALI is 'to promote the clarification and simplification of the law and its better adaptation to social needs, to secure better administration of justice, and to encourage and carry on scholarly and scientific legal work.'[6] The first Restatement which the ALI published was the Restatement of Contracts (1932). Since then, Restatements have been published relating to many fields of the law including Agency, Conflict of Laws, Property, Torts, Trusts. In 1952 the ALI started the drafting of the Restatements (Second), most of which were completed half way through the 1980s. Currently, the Restatements (Third) are being drafted[7]. It is important to note that Restatements are not law in a formal sense. The courts are not bound by them. The Restatements do not have a formal but only a substantive authority which heavily depends on the reputation of the ALI and of the specific Reporter[8].

Interestingly, establishing unity among the states of the Union is neither mentioned as one of the objects of the ALI nor as one of the purposes of the Restatements. In his Introduction to the Restatement of Contracts (First), W.D. Lewis, the Director of the ALI, said: 'The vast and ever increasing volume of the decisions of the courts establishing new rules or precedents, and the numerous instances in which the decisions are irreconcilable has resulted in ever increasing uncertainty in the law. The American Law Institute was formed in the belief that in order to clarify and simplify the law and to render it more certain, the first step must be the preparation of an orderly restatement of the common law, including in that term not only the law developed solely by judicial decision but also the law which has grown from the application by the courts of generally and long adopted statutes.' Thus the ALI was mainly concerned with uncertainty with regard to the law as a result of an unmanageable number of cases and with contradictions among precedents, and not primarily with inconsistency between the various American jurisdictions.

The first restatements, which were characterised by classical legal thought and inspired by Hohfeld and others in their analytical attempt to create a coherent system of rules, a uniform terminology, and to eliminate

[6] Certificate of Incorporation, reproduced in: *The American Law Institute Annual Reports, 77th annual meeting 1999*, p. 57.

[7] The ALI was also involved in various codifications, studies and other projects, including the Uniform Commercial Code. See *infra*.

[8] See W.D. LEWIS, 'Introduction', in: *Restatement of the Law of Contracts, as adopted and promulgated by the American Law Institute at Washington D.C. May 6, 1932*, Vol. I, p. xi: 'The function of the courts is to decide the controversies brought before them. The function of the Institute is to state clearly and precisely in the light of the decisions the principles and rules of the common law. The Sections of the Restatement express the result of careful analysis of the subject and a thorough examination and discussion of pertinent cases - often very numerous and sometimes conflicting. The accuracy of the statements of law made rests on the authority of the Institute. They may be regarded both as the product of expert opinion and as the expression of the law by the legal profession.'

contradictions[9], met with some severe criticism[10]. The black-letter rules were thought to be too abstract and therefore of little relevance in deciding cases. Moreover, because of their abstraction the black-letter rules were said to be too detached from the cases they were said to be based on, and the link between the restatements and the authorities they were supposed to be based on was generally held to be insufficiently documented. Another point of criticism, which came from the then emerging Realist movement, was that the restatements would never create certainty and coherence - which was, as said, the main purpose of the ALI - because the real law is made by men and is therefore inherently uncertain and it changes all the time. Many authors were critical because, in their view, the focus on coherence had led to artificial closure and had killed off fruitful debates. Finally, the first restatements were criticised because they did not bring the announced improvement of the law; they merely restated the law as it was. One of the harshest critics was Charles E. Clark, the then Dean of the Yale School of Law, and Adviser to the ALI on Property[11]. He said[12]: 'I see my own group so often turn in impatience if not disgust from the attempt to force a black letter sentence do what it can never do - state pages of history and policy and honest study and deliberation - and long for freedom of expression which scholars should have.' See also Yntema[13]: 'The decision to restate the law as it is, rather than to put forth a candid effort to improve the law by critical formulation, as originally designed; the omission of the treatises; the imperfect provision for incisive independent criticism of tentative restatements as the condition *sine qua non* of their submission for approval: these are phenomena which are difficult to explain except upon the supposition that the policy of securing the public acceptance of the restatement has affected its content and perhaps even partially diverted the fundamental purpose.' See finally (and more recently) Lawrence Friedman[14]: 'They took fields of living law, scalded their flesh,

---

[9] See LAWRENCE M. FRIEDMAN, *A History of American Law*, p. 676: 'perhaps the high-water mark of conceptual jurisprudence'.

[10] See G. EDWARD WHITE, 'The American Law Institute and the Triumph of Modernist Jurisprudence', *Law and History Review* (1997) Vol. 16, p. 1, and RICHARD HYLAND, 'The American Restatements and the Uniform Commercial Code', A.S. Hartkamp et al. (eds.), *Towards a European Civil Code*, 2nd ed., Nijmegen and The Hague, London, Boston 1998, pp. 55, both with further references.

[11] Another fervent critic of the Restatements was ALBERT A. EHRENZWEIG, 'Das Desperanto des zweiten "Restatement of Conflict of Laws', in: Ernst van Caemmerer et al. (eds.), *Ius Privatum Gentium (Festschrift Max Rheinstein)*, Vol. I, pp. 343 ff., p. 344, p. 345: 'dieses unglücklichster Weise die bedeutsamste Schwäche europäischer Kodifikationen, nämlich ihre Starre, mit der des common law, nämliche seine Systemlosigkeit, verbindet und damit gleichzeitig auf die Stärken beider, Systematik einerseits und Beweglichkeit andererseits, verzichtet.'

[12] CHARLES E. CLARK, 'The Restatement Of The Law Of Contracts', 42 *Yale L J* 643-667, p. 646.

[13] HESSEL E. YNTEMA, 'What Should The American Law Institute Do?', 34 *Michigan Law Review* (1936) 461-473, on p. 468.

[14] LAWRENCE M. FRIEDMAN, *A History of American Law*, p. 676. He continues: 'The restatements were, basically, virginally clean of any notion that rules had social and economic consequences. The arrangements of subject matter were, on the whole, strictly logical; the aim was to show order and unmask disorder. (Courts that were out of line could cite the restatement

drained off their blood, and reduced them to bones. The bones were arrangements of principles and rules (the black-letter law), followed by a somewhat barren commentary.'

The criticism was taken into account by the ALI and they soon started the preparation of a second Restatement[15]. In the Restatement (Second) there is a clear shift in emphasis from the black-letter rule to the comments, which are much more extensive than before. The Restatements (Second) do not attempt to put an end to the debate, but rather try to state which positions are taken and leave it for the courts to decide. As a result there is also a shift in interest from the black-letter rule to the comment. The new restatements are also much less rigidly formulated. The black-letter rules frequently confine themselves to listing a number of aspects that should be taken into account when resolving the conflict. The Restatements (Third), however, which are currently being drafted seem to be characterised by an attempt to attain fine-tuned detailed momentary compromises between all the interests at stake and between the interest groups affected by the issue. The result is a less elegant draft characterised by lengthy technocratic wording[16].

Although, as said, this was not the initial aim, the restatements have certainly also had a unifying effect on adjudication, teaching and academic debate. At the very least they have provided a common framework for debate. Compare Hyland[17]: 'In sum, the dichotomous structure of the common law convinced the drafters of the Restatement (second) and the UCC to prefer a dialogic form for its systemisation. Both are flexible and open-textured. Neither truly resolves the difficult questions - in fact, they seem to suggest that no final resolution will ever be achieved. Their goal is rather to provide the long term discussion with a convenient framework.'

2. The Restatements of Contracts. - As for contract law, the first Restatement of Contracts was published in 1932. The Reporter was Samuel Williston, Arthur L. Corbin serving as a Special Reporter on Remedies. Although this Restatement was also met by some sharp criticism right after its publication (see above), it did become a success, both because it was generally held to clarify the law (it was cited in contract cases in virtually all American states), and because it contributed to a more uniform contract law in the United States[18]. The Restatement (Second) of Contracts was drafted between 1962 and 1979 and was published in 1981. The general reporter was

---

and return to the mainstream of common-law growth.) The chief draftsmen (...) expended their enormous talents on an enterprise which, today, seems singularly fruitless, at least to those legal scholars who adhere to later streams of legal thought. Incredibly, the work of restating (and rerestating) is still going on.'

[15] RICHARD HYLAND, 'The American Restatements and the Uniform Commercial Code', p. 63; G. EDWARD WHITE, 'The American Law Institute and the Triumph of Modernist Jurisprudence', p. 46.

[16] See RICHARD HYLAND, 'The American Restatements and the Uniform Commercial Code', p. 65. He does not seem to be very impressed by it, and rather favours the second style.

[17] RICHARD HYLAND, 'The American Restatements and the Uniform Commercial Code', p. 64.

[18] STEVE J. BURTON & MELVIN A. EISENBERG, *Contract Law: Selected Source Materials*, St. Paul 1999, p. 2.

first Robert Braucher and then E. Allan Farnsworth. The Restatement (Second) of Contracts was also clearly influenced by American Legal Realism. It is much less conceptual, more functional and more open to dialogue. Also many provisions of the UCC, that were published in the meantime, have been taken into account. The Restatement (Second) has had considerable success as well, but has not been accepted by all the courts. Some courts, in some cases, continue to rely on the Restatement (First)[19]. Compare Melvin A. Eisenberg: 'The restatements may be most helpful when there is no clear law on the point or when there is reason to believe that the courts might change the law. In the latter respect, the Restatement (Second) serves as a conventional statement of "the modern view" of the law, even when it differs from the formal law in a particular jurisdiction. It has considerable "persuasive authority".'

3. The Uniform Commercial Code. - Another source of inspiration for the Lando Commission has been the Uniform Commercial Code[20]. One of its purposes was to create unity among the various states of America[21]. It was drafted by the National Conference of Commissioners on Uniform State Laws and the ALI[22] between 1942 and 1954, under Chief Reporter Karl Llewellyn. Llewellyn was one of the leading figures in the American Legal Realist movement and his anti-formalist, functional approach is easy to recognise, e.g. in its structure: no abstract concepts and general parts, but articles on Negotiable Instruments, Bulk Sales, Secured Transactions et cetera. See also UCC § 1-102 (1): 'This Act shall be liberally construed and applied to promote its underlying purposes and policies.'[23] The underlying purposes and policies of the act are to simplify, clarify, and modernise the law governing commercial transactions; to permit continued expansion of commercial practice through custom, usage, and agreement of the parties; and to make uniform the law among the various jurisdictions[24]. The style of the UCC is very similar to the second wave of restatements (or rather the other way

[19] STEVE J. BURTON & MELVIN A. EISENBERG, *Contract Law: Selected Source Materials*, p. 3. See on the relationship between the Restatement (First) and the Restatement (Second), Herbert Wechsler, the then director of the ALI: 'The Reporters, their Advisers and the Institute approached the text of the first Restatement with the respect and tenderness that are appropriate in dealing with a classic. As the work proceeded, it uncovered relatively little need for major revision, in the sense of changing the positions taken on important issues, although the Uniform Commercial Code inspired a number of significant additions. (...) It does not denigrate the 1932 volumes to say that the revisions and additions here presented greatly augment their quality. This is, indeed, very close to a new work.' ('Foreword', in Restatement (Second) of Contracts (1981), p. viii).

[20] See PECL, Introduction, p. xxvi.

[21] STEVE J. BURTON & MELVIN A. EISENBERG, *Contract Law: Selected Source Materials*, p. 4.

[22] The Commissioners are appointed by the governors of each state.

[23] U.C.C. § 1-102 (1) seems to have inspired art. 1:106 PECL, which, however, is less liberal.

[24] See for scepticism LAWRENCE M. FRIEDMAN, *A History of American Law*, pp. 675-676, on the UCC: 'It took a heavy effort to sell it to the legislators, who had no idea they needed a code.' 'It was, in a way, curiously old fashioned.' 'The Code was a product of a time that now seems as quaint and old-fashioned as the era of high-button shoes.'

around). Compare Hyland[25]: 'the Code itself, especially the Sales article, which has proved to be one of the great achievements of American codification, rarely provides a specific answer to any question.' In contrast to the restatements the UCC is law in a formal sense. It consists of 11 'articles', which each consist of several 'Sections'. Each Section is followed by a Comment. Although these Comments are formally not part of the law, courts often give considerable importance to them[26]. Article 2, on Sales, which has clearly inspired the Lando Commission, has been adopted in 49 American states. The UCC is under continual revision by the Permanent Editorial Board for the Uniform Commercial Code. At this moment art. 2 (Sales) is under revision.

4. UNIDROIT Principles. - By far the most important source of inspiration have clearly been the UNIDROIT Principles of International Commercial Contracts (UP) which were published in 1994. The PECL look very similar to the UP in all respects[27] and the Lando Commission has followed the UP (often literally) on many points[28]. This is not surprising because there has been an important overlap between the commissions that prepared the two sets of Principles and they have worked contemporaneously most of the time[29]. It should be noted, however, that the Working Group that drafted the UP themselves of course were not working in splendid isolation. They were inspired by the Vienna Sales Convention[30], the UNIDROIT draft on the validity of sales contracts[31], the Restatement (Second) of Contracts[32], and the UCC[33].

5. The PECL as a restatement. - It is clear that the American Restatements had a different objective from the PECL. The ALI presumed the unity of the common law but was concerned with its uncertainty as a result of an

---

[25] RICHARD HYLAND, 'The American Restatements and the Uniform Commercial Code', pp. 55, p. 64.

[26] STEVE J. BURTON & MELVIN A. EISENBERG, *Contract Law: Selected Source Materials*, p. 4.

[27] An important point of difference, however, is that only the PECL contain Notes. See further *infra*.

[28] On other points the drafters of the UP followed the Lando Commission, especially with regard to non-performance and remedies. Compare MICHAEL JOACHIM BONELL, *An International Restatement of Contract Law; The UNIDROIT Principles of International Commercial Contracts*, 2nd ed., New York 1997, p. 87, and EWOUD HONDIUS, 'De betekenis van de Principles of European Contract Law voor het Nederlandse recht / inleiding', *NTBR* 2000, p. 428 ff.

[29] Professors Joachim Bonell, Ulrich Drobnig, Arthur Hartkamp, Ole Lando and Denis Tallon were members of both Commissions.

[30] See UP, Introduction, p. viii.

[31] *Projet de loi pour l'unification de certaines règles en matière de validité des contrats de vente internationale d'objets mobiliers corporels, R.D.U.* 1973, p. 60.

[32] It is important to note that E. Allan Farnsworth, as said the Reporter of the Restatement (Second) of Contracts, was also the Chairman of the Editorial Committee for the UNIDROIT Principles.

[33] See on the American influence E. ALLAN FARNSWORTH, 'The American Provenance of the UNIDROIT Principles', *RDU* 1997, p. 397 ff., and JAMES GORDLEY, 'An American Perspective on UNIDROIT Principles', in: Centro di studi e ricerche di diritto comparato e straniero (lead by M.J. Bonell), *Saggi, conferenze e seminari*, no. 23, Roma 1996.

unmanageable number of cases and with its internal contradictions. What the law in the US was lacking, according to the ALI, was a systematic restatement in general rules of the law which had developed on a case to case basis. In Europe, however, the law of contract in all countries except England and Wales, Ireland and Scotland, is formulated as a coherent system of abstract rules in civil codes (though interpreted and further developed on a case to case basis). Therefore the concern in Europe is rather with a reconciliation of the different abstract formulas and their tradition of interpretation. The Lando Commission is concerned with the diversity among the various European legal systems and tries to create some unity. On the other hand, however, the Lando Commission also presumes the presence of a common core of European contract law, and has tried to restate it.

It is interesting to see that in the U.S. the first approach to the restatement endeavour did not work out. The strong emphasis on abstract black-letter rules in the Restatements (First) met with broad criticism. It seems likely that today in Europe such an approach would not work either. The days of strong formalism in Europe (*École de l'exégèse, Begriffsjurisprudenz, legisme*) are long gone, and, although Europe is still much more formalist than the US, it does not seem very likely that many European courts would 'apply' a European restatement in a rigid way when that would lead to a result which would be, in their view, patently unfair, particularly if they would regard the solution under their own national law as being fairer. Also, a restatement of such a kind would be likely to remain sterile since, as a result of the high degree of abstraction of black-letter rules, it would be of little use as a source of inspiration to national legislators, courts, teachers and scholars. However, the approach of the Restatement (Second) could be successful in Europe. A restatement which provides a framework for dialogue could be extremely helpful[34]. There does not seem to be anything against such a framework. It could even help to make our law 'better'. The PECL clearly look more like the Restatement (Second) than the Restatement (First). In particular, they contain extensive and highly informative Comments. On the other hand, however, they sometimes give more of an impression of closure (as opposed to being open to dialogue) than is the case with the Restatement (Second). They are therefore somewhat ambivalent[35].

Whether the PECL will be successful as a European restatement of contracts will, of course, in the end depend entirely on how European lawyers are going to deal with them, on whether the parties, courts, legislators and the

[34] Compare also J.M BARENDRECHT, 'What kind of European Liability Law?; About the optimal level of detail in rules regarding (tort) liability in a European civil code', published on the Internet (http://dlo.kub.nl:8080/courses/650062/index.html) and JÜRGEN BASEDOW, 'Europäische Vertragsvereinheitlichung und deutsches Recht - Einführung', in: Jürgen Basedow (ed.), *Europäische Vertragsvereinheitlichung und deutsches Recht*, Tübingen 2000.
[35] See also RICHARD HYLAND, 'The American Restatements and the Uniform Commercial Code', p. 60.

EU directives will quote them and be inspired by them. As said, the success of a restatement depends on its authority[36].

B. The Basis for Unification

1. The Need for the Unification of Contract Law in Europe. - Providing an authoritative statement of the law similar to the American Restatements is not the only purpose of the PECL. The Lando Commission also has other purposes in mind. Contrary to the drafters of the American Restatements the Lando Commission hopes that its Principles will one day be enacted as law in a formal sense, preferably as a European Code of Contracts[37].

The Lando Commission makes a clear choice with regard to the need for uniform rules of contract law in Europe. Why do we need uniformity? The Lando Commission tells us explicitly. First, uniform law would facilitate cross-border trade within Europe[38]: 'both within and outside Europe there is a growing recognition of the need for measures of harmonisation to eliminate those differences in national laws which are inimical to the efficient conduct of cross-border business within Europe.' More specifically, in the view of the Lando Commission, a uniform European contract law would help to strengthen the Single European Market[39]: 'The harmonisation of principles of contract law is of especial importance to the proper functioning of the Single European Market, the very essence of which is a broadly unitary approach to law and regulation that surmounts the obstacles to trade and the distortions of the market resulting from differences in the national laws of Member States affecting trade within Europe.'

The Commission does not say anything as to the possible benefits that could (and may now) be derived from 'those differences in national laws which are inimical to the efficient conduct of cross-border business within Europe', both specifically and more in general. It is, of course, possible that those differences in the law are differences that people care about. Admittedly, general contract law is not likely to provoke strong patriotic feelings among most European citizens, but some English tradesmen might prefer the tougher English rule on 'frustration of contract' to art. 6:111 PECL ('Change of Circumstances'), whereas a Scandinavian consumer might prefer a more general test of the fairness of all contract terms than art. 4:109 PECL ('Excessive Benefit or Unfair Advantage') would allow. In other words, many Europeans may regard their law on some points not merely as different from that of other European countries but also as better. Moreover, we might derive a benefit from difference in another way. Mattei and other proponents of the

---

[36] For a parallel see the European Charter of Fundamental Rights, promulgated in December 2000 in Nice which, in spite of its unclear formal status, may be regarded as binding in substance by European institutions. See STEFANO RODOTÀ, 'Ma l'Europa già applica la nuova Carta dei diritti', *la Repubblica*, 3 January 2001.

[37] PECL, Introduction, p. xxiii.

[38] PECL, Introduction, p. xxi.

[39] PECL, Introduction, p. xxi.

theory of comparative law & economics tell us that international competition between legal rules and doctrines may lead to an improvement in the quality of each of our legal systems[40]. Finally, the need for a unity of private law in Europe is strongly contested by Legrand. He derives his arguments from arguments that are put forward against European unification in general, most of which are concerned with the preservation of national culture. He argues that law is culture and that diversity is richness and that in this post-modern age we rather need legal pluralism[41]. I will come back to these objections in the following Sections[42].

Another question is whether the unification of contract law should be limited to Europe. Certainly, there is a clear development towards further integration in Europe, in all sorts of ways. However, that is not the only, and possibly not even the most important, trend today. If uniform rules are needed in order to facilitate international trade, it is doubtful that such unification should stop at the European borders. Rather, there seems to be a trend towards globalisation of the economy, a trend that seems to be enhanced by the Internet and the related New Economy[43]. As a matter of fact, also in contract law until the publication of the PECL the unificatory trends seemed to be rather in the direction of sustaining those developments. In 1980 the United Nations Convention for the International Sale of Goods (CISG) was adopted. It has now been ratified by 61 countries all over the world[44]. And in 1994 the UP were published, which also have a global scope. One could ask whether we really need European Principles, especially since they seem to differ so little from the UP[45]. On the other hand, however, the risk for the PECL to compromise trends towards global unity seems to be rather limited. First, because there is no formal conflict since neither of them is law in a formal sense. Secondly, because they are very similar to both the UP and CISG.

---

[40] See UGO MATTEI, *Comparative Law and Economics*, 1998. There are also risks of a race to the bottom, which would make the most liberal rule survive. See for the United States, LAWRENCE M. FRIEDMAN, *A History of American Law*, New York 1985, p. 410.

[41] PIERRE LEGRAND, *Fragments on Law-as-Culture*, Deventer 1999. See also JAN SMITS, 'Een Europees privaatrecht als gemengd rechtsstelsel', *NJB* 1998, p. 61, JAN SMITS, 'Eenheid en verscheidenheid in het contractenrecht; Over het gedetermineerde verleden en de postmoderne toekomst van het privaatrecht', *R&R* 1998, p. 10 ff, on p. 46.

[42] See *infra* Sections VI Politics, VII Culture and VIII Economics.

[43] See GUNTHER TEUBNER, *Global Law Without a State*, Dartmouth, 1997, WILLIAM TWINING, *Globalisation & Legal Theory*, London, Edinburgh, Dublin 2000, STEFANO RODOTÀ, 'Ma l'Europa già applica la nuova Carta dei diritti'.

[44] See UNCITRAL Status of Conventions and Model Laws, update 14 March 2002 (see www.uncitral.org).

[45] See on the differences ARTHUR HARTKAMP, 'The UNIDROIT Principles for International Commercial Contracts and the Principles of European Contract Law', *ERPL* 1994, 2, pp. 341-357, MICHAEL JOACHIM BONELL, *An International Restatement of Contract Law; The UNIDROIT Principles of International Commercial Contracts*, p. 85 ff. It is interesting to note that the UP have found their way into many a book on cases and materials for contracts courses in the US, e.g. STEVE J. BURTON & MELVIN A. EISENBERG, *Contract Law: Selected Source Materials*.

There is another problem with regard to the Lando Commission's claim of a need for unification. It seems to be in contradiction with their claim that the PECL 'represent the common core of the European systems'. There is some tension between, on the one hand, the strong assertion that unification is needed because diversity is an obstacle to trade, and, on the other, the equally strong claim that the PECL represent the common core of European contract law. Is there great diversity or overwhelming unity? To the extent that the PECL are a reliable restatement of the common core of European contract law, they actually form a strong statement against unification efforts for the simple reason that unity already exists. Conversely, if there are important differences between the European systems of contract law, how was it possible for the Lando Commission to find a common core? Compare Yntema on the American restatements[46]: 'This much is certain, that the notion of improving the law by restating it as it is, is unsatisfactory. (...) Where there is diversity in the law, how can it be stated in a single rule? Where there is uniformity, what is the need for restatement?' To some extent, of course, both claims can be reconciled: the Lando Commission's largely implicit[47] but very plausible[48] assumption seems to be that the commonalties and differences are different in kind (commonalties in substance and differences in form) and that one is more important than the other.

2. *The PECL as a Foundation for European Legislation.* - Like many others, the Lando Commission is clearly concerned with the impressionistic way in which the European Union is harmonising private law, especially contract law[49]. Frequently the European Commission seems to possess a very narrow-minded view (the view of its Brussels Directorate-General) and does not seem to care about the broader picture, i.e. the rest of the national legal system into which the directive must be implemented. The implementation of directives on unfair terms[50], consumer guarantees[51], and, most recently, on late payment of money debts[52], have raised some very difficult systematic questions in various legal systems in Europe[53]. Moreover, directives

[46] HESSEL E. YNTEMA, 'What Should The American Law Institute Do?', p. 468.

[47] See however, PECL, Introduction: 'systems often reach the same solution in different ways.'

[48] See further *infra*.

[49] P. xxii.

[50] 1993/13/EEC.

[51] 1999/44/EC.

[52] 2000/35/EC.

[53] On the other hand, the need for the implementation of directives may also sometimes be beneficial to the system. In Germany, for example, there are plans to use the implementation of the directives on consumer guarantees and on late payment of money debts to establish some order in the very complicated system of remedies for non-performance. See the *Diskussionsentwurf eines Schuldrechtsmoderniserungsgesetzes* issued by the *Bundesministerium der Justiz* on August 4th, 2000. A similar operation was attempted in France when the directive on product liability had to be implemented but unfortunately failed due to a strong producers' lobby. See JACQUES GHESTIN, 'Le nouveau titre IV bis du Livre III du Code civil "De la responsabilité du fait des produits défectueux"; L'application en France de la directive dur la responsabilité du fait des produits défectueux après l'adoption de la loi n° 98-389 du 19 mai 1998', *JCP*, 1998, no.

sometimes seem to contradict one another. Therefore, another purpose (the first) of the PECL mentioned by the Lando Commission is to provide a foundation for European legislation, in order to assure a more orderly development of the law.

3. A European Code of Contracts?. - However, the PECL are not only meant to assist the institutions of the European Union in drafting directives et cetera. The PECL are also explicitly meant to provide a basis for a future European civil code: 'One objective the Principles of European Contract Law is to serve as a basis for any future European Code of Contracts'[54]. This may explain why in its deliberations the Lando Commission has paid most attention to the formulation of the black-letter rules[55].

On this point there is a clear difference between the PECL and the American Restatements of the Law. The Restatements have never been meant to provide a basis for a code. However, it is not immediately clear what the benefit of adoption as a code would be as compared to its status as a restatement, particularly if the code would only consist of the black-letter rules. As said before, much of the substantive value of the PECL lies in the Comments. And it is not all that clear whether the adoption of only the black-letter rules of the PECL as a European Code of Contracts without any harmonisation of regulations concerning specific contracts, without a common law of civil procedure, and without a common jurisdiction that would guarantee uniform interpretation, would lead to a significant degree of uniformity in Europe. However, if it was decided to enact such a European code of general contract law, the PECL would obviously provide an eminent basis for such a purpose.

C. Applicable Law Today

1. Incorporation. - The PECL are not only meant to serve as a basis for future law. They are also intended to be used by contracting parties in Europe today. Of course, the incorporation of the PECL by the parties into their contract is one possibility[56]. In principle parties are free to declare the PECL to be part of their contract (freedom of contract). This may be useful to parties who wish to have a neutral set of contract clauses without time-consuming negotiations and delicate drafting exercises. For example the famous Channel-tunnel contract, that now refers to the law common to France and England, could have adopted the PECL as part of their contract[57].

27, pp. 1201 ff.

[54] See PECL, p. xxiii. Explicit reference is made to the European Parliament Resolutions calling for the preparation of a European Code of Private Law, one in 1989 (Resolution of 26 June 1989, OJEC No. C 158/401) and the other in 1994 (Resolution of 6 May 1994, OJEC No. C 205 (519)).

[55] P. xv.

[56] Art. 1:101 (2).

[57] See OLE LANDO, 'The Principles of European Contract Law after Year 2000', in: Franz Werro (ed.), *New Perspectives on European Private Law, Forum Europarecht*, no. 4, Fribourg 1998, EWOUD HONDIUS, 'De betekenis van de Principles of European Contract Law voor het

2. Choice of law. - However, a choice of law in favour of the PECL, as art. 1:101 (2) also suggests, seems to be more problematic. It is not at all certain that in many European legal systems conflict rules would allow parties to make a choice of law in favour of the PECL[58]. The argument in favour is obvious: the PECL are truly European and therefore probably better adapted to international situations[59]. However, the argument against is equally obvious: the PECL are not 'law' in a formal sense. They have not been enacted by any public authority, nor are they democratically justified in any other way (e.g. consultation with those interested, et cetera). They *are* no more the law than, say, Kötz's book 'European Contract Law'[60]. Nevertheless, several European authors have argued that a choice of law in favour of the PECL should be possible[61]. However, these authors have been met with criticism[62].

3. Formulation of the Lex Mercatoria. - Another purpose mentioned by the Lando Commission is that the PECL may be applied when an international contract states that the arbitrators are to resolve their dispute on the basis of the Lex Mercatoria[63]. The PECL may then be regarded as a restatement of the Lex Mercatoria[64].

When contracting parties instruct arbitrators to apply the Lex Mercatoria, a problem might arise with regard to the choice between the PECL and the UP. The PECL claim that they are 'a modern European Lex Mercatoria'. However, they also claim that they contain rules of general contract law, not only for international commercial contracts, but also for national and consumer contracts. The UP, on the other hand, claim to be the Lex Mercatoria for international commercial contracts[65]. And there is also the

---

Nederlandse recht / inleiding', *NTBR* 2000, p. 428 ff.

[58] The same problem arises with regard to the UP.

[59] This argument is even stronger for the UP, that are exclusively intended for international (commercial) contracts.

[60] HEIN KÖTZ, *European Contract Law*, Part I (translated by Tony Weir), Oxford 1997. Indeed the American Restatements never seem to have aspired to be the object of a choice of law.

[61] See ARTHUR HARTKAMP, 'The Use of the UNIDROIT Principles of International Commercial Contracts by National and Supranational Courts', in *UNIDROIT Principles for International Commercial Contracts: A New Lex Mercatoria, ICC/Dossier of the Institute of International Business Law and Practice* 1995, p. 253 ff.; OLE LANDO, 'Each contracting party must act in accordance with good faith and fair dealing', in: *Festskrift till Jan Ramberg*, Stockholm 1996; KATHARINA BOELE-WOELKI, *Principles en IPR; Enkele beschouwingen over de toepassing van de UNIDROIT Principles of International Commercial Contracts en de Principles of European Contract Law op internationale overeenkomsten*, Lelystad 1995, KATHARINA BOELE-WOELKI, 'Principles and Private International Law', *Uniform Law Review* 1996, 652 ff.

[62] Very sceptical is CATHERINE KESSEDJIAN, 'Une exercise de rénovation des sources du droit des contrats du commerce international: les Principes proposées par l'Unidroit', *Rev. crit. dr. internat. privé.*, 84 (4) October-December 1995, pp. 641-670.

[63] The *Lex Mercatoria* is not recognised in all countries. See FILIP DE LY, *De lex mercatoria: inleiding op de studie van het transnationaal handelsrecht*, Antwerpen 1989 and FILALI OSMAN, *Les principes généraux de la lex mercatoria; contribution à l'étude d'un ordre juridique anational*, Paris 1992.

[64] Art. 1:101 (3).

[65] See UP, Preamble (p. 10), and MICHAEL JOACHIM BONELL, *An International Restatement of*

Central project, led by Berger, which is specifically meant to provide guidelines for arbitrators[66]. However, in practice the difficulties will not be as great as they seem: as said, the UP and the PECL are very similar[67].

D. A Common Language

One of the most important benefits of the European private law movement has been that academic debate on private law has rapidly become international. In my view the most important achievement of the Lando Commission is that it has provided us with a common language for that debate.

Probably the most important function of the PECL will be that they provide us with a common European language for discussions on contract law[68]. This common language provides us with a clear, efficient and sufficiently neutral framework for a fruitful European discussion on contract law[69]. It helps us to formulate the various conflicts[70]. And it is highly accessible and thus allows everyone to participate in the debates.

This common language is not meant to replace the national languages. It simply helps us when we want to talk about the commonalties and differences between our systems. Many commonalties in substance are hidden by differences in terminology (Babel) and, vice versa, many differences in substance are hidden by common terms (false friends). The use of a common language may make communication easier[71]. For the first time in recent history we now have in Europe a sort of meta-language for debates on

---

Contract Law.

[66] See CENTER FOR TRANSNATIONAL LAW (ed.), *Transnational Law in Commercial Legal Practice*, Münster 1999 and www.uni-muenster.de/Jura.iwr/central/english/central.html

[67] See also MICHAEL JOACHIM BONELL, *An International Restatement of Contract Law*, p. 87 ff.

[68] See p. xxv: 'Those attempting to unify European contract law, particularly within the Community, need above all uniform principles and a uniform terminology.' Strangely enough one other, and in my view very important, possible function of the PECL is not mentioned by the drafters: education. First, of course, they can be extremely useful in optional courses on 'European Contract Law' as we have seen in many Dutch universities for some years now. But, secondly, in my view the PECL provide excellent material for teaching the ordinary (mandatory) contract law course in a less positivist, more problem-oriented way. And it is obvious that if all over Europe in contract law courses attention would be paid to the PECL this would contribute enormously to unification. See further HEIN KÖTZ, 'A common private law for Europe: perspectives for the reform of European legal education', in: Bruno De Witte, Caroline Forder (eds.), *The common law of Europe and the future of legal education*, Deventer 1992, MARTIJN W. HESSELINK, *De redelijkheid en billijkheid in het Europese privaatrecht*, Deventer 1999, p. 17 and JÜRGEN BASEDOW, 'Europäische Vertragsvereinheitlichung und deutsches Recht - Einführung', in: Jürgen Basedow (ed.), *Europäische Vertragsvereinheitlichung und deutsches Recht*, Tübingen 2000.

[69] See on taxonomy: UGO MATTEI, 'Three Patterns of Law: Taxonomy and Change in the World's Legal Systems', 45 *AJCL* (1997), p. 5 ff.

[70] See also J.M BARENDRECHT, 'What kind of European Liability Law?; About the optimal level of detail in rules regarding (tort) liability in a European civil code': 'giving the problem a name'. It should not be understood too much as an answer to those conflicts. See RICHARD HYLAND, 'The American Restatements and the Uniform Commercial Code', p. 65-67: 'What the American experience teaches is that differences disappear very slowly if at all. If they are suppressed in one domain, they resurface elsewhere. The only question is how best to take advantage of them.'

[71] On the other hand, the use of a third language may also complicate matters.

contract law. This may reduce to some extent - but not completely! - the Babylonian conversations between scholars and practitioners from different European jurisdictions[72].

Of course this language is by no means completely neutral. The choice of concepts et cetera made by the Lando Commission implies cultural, political and other choices. I will return to this later.

Although the PECL's language is limited to Europe, it will not isolate Europeans from the rest of the world since it is very similar (though not identical) to CISG and the UNIDROIT Principles.

III. Authors and Working Method

A. Authors

Who drafted the Principles of European Contract Law? The PECL were prepared by the Commission on European Contract Law, and edited by Ole Lando and Hugh Beale. The Commission on European Contract Law consists of members from each country of the European Union, including from Scotland. With the expansion of the Union the number of members of the Commission has increased over the years[73].

Who asked this Commission to draft the PECL? The answer is in fact: nobody. In 1974 Professor Ole Lando concluded that the EEC Convention on the Law Applicable to Contractual and Non-Contractual Obligations would be insufficient: 'They would never establish the legal uniformity necessary for an integrated European market.'[74] Although funds were provided by the European Commission[75], the Commission never asked them to draft Principles of European Contract Law. Therefore the Lando Commission cannot be said to represent the European Union in any official capacity. Nor do its members formally represent their countries. Their countries are not bound by them and they are not bound by directives or guidelines from their respective governments. To be clear: the Lando Commission do not claim that they represent anybody. On the contrary, they emphasise the fact that they have worked with great independence.

---

72 And the world. See JAMES GORDLEY, 'The Common Law in the Twentieth Century: Some Unfinished Business', *California Law Review* 2000: 'If we break our last ties with the traditional English common law, the number of [legal] families will be reduced to one. I have argued that we must do so simply in the interest of coherent thinking and sensible outcome. If we do, however, we may also discover that coherence and good sense have little to do with national boundaries. We will have moved toward a world in which jurists everywhere recognize that the fundamental problems are the same, and can talk to each other about them in the same vocabulary.'

73 The Commission only has members from the current EU Member States. Therefore the laws of prospective new members have not been explicitly taken into account.

74 PECL, Preface, p.xi.

75 The EC paid most of the expenses up to 1994. Other funds were provided by some 15 private and public sponsors. See PECL, Preface, p. xv.

The members of the Commission on European Contract Law are virtually all university professors. However, several of them are also practising lawyers[76]. How were the members selected? The Preface to the PECL does not explicitly mention anything with regard to the selection of Commission members, but it is clear that they were selected by co-option. Although the Commission consists of specialists of the highest international esteem, the Commission is not democratically legitimised in any formal way. For most of the purposes for which the PECL are intended (see above) this is not a problem whatsoever, but for some (especially the model for a European Code) it may be questionable from a political perspective.[77] On the other hand, even if the PECL were to be the basis for a European code of contact law, from the perspective of most European countries it is not at all extraordinary for a code to be drafted mainly by scholars. Especially in Germany there is a long-standing tradition of this from the drafting of the BGB until the recent proposals for a *Schuldrechtreform*[78]. And in the Netherlands Meijers and most of his successors who drafted the 1992 Civil Code were academics[79]. Also in Great Britain many statutes and law reforms are prepared by the Law Commissions, which also (but not exclusively) include academics[80]. And in France many pieces of private law legislation, like family law (Carbonnier), traffic liability (Tunc) and product liability (Ghestin) have been prepared by academics. The main difference seems to have been that the members of the Commission on European Contract Law were not formally appointed by their governments to do the drafting[81].

Many of America's prominent law professors, judges, and attorneys are members of the ALI, and, more or less actively, are involved in the drafting and final adoption of the Restatements. This, of course, helps considerably in broadening the support for the restatements. The PECL have not undergone such an elaborate drafting process where literally thousands of people have been involved. They were drafted by some 20 professors. This could of course lead to indifference or scepticism or even hostility on the part of those academics who were not involved in the drafting. In order to broaden support for the project it would be desirable if a European Law Institute, similar to the ALI and UNIDROIT, were to be established, and the EU should invest in

---

[76] PECL, Preface, p. xiii.

[77] Compare G. EDWARD WHITE, 'The American Law Institute and the Triumph of Modernist Jurisprudence', p. 1, on the ALI: 'an organization of elite lawyers and judges'.

[78] Among the members of the *Kommission zur Überarbeitung des Schuldrechts* which presented its proposals in 1992 were Professors Hein Kötz, Dieter Medicus, and Peter Schlechtriem, The recent reform of the law of obligations (on which see further *infra*) is largely based on the findings of that committee (see 'Abschlußbericht der Kommission zur Überarbeitung des Schuldrechts, herausgegeben vom Bundesminister der Justiz', *Bundesanzeiger*, Köln 1992).

[79] Snijders, however, was a senior judge.

[80] E.g. at this moment Professor Hugh Beale, a prominent former member of the Lando Commission.

[81] See for some very formalist criticism CATHERINE KESSEDJIAN, 'Une exercise de rénovation des sources du droit des contrats du commerce international: les Principes proposées par l'Unidroit'.

this[82]. Such an institute could provide the infrastructure for the successor of the Lando Commission, the Von Bar group, which is currently working on the European Civil Code project. It could also guarantee the continuity of the project (similar to Restatements Second and Third).

Of course, all this could not be expected from the Lando Commission. The publication of the PECL is a major achievement. However, it should also be openly recognised that it is essentially an academic achievement, albeit, I repeat, a collective achievement by some of Europe's most renowned experts in the field. The PECL are the private academic work of a group of the most outstanding European scholars with an undisputed reputation in general contract law, most of them with an inclination towards comparative law.

B. *Working Method*

The working method adopted by the Lando Commission is described clearly in the Preface: First, a Reporter drafts Articles and Comments on a certain subject which he presents to the Drafting Group. That group prepares the text for submission to the whole Commission. After the Commission has accepted the texts they are sent to the Editing Group which takes special care of the terminology and presentation of the texts[83]. It is important to note that the Commission left it to the Drafting Group and the Editing Group to finalise the Comments[84], apparently considering the black-letter Principles to be the most important part of their work. The Notes to each article were written by its Reporter on the basis of information provided by the Commission Members[85].

As said above, the American Restatements are also drafted by a private organisation, the American Law Institute. However, there is a major difference between the way the PECL were drafted and the way in which in the US the Restatements of the Law and the UCC are drafted. The drafts for the Restatements and for the UCC are explicitly exposed to interest groups. Moreover, representatives from all parties concerned with a certain branch of the law are involved (in great numbers) in the debates concerning the drafts during the Annual Meeting of the ALI.

The Commission does not say why it has not exposed its draft to explicit lobbying[86]. It could be argued that there is no need to do so because the PECL deal with general contract law which is a fairly neutral part of the law, and the matters which the Commission had to deal with were highly technical issues

---

[82] See W. SNIJDERS, 'The organisation of the drafting of a European Civil Code: a walk in imaginary gardens', *ERPL* 1997, p. 483 ff., MARTIJN W. HESSELINK, *De redelijkheid en billijkheid in het Europese privaatrecht*, p. 21.

[83] Preface p. xv. Especially the Editing Group ensured that the terminology which was used could be readily translated into French and other languages.

[84] See PECL, Introduction, p. xv.

[85] See PECL, Introduction, p. xv.

[86] The PECL were discussed, in view of their comprehensiveness, with practising lawyers from six Member States. See PECL, Introduction, p. xxvi.

which could best be left to specialists[87]. However, the most likely reason seems to be that sufficient funds were simply not available to organise such an endeavour in a serious way. Contrary to the ALI, which, as said above, is a highly professional organisation with thousands of members, the Lando was rather a Commission of idealist volunteers[88].

C. *Presumptio Similitudinis*

The Commission rather looked for similarities than for differences between the systems. They adopted the *presumptio similitudinis* as the basis for their working method. This method was previously successfully applied by Hein Kötz in his *European Contract Law*[89]: the book mainly concentrates on the common core; the local peculiarities can be found in the footnotes. Similarly, the Lando Commission has concentrated on commonalties rather than on divergences. However, the differences are not hidden altogether: they are spelled out in the comparative Notes.

Some scholars are very critical of this method[90]. They maintain that it is 'unscientific'. A true comparative lawyer should look for differences rather than for common factors. However, in the light of their objectives the Lando Commission's choice is perfectly understandable. As said above, the main purposes the PECL should serve are the following: to serve as a restatement of the common core of European contract law; to provide a basis for the future unification of contract law in Europe; to be applied as law from now on in certain specific situations; and to provide a common language. For all these purposes it makes perfectly good sense to concentrate on the similarities rather than on the differences between the various European systems of contract law. If one wishes to draft a set of rules which can be said to be based to some extent on all these systems, and if one wishes to encourage further European integration this method is likely to be the most effective. Clearly, the method of *presumptio similitudinis* is far from being politically neutral. It is typically adopted by idealists who believe in a uniform private law for Europe. It would never be used by adversaries of European integration. But, of course, the alternative method which emphasises differences is not politically neutral either. Apart from a few naive scholars who regard the method as 'objective' or 'scientific', it is mainly employed by those who have other ideals and political aims. They want to preserve local particularities because they regard them as an important part of the national cultural heritage.

---

[87] Whether that position would be tenable will be discussed *infra*.

[88] See Lando's preface (p. xvi): 'However, the most important support was provided by my colleagues, the members of the two Commissions, who without being paid for it gave their time and efforts for the cause.' See on the need for a European Law Institute which could provide the infrastructure for the European Civil Code Project, *supra*.

[89] HEIN KÖTZ, *European Contract Law*. See also KONRAD ZWEIGERT & HEIN KÖTZ, *Introduction to Comparative Law*, 3rd ed., Oxford 1998, p. 40.

[90] See especially PIERRE LEGRAND, 'On the Unbearable Localness of the Law: Academic Fallacies and Unseasonable Observations', 10 *ERPL* 2002, pp. 61-76.

And, clearly, they will not only attack the method but also the purposes envisaged by the Lando Commission.

It should be noted, however, that the members of the Commission did not limit themselves to establishing the common core. They went further. They wanted to build something new, mainly (but not only[91]) based on the foundation provided by the national European legal systems. The Commission stated: 'The method adopted may be compared with the American Restatement of Contract, the second edition of which was published in 1981. However, the task is different. The restatement is broadly intended as a formulation of existing law, since in almost all states the law of contract is based on the common law. In the Union, which is characterised by the existence of a number of divergent legal systems, general principles applicable across the Union as a whole must be established by a more creative process whose purpose is to identify, so far as possible, the common core of contract law of all the Member States of the Union and on the basis of this common core to create a workable system.'

Apart from whether there is here any true difference in principle with the Restatements (it rather seems to be one of degree), it seems appropriate that the Commission explicitly stated that they intended to create something new since this will avoid the risk of the PECL being scrutinised by dedicated positivist 'legal scientists' who wish to reproach the Commission for the fact that the PECL are not an accurate or objective or true statement of the common core. However, as a result, the PECL, at first sight, seem to suffer from ambiguity[92]. On the one hand, they pretend to present the common principles, the common core. They make a strong statement of communality. On the other hand, they pretend to be progressive and tell us that they have not seen it as their task to make interpolations or compromises. They actually acknowledge that some of the provisions in the PECL reflect ideas which have 'not yet' (!) materialised in the law of any State[93]. Probably this ambiguity has something to do with the position of the Lando Commission. On the one hand, the members are academics who want to demonstrate how much the present contract laws of Europe actually have in common, while, on the other, they are also would-be European legislators who want to show us what a good European Contract Code could look like. However, on second thoughts, this ambiguity should not be regarded as problematic. Instead of investigating to what extent the PECL really represent the common *core* they can best be seen as the common *view* (there are no dissents) on general contract law of some of the most eminent scholars in the field from all across Europe. This in itself is a very strong and relevant statement. I do not think that the Commission should or can (or indeed does) pretend that the PECL are anything more than this.

---

[91] Some rules emanate from outside the EU (UCC, Restatements), and some from no system at all!

[92] This ambiguity is not the same as the one discussed *supra*.

[93] See PECL, Introduction, p. xxvi.

IV. Format and Style

A. Format

The format chosen by the Lando Commission is that of Principles. At first sight, to some legal theorists the term 'principles' may be somewhat misleading. Far from being principles as Ronald Dworkin has used them in order to sustain his claim of the law's integrity[94], the black-letter text of Principles of European Contract Law looks very much like rules, similar to those that can be found in many of the civil codes in Europe and, across the ocean, for example in the Uniform Commercial Code[95]. Indeed, similar to the Restatements the black-letter text is often referred to as 'black-letter *rules*' and the Lando Commission itself frequently refers to 'the rule' in one article or the other. Why are the PECL called 'principles'? The members of the Commission never explicitly say so but it seems likely that they were attracted by the connotation of 'basic', 'fundamental', 'general', et cetera[96]. Moreover, they may have been reluctant to speak of rules for fear of being labelled as self-proclaimed European legislators. Finally, of course, the direct source of inspiration were clearly the UNIDROIT Principles.

The Principles are accompanied by Comments and Notes. Since some of the Articles are (necessarily) rather abstract[97], the Comments provide a very important source of information. The Comments ensure that lawyers from the various European traditions have a clear idea of what the Lando Commission means by the abstract formulas contained in the Articles. They are an invaluable product of collective, international scholarship, which may also, together with a casebook, provide excellent materials for teaching the law of contract in Europe. For that reason it is of particular importance that Ole Lando has made sure that a student's edition would be available. (Frankly, for optimal dissemination it would have been better if the whole document had been made freely available on the Internet[98].)

In my view, the format is very appropriate for all the purposes which the PECL are meant to serve[99]. Because of the Comments, which contain many very helpful Illustrations, the PECL are much less abstract and provide much more information and certainty than a classical code. In that sense the adoption of the PECL as a European Code of Contracts would mean important progress for many legal systems. On the other hand, for the same reason, it

---

[94] See especially, RONALD DWORKIN, *Law's Empire*, London 1986.

[95] See *supra*.

[96] This, of course, does ring a bell as regards Dworkin's integrity and other (crypto-) natural law theories.

[97] See on abstraction *infra*, Section V, A.

[98] On p. iv it is stated: 'Permission is given by the copyrightowner for unlimited reproduction for non-commercial purposes only of the pages containing the texts of the articles.' On the risk of separating the Articles from the Comment, see *infra*. See now the UNIDROIT Principles at www.unidroit.org/english/principles/ contents.htm.

[99] On these purposes see *supra*, Section II.

would be an inexcusable mistake to cut off the Comments and Notes and to adopt only the black-letter articles as a European code.

B. Style

1. Accessible - The PECL are written in an elegant style. Fortunately, the Lando Commission has neither adopted the very learned, dogmatic style of *Professorenrecht*, full of concepts and abstractions, such as e.g. the German, Greek, Portuguese and Dutch civil codes (although, as said, the members of the Lando Commission are all professors!), nor the extremely detailed and bureaucratic style of most English statutes. Obviously, this very fortunate result was not attained by chance. It was rather an explicit objective of the Lando Commission: 'Every effort has been made to draft short and general rules which will be easily understood not only by lawyers but also by their clients.'[100] And this effort has been very successfully accomplished by the Editing Group.

2. Open. - The style is also rather open. The PECL explicitly leave a great deal of discretion to the courts. There is no explicit attempt at 'closure': 'The rules are supple, leaving judges considerable latitude. Moreover, the rules may point in opposite directions. It will then be for the judge to choose which is most appropriate in the circumstances of the case and which to disregard.'[101] As a restatement the PECL are also meant to stimulate debate (both between the contracting parties and in the legal community). As we saw above, the American experience has shown that for a restatement too much closure in rigid black-letter rules is not the appropriate style. Indeed, the style of the PECL is rather discursive. Sometimes they do little more than provide the relevant elements for debate. Often they merely mention a set of factors which should be taken into account. See, for example, art. 4:107 (3) (Fraud): 'In determining whether good faith and fair dealing required that a party disclose particular information, regard should be had to all the circumstances, including: (a) whether the party had special expertise; (b) the cost to it of acquiring the relevant information; (c) whether the other party could reasonably acquire the information for itself; and (d) the apparent importance of the information to the other party.'[102] More specifically, the PECL make extensive use of open standards like 'good faith and fair dealing', 'reasonableness' et cetera.

---

[100] PECL, Introduction, p. xxvi.

[101] PECL, Introduction, p. xxxiv.

[102] Another typical example is art. 5:102 (Relevant Circumstances), on interpretation: 'In interpreting the contract, regard shall be had, in particular, to: (a) the circumstances in which it was concluded, including the preliminary negotiations; (b) the conduct of the parties, even subsequent to the conclusion of the contract; (c) the nature and purpose of the contract; (d) the interpretation which has already been given to similar clauses by the parties and the practices they have established between themselves; (e) the meaning commonly given to terms and expressions in the branch of activity concerned and the interpretation similar clauses may already have received ; (f) usages; and (g) good faith and fair dealing.'

There is a persistent view that commercial practice needs hard and fast rules whereas in a non-commercial sphere (especially consumer contracts) more general standards and open-textured rules are preferable. The underlying ideas seem to be that commerce needs certainty more than individual fairness: it is more important to know exactly what the law is than that the resolution of each specific case is fair to both parties; professional parties conclude the same types of contracts all the time and all they want is to be able to calculate their risk and set their prices on the basis of what they know to be the law. This is what many scholars say about commercial practice[103]. If this is true, then the PECL are not as well adapted to commercial contracts as the Lando claims.

However, this view does not seem to be unequivocally confirmed, to say the least, by commercial practice[104]. Many important international commercial contracts contain very vague 'hardship clauses', which often do not say much more than that in case of 'hardship' both parties will be under a duty to renegotiate the contract in good faith. Moreover, some of the most important commercial contracts instruct the arbitrators to apply the 'lex mercatoria', 'general principles of the law', et cetera. And quite frequently arbitrators find as the most important content of the lex mercatoria the general duty of good faith[105]. Interestingly, the concept of good faith was first introduced in American law in the Uniform Commercial Code[106]. And, more generally, the UCC is full of very broad standards. The reason for this is that the drafters thought that such standards would be more suited to commercial practice[107]. Other interesting examples include the UNIDROIT Principles of International Commercial Contracts, which cannot be said to be a set of hard and fast rules, and Klaus-Peter Berger's Central Project, which compiles a list of (now 70)

---

[103] According to DUNCAN KENNEDY, 'Form and Substance in Private Law Adjudication', 89 *Harv. L. Rev.* (1976), p. 1685 ff., p. 1704, with references, this line of thought goes back to Max Weber. See recently in the Netherlands C.J.H. BRUNNER, 'De billijkheid in het nieuwe BW', in: *Rechtsvinding onder het NBW. Een Groningse kijk op het nieuwe vermogensrecht*, 1992, p. 87 ff., and RIEME-JAN TJITTES, 'Naar een bijzonder contractenrecht voor ondernemers', in *Onderneming en 5 jaar Nieuw Burgerlijk Recht*, Deventer 1997, p. 375 ff; RIEME-JAN TJITTES, 'Zaken zijn zaken', *RM Themis* 2000, p. 321-322.

[104] In the same sense M.M. MENDEL 'Welke rol spelen in het handelsrecht de redelijkheid en billijkheid - met name in hun beperkende werking - in rechtsverhoudingen tussen ondernemers en wat behoort die rol te zijn?', in: *Preadvies van de Vereniging Handelsrecht 2000; Het eigen gezicht van het handelsrecht*, Deventer 2000, p. 230 ff.

[105] See e.g. the famous Norsolor case (C.C.I. 26 October 1979, no 3131); NAGLA NASSAR, *Sanctity of Contract Revisited: A Study in the Theory and Practice of Long-Term International Commercial Transactions*, Dordrecht, Boston, London 1995, FILALI OSMAN, *Les principes généraux de la lex mercatoria*, Paris 1992; CENTER FOR TRANSNATIONAL LAW (ed.), *Transnational Law in Commercial Legal Practice*, Vol. 1, Münster 1999 (where good faith is listed as the Lex Mercatoria's no. 1 principle (see p. 148)).

[106] See § 1-203 *UCC*. In addition, more than 50 other provisions make reference to the concept of good faith.

[107] See WILLIAM TWINING, *Karl Llewellyn and the Realist Movement*, London 1973, p. 336: Llewellyn believed that tight drafting will often be at least as likely to defeat commercial expectations as to provide a basis for them.

principles which are said to be generally accepted in commercial practice, most of which are very broad[108].

3. Flexible. Finally, the style is meant to create maximum flexibility. Therefore the drafters have refrained from excessive detail and specificity in order not to inhibit future development[109]. In addition, Article 1:106 provides a liberal rule on interpretation and supplementation of the PECL. See the Comment[110]: 'The 'liberal' interpretation has a static and a dynamic aspect. The first envisages situations which may occur today but which have been overlooked or omitted, the second situations which we cannot imagine today, as the authors of the French civil code could not imagine an industrialized society.'

C. Language

1. Choice of language. - The PECL were published in English. This was an obvious choice since today English is not only the undisputed world language, it has also become the European *lingua franca* among lawyers, both practising lawyers (mainly due to the economic power of the London and New York based law firms) and academics (virtually all European private law projects use English as their working language)[111].

A French translation of the first part of the PECL was published soon after the English version[112]. And no doubt there will also be a French translation of this edition[113]. Are translations into other European languages necessary? There is no doubt that such translations would considerably enhance their circulation, and, as a result, the familiarity of European lawyers with them, and, eventually, the realisation of their goals. The potential risk of a loss of uniformity as a result of inadequate translation, seems to be of minor importance, since the substantive ideas contained in the PECL are far more important than the precise way in which they are formulated. However, if there are going to be translations it is crucial that they should contain not only the black-letter rule but also the Comments (with Illustrations)[114].

---

108 See KLAUS-PETER BERGER, *Formalisierte oder "schleichende" Kodifizierung des transnationalen Wirtschaftsrechts*, Berlin, New York 1996 and KLAUS-PETER BERGER, *The Creeping Codification of the Lex Mercatoria*, The Hague, London, Boston 1997.

109 P. xxvii. Compare UP, Introduction, p. viii: 'the UNIDROIT Principles are sufficiently flexible to take account of the constantly changing circumstances brought about by the technological and economic developments affecting cross-border trade practice.'

110 Art. 1:106, Comment C.

111 See on the important purpose of the PECL as a 'common language', *supra*, Section II, D.

112 *Les principes du droit européen du contrat, L'exécution, l'inexécution et ses suites. Version française*, Paris 1997, translated and edited by ISABELLE DE LAMBERTERIE & GEORGES ROUHETTE & DENIS TALLON.

113 This edition already contains the French translation of the black-letter text.

114 A German translation of only the black-letter articles was published in *Zeitschrift für europäisches Privatrecht* 1995, p. 864, a Spanish one in LUIS DÍEZ-PICAZO & E. ROCA TRIAS & A.M. MORALES, *Los principios del derecho europeo de contratos*, Madrid 2002 (with an extensive commentary from the Spanish perspective), and an Italian one, edited by Professor GUIDO ALPA in *Rivista Critica del Diritto Privato* 2000, 3.

Nevertheless, it seems likely that international academic debate and international practice will mainly use the English version[115]. Thus, eventually the English version may well become the one which is used most frequently. Would that be a dangerous development? It does not seem so. Even the most ardent French preservationist will have to admit that today there is not a great risk that the British will want to dominate Europe. Moreover, it should be emphasised that the terminology used in the PECL is not the terminology of English law. It is rather a new legal language[116].

2. *Some terminological choices.* - It is clear that the Lando Commission had to make many choices also with regard to terminology. Some of the most significant include the following. The PECL use[117] 'good faith *and fair dealing*', like the Restatement (Second) of Contracts and like the UP, not 'good faith', like many European systems and the EC Directive on Unfair Terms[118]; 'termination', not 'rescission' like many English judges[119] or 'avoidance' like the CISG[120]; 'avoidance', like the UP, not 'to annul' which is frequently used in international academic debate[121]; 'debtor' and 'creditor', like many European systems, but unlike English law which uses these terms only as regards monetary debts, and unlike the UP, which use 'obligor' and 'obligee'[122]; 'non-performance', like the UP, but unlike the CISG ('breach')[123]; 'specific performance', like in England and not 'implement' like in Scotland[124]; 'recovery'[125], and not 'restitution', like in England and in the UP[126].

---

[115] Indeed a recent commentary which compares the PECL with Dutch law is based on the English version (and is written in English). See DANNY BUSCH & EWOUD HONDIUS & HUGO VAN KOOTEN & HARRIET SCHELHAAS (GENERAL EDITOR) & WENDY SCHRAMA (eds.), *The Principles of European Contract Law and Dutch Law: A Commentary*, Nijmegen and The Hague, London, New York 2002.

[116] See p. xxv: 'In fact no single legal system has been made the starting point from which the Principles and the terminology which they employ are derived.' This seems to be true. Here again there is a clear parallel with the UP (Introduction, p. viii): 'As to their formal presentation, The UNIDROIT principles deliberately seek to avoid the use of terminology peculiar to any given legal system.'

[117] Emphasis added.

[118] Art. 3, Council directive 93/13/ECC on Unfair Terms in Consumer Contracts, 5 April 1993, *OJ* no. l095, p. 29, 1993/04/21.

[119] Which is confusing in England because the same concept is also used in the case of misrepresentation, i.e. both for termination *ex nunc* and *ex tunc*. See Lord Wilberforce and Lord Diplock in *Photo Production Ltd.* v *Securicor Transport Ltd.* [1980] AC 827 (p. 844 and p. 851 respectively). See on the debate G.H. TREITEL, *The Law of Contract*, 10th ed., London 1999, p. 702 ff.

[120] Arts. 49 and 64 CISG.

[121] NB: in CISG, as said, 'avoidance' is what the PECL call 'termination'.

[122] In most of the drafts (and in the published Part I) the PECL also used 'obligor' and 'obligee' but these terms were substituted in the final draft, a very fortunate choice. CISG, of course, uses 'buyer' and 'seller'.

[123] See on the general concept of non-performance *infra*, Section VII, C.

[124] HECTOR L. MACQUEEN & J. THOMSON, *Contract Law in Scotland*, Edinburgh 2000, p. 221 ff.

[125] Arts. 9:307-9:309 PECL.

[126] Art. 7.3.6 UP.

Some interesting French translations of the articles include: *dol* (not *fraude*) for 'fraud'; *contrainte* (not *violence*) for 'threat'; *droit de suspendre l'exécution* (not: *exception d'inexécution*) for 'right to withhold performance'[127]; and *moyens* for 'remedies'.

V. Subject Matter

A. Abstraction

The law relating to contracts could be in theory, and is in practice in the various European legal systems, stated on various levels and in various modes of abstraction. The Lando Commission has opted for general contract law. Other alternatives include:

1. Legal acts (Rechtsgeschäfte). - In the systems of the German legal family (Germany, Greece, Portugal (*negócio jurídico*), the Netherlands (*rechtshandeling*)) contracts are regarded as just one type of *Rechtsgeschäft*. This concept has had some success in legal doctrine in Italy, but it was not introduced into the new 1942 civil code[128]. In France the concept has been even less successful[129] and in English law it is not known at all. It is a very abstract concept, which is to be found in the most general (i.e. abstract) parts of the code, in Germany in Book 1 (General Part), in Greece in Book 1 (General Principles), in Portugal in Book 1 (General Part), and in the Netherlands in Book 3 (General Part of Patrimonial Law) and is applicable, for example, to such different acts as the formation of a contract, the recognition of a child and the acceptance of an inheritance. It was developed in the heyday of *Begriffsjurisprudenz* and it is very strongly related to the 19th century idea of party autonomy[130].

The concept now seems outdated. As said, it was not included in the Italian Civil Code. The Hungarian, Russian and other Eastern European codes do not use it, and it is neither included in the UP[131], nor in the Scottish plans for a civil code[132] or the English proposals for a commercial code. And although, as said, it is included in the 1992 Dutch code it should be kept in mind that the first drafts for that code date from the 1950s[133]. Moreover, today

---

[127] Art. 9:201 PECL. Compare CISG: 'suspend performance'. But see the Title of Section 9.2 (Withholding Performance): *Exception d'inexécution*.

[128] See C. MASSIMO BIANCA, *Diritto Civile*, III, *Il contratto*, Milano 1987 (reprinted in 1992), 3, with references.

[129] But see JACQUES FLOUR & JEAN-LUC AUBERT, *Les obligations; 1. L'acte juridique*, 6th ed., Paris 1994.

[130] See WERNER FLUME, *Allgemeiner Teil des Bürgerlichen Rechts;* Vol. II. *Das Rechtsgeschäft*, 4th ed. Berlin, Heidelberg, New York 1992, esp. pp. 28 ff.

[131] Neither is it to be found in the American Restatements (First) and (Second) of Contracts or in the UCC

[132] See HECTOR MACQUEEN, 'Scots Law and the Road to the New Ius Commune', *Ius Commune Lectures on European Private Law*, 1, Maastricht 2000.

[133] See E.M. MEIJERS, *Ontwerp voor een Nieuw Burgerlijk Wetboek (Groene Boeken), Tekst eerste gedeelte (Boek 1-4)*, The Hague 1954, p. 117. The first drafts reflect a clear preference for

in legal doctrine and in legal education in most European countries emphasis seems to be more on the law of obligations (with contract as one source of obligations) and on the law of contract.

The Lando Commission was right in choosing not to draft Principles of European Legal Acts. The concept is too abstract: even for those who are not completely convinced by post-modernism[134], this degree of rational, systematic abstraction goes too far, especially as far as the law is concerned (as opposed to textbooks). It is also too closely related to the 19th century conception of party autonomy for it to be acceptable as a central concept in the law of the 21st century[135]. And, finally, it is too closely related to only the German legal family, whereas it is completely unknown in English law[136].

2. Law of obligations, liability law, the death of contract. - In most European legal systems lawyers think in terms of the law of obligations and are familiar with general rules on obligations[137]. Systematically, in these countries contracts are regarded primarily as one of the sources of obligations. The concept of 'obligation' has been central in the legal systems on the Continent since Roman law[138] and it lies at the heart of all European codes and at the universities in most civil law countries courses and textbooks are based on it. This is different in the legal systems of England and Wales, Ireland, and Scotland, where emphasis is more on 'contracts', 'torts' and, more recently, on 'restitution'[139], and in Scandinavian countries, where sales law and general contract law are the central concepts[140].

The Lando Commission has not opted for Principles of European Obligations. They do not explain why. Therefore we can only hazard a guess. The most obvious reason seems to be that drafting Principles of European Contract Law was a sufficiently ambitious endeavour. Another plausible reason might be that in the law of contracts a great deal of work had already been done (ULIS, CISG, Restatements First and Second, UP). Finally, they may have regarded the PECL as just a first step. Eventually, within the ECC project where the PECL will be the general contract law, it may be decided to

---

abstractions which was typical of Meijers, the author of the first drafts. See JAN SMITS, 'Eenheid en verscheidenheid in het contractenrecht', p. 17.

134 See on abstraction MARTIJN W. HESSELINK, *De redelijkheid en billijkheid in het Europese privaatrecht*, p. 406 f, and on modernism and abstraction JAN SMITS, 'Eenheid en verscheidenheid in het contractenrecht', p. 16 ff.

135 See on this *infra*, Section VI, A.

136 See BASIL. S. MARKESINIS & W. LORENZ & G. DANNEMANN, *The German Law of Obligations*, Vol. I *The Law of Contracts and Restitution: A Comparative Introduction*, Oxford 1997 and my 'Review', 3 *The Edinburgh Law Review* (1999), p. 412 ff.

137 This is also true for the systems of the Germanic legal family, which also contain a general law of obligations.

138 See REINHARD ZIMMERMANN, *The Law of Obligations*, Oxford 1996.

139 See, however, GEOFFREY SAMUEL & JAC RINKES, *The English law of obligations in comparative context*, Nijmegen 1992 and ANDREW BURROWS, *Understanding the Law of Obligations; Essays on Contract, Tort and Restitution*, Oxford 2000.

140 See for Sweden CHRISTINA HULTMARK, 'Obligations, Contracts and Sales', in: Michael Bogdan (ed.), *Swedish Law in the New Millennium*, Stockholm 2000, p. 273.

adopt general rules on obligations. Many of the rules contained in the PECL may be easily transformed into rules of obligations. As a matter of fact, during the drafting of many rules (especially those relating to liability in damages) their possible application to types of liability other than contractual has been taken into account.

Neither has the Lando Commission opted for 'liability law'. In some legal systems there is a tendency to concentrate mainly on liability and to move towards a 'liability law'. This is so in France[141] and the Netherlands, where the University of Tilburg has a 'Centre for Liability Law'[142]. This tendency is inspired by the idea that in many cases it does (or should) not matter whether liability is contractual or delictual[143]. This seems to be particularly true in case of accidents and other cases of physical harm and damage to property, where indeed it should not make any difference whether or not parties have a contractual or similar relationship (*Sonderverbindung*), but for 'pure economic loss' some legal systems (especially German and English law) make a distinction[144].

The notion of a general 'liability law' is related to the idea of 'the death of contract' which was proclaimed by Grant Gilmore in 1974[145]. (See also the theories of *gesetzliches Schutzverhältnis* (Canaris) and *dritte Spur*[146]). But today in most legal systems contract law seems alive and well. One of the reasons seems to be that there is more to contract law than just the 'law of accidents' or 'injury law' or even 'liability law'. This is particularly true for long-term contracts where even in case of conflict liability is frequently not the main issue since, because of their mutual dependence, parties are more interested in how they should continue their relationship[147]. Therefore under the PECL, as in most European legal systems, liability in damages is just one of the remedies for non-performance. Another reason is that most people still believe that it makes a difference for the existence and extent of rights and obligations between parties whether or not such rights and obligations were

[141] See especially GENEVIEVE VINEY, *Traité de droit civil; Les obligations; Introduction à la responsabilité*, 2nd ed., Paris 1995. See also PHILIPPE LE TOURNEAU, LOÏC CADIET, *Droit de la responsabilité*, Paris 1996.

[142] See also J.M BARENDRECHT, 'What kind of European Liability Law?; About the optimal level of detail in rules regarding (tort) liability in a European civil code'.

[143] See the structure of the Dutch 1992 Civil Code, which provides general rules for liability in damages (Section 6.1.10), from whichever source (contract, tort, *negotiorum gestio*, unjust enrichment or other).

[144] Compare CHRISTIAN VON BAR, *Gemeineuropäisches Deliktsrecht, München 1996*, and MARTIJN W. HESSELINK, *De redelijkheid en billijkheid in het Europese privaatrecht*, p. 220 ff., with further references.

[145] GRANT GILMORE, *The Death of Contract*, Ohio 1997.

[146] Rejected for the Netherlands by MARTIJN W. HESSELINK, *De redelijkheid en billijkheid in het Europese privaatrecht*, p. 210 ff. and A.S. HARTKAMP, *Mr. C. Asser's handleiding tot de beoefening van het Nederlands burgerlijk recht; Verbintenissenrecht;* Vol. II *Algemene leer der overeenkomsten*, 11th ed., Deventer 2001, no. 48b.

[147] See IAN MACNEIL 'Relational Contract Theory as Sociology', 143 *Journal of Institutional and Theoretical Economics* (1987), p. 272, and STEWART MACAULAY, 'Non-Contractual Relations in Business: A Preliminary Study', 28 *American Sociological Review* (1963), p. 55.

intended by the parties or not, particularly in the case of 'negotiated contracts'. This view seems to have been embraced by the Lando Commission as well. Therefore, also in the view of the Lando Commission, contract is alive and kicking.

3. Specific contracts. - Another alternative would have been only to make rules for all (or some) known types of specific contracts. The obvious advantage of such an approach would be that the rules would be much less abstract. And, clearly, such specific rules would much better fit the specific type of contract concluded by the parties. But the drawbacks of such an approach are equally evident. First, as a result of freedom of contract the work on such principles would never be finished because people invent new types of contracts every day in order to best serve their particular interests[148]. Secondly, such separate sets of rules for each type of contract would inevitably be very repetitive, because many of the rules would be the same for all (or most) types of contract. These seem to be the main reasons why since the acceptance of consensual contracts in Roman law such an approach has been gradually abandoned and why today all European legal systems contain general rules of contract law (and/or the law of legal acts and/or the law of obligations)[149]. On the other hand, it is clear that having *only* the general law of contract leaves many specific questions unanswered. That is why within the framework of the European Civil Code project principles of specific contracts (sales, services, long-term contracts) are being prepared.

4. Commercial and consumer contracts. - Some legal systems distinguish between commercial and civil law. In the first wave of codifications most continental European legal systems adopted both a civil code and a commercial code. However, since the first half of the 20th century the significance of this distinction has significantly decreased. And some countries, notably Italy (1942) and the Netherlands (1992), officially abolished the distinction on the occasion of the implementation of their new civil codes[150].

However, interestingly, during the last decades of the 20th century a counter-development started to occur as a result of the birth of 'consumer law'. Thus a new distinction arose, between general civil law, which was thought to be largely based on party autonomy, and specific consumer law, which exceptionally was more protective[151]. In the course of the 1980s and '90s in many European countries consumer law developed into an important branch of the law (not least as a result of the many European directives), with

---

[148] See MARCO B.M. LOOS, 'Naar een Europees dienstverleningsrecht', *NJB* 2000, p. 452 ff.

[149] In Scandinavian systems the Contract Act only covers a limited number of issues. See for Sweden CHRISTINA HULTMARK, 'Obligations, Contracts and Sales', p. 274.

[150] In the Netherlands the distinctions between *kooplieden* and other persons, and between *daden van koophandel* and other acts was abolished as early as in 1934. See R.J.Q. KLOMP, *Opkomst en ondergang van het handelsrecht*, Nijmegen 1998; R.J.Q. KLOMP, 'Geschiedenis, bij wijze van inleiding', in: *Preadvies van de Vereniging Handelsrecht 2000*, Deventer 2000.

[151] See R.P.J.L. TJITTES, *De hoedanigheid van contractspartijen*, Deventer 1994.

a great deal of autonomy. In France all consumer regulations have even been brought together in the *Code de la Consommation.* This development was enhanced by the way in which European Union bureaucracy in Brussels is organised. Different Directorates-General are responsible for the Common Market and for Consumer Protection, which has significantly increased the tendency to make separate rules for consumers and commercial parties.

There are many international examples of the new dichotomy: the UCC, CISG and UP are only intended for commercial contracts; in England plans are being made for a commercial code whereas, as said, France has adopted a consumer code. However, there are also counter-examples: the American Restatements (First) and (Second) of Contracts are intended for all contracts, and in Europe many countries have tried to integrate consumer law into their civil codes as far as possible, thus trying to maintain the integrity of civil law. A clear example is the 1992 Dutch Civil Code.

The Lando Commission has expressly opted for unitary contract law. This seems to be the right choice for many reasons. First, the distinction between consumer contracts and commercial contracts is very problematic. Smits argues that each has its own distinct logic[152]: commercial contracts are concluded with a view to making profits whereas 'domestic contracts' (concluded by consumers, et cetera) would not have this purpose. This position does not seem to be tenable. First, this distinction ignores the importance of a major group of contracts, the mixed contracts, i.e. the ones concluded between a consumer and a professional. There are very few purely domestic contracts, and there is even less litigation on such contracts. In many systems many domestic agreements are even considered to be outside the scope of the law[153]. But more importantly: every party who concludes a contract usually does so because she believes it will make her better off. More specifically, most consumers will buy their goods and services where it is most favourable in terms of price, service et cetera, whereas most sellers and service providers are doing their best to make a profit. Compare Mattei[154]: 'Since there is no such thing as a separate market for consumers (demand) and a separate market for producers (supply), contract law has to face the problem of how to merge supply and demand into a single market. The creation of two different bodies of law at odds with each other would ignore this reality, and, as a result, reduce the chance of building efficient private law institutions for modern Europe.' Secondly, by (re)introducing 'schizophrenic contract law', as Mattei has called it[155], the definition and proof of status (consumer or

---

[152] In favour of such schizophrenia is also the 'Groningen school': see e.g. C.J.H. BRUNNER, 'De billijkheid in het nieuwe BW', and, especially, R.P.J.L. TJITTES, *De hoedanigheid van contractspartijen*, RIEME-JAN TJITTES, 'Naar een bijzonder contractenrecht voor ondernemers', RIEME-JAN TJITTES, 'Zaken zijn zaken'.

[153] See JAMES GORDLEY (ed.), *The Enforceability of Promises in European Contract Law*, Cambridge 2001.

[154] UGO MATTEI, 'Efficiency and Equal Protection In The New European Contract Law: Mandatory, Default and Enforcement Rules', 39 *Va. J. Int'l L.* (1999), p. 538

[155] UGO MATTEI, 'Efficiency and Equal Protection In The New European Contract Law'.

professional) becomes all important, whereas it seems much more efficient to concentrate on contract rather than on status.

However, for one of the purposes which the Lando Commission has in mind for its PECL (maybe it is even its final goal), in admittedly rather opportunistic terms, it might have been preferable to opt either for a consumer code or for a commercial code since, precisely because of the way Brussels' bureaucracy is organised, the adoption of a Consumer Code (institutional basis and political aim: consumer protection) or a Commercial Code (institutional basis and political aim: common market) seems to be much easier to achieve[156]; the concept of general 'contract law' may be somewhat too abstract from a European institutional and political perspective.

Interestingly, the PECL are very similar to the UP which are intended exclusively for commercial contracts[157]. If commercial law and consumer law have their own respective logic, does this mean that the PECL have applied business logic to consumers (or the other way around)?[158]. Or are the rules so abstract that the real choices will have to be made when the rules are applied? Or do the PECL provide evidence against the necessity of this dichotomy[159]?

5. National and international. - Whereas the UP are only meant for international contracts, the PECL are explicitly intended to apply also to internal contracts[160]: 'But while the Principles will be found particularly useful in international trade transactions within Europe, they are not confined to such transactions and may be applied equally to purely domestic transactions.' A distinction between national and international contracts was proposed by Drobnig: he suggested unifying only the law of international contracts[161]. However, this suggestion was rejected by most other scholars as being impracticable and as being a source of new discrimination which would obstruct the proper functioning of the common market.

6. Some consequences. - The Lando Commission has chosen for general contract law. For the purpose of creating a common language the choice of general contract law is probably the most suitable. Rules of general contract law may, however, be less appropriate for some of the other purposes. For a code, a choice of law, or incorporation into a contract some more specific rules are usually (also) needed. In the ECC project work has now started on 'nominate contracts', especially sales, services, long-term contracts,

[156] Compare what Staudenmayer, a senior civil servant at the European Commission, said in Utrecht in December 1999 (see Martijn W. HESSELINK, *AA Katern* 74).

[157] See *supra*, Section II, A.

[158] In their Preface and Introduction the PECL frequently refer to business. See e.g. p. xxv ('international business community').

[159] See on the political relevance of this distinction *infra*, Section VI, A, on the relevance of the distinction for the style of drafting (closed rules or open standards) *supra*, Section II, A.

[160] P. xxv.

[161] ULRICH DROBNIG, 'Private Law in the European Union', *Forum Internationale*, no. 22, September 1996 and ULRICH DROBNIG, 'Scope and general rules of a European civil code', *ERPL* 1997, p. 489 ff.

insurance, monetary loans and personal guarantees[162]. Among these rules there will probably be some specific rules on e.g. consumer sales and commercial sales respectively.

Also, from a (left-wing) political perspective, as a result of the absence of (usually mandatory) protective rules for consumers, employees, tenants and other weaker parties, which are usually to be found in the part on specific rules of contract law, the PECL may look rather individualist (as opposed to social) and sterile (the important rules are simply not there)[163].

Another consequence of the Lando Commission's choice for general contract law is of a more institutional kind. General rules of contract law are necessarily rather abstract and abstract rules in practice leave many of the real choices to the discretion of the courts[164].

B. Functional Approach

The Commission on European Contract Law has adopted the 'functional approach'[165]. This means that it has dealt with (more or less) all matters which are relevant for contracts even though some of these matters could be, and in many systems actually are, dogmatically regarded as part of another or a broader field of law, based on a different type or degree of abstraction (see above). First, the PECL deal with some matters that are regarded in many jurisdictions as matters of tort law. See, for example, Section 2.3 (articles 2:301 and 2:302) on pre-contractual liability[166] and art. 4:117 on damages in case of (possible) avoidance for mistake et cetera. The PECL also include rules on matters that are regarded in some countries as part of the law of *Rechtsgeschäft* (see above), for example many issues of formation (Chapter 2) and validity (Chapter 4)[167]. In addition, the PECL contain many examples of subjects that in most European countries are regarded as part of the general law of obligations. See, for example, the rules on Performance and Non-

[162] A team based in Amsterdam, Tilburg, and Utrecht is preparing the draft rules on sales, services and commercial contracts. In Hamburg a team is working on personal guaranties. Recently in Luxembourg/Paris a team has started to work on monetary loans. And in Hamburg an associated team is currently drafting principles of insurance contracts in collaboration with a group led by Professor Reichert-Facilides).

[163] See on this further *infra*, Section VI, B.

[164] Compare HESSEL E. YNTEMA, 'What Should The American Law Institute Do?', p. 468: 'European codes, which confide excessive discretion to the courts on account of the generality of their prescriptions'.

[165] P. xxv.

[166] See for example France, Belgium, and Italy. See MARTIJN W. HESSELINK, *De redelijkheid en billijkheid in het Europese privaatrecht*, p. 80, MARTIJN W. HESSELINK, 'Precontractual Good Faith', in: Hugh Beale et. al. (eds.) *Cases, Materials and Text on Contract Law, Oxford and Portland*, Oregon 2002, Chapter 2, Section 2 (pp. 237-293), and EWOUD H. HONDIUS, 'General Report', in: *Precontractual Liability; Reports to the XIII Congress International Academy of Comparative Law; Montreal, Canada 18-24 August 1990*, Deventer/Boston 1991, pp. 11-12, all with further references.

[167] See notably Germany (arts. 116 ff. *BGB*), Portugal (arts. 240 ff. *Código civil*) and the Netherlands (arts. 3:32 ff. *BW*).

Performance (Chapters 7, 8 and 9)[168]. Moreover, the PECL deal with some issues that in many systems are regarded as part of the law of restitution. The most prominent examples are articles 4:115 and 9:307-9:309 on recovery after avoidance or termination of a contract which has already been (partially) performed[169]. Finally, the PECL contain some rules, especially some remedies, which in some jurisdictions are only available with regard to some specific contracts, particularly sales (example: art. 9:401 on price reduction[170]).

The Commission could have made different, more radical functional choices. Some will find the functional choice of contracts still too dogmatic and would have preferred the functional choice of liability law[171]. However, as said, there is more to contract law than liability, and it is likely that the choice of contract law will be the one which is most easily accepted by (and thus: functional to) both legal doctrine and practice[172].

C. Subjects Covered

Most of the subjects relating to general contract which codes, contracts courses and commentaries in Europe deal with today are covered by the PECL. The choice of subjects and their presentation are very similar to the UP. However, contrary to the UP the PECL also deal with the difficult subject of the authority of agents (Chapter 3)[173].

A few classical subjects of contract are still missing, but the Lando Commission is currently working on them[174]: 'Additional chapters will deal with the effects of illegality and immorality, compound interest, conditions, extensive prescription of claims and with topics which cover both contractual and non-contractual obligations such as assignment of claims, assumption of debts, plurality of debtors and creditors, and set-off.'

The structure of the PECL is quite straightforward. It consists of 131 articles which are divided into 9 chapters, four of which are sub-divided into two or more sections. The structure looks very similar to the UP, but in

---

[168] See for example Italy (arts. 1176 ff.), the Netherlands (arts. 6:27 ff. and 6:74 ff.).

[169] Compare arts. 7.3.6 UP and 81 (2) CISG.

[170] See for example France (art. 1644 Cc), Germany (art. 462 *BGB*) and Italy (1492). See also art. 3 (2) Directive 1999/44/EC on consumer guarantees.

[171] This approach seems to be favoured by J.M BARENDRECHT, 'What kind of European Liability Law?; About the optimal level of detail in rules regarding (tort) liability in a European civil code'.

[172] See on taxonomy UGO MATTEI, 'Three Patterns of Law: Taxonomy and Change in the World's Legal Systems'.

[173] The rules are based on, and are very similar to, the UNIDROIT Convention on Agency in International Sale of Goods. See DANNY BUSCH, 'Indirect Representation and the Lando Principles', vol. 2.3 EJCL (December 1998) (http://law.kub.nl/ejcl/23/art23-1.html); A.S. HARTKAMP, 'Indirect Representation According to the Principles of European Contract Law, the Unidroit Agency Convention and the Dutch Civil Code', in Jürgen Basedow, Klaus J. Hopt and Hein Kötz (eds.), *Festschrift für Ulrich Drobnig zum siebzigsten Geburtstag*, Tübingen 1998, pp. 45 ff.

[174] PECL, Preface xiv.

Europe there does not seem to be a Code with such a plain structure. This is clearly one of the 'progressive' aspects of the PECL[175]. The PECL are much more straightforward than, for example, the recent (1992) Dutch Civil Code, where one has to 'collect' the law relating to a consumer sales contract from 6 different degrees and types of abstraction.

Nevertheless the PECL still provide a rather 'learned' view of contract law. Their structure reveals that they were drafted by academics. Barendrecht has suggested a different, more inductive approach[176]. In his view a codifier should start by identifying which problems require specific rules and draft specific rules for those problems. Would the result have been very different from the PECL? It probably would. In the alternative approach the Principles would probably have been less abstract (no general contract law), and concerning some specific issues (e.g. offer and acceptance (Section 2.2)) there would probably have been less detailed rules whereas concerning other subjects (e.g. measure of damage (9:502)) the rules would probably have been more detailed.

VI. Politics

A. Law & Politics

1. Conflict. - Contract law is meant to resolve conflicts between parties to contracts. These parties have conflicting interests and invoke conflicting arguments in favour of their respective positions[177]. Each system of general contract law has balanced those interests in its own way. The way the balance is struck depends on many factors. One is the type of contract most frequently involved in the cases that have come before the courts, or the type of cases the legislator had in mind when stating the law[178]. General contract law differs if it has been developed in labour or in construction cases, in negotiated or non-negotiated contract cases and in long-term (e.g. franchise) or discrete (e.g. sales) contract cases. Another factor is the types of parties that were involved in most cases in which general contract law was developed. It makes a difference whether in most cases both parties were large multinational companies which were each assisted by a whole team of specialised lawyers,

---

[175] On progress see further *infra*, Section IX.

[176] See J.M BARENDRECHT, 'What kind of European Liability Law?; About the optimal level of detail in rules regarding (tort) liability in a European civil code'.

[177] See generally RUDOLPH VON JHERING, *Der Kampf ums Recht*, Darmstadt 1874, and J.H. NIEUWENHUIS, *Confrontatie en compromis; Recht, retoriek en burgerlijke moraal*, Deventer 1992.

[178] See HEIN KÖTZ, 'The Trento Project and Its Contribution to the Europeanization of Private Law', in: Mauro Bussani, Ugo Mattei (eds.), *Making European Law; Essays on the 'Common Core Project'* Trento 2000, HEIN KÖTZ, 'How to Achieve A Common European Private Law', in: Franz Werro (ed.), *New Perspectives on European Private Law, Forum Europarecht*, no. 4, Fribourg 1998, p. 20; MARTIJN W. HESSELINK, *De redelijkheid en billijkheid in het Europese privaatrecht*, p. 419.

or whether in most cases one party was a consumer, or the state. It may also make a difference at which point in time the most important part of contract law developed, a long time ago or relatively recently. Finally, and probably most importantly, it makes a difference who developed contract law and what their views were. Lawmakers with different views make different choices. Therefore all coherent theories of contract law that have attempted to consider contract law as the expression of just one underlying idea and which have tried to explain contract law in its entirety in terms of that particular idea (including the one that proclaimed the death of contract) have failed[179]. And there is not much hope for new theories.

2. Autonomy (Individualism) v Solidarity (Altruism). - One of the basic conflicts underlying contract law is the conflict between autonomy and solidarity. Or, as it is often put, the conflict between the right to be free and the obligation of solidarity (but it could also be stated in the opposite way: the obligation to leave others free and the right to solidarity). Many conflicts concerning contracts may ultimately be reduced to that conflict[180]. This was first argued with great force by Duncan Kennedy[181]. It is clear that there is here an analogy with the traditional political opposition, that most European countries (and many others) have known throughout the 20th century, between liberalism and socialism or the right and left[182]. These political currents reflect different views concerning the economy and the role of the law within it. One is usually associated with a free market, the other with state intervention (regulation), one with mere allocation, the other with redistribution. More broadly speaking, the idea of party autonomy (individualism) is usually historically connected to Enlightenment, philosophically to rationalism (Kant), socially to the 18th and 19th century dominance of citizens, economically to classical capitalism (*laissez-faire*), and politically to liberalism ('the right'). Basic ideas include 'free will', 'certainty', 'self-reliance' and 'competition'[183]. Typical legal dogmas are 'freedom of contract', 'absolute property' and 'fault liability'. On the other hand, the idea of solidarity (altruism) is usually historically associated with Industrialisation, philosophically to Marxism, socially to the late 19th and early 20th century attack on capitalism and emancipation movements (the working class, women,

[179] In the same sense RICHARD CRASWELL, 'Contract Law, Default Rules, And The Philosophy Of Promising', 88 *Mich. L. Rev.* (1989), p. 489-529, and JAN SMITS, 'Eenheid en verscheidenheid in het contractenrecht', p. 10 ff.

[180] I do not pretend that all contract law can be explained in terms of this dichotomy, nor do I pretend that this is the only important conflict underlying contract law, this dichotomy is all there is to contract law. Quite the opposite. *Supra* I said that contract law can best be regarded as a relatively incoherent result of balancing a great variety of conflicts.

[181] See DUNCAN KENNEDY, 'Form and Substance in Private Law Adjudication'. This Section owes a great deal to his analysis in both that classical article and in his recent book, DUNCAN KENNEDY, *A Critique of Adjudication {fin de siècle}*, Cambridge Massachusetts 1997.

[182] Of course, in countries with a proportionate electoral system there were many other parties as well, including, typically, a Christian-Democratic party in the centre.

[183] See DUNCAN KENNEDY, 'Form and Substance in Private Law Adjudication', pp. 1713 ff.

cultural minorities, consumers), economically to the welfare state (regulation), and politically to socialism ('the left'). Basic ideas include 'protection', 'fairness', 'sacrifice and sharing', and 'regulation'[184]. Typical legal dogmas are 'the duty of good faith', 'abuse of right' and 'strict liability'.

Whether this distinction will continue to have a prominent role in the 21st century is uncertain. It is clear that in many European countries the political conflict is much less poignantly present today than it was during the Cold War. And maybe today's political spectrum can best be characterised by the attempt to overcome this dichotomy. But, on the other hand, it is striking to see that the political movements ('Third Way'[185], *'l'Ulivo'*) or models ('Polder Model') that pretend to have overcome the classical distinction define themselves exactly in terms of the old distinction; they claim to be a compromise between the two extremes[186].

3. A Matter of Choice. - Left versus right, freedom versus equality, individual versus the state, market versus regulation, individual versus collective, egotism versus altruism. I do not claim that these distinctions either completely or necessarily overlap, but I do think that they have been sufficiently connected and recognisable in Europe over the last century. In each European system balances have been reached between these extremes, in each field of the law including contract. I also think that the more a legal system tends to opt in all the choices just mentioned for the first alternative the more most people will regard it as left wing, whereas systems that tend to opt for the latter will be regarded more as right wing. Where did the Lando Commission strike the balance?[187].

4. *Comparative Law & Politics.* - Interestingly, with regard to political preferences there may sometimes be more harmony within one political family across the European borders than within a legal family of conceptually and historically related European legal systems. The question then arises for European citizens (as it arises more generally within the European Union) whether they feel, for example, more 'right' or more 'French' (the clash between culture and politics).

5. No Integrity. - Before embarking upon a political evaluation of the PECL, a few preliminary remarks should be made. First, there is nothing natural, logical or necessary about one way or another of balancing autonomy and solidarity. There is a policy (or political) choice to be made here on which different people have different views (law is politics). Assertions that contract is really only (or mainly) based on freedom, will, promise et cetera are based

---

[184] See DUNCAN KENNEDY, 'Form and Substance in Private Law Adjudication', pp. 1717 ff.

[185] See for a philosophy of the third way RONALD DWORKIN, *Sovereign Virtue; The Theory and Practice of Equality*, Cambridge Massachusetts, London 2000.

[186] Maybe in some countries like the Netherlands the underlying conflict is merely hidden under compromise but will re-emerge in days of less (or even more) economic prosperity when real choices will again have to be made.

[187] The general part of contract law is often thought to be 'politically neutral', technical. This is forcefully contested by DUNCAN KENNEDY, 'The Political Stakes in "Merely Technical" Issues of Contract Law', 10 *ERPL* 2002, pp. 7-28.

on a rhetoric that calls for deconstruction[188]. I do not think that in any European country today a set of general contract law rules would be accepted that were exclusively based on either freedom of contract or contractual solidarity. Therefore a balance must be found. There are different political views in all countries on where the balance should lie[189].

Secondly, for a legislator there are only two ways to avoid striking the balance in the conflict at some specific point. One is by drafting a very vague or open-textured or abstract rule, that leaves the actual choice to the courts. The other is by providing no rule at all, and thus leaving the matter completely to the courts to decide (or to the negotiating parties). However, it should be noted that in most cases choosing not to make specific rules is also a choice in the conflict, because where there is no specific derogating rule (e.g. relief in case of a change of circumstances), the general rule (e.g. the binding force of contract) will apply.

Finally, it should be noted that, exactly because of the various factors that play a role in the development of the law (there are probably many others), the system of contract law in a country is never, and can never be, the consistent expression of one specific balance in just one of the many conflicts that underlie it, say 70% freedom of contract and 30% solidarity. No legal system is consistently to be found in one specific place on the line between the two poles[190]. To give an example, French law has a tough rule on *imprévision* (*pacta sunt servanda*: autonomy) but also has extensive 'implied' duties to inform (*obligation d'information*)[191] and to protect (*obligation de sécurité*)[192] the other party (*forçage du contrat*: solidarity). Similarly, in most countries both 'commercial' and 'consumer' contract law are based on both notions[193]. In the Netherlands some authors have recently argued for two distinct bodies of contract law, one for tradesmen and one for consumers[194]. The strongest separation thesis is proposed by Jan Smits[195]. He maintains that the law of commercial contracts and the law of consumer contracts have a completely different logic[196]. Smits bases his theory on post-modernist philosophy and on the related theory of legal pluralism. It is very surprising that Smits should

[188] Which is not the same as destruction.

[189] See recently in favour of more freedom of contract in the Netherlands TON HARTLIEF, *De vrijheid beschermd*, Deventer 1999.

[190] See DUNCAN KENNEDY, 'The Political Stakes in "Merely Technical" Issues of Contract Law'.

[191] See MARTIJN W. HESSELINK, *De redelijkheid en billijkheid in het Europese privaatrecht*, pp. 262 ff., with many examples.

[192] See MARTIJN W. HESSELINK, *De redelijkheid en billijkheid in het Europese privaatrecht*, pp. 191 ff., with many examples.

[193] See also *supra*.

[194] See C.J.H. BRUNNER, 'De billijkheid in het nieuwe BW', RIEME-JAN TJITTES, 'Naar een bijzonder contractenrecht voor ondernemers', RIEME-JAN TJITTES, 'Zaken zijn zaken'.

[195] JAN SMITS, 'Eenheid en verscheidenheid in het contractenrecht' and repeated in JAN SMITS, *The Good Samaritan in European Private Law; On the Perils of Principles without a Programme and a Programme for the Future*, Deventer 2000.

[196] The logic of trade is to maximise profit and the logic of a 'house and garden' contract is to obtain a specific result.

invoke post-modernism for introducing (or rather reintroducing) what is of course a very modernist abstraction: the whole world of people entering into contracts can be divided into two distinct groups, each with their own exclusive logic. As I explained above, general contract law is best understood as being based on a whole variety of different logics. (That is pluralism!) But this philosophical argument cannot in itself completely disqualify the separation thesis. The weakness of the theory rather lies in its assumption of these two different logics. Is commercial practice a jungle that needs a tough freedom of contract logic? There are many examples that rather show the opposite. First, the doctrine of unforeseen circumstances, which is usually regarded as an example of solidarity in contract. In virtually all countries this doctrine was accepted in purely commercial cases[197]. In the Netherlands the pre-contractual duty to inform, another classical example of a more social contract law, was developed in commercial cases[198], just like the doctrine against formalist, literal interpretation[199], and liability for breaking-off negotiations[200]. Another example is provided by the theory of relational contracts, which emerged in commercial settings (distribution, franchise, agency, joint ventures)[201]. And the doctrines of good faith and unconscionability were first introduced into the law of the United States in the Uniform Commercial Code[202]. More recent examples include the UNIDROIT Principles of International Commercial Contracts which contain many very 'social rules', e.g. art. 3.10 (gross disparity)[203].

B. Autonomy v. Solidarity

Which political choices has the Lando Commission made with regard to the conflict between autonomy and solidarity? Of course, the most obvious examples of this are to be found among the rules that determine the

[197] See MARTIJN W. HESSELINK, *De redelijkheid en billijkheid in het Europese privaatrecht*, pp. 319 ff., with examples from many European jurisdictions.
[198] HR, 15 November 1957, *NJ* 1958, 67, note Rutten (Baris/Riezenkamp), HR, 21 January 1966, *NJ* 1966, 183 (Booy/Wisman).
[199] HR, 13 March 1981, *NJ* 1981, note Brunner, 635, *AA* 1981, p. 355, note Van Schilfgaarde (Ermes/Haviltex).
[200] HR, 18 June 1982, *NJ* 1983, 723, note Brunner, *AA* 32 (1983), 758, note Van Schilfgaarde (Plas/Valburg), HR, 23 October 1987, *NJ* 1988, 1017, note Brunner (VSH/Shell), HR, 14 June 1996, *NJ* 1997,481, note HJ Snijders (De Ruiterij/Ruiters).
[201] See especially Macneil (e.g. IAN MACNEIL, 'Restatement (Second) of Contracts and Presentiation' 60 *Virginia LR* (1974), p 589 ff.; IAN MACNEIL, 'Contract Adjustment of long-term economic relations under classical, neo-classical and relational contract law', 72 *Northwestern University LR* (1978), p. 854 ff., IAN MACNEIL, 'Relational Contract Theory as Sociology').
[202] See especially § 1-203 UCC: 'Every contract or duty within this Act imposes an obligation of good faith in its performance or enforcement.' In addition, more than 50 other Sections in the UCC refer to the concept of good faith.
[203] See also the many examples of duties to co-operate et cetera accepted in international arbitration. See NAGLA NASSAR, *Sanctity of Contract Revisited: A Study in the Theory and Practice of Long-Term International Commercial Transactions*, Dordrecht, Boston, London 1995.

enforceability of promises and the scope of an obligation. However, it is clear that, upon final analysis, most of contract law deals with these questions. One could even define contract law as the law that determines to what extent promises are binding. Therefore most questions of contract can be analysed in terms of autonomy versus solidarity.

1. General Contract Law. - Of course, the choice made by the Lando Commission to concentrate on the general part of contract law, thus leaving aside most statutory regulations which give protection to employees, tenants, consumers and other presumably weaker parties, gives an impression of a greater freedom of contract than actually exists with regard to many important contracts in most European systems[204]. Or, to put it in more explicitly political terms: from a left-wing perspective most of the important law (most of the political achievements in the 20th century) is missing in the PECL. Therefore, for a left-wing politician the PECL as a first European Code may seem rather poor and old-fashioned; and she would probably be rather more impressed by a Labour Code or a Housing Code or a Consumer Code.

The Commission says that it does not deal with such specific types of contract because policy questions were involved[205]. But is this not also true for the general part of contract law? As demonstrated by the American Legal Realist and the Critical Legal Studies Movements and as we will see in the following, also with regard to issues of general contract law between equal parties et cetera, policy/political choices will have to be made[206]. These choices may not be very politically controversial, but choices have to be made nevertheless.

2. Freedom of contract. - Unlike most civil codes in Europe the PECL dedicate a specific article to 'freedom of contract', which is placed right at the beginning of the PECL (art. 1:102). It starts as follows: 'Parties are free to enter into a contract and to determine its contents'. However, this general statement is immediately qualified, after the comma, by the following phrase 'subject to the requirements of good faith and fair dealing, and the mandatory rules established by these Principles'. Thus, under the PECL the mechanism is the following: freedom in principle, subject to exceptions provided by mandatory law and good faith.

Where freedom of contract forms, like in most legal systems, the point of departure (parallels: free market, absolute property, fault liability), the solidarity rules are to be found in the limitation and regulation of that freedom, often in mandatory rules. Many of these rules are made in order to impose solidarity with (i.e. to protect) a specific type of party which is presumed to be weaker, because of its status and its typical position in the

---

[204] See for similar criticism with regard to the Restatement (First) of contract, CHARLES E. CLARK, 'The Restatement Of The Law Of Contracts', p. 658, and HESSEL E. YNTEMA, 'What Should The American Law Institute Do?', p. 466.

[205] P. xxv.

[206] See on the political stakes in "merely technical" issues of contract law DUNCAN KENNEDY, 'The Political Stakes in "Merely Technical" Issues of Contract Law'.

type of contractual relationship it is involved in. The most classical examples are to be found in the mandatory rules of labour law, landlord and tenant law, and consumer law. Of course, for those types of contracts the most relevant part of contract law is not general contract law. Especially in the heavily regulated fields of contract law, where there is not much freedom of contract remaining, general contract law is of little relevance.

Many scholars favour a more radically social 'general contract law'[207]. And indeed the emphasis given by the Lando Commission to freedom of contract seems somewhat out of place. First, because it gives the wrong impression: in most European systems with regard to many contracts there is not as much freedom of contract as the Principles suggest. Secondly, because it gives just one side of the picture. From a political perspective it would probably have been more balanced to place freedom of contract (autonomy) and the duty to co-operate (solidarity) side by side in the same article, in order to emphasise that European contract law is based on both these (conflicting) ideas.

3. Good Faith and Fair Dealing. - The PECL represent the international triumph of the principle of good faith: they contain innumerable references to 'good faith and fair dealing', both in Articles and in Comments, far more than any civil code in Europe. What will be the role of good faith in article 1:201 and others?

In many European legal systems the good faith principle has developed over the last century into a means by which the courts have imposed solidarity (altruism) and limited autonomy, both within contract law and outside. Indeed, the duty of good faith is frequently defined as the duty to take the other party's interests into account[208]. Many of the typical applications of good faith (*Fallgruppen*) which were developed by legal doctrine translate

---

[207] THOMAS WILHELMSSON, *Social Contract Law and European Integration*, Dartmouth, 1995; THOMAS WILHELMSSON, 'Private Law in the EU: Harmonised or Fragmented Europeanisation?', 10 *ERPL* 2002, pp. 77-94; BRIGITTA LURGER, *Vertragliche Solidarität, Entwicklungschancen für das allgemeine Vertragsrecht in Österreich und in der Europäischen Union*, Baden-Baden 1998; DANIELA CARUSO, 'The Missing View of the Cathedral: The Private Law Paradigm of European Legal Integration'; BRIGITTA LURGER, *Grundfragen der Vereinheitlichung des Vertragsrechts in der Europäischen Union*, Wien, New York 2002. See also CHRISTOPHE JAMIN, 'Plaidoyer pour le solidarisme contractuel', in: Gilles Goubeaux et al. (ed.), *Études offertes à Jacques Ghestin; Le contrat au début du XXIe siècle*, Paris 2001; JAN B.M. VRANKEN, 'Over partijautonomie, contractsvrijheid en de grondslag van gebondenheid in het verbintenissenrecht' in: J.M. Barendrecht, M.A.B. Chao-Duivis and H.A.W. Vermeulen (eds.), *Beginselen van contractenrecht: Opstellen aangeboden aan B.W.M. Nieskens-Isphording*, Deventer 2000; GUIDO ALPA, *Trattato di diritto civile, I Storia, fonti, interpretazione*, Milano 2000, p. 604 ff. See further *infra*, Chapters 5 and 6.

[208] See e.g. C. MASSIMO BIANCA, *Il contratto*, no. 224; A.S. HARTKAMP, *Verbintenissenrecht II* (in: *Asser* series), no. 300; MICHAEL P. STATHOPOULOS, *Contract law in Hellas*, The Hague, London, Boston, Athens 1995, no. 51; ARNDT TEICHMANN, in: *Soergel Bürgerliches Gesetzbuch mit Einführungsgesetz und Nebengesetzen*, Vol. 2 *Schuldrecht I (§§ 241-610)*, 12th ed., § 242, no. 4. See further MARTIJN W. HESSELINK, *De redelijkheid en billijkheid in het Europese privaatrecht*, p. 44.

aspects of a duty to take the other party's interests into account (altruism)[209]: duty of care, duty of loyalty, duty to co-operate, duty to inform, *venire contra factum proprium non valet* (similar to estoppel), proportionality. At first sight, therefore, it seems that good faith is the intrinsically altruist concept that imposes solidarity and counterbalances party autonomy.

However, in my view, good faith, as it developed in European legal systems like the German and the Dutch, should not (or should no longer) be regarded as a separate normative concept[210]. It is best conceived as a means to compensate for a formalist approach towards rules and rights[211]. Similar to the way, under Roman law, the primitive formalist approach towards the *legis actiones* (*ius civile*) was compensated by the law developed by the magistrates (*ius honorarium*), and to the way, in England, the initial formalism of the common law (forms of action) was balanced by the Lord Chancellor's Equity, on the Continent good faith became the tool which the courts had found to counterbalance the consequences of a formalist approach towards the new phenomenon of codes[212]. In contract law most of the anti-formalism judicial activism was aimed at limiting the absolute (i.e. formal) application of the rule *pacta sunt servanda*, which, of course, is closely related to party autonomy. Therefore, today in Europe most of the 'content of the good faith norm' consists of social, altruist norms. However, this could be different if the norms in the code with regard to which a party tries to adopt a formalist approach were social norms[213]. Under a more social system of contract law anti-formalism might also be directed against parts of the law that are based more on solidarity, such as a rule that protects contracting parties (consumers and others) against surprising standard terms[214]. But most of the norms in the European codes were based on 19th century liberalism (freedom of contract, absolute property rights et cetera) and the formalist attitude towards those rules was attacked with the weapon of good faith.

---

209 See MARTIJN W. HESSELINK, *De redelijkheid en billijkheid in het Europese privaatrecht*, pp. 58 ff.

210 See *infra*, Chapter 7. See earlier J. SCHMIDT, *J. von Staudingers Kommentar zum Bürgerlichen Gesetzbuch mit Einführungsgesetz und Nebengesetzen; Zweites Buch Recht der Schuldverhältnisse; Einleitung zu §§ 241 ff.; §§ 241-243*, Berlin 1995, § 242.

211 See on form and substance in private law DUNCAN KENNEDY, 'Form and Substance in Private Law Adjudication' and DUNCAN KENNEDY, *A Critique of Adjudication {fin de siècle}*.

212 MARTIJN W. HESSELINK, *De redelijkheid en billijkheid in het Europese privaatrecht, passim*, especially pp. 429 ff. As a consequence, to the extent that a formalist approach towards the civil code (and towards rules in general) is abandoned, good faith will no longer be needed as a counterbalance. Historical parallels: the merger between *ius civile* and *ius honorarium* and the gradual integration of common law and equity as a result of the Judicature Acts of 1873 and 1875.

213 In the same sense SIMON WHITTAKER & REINHARD ZIMMERMANN, 'Coming to terms with good faith', in: Reinhard Zimmermann & Simon Whittaker (eds.), *Good Faith in European Contract Law*, Cambridge 2000, p. 699.

214 See, as a recent Dutch example, *HR*, 1 October 1999, *NJ* 2000, 207 (Geurtzen/ Kampstaal) where the concept of good faith was used to limit the (protective) statutory rule that standard terms may be avoided if they have not been made available for consultation (art. 6:234 *Civil Code*).

It seems likely that under the PECL good faith will continue to be used as a tool against a formalist approach to rules of contract law and contractual rights and obligations. To the extent that the PECL will be approached in a formal way, good faith will continue to be needed as a limit to party autonomy and as a gateway for solidarity rules. To the extent that the PECL are less individualist than the 19th century codes and more social (which they definitely are), we will start to see some more 'party autonomy' inspired exceptions to 'social' rules as part of the 'content of the good faith norm'[215].

4. Duty to Co-Operate. - Article 1:202 proclaims a duty for the parties to co-operate. At first sight this article seems to be the recognition by the Lando Commission of the importance of the other basic idea underlying today's European contract law: solidarity. However, as seems to follow from the Comment, the Lando Commission rather seems to understand it in a more limited and technical sense. Under the PECL the duty to co-operate is especially meant to play the role that is fulfilled in many civil law systems by the doctrine of *mora creditoris*[216]. However, in contrast with the latter doctrine under the PECL the duty to co-operate is a real, enforceable 'obligation'. Failure to co-operate may constitute 'non-performance'(art. 1:301), which means that in principle the other party has recourse to the remedies given in Chapter 9[217].

A duty to co-operate is recognised, on the basis of good faith, in many European legal systems[218]. It was developed in France by the great René Demogue who said: 'Les contractants forment une sorte de microcosme; c'est une petite société où chacun doit travailler pour un but commun qui est la somme des buts individuels poursuivis par chacun, absolument comme dans la société civile ou commerciale.'[219]. Today, in many European systems it plays an important, though admittedly rather indeterminate role[220]. Although

---

[215] See further *infra*, Chapter 7.

[216] Art. 1:202, Comment A. See MARTIJN W. HESSELINK, *De redelijkheid en billijkheid in het Europese privaatrecht*, p. 244 ff.

[217] See arts. 8:101 in connection with art. 1:301. See also art. 8:101, Comment A.

[218] For example France, Germany, and Italy. See MARTIJN W. HESSELINK, *De redelijkheid en billijkheid in het Europese privaatrecht*, p. 238 ff., with references.

[219] R. DEMOGUE, *Traité des obligations en général, II Effets des obligations*, Part VI, Paris, 1931, no. 3. However, JEAN CARBONNIER, *Droit Civil*, Vol. IV *Les Obligations*, 22nd ed., Paris 2000, no. 114 (p. 227), warns that one should not exaggerate: 'L'outrance peut perdre une idée juste. On s'étonnera qu'à une époque où le mariage s'était peut-être trop transformé en contrat, d'aucuns aient rêvé de transformer tout contrat en mariage.'

[220] See J.B.M. VRANKEN, 'Vertrouwen en rechtszekerheid in het overeenkomstenrecht', in: *Vertrouwensbeginsel en rechtszekerheid, Preadviezen Vereniging voor de vergelijkende studie van het recht van België en Nederland*, Deventer 1997, p. 22, J.B.M. VRANKEN, 'Over partijautonomie, contractsvrijheid en de grondslag van gebondenheid in het verbintenissenrecht' in: J.M. Barendrecht, M.A.B. Chao-Duivis and H.A.W. Vermeulen (eds.), *Beginselen van contractenrecht: Opstellen aangeboden aan B.W.M. Nieskens-Isphording*, Deventer 2000, MARTIJN W. HESSELINK, 'De opmars van de goede trouw in het Franse contractenrecht', *WPNR* 6154 (1994), pp. 694-698; MARTIJN W. HESSELINK, *De redelijkheid en billijkheid in het Europese privaatrecht*, pp. 238 ff. See also the central role of co-operation in Macneil's relational contract theory (IAN MACNEIL, 'Restatement (Second) of Contracts and Presentiation' ; IAN

article 1:202 PECL is intended by the Lando Commission to have a more limited function, if the PECL were to be enacted as a European Code of Contracts, it might nevertheless develop as the main anchor-point under the European code for the further development of social contract law. It seems perfectly suitable as a basis for social rules that courts might wish to develop.

5. Excessive Benefit or Unfair Advantage. - With regard to the kind of cases art. 4:109 is meant to deal with, one extreme position (freedom of contract) would be: the contract is binding upon the parties since consensus was reached. This is what seems to have been the rule in many European countries in the 19th century before doctrines like undue influence, *misbruik van omstandigheden* et cetera were developed. A more moderate version of this approach would aim to restore the (imaginary) 'initial position'. It would concentrate on the contract the parties would presumably have concluded if the weaker party was an ordinary party. An advantage of this approach is that it provides incentives for creating an equal bargaining situation[221]. A disadvantage is that it leads to fictions. Who knows what the parties would have done? (would the seller have accepted the market price? et cetera).

The other extreme (contractual solidarity) would be: the state imposes the price included in any contract. In more moderate versions it would be held that courts should only enforce contracts with fair prices. The law could either indicate a certain absolute or presumptive balance between the price actually paid and the market price, or leave it to the courts to decide in every individual case. Scandinavian countries (most explicitly) and German and Austrian law (in some cases) seem to rely on a version of the latter approach, and French law in the case of some contracts (*lésion*)[222]. An advantage of this approach is that it is straightforward. The difficulty lies in deciding what a fair price is, i.e. where the balance should lie between the price the parties agreed upon and the market price.

To put it in other words, in cases like this an individualist is more likely to favour the approach of procedural fairness, which is more respectful of party autonomy (although in a rather fictitious way: it is said to provide incentives, but incentives for what?; to reach a fair price or just to inform?), whereas an altruist would rather favour a substantive fairness approach, which

---

MACNEIL, 'Relational Contract Theory as Sociology').

221 See *infra*, on law & economics.

222 In the Nordic countries on the basis of § 36 Contract Act any clause in any contract may in principle be policed in view of substantive unfairness. See THOMAS WILHELMSSON, 'Standard Form Conditions', in: A.S. Hartkamp et al. (eds.) *Towards a European Civil Code*, 2nd ed., Nijmegen and The Hague, London and Boston 1998, pp. 255 ff., on p. 259, RUTH NIELSEN, *Contract Law in Denmark*, The Hague, London and Boston 1997, no. 128, CHRISTINA HULTMARK, 'Obligations, Contracts and Sales', p. 278, and *infra*. Under German (§ 138 (2) BGB), Austrian (§ 879 *ABGB*) and Greek (arts. 178 and 179 civil code) law contracts with a gross disparity between the obligations are considered to be against good morals. Under French and Belgian law (arts. 1674-1685 Cc) a sale of immovable property may be rescinded in case of *lésion* (price less than 5/12th of the value).

acknowledges that some people under certain circumstances even make the wrong choices when they are provided with all the relevant information.

The PECL have reached a compromise (third way): a combination (or rather cumulation) of procedural and substantive unfairness. Neither of them suffices in isolation[223]. At first sight, that seems a rather harsh rule. However, as it seems, in most cases it should be relatively easy to prove one of the weaknesses or needs indicated in art. 4:109[224]. Then everything will depend on the court's appreciation of excessiveness. It seems likely that, if the PECL were to be enacted as a European Code of Contracts, at least in the beginning, different courts could decide differently according to their traditions et cetera. In order to create more legal certainty the PECL could have indicated in the Comments what proportion is presumed to be excessive, as indeed the UP did in their Comment on the rule concerning unforeseen circumstances (hardship)[225].

6. Unfair terms. - Standard terms are a classical instance where the principle of freedom of contract came under attack. With regard to such terms the individualist conception of contract as consensus was obviously highly fictitious. When signing a contract which contains a set of standard terms or refers to them a party usually gives its consent without fully knowing the content and implications of these terms, either because she has not read them or because she does not understand them. Moreover, even if she does understand them she is frequently left with no alternative because the other party (typically an economically more powerful one) is not prepared to contract on terms other than these whereas all the other actors in the industry use similar conditions. In the course of the 20th century in all European legal systems the question arose of how to deal with standard terms.

In an extremely individualist view all such contracts would simply be valid and enforceable: the general conditions were freely accepted when the contract was signed; each party should take care of its own interests when signing a contract. This view has been abandoned in all European countries. Less extreme versions of the individualist approach concentrate on bringing the general terms to the attention of the other party. If that party accepts these conditions after having read them and understood them they should then be binding upon her. This approach was adopted by the 1942 Italian civil code, the first code to deal with the problem[226]. It provided protection by trying to restore the 'initial position' of true consent: it declared a number of onerous standard terms to be void unless the other party explicitly agreed to them in

[223] Art. 4:109, Comment B. A similar approach was earlier adopted in Italy (art. 1448 cc) and in Portugal (art. 282 *CC*).
[224] See (1)(a): '[the party] was dependent on or had a relationship of trust with the other party, was in economic distress or had urgent needs, was improvident, ignorant, inexperienced or lacking bargaining skill'.
[225] An alteration amounting to 50% or more of the cost or the value of the performance is likely to amount to a "fundamental" alteration, which may allow relief. See art. 6.2.2., Comment 2.
[226] Art. 1341 cc. Since 1996 see also arts. 1469 bis ff. which implement the EC Directive on unfair terms in consumer contracts.

writing. In most other systems it took a long time for the legislator to intervene. In the meantime the courts tried to solve the problem on a case by case basis. They often did so with the help of the concept of good faith: in specific cases they declared the invocation of a specific clause in standard terms as being contrary to good faith, thus upholding the formal validity of the clause (no interference with freedom of contract). Later, a more straightforward check of the content of such clauses was adopted (*Inhaltskontrolle*)[227]. In most systems the legislator intervened during the 1970s[228]. After the German example (*AGBG*) most of these statutes mainly focus on checking the content of standard terms, thus openly limiting the freedom of contract. They even contain blacklists of clauses that are deemed to be voidable in general conditions in consumer contracts. In 1993 a European directive on unfair terms in consumer contracts was adopted[229]. This directive has now been implemented in most European legal systems.

Just like most European statutes and the EC Directive, art. 4:110 also aims to directly police the content of standard terms (substantive fairness) rather than limiting itself to procedural fairness: a party may avoid a standard term if the term causes a significant imbalance in the parties' rights and obligations. However, the *Inhaltskontrolle* is limited in two significant ways. First, art. 4:110 only deals with unfair terms 'which have not been negotiated'. Thus for clauses that have been individually negotiated freedom of contract and self-reliance continue to prevail. Secondly, section 2 excludes application to terms which define the main subject matter and to the price, thus rejecting the *iustum pretium* theory. These two limitations are also to be found in the EC Directive and were also present in most European legal systems before the implementation of the directive. Moreover, most European legal systems also reject the adoption of the *iustum pretium* theory as such[230]. However, in the Scandinavian countries protection extends further[231]. In the Nordic countries the checking of contract clauses is not limited to standard terms. See art. 36 Contract Act[232]: '(1) An agreement may be amended or set aside, in whole or in part, if its enforcement would be unreasonable or contrary to principles of fair conduct. The same applies to other legal transactions. (2) In applying subsection 1 of this provision, consideration shall be given to the circumstances at the time of the conclusion of the agreement, the content of the agreement, and later developments.' On the basis of this article even the price may be controlled[233].

---

[227] See in Germany *BGH*, 29 October 1956, *BGHZ* 22, 90.

[228] For example in Germany (1976), in England (1977), and in France (1978). See MARTIJN W. HESSELINK, *De redelijkheid en billijkheid in het Europese privaatrecht*, pp. 97 ff., with further references.

[229] Council Directive 93/13.

[230] See Hein Kötz, *European Contract Law*, p. 130 ff.

[231] See THOMAS WILHELMSSON, 'Private Law in the EU: Harmonised or Fragmented Europeanisation?'.

[232] See RUTH NIELSEN, *Contract Law in Denmark*, nos. 128 ff. and 382 ff.

[233] See THOMAS WILHELMSSON, 'Private Law in the EU: Harmonised or Fragmented

In another respect, however, protection (and therefore: limitation of freedom of contract) under the PECL goes further than that provided by the directive. Art. 4:110 extends the scope of application of the general clause of the EC Directive to contracts between private persons and to commercial contracts[234]. Even the directive's blacklist of clauses that are deemed to be unfair, although not directly applicable, is quoted in the Comment as a possible source of inspiration for judges and arbitrators[235].

7. Implied terms. - Chapters 6 on 'Contents and Effects' and Chapter 7 on 'Performance' look very classical, and are very much based on party autonomy. Especially the way in which the PECL deal with 'implied terms' is somewhat disappointing. The PECL do not explicitly take into account all the 'implied terms' that courts in Europe have developed during the course of the 20th century, especially on the basis of good faith[236], and that have radically changed contractual relationships and the rights and obligations of the parties to a contract[237]. Art. 6:102 (Implied Terms) only mentions possible sources of implied terms. But, as Oliver Wendell Holmes said[238], 'you always can imply a term in a contract'. The Lando Commission has made no attempt to state when a term should be implied or what its content should be. The only heteronomous obligations they explicitly mention are the duty of good faith and fair dealing (art. 1:201) and the duty to co-operate (art. 1:202), but, as said, these duties are too vague.

Also the choice of the term 'implied term' is itself unfortunate because it makes one think of an implicit agreement by the parties (intent, autonomy). The PECL even mention as the first source of implied obligations the intention of the parties[239]. This means: the unexpressed intention of the parties[240]. In reality, however, these are obligations that parties would often not have contemplated, and if they had one of them (the one who is now accused of non-performance) would probably not have agreed to such an obligation[241]. In France some of these obligations cannot even be excluded or

---

Europeanisation?', and PECL, art. 4:110, Notes, 4 (p. 271).

[234] Art. 4:110, Comment A.

[235] Art. 4:110, Comment B. See on *reflexwerking* in the Netherlands A.S. HARTKAMP, *Verbintenissenrecht II* (in: *Asser* series), no. 368.

[236] See for hundreds of examples from many European jurisdictions MARTIJN W. HESSELINK, *De redelijkheid en billijkheid in het Europese privaatrecht*, Deventer 1999, pp. 173-273.

[237] See on the importance of these obligations W. SNIJDERS, 'Boekbespreking', *WPNR* 6376 (1999), p. 792 ff, J.B.M. VRANKEN, 'Over partijautonomie, contractsvrijheid en de grondslag van gebondenheid in het verbintenissenrecht', and J.M. BARENDRECHT, 'Contractuele gebondenheid en het beginsel van belangenmaximalisatie', in: J.M. Barendrecht, M.A.B. Chao-Duivis and H.A.W. Vermeulen (eds.), *Beginselen van contractenrecht: Opstellen aangeboden aan B.W.M. Nieskens-Isphording*, Deventer 2000.

[238] OLIVER WENDELL HOLMES JR., 'The Path of the Law', in: Sheldon M. Novick (ed.) *The Collected Works of Justice Holmes; Complete Writings and Selected Judicial opinions of Oliver Wendell Holmes*, Vol. III, Chicago and London 1995, pp. 391 ff. (originally published in 1897 in 10 *Harvard Law Review*, 457).

[239] Art. 6:102 (a).

[240] The UP (art. 5.1) do not mention the parties' intention as a source of implied obligations.

[241] See PHILIPPE MALAURIE & LAURENT AYNES, *Cours de droit civil*, part IV, *Les obligations*,

limited in the contract[242]. And in all systems, exclusion is often effectively difficult because these obligations are 'implied' by the courts after the fact. Compare in the Netherlands the so-called implied warranties[243].

The wording of the article, the Comment on it, and the Survey of Chapters 1-9 suggest that art. 6:102 is only a 'gap-filling' device, which is elaborated in more specific rules on instances of failure to fix the price (art. 6:104), the absence or disappearance of a factor of reference (art. 6:107) and the quality of performance (art. 6:108). That is a very narrow view of the concept of implied terms, which does not reflect the achievements in European case law during the 20th century[244]. To put it in German terms: the PECL only deal with *ergänzende Vertragsauslegung*, not with *Nebenpflichten* (*Schutzpflichten*). However, in the course of the 20th century in hundreds of cases all over Europe a host of obligations have been developed by the courts. This is what Barendrecht has rightly called the 'living law of contract'[245]. It would be fictitious, and politically wrong, to regard the acceptance of these obligations by the courts as being based on party autonomy. As said, it is sometimes even impossible to exclude them effectively. In my view the Lando Commission should have tried to 'codify' this very important part of contract law. It could have relied on the achievements attained by the courts and legal doctrine, especially in Germany, where sets of detailed obligations have been elaborated. At the very least they could have codified four types of basic obligations which have been accepted in many European systems: duties of care or protection[246], duties of loyalty[247], duties to co-operate[248] and duties

10th ed., Paris 1999, no. 632 ('le juge ajoute au contrat une obligation à laquelle les parties n'avaient pas songé, et peut-être même qu'elles avaient implicitement écartée') ; JACQUES FLOUR & JEAN-LUC AUBERT, *Les obligations; 1. L'acte juridique*, no. 406 ('Dans les mots, les tribunaux feignent toujours de rechercher la volonté des parties. Dans la réalité, ils se fondent sur l'équité plus souvent qu'ils ne le disent: et ce, au mépris parfois de ce qui a été le plus probablement voulu.') ; G.H. TREITEL, *The Law of Contract*, 10th ed., London 1999, p. 190 ('In many cases of this kind, the same process can with equal plausibility be described (...) as the imposition of a legal duty').

242 GENEVIEVE VINEY, *Introduction à la responsabilité*, no. 186.

243 HR, 9 October 1992, *NJ* 1994, 287, 289 (Steendijkpolder) (an implied warranty by the seller of land to the buyer who is under a contractual obligation towards the seller (a municipality) to build on it, that the land is in all respects suitable as a building site), HR, 25 June 1993, *NJ* 1994, 291, note Brunner (implied warranty that a second-hand car's milometer indicates the correct mileage).

244 Compared to the PECL the UP place somewhat greater emphasis on the importance of 'implied' obligations. Art. 5.1 (Express and implied obligations), the first article of chapter 5 (Content), states: 'The contractual obligations of the parties may be express or implied.' Also the term 'implied *obligations*' is more appropriate than 'implied terms' because it relates less to the fiction that these terms are part of the contract (autonomy, et cetera).

245 J.M. BARENDRECHT, 'Contractuele gebondenheid en het beginsel van belangenmaximalisatie'.

246 *Schutzpflichten, obligations de sécurité, obblighi di protezione.* See MARTIJN W. HESSELINK, *De redelijkheid en billijkheid in het Europese privaatrecht*, p. 186 ff. with many examples from case law, and with further references.

247 *Leistungstreuepflichten, obligations de loyauté, obblighi di salvaguardia.* See MARTIJN W. HESSELINK, *De redelijkheid en billijkheid in het Europese privaatrecht*, p. 225 ff. with many examples from case law, and with further references.

248 *Mitwirkungspflichten, obligations de coopération, obblighi di cooperazione.* See MARTIJN W.

to inform[249]. Admittedly, the PECL did codify the duty to co-operate, but, as said, the examples in the Comment mainly cover traditional *mora creditoris* situations[250].

8. Change of circumstances. - The problem of changing circumstances provides a good illustration of the phenomenon that legal systems are not consistently more liberal or social. French contract law which, as we saw, contains many social rules and doctrines, refuses to assist a party who has found herself in serious trouble because of an unexpected change of circumstances. The law on this point was established in the 19th century (in a case which involved a contract concluded in 1567), and has remained unchanged since then: *pacta sunt servanda* and the court should not come to the rescue on account of the judges' sense of equity[251]. Today, all other European legal systems assist a party when the performance of the contract unexpectedly becomes excessively onerous, although for some systems this has taken a long time (the Netherlands) and in others this assistance is rather limited (England)[252]. In most jurisdictions the rules have been developed by the courts on a case to case basis, usually on the basis of the doctrine of good faith. Today, Italy, Greece and the Netherlands have codified rules[253]. Articles 6.2.1. UP and 6:111 PECL are the first to introduce the duty to negotiate, which is similar to the contractual provisions in many international commercial contracts (hardship clause)[254].

In the course of the 20th century, with regard to a change of circumstances, most European legal systems have moved from a very individualist rule to a more social one. The conflict is usually expressed, in less straightforward language, as the conflict between the principle of *pacta*

HESSELINK, *De redelijkheid en billijkheid in het Europese privaatrecht*, p. 238 ff. with many examples from case law, and with further references.

[249] *Aufklärungs-* and *Auskunftpflichten*, *Obligations d'information*, *obblighi d'informazione*. Duties to inform not only exist in the pre-contractual stage but also during performance. See MARTIJN W. HESSELINK, *De redelijkheid en billijkheid in het Europese privaatrecht*, pp. 262, with many examples from case law, and with further references.

[250] The obligation is stated at the beginning. The UP have placed the equivalent (art. 5.3 UP) in the chapter on 'Content'.

[251] *Civ.*, 6 March 1876, *D.* 1876, 1, 193, note Giboulot, *Les grands arrêts*, no. 94. It should be noted that the legislator intervened by way of specific legislation after both World Wars. See further MARTIJN W. HESSELINK, *De redelijkheid en billijkheid in het Europese privaatrecht*, p. 321 ff., with further references.

[252] Art. 6:111 goes further than English law. See Comment, p. 325, which would allow relief in Suez cases where the English courts refused to help (*Tsakiroglou & Co Ltd* v *Noblee Thorl GmbH* [1962] AC 93).

[253] Arts. 1467 *codice civile*, 388 Greek civil code, 6:258 *BW*. In the Dutch case one cannot really speak of codification. Rather, the *Hoge Raad* abandoned its extreme position (established in HR, 8 January 1926, *NJ* 1926, 203 (Sarong case), 19 March 1926, *NJ* 1926, 441, note Scholten, HR, 2 January 1931, *NJ* 1931, 274 (Mark = Mark)) when it had become certain that the new code would include this new rule (HR, 27 April 1984, *NJ* 1984, 679, note Van der Grinten (Sipke Helder/NVB)).

[254] See MARTIJN W. HESSELINK, *De redelijkheid en billijkheid in het Europese privaatrecht*, p. 348.

sunt servanda and the principle of good faith, or, as the Lando Commission puts it[255], the 'tension between two conflicting principles, *pacta sunt servanda* (agreements must be observed) and *rebus sic stantibus* (undertakings are based on the premise that circumstances remain as they are).' However, in the next sentence the language is more openly moralist (altruism): 'Article 6:111 stresses that normally *pacta sunt servanda* is the paramount principle; but that in certain extreme circumstances it would be considered inequitable for one party to insist on strict performance when that would be excessively onerous for the other.'

Some authors, relying on theories on relational contracts and extensive duties to co-operate[256], and on law & economics, suggest that art. 6:111 may be too restrictive[257]. Parties should have incentives to renegotiate much earlier, not only when performance becomes excessively onerous. In contracts which are characterised by great uncertainty concerning the future, on the one hand, and strong mutual dependence, on the other, parties should be under an obligation to renegotiate in order to deal with foreseen incidents. The UP actually seem to go further (and are clearer) than the PECL: the Comment says that an alteration amounting to 50% or more of the cost or the value of the performance is likely to amount to a "fundamental" alteration[258]. The PECL do not contain a similar rule, neither in the black-letter text nor in the Comments.

9. Choice of remedy. - Under the heading 'Freedom to choose remedies' the 'Survey Chapters 1-9' proclaims[259]: 'When there has been a non-performance, the aggrieved party should be given the greatest possible freedom to choose its remedy to fit for its needs, subject only to the requirements of good faith and fair dealing already mentioned'. This statement of principle is a very strong statement of individualism[260], although it is moderated to some extent by the reference to good faith. A more altruistic approach would require the innocent party to take the legitimate interests of the other party into account when choosing a remedy.

The phrase 'the requirements of good faith and fair dealing already mentioned' refers to an earlier passage where three examples are given of the limitation of remedies by 'good faith and fair dealing': art. 9:201 PECL (a right to withhold performance only in as far as it is reasonable), art. 9:505 (the right to damages limited to losses which the creditor could not reasonably have avoided), and art. 9:301 PECL. The last-mentioned article limits the availability of the remedy of termination to cases of 'fundamental non-

---

[255] PECL, Survey Chapters 1-9, p. xxxvii.

[256] See IAN MACNEIL, 'Relational Contract Theory as Sociology'.

[257] J.M. BARENDRECHT, 'Contractuele gebondenheid en het beginsel van belangenmaximalisatie'.

[258] Comment 2 (p. 147). It should be noted that the UP are intended exclusively for commercial contracts.

[259] P. xxxix.

[260] It also follows from the wording of art. 8:101 (1) (Remedies available): '*Whenever* a party does not perform an obligation under the contract (...), the aggrieved party may resort to *any* of the remedies set out in Chapter 9.' Compare also Section (2).

performance'. Fundamental non-performance is defined in art. 8:103[261]. Here the interest of the non-performing party is clearly taken into account. Much more so than in the Netherlands where the *Hoge Raad* maintains an extremely individualist position in this matter[262], although there has been some fierce and justified opposition in legal doctrine[263]. These are important limitations to the free choice of remedies. And the PECL contain some further examples that show that 'the greatest possible freedom to choose a remedy' may be limited in practice ('by good faith').

Nevertheless, one wonders whether the Lando Commission should not have gone further. It could have adopted a general rule to the effect that the election of remedies is subject to principles of proportionality and subsidiarity, the former meaning that a specific remedy should not be available if the benefit the creditor would derive there from would be extremely disproportionate to the burden it would impose on the debtor, and the latter meaning that if each of a number of remedies would result in bringing the creditor into the same position (in the specific circumstances of the case; not merely in the abstract!), then the creditor should opt for the remedy which (to his knowledge!) is less detrimental to the debtor[264]. Of course such a rule could be read into art. 1:201, but, as said above, this could be said of *any* rule. It would have been desirable if such a more specific rule could have been established in Chapter 8.

An additional argument is provided by the recent EU directive on consumer guarantees where the choice of remedy for the buyer is far from free[265]. On the contrary, the Directive provides for a hierarchy of remedies[266].

10. Balance. - On balance, also taking the other articles into account which cannot be discussed in detail here for reasons of limited space, I think that the

---

[261] Compare art. 7.3.1 UP. See RUTH SEFTON-GREEN, *La notion d'obligation fondamentale: comparaison franco-anglaise*, Paris 2000.

[262] See HR, 24 November 1995, *NJ* 1996, 160 (Tromp/Regency), HR, 22 October 1999, NJ 1999, 159, note Bloembergen, where the lower court had interestingly adopted a distinction very similar to the English distinction between conditions and warranties, and HR, 4 February 2000, *NJ* 2000, 562, note Vranken.

[263] See F.B. BAKELS, *Ontbinding van wederkerige overeenkomsten*, Deventer 1993, p. 225 ff.; TON HARTLIEF, *Ontbinding: over ongedaanmaking, bevrijding en rechterlijke bevoegdheden bij ontbinding wegens wanprestatie*, pp. 185, 204 ff. See further, with references, A.S. HARTKAMP, *Verbintenissenrecht II* (in: *Asser* series), no. 516 and *Verbintenissenrecht*, art. 265 (HARTLIEF). In my view the *Hoge Raad* should, more in general, subject the choice of the remedy to proportionality and subsidiarity tests as described *supra*. Such a test could be based on good faith (*redelijkheid en billijkheid*), although, in my view, such a formal foundation would not add a great deal.

[264] In the Netherlands some authors have recently proposed subjecting the exercise of the remedy of termination to these two principles. See M.M. STOLP, 'De bevoegdheid tot ontbinding ex art. 6:265 lid 1 BW in het licht van subsidiariteit en proportionaliteit', *NTBR* 2000, p. 352 ff, with further references.

[265] See art. 3 Directive 1999/44/EC on consumer guarantees.

[266] See for criticism JAN SMITS, 'Naar een nieuw Europees consumentenkooprecht; Over de Europese richtlijn verkoop van en garanties voor consumentengoederen in het Nederlandse recht', *NJB* 2000, p. 1825 f.

PECL are rather more 'social' (to the left) than most of the European codes, although because of their abstraction very much will ultimately depend on how they will be applied by the courts (if they are going to be enacted as a European Code of Contracts). This is not to say that they are more social than the contract laws of most European jurisdictions. Much of the 'social' contract law can be found in 20th century case law and statutory regulations.

The basic structure of the PECL seems to be rather classical, in the sense that the general rule is autonomy, which is (frequently and extensively) supplemented and corrected by good faith related doctrines. One wonders whether the Lando Commission could not have gone further so as to take the development of contract law in the 20th century fully into account and to base its general contract rules more explicitly on both autonomy and solidarity. It is clear that many of the conflicts emanating from contracts will be between one party relying on autonomy and the other on solidarity. In that conflict a balance has to be struck. Under the PECL the former party still has a rhetorical (and evidentiary?) advantage over the other. Or is this the price we will have to pay if we want to keep the conservatives on board the European private law movement?

VII. Culture

A. Law as Culture

1. Comparative Law & Culture. - There exist considerable differences in style between the various European legal systems[267]. These differences in style and in *mentalité* are regarded by some legal scholars as an important part of our culture[268]. And in their view these differences in legal culture should therefore be cherished. Other legal scholars, however, hold the opposite view. They regard national idiosyncrasies as provincialism[269]. In their view most

[267] See KONRAD ZWEIGERT & HEIN KÖTZ, *Introduction to Comparative Law*, p. 67 ff.; OLIVIER REMIEN, 'Über den Stil des europäischen Privatrechts', 60 *RabelsZ* (1996), pp. 1-39.

[268] See HUGH COLLINS, 'European Private Law and Cultural Identity of States', *ERPL* 1995, pp. 353-365, TONY WEIR, 'Die Sprachen des europäischen Rechts; Eine skeptische Betrachtung', *ZeuP* 1995, p. 368 ff, PIERRE LEGRAND, 'European legal systems are not converging', 45 *International and Comparative Law Quarterly* (1996), pp. 52-81, PIERRE LEGRAND, 'Against a European Civil Code', 60 *MLR* (1997), pp. 44-62, PIERRE LEGRAND, *Fragments on Law-as-Culture*, Deventer 1999, PIERRE LEGRAND, *Que sais-je? Le droit comparé*, Paris 1999, PIERRE LEGRAND, 'On the Unbearable Localness of the Law: Academic Fallacies and Unseasonable Observations', 10 *ERPL* 2002, pp. 61-76.

[269] See UGO MATTEI & ANNA DI ROBILANT, 'The Art and Science of Critical scholarship; Postmodernism and International style in the Legal Architecture of Europe', 10 *ERPL* 2002, pp. 29-59. The locus classicus is RUDOLPH VON JHERING, *Geist des römischen Rechts auf den verschiedenen Stufen seiner Entwicklung*, 8th ed. (1924), Part I, p. 15: 'legal science has degenerated into jurisprudence of states, limited them by political boundaries - a discouraging and unseemly posture for a science! But it is up to legal science itself to cast away these chains and to rediscover for all time that quality of universality which it long enjoyed: this it will do in the different form of comparative law. It will have a distinct method, a wider vision, a riper judgement, a less constrained manner of treating its material: the apparent loss will in reality

differences between the various legal systems are merely a nuisance which, moreover, obstructs the proper functioning of the common market. The Lando Commission has made a clear choice for a new common European legal culture rather than for the mere preservation of local legal cultures.

2. Cultural Ingredients of the PECL. - Obviously, the PECL are not culturally neutral; they have been inspired by the various European cultures. The Lando Commission does not try to hide this. On the contrary, it claims that its PECL are, among other things, a restatement of the contract laws from the various European legal cultures. However, it is excluded that the PECL should be inspired by each legal system to the same degree. It is evident that the Lando Commission had to make (implicit or explicit) cultural choices. See the Introduction where it is stated[270]: 'The Principles are designed primarily for use in the Member States of the European Union. They have regard to the economic and social conditions prevailing in the Member States. The Commission on European Contract Law has therefore drawn in some measure on the legal systems of every Member State. This does not, of course, imply that every legal system has had equal influence on every issue considered. In fact no single legal system has been made the starting point from which the Principles and the terminology which they employ are derived. Nor have the draftsmen of the Principles seen it as their task to make interpolations or compromises between the existing national laws, except as is necessary in order to weld the Principles into a workable system.' In this Section I will try to assess the cultural choices which the Lando Commission has made. Of course, it is impossible to determine precisely for each legal culture how much and in what way it is represented in the PECL. But, on the other hand, I think it is possible to say something in this respect.

3. Legal Formants. - Cultures in Europe differ in many different ways. Such cultural differences may also determine important differences in the law in a broad sense of 'law as legal culture' (law in society). Even if the rules are very similar there may be great differences in (for example) the way disputes are resolved. However, such differences, interesting as they are, are difficult to describe and even more difficult to measure. They easily slip into cliché and prejudice. The interest private law scholars in Europe have taken in legal culture is only rather recent[271]. Moreover, with regard to the PECL today we do not have anything more than black-letter rules, comments and illustrations; we cannot say anything concerning the way in which they will be applied, the context they are embedded in et cetera[272]. Therefore I will mainly (but not

---

prove a great gain, by raising law to a higher level of scientific activity.' (English translation taken from KONRAD ZWEIGERT & HEIN KÖTZ, *Introduction to Comparative Law*, p. 44).

[270] PECL, Introduction, p. xxv.

[271] See e.g. RODOLFO SACCO, 'Legal Formants: A Dynamic Approach To Comparative Law', 39 AJCL (1991), pp. 1-34, pp. 343-401, WILLIAM TWINING, *Law in Context; Enlarging a Discipline*, Oxford 1997.

[272] This is also one of the reasons why Legrand and others object to a European Code: we do not know what it means because rules only have meaning in context. See PIERRE LEGRAND, 'Against a European Civil Code'.

only) concentrate here on the cultural roots of legal rules and doctrines. I also will mainly limit myself to the difference between the common law and the civil law tradition which is generally held to be the most important cultural divide in Europe.

B. Common Law v Civil Law

1. Divergence.- The common law and civil law legal cultures are usually said to be fundamentally different in many respects[273]. For example, the way of legal reasoning: a common lawyer is said typically to draw a direct comparison between two cases whereas a civil lawyer would compare the cases indirectly, via an abstract rule. Moreover, a civil lawyer is said typically to think in terms of rights whereas a common lawyer would rather think in terms of remedies (causes of action): one only has a right if one has a remedy. Finally, the civil law is said to be a systematic whole (codes), whereas the common law is traditionally merely meant to resolve conflicts (precedents). More specifically with regard to contract law, the common law is said to be based on exchange (bargain theory) whereas the civil law is said to be based on consensus; therefore under common law the parties bargain at arm's length whereas under civil law they should bargain in good faith.

2. Convergence. - It is not surprising that those who are against the unification of private law in Europe (especially against a Code) tend to emphasise these differences[274], whereas those who are part of the European private law movement either claim that their opponents exaggerate[275], or that today the differences are diminishing[276] or even that they never really existed at all (the important civil law influence on English law)[277], or that they are simply not very relevant (political, socio-economic and institutional similarities are more important)[278].

---

[273] According to Legrand a common lawyer and a civil lawyer have fundamentally different views on what 'law' means. See on epistemology PIERRE LEGRAND, 'European legal systems are not converging'.

[274] Especially PIERRE LEGRAND, 'European legal systems are not converging' and PIERRE LEGRAND, 'Against a European Civil Code'. See also JAN SMITS, *Europees Privaatrecht in wording: naar een Ius Commune Europaeum als gemengd rechtsstelsel*, Antwerpen, Groningen 1999, pp. 85 ff.

[275] See H.G. BEALE, Paper presented at the 4th Ius Commune Conference, Corsendonk, December 1999 (unpublished), H.G. BEALE, Paper presented in Rome at the European Civil Code conference, June 2000 (unpublished), and EWAN MCKENDRICK, 'Traditional Concepts and Contemporary Values', 10 *ERPL* 2001, pp. 95 ff.

[276] See BASIL MARKESINIS (ed.), *The gradual convergence; Foreign Ideas, Foreign Influences, and English Law On the Eve of 21st Century*, Oxford 1994.

[277] See REINHARD ZIMMERMANN, 'Roman Law and European Legal Unity', in: A.S. Hartkamp et al. (eds.) *Towards a European Civil Code*, 2nd ed., Nijmegen and The Hague, London, Boston 1998, pp. 21 ff., and JAMES GORDLEY, 'Common law und civil law: eine überholte Unterscheidung', *ZeuP* 1993, p. 498 ff.

[278] See UGO MATTEI, *Comparative Law and Economics*, p. 69 ff. See also above, Chapter 2, Section IV, H, 4.

3. Bridging the Gap. - The Lando Commission explicitly addresses the gap between common law and civil law. As a matter of fact, according to the Commission, one of the benefits to be derived from the PECL is that they may provide a bridge across the Channel[279]: 'One of the most intractable problems of European legal integration is the reconciliation of the civil law and the common law families. It is of course true that there are significant differences even between one civil law system and another; it is also true that in many cases common problems will be solved in much the same way by the various legal systems, to whichever legal family they may belong. But there remain major differences between civil law and common law systems in relation to legal structure and reasoning, terminology, fundamental concepts and classifications and legal policies. (...) Differences of these kinds are inimical to the efficient functioning of the single Market. One of the major benefits offered by the Principles is to provide a bridge between the civil law and the common law by providing rules designed to reconcile their differing legal philosophies.' Thus, rather than consistently adopting either the common law or the civil law approach, which would obviously have made the Principles unacceptable to the other side, the Lando Commission opted for the more difficult approach of trying to reconcile both cultures (and thus to create a new, common European legal culture!). However, obviously even when building a bridge many choices have to be made. What choices did the Lando Commission make?

4. Common Law Influence. - In a number of issues the Commission has clearly opted for the common law tradition. Generally, it should be reiterated that the PECL have been strongly influenced by the UP and that the UP, especially the part on non-performance and remedies, are very much based on - both directly and indirectly, via CISG - art. 2 UCC and the Restatement (2nd) of Contracts in the United States, a common law system[280]. Moreover, it should also be reiterated that the PECL have 'contract law' as their object, which is the abstraction most familiar to common law lawyers (see e.g. most English textbooks and university courses and the American Restatements of Contracts), whereas in civil law systems the codes, textbooks and commentaries usually concentrate on 'the law of obligations'[281]. Finally, the reader should be reminded that the idea of a restatement, which is one of the main objects of the PECL, and its format and style have been borrowed from the American (common law) tradition of Restatements.

As for specific rules and doctrines, probably the clearest common law influence is to be found in the PECL's elaborate set of rules on remedies for

---

[279] Pp. xxii-xxiii.

[280] See E. ALLAN FARNSWORTH, 'The American Provenance of the UNIDROIT Principles'; JAMES GORDLEY, 'An American Perspective on UNIDROIT Principles'; MICHAEL JOACHIM BONELL, *An International Restatement of Contract Law; The UNIDROIT Principles of International Commercial Contracts*, pp. 18, 65 and *passim*.

[281] See *supra*.

non-performance[282]. The emphasis on remedies clearly reflects the common law tradition. In his Preface Lando says[283]: 'Believing that, within the law of contracts, the rules on due performance and the remedies for non-performance were of paramount importance, the first Commission chose these subjects for the first phase of its work.' Whereas this observation may sound obvious to most common law lawyers, many civil law scholars would typically regard formation, defects of consent (validity) and contents and effects as more important, and formation as the natural starting point[284].

Another very clear example of the common law influence is the use in the PECL of the concepts of 'implied and express terms'[285]. Although civil law courts probably imply more terms into contracts than the English courts do, they do this under different headings; the concept of 'implied terms' is clearly of English origin.

Since the first half of the 19th century English law has made a distinction between the terms of a contract according to their importance[286]. A breach of condition always allows the innocent party to terminate the contract, whereas in the case of a breach of warranty, the innocent party is never allowed to rescind. A term can be a condition because the parties or statute or the courts say so[287]. When this sharp distinction proved unsatisfactory the courts developed a third category of 'intermediate' or 'innominate terms'. The PECL do not make such a distinction between types of contractual terms. However, the rules on non-performance and remedies, although admittedly they are organised in a different way, seem to reflect much of the English case law (and debates) with regard to remedies and, on the whole, it seems to be more similar to the common law than to the civil law tradition. One example is Lord Diplock's definition of an innominate term[288]: 'There are many contractual undertakings of a more complex character which cannot be categorised as being "conditions" or "warranties", (...). Of such undertakings, all that can be predicated is that some breaches will, and others will not, give rise to an event which will deprive the party not in default of substantially the whole benefit which it was intended that he should obtain from the contract.' This definition was adopted as one of the three situations in which non-performance is

---

[282] See H.G. BEALE, *Paper presented in Rome at the European Civil Code conference*, June 2000: an elaborate set of rules on 'defects of consent' is more typical of civil (especially French) law, elaborate rules on remedies are more typical of common (especially English) law.

[283] P. xiv.

[284] See e.g. J.M. BARENDRECHT, 'Contractuele gebondenheid en het beginsel van belangenmaximalisatie', p. 3: rules on interpretation, implied terms and good faith are probably the most important rules of contract law.

[285] Art. 6:102 PECL.

[286] See G.H. TREITEL, *The Law of Contract*, p. 731 ff.; H.G. BEALE & W.D. BISHOP & M.P. FURMSTON, *Contract Cases and Materials*, London, Dublin, 4th ed. Edinburgh 2001, p. 560 ff.; EWAN MCKENDRICK, *Contract Law*, 4th ed., London 2000, p. 207.

[287] See G.H. TREITEL, *The Law of Contract*, p. 732; H.G. BEALE & W.D. BISHOP & M.P. FURMSTON, *Contract Cases and Materials*, p. 560; EWAN MCKENDRICK, *Contract Law*, p. 208 ff.

[288] *Hong Kong Fir Shipping Co Ltd* v *Kawasaki Kisen Kaisha Ltd* [1962] 2 QB 26.

fundamental under the PECL[289] (and therefore gives the innocent party the right to terminate[290]): 'A non-performance of an obligation is fundamental to the contract if: (...) the non-performance substantially deprives the aggrieved party of what it was entitled to expect under the contract, unless the other party did not foresee and could not reasonably have foreseen that result'[291].

On the other hand, some typical common law doctrines have not been adopted by the PECL. The most prominent is probably the doctrine of consideration[292]. In art. 2:101 (1) the PECL explicitly state: 'a contract is concluded if: (a) the parties intend to be legally bound, and (b) they reach a sufficient agreement *without any further requirement*'[293]. The doctrine of consideration is frequently regarded as the basis of English contract law. However, not only is this view incorrect from a historical perspective (the bargain principle is actually quite recent), but the doctrine has also become rather problematic in many respects and, as a consequence, controversial as well. In practical terms the doctrine has lost most of its relevance because a deed is easily made and otherwise (nominal) consideration is easily found[294].

The PECL contain no strong privity rule. For a long time the doctrine of privity of contract (which is related to the doctrine of consideration) provided a major difference between common law and civil law[295]: under English law a contract could not confer rights or obligations on a third party. However, recent law reform has relaxed the English privity rule considerably[296]. Today, under English law it is possible for two parties to stipulate an enforceable promise towards a third party in their contract. Therefore art. 6:110 (Stipulation in Favour of a Third Party[297]) can now be said to reflect also the common law. Apart from the 'Stipulation in Favour of a Third Party' (and Agency) there is little attention in the PECL to the problem of 'contract and third parties'.

2. Civil Law Influence. - There are many typical examples of a civil law influence in the PECL. The most striking example is probably the omnipresence of the concept of good faith. The Lando Commission has clearly embraced the concept[298]: it is used on a very large scale, far more than

[289] Art. 8:103 (b) PECL. See also art. 25 CISG and art. 7.3.1 (2) (a) UP.
[290] Art. 9:301 (1) PECL.
[291] See on fundamental non-performance in French and English law RUTH SEFTON-GREEN, *La notion d'obligation fondamentale: comparaison franco-anglaise.*
[292] It should be noted, however, that the similar civil law doctrine of *causa* was rejected by the Lando Commission in the same manner. See *infra*.
[293] Emphasis added. See also Comment (D): 'Nor is it necessary that a promisee undertakes to furnish or furnishes something of value in exchange for the promise (consideration).'
[294] See EWAN MCKENDRICK, 'Traditional Concepts and Contemporary Values', 10 *ERPL* 2001, pp. 95 ff.
[295] See EDGAR DU PERRON, 'Contract and Third Parties', in: A.S. Hartkamp et al. (eds.), *Towards a European Civil Code.*, 2nd ed., Nijmegen and The Hague, London, Boston 1998, pp. 211 ff.
[296] See the Contracts (Rights of Third Parties) Act 1999.
[297] Although the 'title' of the article has a typical civil law, especially French, sound.
[298] See for criticism, MARTIJN W. HESSELINK, *De redelijkheid en billijkheid in het Europese privaatrecht, passim*, especially p. 437 ff. See further *supra*, Section VI, B, and *infra*, Chapter 7.

in any civil code in Europe. Although clearly of civil (Roman) law origin, today, as a result of the EU Directive on Unfair Terms, the concept is no longer completely alien to English law[299].

As to specific rules, like all civil law systems[300] but unlike English law[301], the PECL accept liability for negotiations contrary to good faith (art. 2:301). Moreover, under the PECL the parties may be under a pre-contractual duty to inform (art. 4:103 (1) (a) (ii) and art. 4:107)[302]. A similar duty is accepted in most European legal systems, but has traditionally been rejected by English, Scots and Irish law[303]. As said, the common law has traditionally allowed parties to bargain 'at arm's length'. Art. 2:202 (3) PECL accepts the irrevocability of an offer when the offer explicitly says so, when it contains a time-limit for acceptance and in case of detrimental reliance by the offeree. This is in line with most civil law systems where an offer can be made irrevocable in many situations. In German and Belgian law irrevocability is even the main rule[304]. In contrast, under English law a party cannot, in principle, make its offer irrevocable, for such an undertaking would lack consideration[305]. Under the PECL penalty clauses are enforceable (art. 9:509 PECL), but courts may reduce the penalty when it is grossly excessive[306]. This is completely in line with the civil law tradition[307], but in common law systems penalty clauses are in principle not enforceable[308]. The 'right to withhold performance' is regarded by the PECL as a 'remedy for non-performance' (9:201), whereas in common law systems it is not usually considered to be a remedy[309].

In civil law systems the ordinary remedy in case of non-performance of a contract has traditionally been the claim for specific performance of the

---

299 See GUNTHER TEUBNER, 'Legal Irritants: Good Faith in British Law or How Unifying Law Ends Up in New Divergences', *MLR* 1998, p. 11 ff. and MARTIJN W. HESSELINK, *De redelijkheid en billijkheid in het Europese privaatrecht*, p. 418, with further references.

300 See MARTIJN W. HESSELINK, 'Precontractual Good Faith', and MARTIJN W. HESSELINK, *De redelijkheid en billijkheid in het Europese privaatrecht*, p. 67 ff., with further references.

301 The duty to conduct negotiations in good faith was explicitly rejected by the House of Lords in *Walford* v *Miles* [1992] 2 AC 128. See for Scotland HECTOR L. MACQUEEN, 'Good Faith in the Scots Law of Contract: An Undisclosed Principle?', in: *Good Faith in Contract and Property*, Oxford 1999, p. 5 ff. and HECTOR L. MACQUEEN & J. THOMSON, *Contract Law in Scotland*, p. 83 ff.

302 This duty is related to the general duty of good faith. See art. 4:107, Comment E.

303 See ALBERTO M. MUSY, *Il dovere di informazione; Saggio di diritto comparato*, Trento 1999, p. 9 ff.

304 See § 145 *BGB*; JACQUES HERBOTS, *Contract Law in Belgium*, Deventer, Boston, Bruxelles 1995, no. 127.

305 G.H. TREITEL, *The Law of Contract*, p. 39. However, in the (common law) system of US law firm offers are sometimes irrevocable (for up to three months) under § 2-205 UCC

306 Section (2).

307 See e.g. the recent Dutch Civil Code, arts. 6:91 ff. *BW*.

308 See further *infra*.

309 Of course, also in civil law systems the right to withhold performance is not an action but an exception. Compare on the history, foundation et cetera MARTIJN W. HESSELINK, *De redelijkheid en billijkheid in het Europese privaatrecht*, p. 283 ff.

obligation. The right to specific performance is usually regarded as the essence of any obligation, whether of contractual or other origin[310]. In common law systems, on the contrary, the order for specific performance has traditionally been regarded as an exceptional remedy, which is only available, at the discretion of the court, when damages are not an adequate remedy[311]. In practice, this equitable remedy has mainly been granted in conflicts concerning rights in land. The Lando Commission decided not to adopt the traditional common law principle that damages are the normal remedy and that an order for specific performance will only be given in exceptional cases: 'The Principles take the approach that, unless non-performance is excused, compelling the non-performing party to perform should not be an exceptional remedy'[312]. However, it should be added that the availability of performance *in natura* is excluded by the PECL in a number of cases (see arts. 9:101 and 9:102 PECL). The result is usually regarded, quite rightly, as a satisfactory pragmatic compromise between both traditions[313].

The distinctions in Chapter 3 (Authority of agents) between direct and indirect representation are familiar to many European systems, whereas the traditional common law distinction between disclosed and undisclosed principals was not endorsed by the Lando Commission[314]. Generally speaking, Chapter 4 (Validity) looks very civilian because of its 'defects of consent' (*vices de consentement*, *Willensmangel*) approach[315]. Chapter 5 (Interpretation) also seems closer to civil law. Art. 5:101 (1) states as a first general rule of interpretation that a contract is to be interpreted according to the common intention of the parties[316]. This is in line with the civil law tradition[317], but in contrast with the common law, where emphasis traditionally lies more on the objective meaning of the contract[318]. However, there is also some gradual convergence to be noticed here. On the one hand, most civil law systems seem to have moved towards a somewhat more

[310] See MURIEL VELDMAN, 'Grenzen aan het recht op nakoming', with further references.

[311] See MURIEL VELDMAN, 'Grenzen aan het recht op nakoming', with further references.

[312] P. xxxix. See also Art. 9:102, Comment D: 'Under these Principles the aggrieved party has a substantive right to demand and to enforce a non-monetary obligation. Granting an order for performance thus is not in the discretion of the court; the court is bound to grant the remedy, unless the exceptions of paragraph (2) and (3) apply. National courts should grant performance even in cases where they are not accustomed to do so under their national law.'

[313] In practical terms the UP seem more effective because they allow the court to impose a judicial penalty (art. 7.2.4), similar to *astreinte* and *dwangsom* (which may cumulate with damages, like the *dwangsom*).

[314] See DANNY BUSCH, 'Indirect Representation and the Lando Principles'; A.S. HARTKAMP, 'Indirect Representation According to the Principles of European Contract Law, the Unidroit Agency Convention and the Dutch Civil Code', pp. 45 ff.

[315] See also Art. 4:101, Comment (p. 227).

[316] See art. 5:101 (1).

[317] Compare e.g. art. 1156 French and Belgian *Cc*, and art. 1362 Italian *c.c.*

[318] See Cozens-Hardy MR's formulation of the 'golden rule' in *Lovell & Christmas Ltd* v *Wall* (1911) 104 LT 85: 'it is the duty of the court, which is presumed to understand the English language, to construe the document according to the ordinary grammatical meaning of the words used therein, and without reference to anything which has previously passed between the parties'.

objective method of interpretation (*normative Auslegung* in Germany, *il significato normale* in Italy, and the *Haviltex criterium* in the Netherlands)[319], whereas, on the other hand, the House of Lords (in a controversial decision) has recently abandoned the 'golden rule' of literal interpretation in favour of an approach which concentrates on the interpretation that a reasonable person with full knowledge of the factual background of the contract would give[320]. This latter test in nearly identical to the subsidiary test in art. 5:101 (3)[321].

---

[319] See further MARTIJN W. HESSELINK, *De redelijkheid en billijkheid in het Europese privaatrecht*, pp. 143-160.

[320] *Investors Compensation Scheme Ltd* v *West Bromwich Building Society (No.1)* [1998] 1 W.L.R. 896; [1998] 1 All E.R. 98. See Lord Hoffmann (Lord Goff concurring): 'I do not think that the fundamental change which has overtaken this branch of the law, particularly as a result of the speeches of Lord Wilberforce in Prenn v. Simmonds [1971] 1 W.L.R. 1381, 1384-1386 and Reardon Smith Line Ltd. v. Yngvar Hansen-Tangen [1976] 1 W.L.R. 989, is always sufficiently appreciated. The result has been, subject to one important exception, to assimilate the way in which such documents are interpreted by judges to the common sense principles by which any serious utterance would be interpreted in ordinary life. Almost all the old intellectual baggage of "legal" interpretation has been discarded. The principles may be summarised as follows: (1) Interpretation is the ascertainment of the meaning which the document would convey to a reasonable person having all the background knowledge which would reasonably have been available to the parties in the situation in which they were at the time of the contract. (2) The background was famously referred to by Lord Wilberforce as the "matrix of fact," but this phrase is, if anything, an understated description of what the background may include. Subject to the requirement that it should have been reasonably available to the parties and to the exception to be mentioned next, it includes absolutely anything which would have affected the way in which the language of the document would have been understood by a reasonable man. (3) The law excludes from the admissible background the previous negotiations of the parties and their declarations of subjective intent. They are admissible only in an action for rectification. The law makes this distinction for reasons of practical policy and, in this respect only, legal interpretation differs from the way we would interpret utterances in ordinary life. The boundaries of this exception are in some respects unclear. But this is not the occasion on which to explore them. (4) The meaning which a document (or any other utterance) would convey to a reasonable man is not the same thing as the meaning of its words. The meaning of words is a matter of dictionaries and grammars; the meaning of the document is what the parties using those words against the relevant background would reasonably have been understood to mean. The background may not merely enable the reasonable man to choose between the possible meanings of words which are ambiguous but even (as occasionally happens in ordinary life) to conclude that the parties must, for whatever reason, have used the wrong words or syntax (see Mannai Investments Co. Ltd. v. Eagle Star Life Assurance Co. Ltd. [1997] 2 W.L.R. 945). (5) The "rule" that words should be given their "natural and ordinary meaning" reflects the common sense proposition that we do not easily accept that people have made linguistic mistakes, particularly in formal documents. On the other hand, if one would nevertheless conclude from the background that something must have gone wrong with the language, the law does not require judges to attribute to the parties an intention which they plainly could not have had. Lord Diplock made this point more vigorously when he said in The Antaios Compania Neviera S.A. v. Salen Rederierna A.B. 1985 1 A.C. 191, 201: "if detailed semantic and syntactical analysis of words in a commercial contract is going to lead to a conclusion that flouts business commonsense, it must be made to yield to business commonsense."' In *Prenn* v *Simmons* Lord Wilberforce had said: '[English law is not] left behind in some island of literal interpretation (...) the time has long passed when agreements were isolated from the matrix of facts in which they were set and interpreted purely on internal linguistic considerations'.

[321] Art. 5:101 (3): 'If an intention cannot be established according to (1) and (2), the contract is to be interpreted according to the meaning that reasonable persons of the same kind as the parties

However, there are also many typical examples from the civil law tradition which have not been followed by the Lando Commission. To mention a few, the PECL are not a (draft) civil code, they are not based on the concepts of a general law of obligations or on *Rechtsgeschäft*[322], they do not require a valid *causa* for the validity of the contract[323], they do not contain the German concepts of *positive Vertragsverletzung* and *Vertrag mit Schutzwirkung für Dritte*[324], and they do not contain specific rules on the distinction between *obligations de moyens* and *obligations de résultat* which is known in many civil law systems[325].

3. Balance. - Although there are important examples of the presence and absence of some very characteristic aspects of both major legal traditions and although the Lando Commission has found some very interesting compromises and new solutions, it is submitted that, on the whole, the PECL seem to be somewhat closer to the civil law tradition than to common law. In terms of numbers this seems to be only fair: in Europe there are far more civil law than common law systems (13-2 plus one mixed system) and many more European citizens belong to the civil law tradition than to the common law. Frankly, the PECL probably adopted many more common law inspired rules and cultural compromises than simple numerical considerations would justify.

However, for cultural preservationists this may not be enough. The point raised by those who argue against a European civil code is that the cultural dominance of the numerically, economically and politically stronger risks annihilating a certain legal tradition in Europe, a legal tradition which incidentally on a world scale is far from marginal (e.g. the United States, Canada, Australia, Hong Kong). Is this too high a price to pay for European unity? The question seems only a variant of the more general question of British participation in Europe.

According to Legrand the adoption of a European Civil Code would never lead to real unity, because such a code would be interpreted differently in countries with different legal cultures[326]. This may be true in the beginning. It is possible that if the PECL were to be enacted as a European Code of Contract Law, in case of 'disappointing contracts'[327] civil law courts would in the beginning resolve conflicts rather more frequently on the basis of doctrines which are to be found in the chapter on Validity, whereas English,

---

would give in the same circumstances.'

[322] See *supra*, Section V, A.

[323] Art. 2:101 (1) PECL.

[324] See MARTIJN W. HESSELINK, *De redelijkheid en billijkheid in het Europese privaatrecht*, pp. 189 ff., and 275 ff. respectively, both with further references.

[325] This distinction, which was first proposed by Demogue, has been adopted in France, Belgium, Italy, and the Netherlands. See also art. 5.4 UP (Duty to achieve a specific result / Duty of best efforts). However, see the Comment on art. 6:102 (Implied Terms), which (under D) endorses the distinction (pp. 303-304).

[326] PIERRE LEGRAND, 'Against a European Civil Code'.

[327] See J.H. NIEUWENHUIS, 'Vernietigen, ontbinden of aanpassen; Wat is het lot van teleurstellende overeenkomsten?', *WPNR* (1995), nos. 6164 (pp. 23-26) en 6165 (pp. 37-41).

Irish and Scots plaintiffs (and courts) would be more likely to rely on doctrines which are to be found in the chapters on Non-Performance and Remedies. Courts from different traditions may even reach different results in substance[328]. However, as soon as a common European legal culture will have started to emerge (European academic debate, education, common textbooks et cetera), and especially if there will be one European supreme court to preside over uniform application[329], this diversity will probably soon diminish.

C. *Other Cultural Choices*

Some rules in the PECL have been clearly inspired by one specific legal system. The concept of 'excessive onerosity' in art. 6:111, for example, has clearly been borrowed from Italian law (*eccessiva onerosità*)[330]. Art. 2:107 (Promises Binding without Acceptance) seems to be based on the Nordic *löftesprincipen*[331], whereas art. 2:210 (Professional's Written Conformation) seems to have been taken from the German Commercial Code[332]. The concept of excused non-performance was clearly inspired by the French tradition (= *force majeure*). Art. 4:103 (Fundamental mistake as to facts or law) is very similar to the Dutch art. 6:228 *BW*[333], but actually both articles are based, like some other rules on validity[334], on a 1973 UNIDROIT draft model law[335].

[328] Although the PECL urge the courts to break with their national traditions. See e.g. art. 9:102, Comment D: 'Under these Principles the aggrieved party has a substantive right to demand and to enforce a non-monetary obligation. Granting an order for performance thus is not in the discretion of the court; the court is bound to grant the remedy, unless the exceptions of paragraph (2) and (3) apply. National courts should grant performance even in cases where they are not accustomed to do so under their national law.'

[329] Compare DAVID HOWARTH, 'The General Conditions of Unlawfulness', in: A.S. Hartkamp et al. (eds.) *Towards a European Civil Code*, 2nd ed., Nijmegen and The Hague, London, Boston 1998, pp. 397 ff.

[330] Art. 1467 *c.c.* The concept has had great international success. It was also introduced in the Greek code (art. 388; see MICHAEL P. STATHOPOULOS, *Contract law in Hellas*, no. 293) and in many Latin American codes (see ANNEMIEKE VAN PLATERINGEN, *Imprévision in Latijns-Amerika; Een rechtsvergelijkend onderzoek naar de toepassingseisen van wettelijke imprévision-regelingen in Latijns-Amerika*, Amsterdam 2001).

[331] See, for Denmark, RUTH NIELSEN, *Contract Law in Denmark*, 238, and, for Sweden, CHRISTINA HULTMARK, 'Obligations, Contracts and Sales', p. 275. See also RODOLFO SACCO, 'Formation of Contracts', in: A.S. Hartkamp et al. (eds.) *Towards a European Civil Code*, 2nd ed., Nijmegen and The Hague, London, Boston 1998, pp. 191 ff.

[332] See CLAUS-WILHELM CANARIS, *Handelsrecht*, 22nd ed., München 1995, p. 339 ff.

[333] On the influence of Dutch law on the PECL see EWOUD H. HONDIUS, 'The Genesis of the Principles of European Contract Law and of Modern Dutch Private Law', in: DANNY BUSCH & EWOUD H. HONDIUS & HUGO J. VAN KOOTEN & HARRIET N. SCHELHAAS (GENERAL EDITOR) & WENDY M. SCHRAMA (eds.), *The Principles of European Contract Law and Dutch Law: A Commentary*, Nijmegen and The Hague, London, New York 2002, pp. 13-27.

[334] See e.g. 4:105 (Adaptation of Contract), which is based on art. 15, which has also inspired 3.13 *UP*, and art. 6:230 para 1 Dutch *BW*, and which was itself inspired by art. 1432 Italian *cc*. See further MARTIJN W. HESSELINK, *De redelijkheid en billijkheid in het Europese privaatrecht*, p. 106 ff.

[335] *Projet de loi pour l'unification de certaines règles en matière de validité des contrats de vente*

Moreover, as said, many rules are similar (sometimes identical) to the UP and, to a lesser extent, to the CISG.

Some other rules clearly imply a choice against a specific legal system, in the sense that if that system were to be replaced by a European code based on the PECL this would imply a radical change in that specific jurisdiction. For example, the PECL have adopted a unitary concept of non-performance. It includes both defective performance, late performance and the total failure to do anything at all[336]. Thus the Lando Commission has rejected the German concept of *positive Vertragsverletzung*[337]. The unitary concept of non-performance also includes both non-excused and excused non-performance, thus deviating from the English concept of 'breach' which does not include excused non-performance[338]. Moreover, as said, the English distinction between breaches of condition, warranty and intermediate terms was not adopted as such by the PECL. Finally, the PECL do not contain any special rules on 'hidden defects' in sales[339]. Another example is provided by art. 4:104: 'inaccuracy in communication' is to be treated as a mistake, which is contrary to the Dutch tradition where *oneigenlijke dwaling* is regarded as a problem of formation and not of defect of consent (validity)[340]. Moreover, as said, the PECL do not allow for the *Inhaltskontrolle* of all contract clauses, as is the case in Scandinavian countries (art. 36 Contract Act).

Finally, the Lando Commission has made no cultural choice (as yet) with regard to illegality and immorality See art. 4:101 (Matters not Covered) and the Comment[341]: 'Because of the great variety among the legal systems of Member States as to which contracts are regarded as unenforceable on these grounds, and the very different consequences which follow from this categorisation, further investigation is needed to determine whether it is

---

internationale d'objets mobiliers corporels (UNIDROIT).

336 The definition of non-performance is not provided, as in the UP, in the chapter on 'Non-Performance and Remedies in General', but in the first chapter, on General Provisions. See art. 1:301 (Meaning of Terms): 'in these Principles, except where the context otherwise requires: (...) (4) "non-performance" denotes any failure to perform an obligation under the contract, whether or not excused, and includes delayed performance, defective performance and failure to co-operate in order to give full effect to the contract' See P. xxxvii.

337 Recently, in Germany, a law reform was enacted which has brought German law very much into line with (the CISG and) the PECL. See *supra*.

338 Under English law liability is strict; non-performance is only 'excused' in the very limited cases of frustration.

339 These rules stem from Roman law and are to be found in sales law in most European codes. However, the Dutch 1992 *BW* abolished them. See, however, the remedy of price reduction (arts. 9:401 ff. PECL) which is very similar to the *actio quanti minoris* and will obtain, under the PECL, general application in the whole of contract law (i.e. not just in sales). See also the recent Directive 1999/44/EC on consumer guarantees, art. 3 (2).

340 In the Netherlands there is no contract, unless the other party was justified in relying (see A.S. HARTKAMP, *Verbintenissenrecht II* (in: *Asser* series), no. 97 ff.); under the PECL the contract is avoidable. The latter solution is preferable, because it is more nuanced.

341 Art. 4:101 PECL, Comment (p. 227).

feasible to draft European Principles on these subjects .' The Commission is currently working on this[342].

VIII. Economics

The Lando Commission has also made economic choices. Different rules of contract law may have different economic effects. Private law is an important part of the institutional framework in which our economy operates. And choices made by lawmakers may have important economic consequences. This is why, since the last few decades, economists, especially in the Unites States, have taken great interest in the economic analysis of the law[343]. After a brief introduction to law & economics (A) I will discuss mandatory rules (B), default rules (C) and some examples of efficient solutions in the PECL (D).

A. Law & Economics

1. Economic analysis of contract law. - The economic analysis of contract law is based on the assumption that contracts are an important economic institution, because they allow the exchange of goods and services, which, in turn, allows an efficient allocation of these goods and services. Contract law is an equally important institution. The main purpose of contract law, according to legal economists, is to facilitate efficient exchange and to repair market failures.

2. *Efficiency.* - Suppose A owns a bicycle that he values at € 50 and B values the same bicycle at € 100. If they decide to exchange the bike against a specific price between € 50 and € 100, say € 75, not only are both parties better off, but society as a whole also benefits (wealth maximisation), assuming that no third parties are harmed (no externalities). Legal economists call a transaction efficient when it makes at least one person better off and nobody worse off (Pareto efficiency) or, in a more sophisticated version, if the winners could fully compensate the losers and still be better off (Kaldor-Hicks efficiency, cost-benefit analysis)[344]. The (utilitarian) assumption on which the economic theory of contract law is based is that efficiency is good, and that therefore the main function of contract law should be to facilitate efficient exchange by making efficient contracts enforceable and by encouraging parties (incentives) to conclude efficient transactions[345].

---

[342] See Lando, Preface, p. xiv, and *supra*.

[343] Law & Economics has been less successful in Europe, probably because legal scholarship in Europe is still largely dogmatic (it has not had the benefit of the Legal Realist revolution; it largely aims to derive right answers to legal questions from a presumably coherent system) and because the Law & Economics movement is associated with right-wing economic policy. See on law & economics in Europe UGO MATTEI, *Comparative Law and Economics*, p. 69 ff.

[344] A situation is fully efficient (optimal) if no change is possible which would make someone better off without making someone else worse off (in their own estimations) (Pareto optimum), or if aggregate benefits outweigh aggregate costs (Kaldor-Hicks optimum).

[345] See ROBERT COOTER & THOMAS ULEN, *Law & Economics*, 3rd ed., Reading etc. 2000, p 177 ff.; RICHARD A. POSNER, *Economic Analysis of Law*, 5th ed., New York 1998, p. 101 ff.;

3. *Market failures*. - Clearly, legal economists have great confidence in the operation of the market, and in freedom of contract, which is essential to a well-functioning market. However, they also recognise that freedom of contract sometimes exists only in a nominal sense, e.g. because a party does not posses enough information to evaluate properly whether a certain transaction will make her better off, or because a party is under pressure to conclude a contract which she knows will not make her better off. Scholars in law & economics regard such problems, from an economic perspective, as market failures. Therefore, although the basic assumption in the economic theory of contract law is that it should make people's promises enforceable, thus helping them to make their commitments credible, in the case of market failures enforceability may have to be limited. Thus, in the economic theory of contract law, another function of contract law is to correct market failures[346].

4. Criticism. - According to its proponents, law & economics can provide a 'neutral' and 'scientific' basis to the law[347]. However, the result of economic analysis very much depends on what economic theory one starts with[348]. Clearly, the prevalent economic theory of contract law (and indeed the prevalent economic theory of law in general) is based on a series of assumptions that, plausible as they may be to many or even most of us, are neither inevitable nor irrefutable. Different choices are possible. Indeed, the economic analysis of law has been contested by several legal theorists and other legal scholars, sometimes very strongly[349]. They reject the economic theory of law because it is based on an economic view (liberal-capitalist[350]) which they do not share, because it depends on unrealistic abstractions (man as a rational wealth maximiser) and because it disregards (or treats as 'irrational') important values (e.g. altruistic and distributional values). Others take a more moderate view. They regard the economic analysis of the law as a useful tool which provides an insight into the way in which rules of contract

---

ANTHONY KRONMAN & RICHARD A. POSNER, *The Economics of Contract Law*, Boston and Toronto 1979, p. 1 ff.; H.G. BEALE & W.D. BISHOP & M.P. FURMSTON, *Contract Cases and Materials*, London, 4th ed., Dublin and Edinburgh 2001, p. 77 ff.; UGO MATTEI, *Comparative Law and Economics*, p. 538 ff.

[346] See ROBERT COOTER & THOMAS ULEN, *Law & Economics*, p 204 ff.

[347] ROBERT COOTER & THOMAS ULEN, *Law & Economics*, p. 3, and RICHARD A. POSNER, 'Foreword', in: MICHAEL FAURE & ROGER VAN DEN BERGH (eds.), *Essays in Law and Economics*, Antwerpen and Apeldoorn 1989, p. 5. Compare UGO MATTEI, *Comparative Law and Economics*, p. 21

[348] Compare JOHN GROENEWEGEN, 'Blind volgen economische school kan ongezond zijn', *NRC Handelsblad*, 20 July 2000.

[349] See e.g. RONALD DWORKIN, 'Is Wealth A Value?' (1980) 9 *Journal of Legal Studies* 191; ARTHUR LEFF, 'Economic Analysis of Law: Some Realism About Nominalism' (1974) 60 *Virginia L. Rev.* 451; DUNCAN KENNEDY & MICHELMAN, 'Are Property and Contract Efficient?' (1980) 8 *Hofstra L.Rev.* 711; M.D.A. FREEMAN, *Lloyd's Introduction to Jurisprudence*, 6th ed., London 1994, p. 374 ff., all with further references.

[350] On the relationship between the law & economics movement and the New Institutionalists, see RICHARD A. POSNER, *Overcoming Law*, Cambridge (Massachusetts) and London 1995, pp. 426 ff.

law may affect the behaviour of the contracting parties, although they are aware that it begs a number of important questions[351].

B. Mandatory Rules

1. Is the Unification of General Contract Law Efficient? - The main argument that is usually proposed in favour of unification of private law in Europe is an economic argument. The diversity between systems of private law, and especially of contract law, is said to be an obstacle to the proper functioning of the Common Market[352]. The Lando Commission has explicitly endorsed this argument. It was one of the main reasons for drafting the PECL[353].

However, there is also an economic argument against a European Civil Code, a European Code of Contracts and other types of unity imposed by the state. This argument of comparative law & economics suggests that competition enhances economic activity and innovation, and therefore economic growth. In that view rather than imposing (code) or suggesting (encouraging restatement) unity the European authorities should encourage competition between law firms who draft different kinds of model contracts (most of the PECL are default rules), and between national legislatures and judiciaries which adopt codes and statutes[354].

2. Unification of Mandatory Rules. - However, there are some rules that parties cannot contract around[355]. These mandatory rules are not subject to the same competition. This leads to the suggestion that it is not the general rules of non-mandatory contract law that should be harmonised or unified but rather regulation, i.e. the mandatory rules of general contract law and especially those of special contract law. Those seem to be the true impediments to the Common Market, not the non-mandatory rules of general contract law[356]. With regard to the latter, from an economic perspective, at best transparency is needed. This could be obtained by the kind of comparative law Legrand favours[357], i.e. the approach which tries to discover where the real differences

[351] H.G. BEALE & W.D. BISHOP & M.P. FURMSTON, *Contract Cases and Materials*, p. 774.
[352] See e.g. JÜRGEN BASEDOW, 'Un Droit Commun des contrats pour le marché commun', *RIDC* 1998, pp. 7-28.
[353] P. xxi.
[354] See UGO MATTEI, *Comparative Law and Economics*. See also JAN SMITS, 'Een Europees privaatrecht als gemengd rechtsstelsel' and JAN SMITS, *The Making of European Private Law; Towards a Ius Commune Europaeum as a Mixed Legal System.*
[355] See generally on the distinction between default rules and mandatory rules MARTIJN W. HESSELINK, *De redelijkheid en billijkheid in het Europese privaatrecht*, p. 184 ff.
[356] See on the economic importance of the right balance between mandatory and default rules UGO MATTEI, 'Efficiency and Equal Protection In The New European Contract Law', p. 546 ('Striking [the right balance] between default rules and mandatory rules in contract law is certainly a key aspect of any system of private law seeking to create the institutional framework for an efficient market.'), and p. 548 ('efficiency requires 1) as small a number of mandatory rules as possible and 2) the general applicability of the ones that are considered unavoidable.').
[357] See PIERRE LEGRAND, *Fragments on Law-as-Culture*; PIERRE LEGRAND, *Que sais-je? Le droit comparé.*

lie[358]. In other words: the opposite of the approach based on the *presumptio similitudinis* which is the dominant mode of comparative law in Europe today[359].

The PECL virtually only 'unify' default rules[360]. This does not mean that the Lando Commission intends all or most contracts only to be governed by default rules. Obviously, it intended that there should be mandatory rules for the protection of, e.g., employees, tenants, commercial agents, consumer buyers et cetera. These rules are simply not contained in the PECL and, if the PECL were to be enacted as a code, in the European Contract Code. This means, presumably, that until the European Civil Code project is completed[361], such rules would have to continue to be taken from the various national legal systems, which vary considerably[362]. Therefore the differences in mandatory rules would presumably continue to exist. Also the absence of adequate information on the extent to which systems differ, which is said to be an important trade impediment[363], will remain in the case of mandatory rules since most scholars concentrate on general European contract law, which mainly contains default rules.

The PECL dedicate a specific provision to mandatory rules: art. 1:103 (Mandatory Law). However, this article seems to deal with a different problem from the one discussed here. Although it says very generally that when the parties choose to have their contract governed by the PECL[364] national mandatory rules are not applicable, unless they are of the type which is applicable irrespective of the law governing the contract[365], it would seem that this article is only meant to deal with rules of general contract law that a choice for the PECL would deviate from; it does not seem to - and indeed should not - mean that a choice of law for the PECL (general contract law) would imply a waiver of protection from special contract law (e.g. the protection of commercial agents).

C. *Default Rules*

1. Efficient Default rules. - Parties can often save transaction costs by (deliberately) leaving gaps in their contracts. If these gaps are filled on the basis of efficient default rules this creates a surplus. Compare Cooter and Ulen[366]: 'Default rules save transaction costs in direct proportion to their

[358] Closest to this approach is the Trento Common Core Project.
[359] See *supra*.
[360] See art. 1:102 (2). Six provisions are mandatory: art. 1:201, 2:105(2)(3), 6:105, 4:118, 8:109, 9:509(2). See PECL, Introduction, pp. xxix.
[361] See *supra*.
[362] See 1:103 (Mandatory Law).
[363] JÜRGEN BASEDOW, 'Un Droit Commun des contrats pour le marché commun'.
[364] See on this purpose of the PECL *supra*, Section II.
[365] Compare the *règles d'application immédiate* in art. 7 Rome Convention. See art. 1:103 PECL, Comment (p. 101).
[366] ROBERT COOTER & THOMAS ULEN, *Law & Economics*, p. 204.

efficiency.' Therefore from an economic perspective it is important that default rules should be efficient. The PECL virtually only consist of default rules. Are they efficient?

2. Hypothetical bargain. - Default rules are generally held to be efficient when they coincide with the result that parties would reach after bargaining in a world without transaction costs, i.e. with what the parties would have wanted (*ex ante*)[367]. Compare Ayres and Gertner: 'The "would have wanted" approach to gap filling is a natural outgrowth of the transaction cost explanation of contractual incompleteness. Lawmakers can minimise the costs of contracting by choosing the default that most parties would have wanted. If there are transaction costs of explicitly contracting on a contingency, the parties may prefer to leave the contract incomplete. Indeed, as transaction costs increase, so does the parties' willingness to accept a default that is not exactly what they would have contracted for.'[368]. Thus to the extent that the PECL reflect what parties would otherwise agree to, they reduce, as default rules, transaction costs[369].

2. Penalty defaults. - Ayres and Gertner have shown that sometimes it is more efficient to provide a default rule that parties would not have wanted (neither the parties to a particular contract nor the majority of parties to such contracts). That is the case when it would be more efficient if parties, before concluding the contract, revealed information to the courts (which have to establish a default rule *ex post*) or to the other party (who has to determine an efficient degree of precaution *ex ante*). Ayres and Gertner argue that sometimes prohibitive transaction costs are not the cause of a gap in a contract but rather a method of strategic bargaining in which a party chooses not to unveil relevant information that would lead to the conclusion of an efficient contract. In such a case the most efficient default rule may be a 'penalty default', a rule that encourages parties to contract around the default rule and thus to encourage them to reveal relevant information to each other[370].

3. Foreseeability. - A clear example of a penalty default in the PECL is the rule on foreseeability (art. 9:503). A party can, as it were, by its reliance on the performance of the contract, increase its expectation interest. Beyond some point it would be inefficient to compensate all this reliance. In most legal systems liability is limited by the doctrine of foreseeability: there is no liability for damage caused to the creditor which the debtor could not reasonably foresee because she could not reasonably expect this excessive

---

[367] See RICHARD A. POSNER, *Economic Analysis of Law*, p. 434; ROBERT COOTER & THOMAS ULEN, *Law & Economics*, p. 202; ANTHONY KRONMAN & RICHARD A. POSNER, *The Economics of Contract Law*, p. 4; H.G. BEALE & W.D. BISHOP & M.P. FURMSTON, *Contract Cases and Materials*, p. 83. IAN AYRES & ROBERT GERTNER, 'Filling Gaps in Incomplete Contracts: An Economic Theory of Default Rules', 99 *Yale L.J.* (1989) 87-130 hold a more nuanced view. See *infra*.

[368] IAN AYRES & ROBERT GERTNER, 'Filling Gaps in Incomplete Contracts', p. 93.

[369] See UGO MATTEI, 'Efficiency and Equal Protection In The New European Contract Law', p. 546, p. 542.

[370] IAN AYRES & ROBERT GERTNER, 'Filling Gaps in Incomplete Contracts'.

investment in reliance on the promise. In common law this doctrine was adopted in the famous case *Hadley* v. *Baxendale*[371]. A miller had agreed with a carrier that the latter would bring his broken shaft to Greenwich where it would be repaired. There was a delay, during which the miller could not work because he had no spare shaft. He claimed the loss of profit as consequential damages. However, on appeal, his claim was rejected because this damage was unforeseeable for the carrier who did not and could not know that the miller had no spare shaft. Ayres and Gertner mention the foreseeability rule as an example of a 'penalty default rule': it provides an incentive to the well-informed party to reveal relevant information which allows the other party to contract around the default and to reach an efficient solution by shifting the risk to the more efficient risk barer (least cost avoider) (in *Hadley* probably the carrier), obviously at a higher price[372].

4. Other examples. - The *contra proferentem* rule, adopted by the Lando Commission in art. 5:103, may also be regarded as a 'penalty default rule': it is not based on the presumption that the interpretation least favourable to the drafter best reflects what the parties (would) have wanted. It is rather meant to provide an incentive to those who draft contracts to formulate their clauses more accurately[373].

Another example is the problem of indefinite offers[374]. The enforcement of indefinite offers drives out inefficient indefinite offers: parties are encouraged to make only very precise offers and not to create erroneous reliance; otherwise they may be bound by a contract they did not want (but the other party thought they wanted). The PECL only enforce an offer if 'it contains sufficiently definite terms to form a contract' (2:201 (1) (b))[375]. This rule, which incidentally is itself rather indeterminate, does seem to be intended as a penalty default.

In the same line of thought the Dutch Plas/Valburg doctrine (liability for the expectation interest when breaking off negotiations after having induced reliance on the imminent conclusion of the contract) may be regarded as a penalty default which is meant to deter negotiating parties from inducing inefficient reliance (incentive to make explicit 'subject to contract' et cetera statements)[376]. On the other hand, extensive liability for breaking off negotiations may have a 'chilling effect' on negotiating parties[377], who do not even start negotiations for fear of liability, which may be inefficient (fewer

---

[371] (1854) 9 Ex. 341.
[372] IAN AYRES & ROBERT GERTNER, 'Filling Gaps in Incomplete Contracts', p. 101.
[373] See IAN AYRES & ROBERT GERTNER, 'Filling Gaps in Incomplete Contracts', p. 105.
[374] IAN AYRES & ROBERT GERTNER, 'Filling Gaps in Incomplete Contracts', p. 105.
[375] See also the related arts. 2:101 (Conditions for the conclusion of a Contract), Section (1) and 2:103 (Sufficient Agreement), Section (1).
[376] See on this doctrine *supra*, Section VI, B.
[377] See E. ALLAN FARNSWORTH, 'Precontractual liability and preliminary agreements: fair dealing and failed negotiations', *Columbia Law Review*, vol. 87, 1987, pp. 217-294.

contracts concluded). This may explain why under the PECL only the reliance interest may be recovered (2:301)[378].

D. Efficient Solutions

In most cases the Lando Commission seems to have adopted efficient solutions. Here are a few examples:

1. Informal. - The PECL contain hardly any formalities. A reduction in formalities reduces transaction costs, which is efficient[379].

2. Self-Help. - The Lando Commission seems to have clearly opted to diminish litigation costs. The PECL encourage 'self-help' by minimising the need for formal steps. An explicit economic argument (in terms of incentives) may be found in the 'Survey Chapters 1-9'[380]: 'Remedies such as withholding performance and termination give the obligor a strong incentive to perform. Thus, if the contract is terminated the obligor may lose all that it has invested in preparing to perform. The more easily the remedy can be operated by the obligee, the more effective it is likely to be to induce the obligor to perform.' Especially court interference is unnecessary[381]. Thus, unlike in many European legal systems, under the PECL a contract may be avoided for mistake, fraud, threats et cetera, or terminated for non-performance, without any court intervention (arts. 4:112 and 9:303 (1) respectively). Moreover, the PECL encourage the parties to adapt the contract in case of mistake (4:105) or a change of circumstances (6:111(2)) rather than to rely on the court's intervention.

3. Enforceability of Promises. - The economic theory of contract law rejects the bargain principle (doctrine of consideration) and wants firm offers and gratuitous promises to be enforceable because that maximises people's well-being. Compare Cooter and Ulen[382]: 'Enforceability apparently makes two people better off, as measured by their own desires, without making anyone worse off. Whenever a change in the law makes someone better off without making anyone worse off, "Pareto efficiency" requires changing the law.' The Lando Commission apparently came to the same conclusion. Therefore it made firm offers enforceable (art. 2:202 (3)), and did not adopt the consideration requirement (art. 2:101(1))

4. Efficient breach. - In some cases the availability of the remedy of specific performance may lead to inefficiency. A court order for specific performance is inefficient when the cost of performance to the debtor is higher than the benefit of the performance to the creditor. In such a case breach plus compensation would be the most efficient solution[383]. Although

[378] See art. 2:301, Comment C.
[379] See UGO MATTEI, 'Efficiency and Equal Protection In The New European Contract Law', p. 541.
[380] P. xxxix.
[381] P. xxxix.
[382] See ROBERT COOTER & THOMAS ULEN, *Law & Economics*, p. 184.
[383] See ROBERT COOTER & THOMAS ULEN, *Law & Economics*, p. 238 ff.

the PECL do not explicitly say so, in practice they may come very close to allowing efficient breach in most cases: whereas art. 9:102 (2) (b) may only apply to extreme cases[384], the exception under (d) seems to open the possibility for efficient breach in most cases: 'Specific performance cannot, however, be obtained where: (...) (d) the aggrieved party may reasonably obtain performance from another source.'[385] Most continental European legal systems do not have such a rule.

IX. Progress v Tradition

A. Modern Solutions

1. Tradition and progress. - Contract law in Europe has a long tradition. Many of the concepts used by the systems of contract law in European countries today date back to the Middle Ages or even to the days of the Roman Empire. Several concepts of Roman law have made it to the European codes[386], and in England, where contract law has not been codified, many of the central concepts have a very long history[387].

At the beginning of the new Millennium two opposite views could be taken by those who wish to create (the basis) for a common law of contract for Europe. One would be to cherish the common traditions we have and to build our new European law on the foundation of the *ius commune* as it was known in most of Europe before the national codifications. This view is taken by Zimmermann and other neo-pandectist scholars[388]. However, this view has met with fierce opposition of various kinds. First, it is submitted that there was never actually a *ius commune*[389]. Secondly, it is argued that this view seems to regard both the national codifications and the subsequent national developments as historical mistakes, whereas most European citizens will

---

[384] 9:102 (2) (b): 'Specific performance cannot, however, be obtained where: (...) (b) performance would cause the debtor unreasonable effort or expenses.'

[385] See MURIEL VELDMAN, 'Grenzen aan het recht op nakoming'.

[386] See REINHARD ZIMMERMANN, *The Law of Obligations.*

[387] See J.H. BAKER, *An Introduction to English Legal History*, London 1979 (reprinted in 1988); S.F.C. MILSOM, *Historical Foundations of the Common Law*, 2nd ed., London 1981.

[388] See e.g. REINHARD ZIMMERMANN, 'Civil Code and Civil Law- The "Europeanization" of Private Law within the European Community and the Re-Emergency of a European Legal Science', *The Columbia Journal of European Law*, 1995, pp. 63 ff.; REINHARD ZIMMERMANN, '"Common law" und "civil law", Amerika und Europa', in Reinhard Zimmermann (ed.), *Amerikanische Rechtskultur und europäisches Privatrecht*, Tübingen 1995; REINHARD ZIMMERMANN, *The Law of Obligations*, Oxford 1996; REINHARD ZIMMERMANN, 'Roman Law and European Legal Unity', in: A.S. Hartkamp et al. (eds.) *Towards a European Civil Code*, 2nd ed., Nijmegen and The Hague, London, Boston 1998, pp. 21 ff.; REINHARD ZIMMERMANN, *Roman Law, Contemporary Law, European Law; The Civilian Tradition Today*, Oxford 2001; see also REINER SCHULZE, 'Gemeineuropäisches Privatrecht und Rechtsgeschichte', in Peter-Christian Müller-Graff (ed.), *Gemeinsames Privatrecht in der Europäischen Gemeinschaft*, Baden-Baden 1993.

[389] See PIO CARONI, 'Der Schiffbruch der Geschichtlichkeit; Anmerkungen zum Neo-Pandektismus', *Zeitschrift für Neuere Rechtsgeschichte* (1994), pp. 85-100.

regard the introduction of labour law, strict product liability et cetera as important achievements of the 20th century[390]. Finally, this view is rejected as very conceptualist, as *Begriffsjurisprudenz* in the Savignian tradition.

In the opposite view the conceptual basis of European legal systems is outdated. The concepts date from Roman law, and the ideological pillars (freedom of contract, liability for fault, and absolute property) belong to the 19th century. They neither fit the present-day political (see above) and economic (see above) views nor our present-day complex and highly organised society (communication, transport, insurance, et cetera). Therefore we should leave our codes et cetera behind us and start afresh, especially with brand new concepts, and a new format[391].

What choice did the Lando Commission make? It has explicitly stated that the PECL can be regarded as 'progressive'[392]. Here are a few aspects of the PECL that could be characterised as 'progressive', in the sense that they are new compared to most systems and may represent or precurse the 'modern trend'.

2. Principles instead of a Code. - The Lando Commission has deliberately chosen for a new format compared to the classical code that Continental European legal systems are familiar with. It has opted for 'Principles' which are presented as Articles, Comments (with Illustrations) and Notes[393]. Thus they are an important source of information for contracting parties, courts, legislators, and academics. This choice represents an important shift from formal to substantive concerns.

3. Informal. - The PECL are informal in many ways. First, the PECL do not require any formality for the conclusion of a contract[394]. Art. 2:101 (2) explicitly states this. Also notices are given in an informal way. See art. 1:303 (1): 'Any notice may be given by any means, whether in writing or otherwise, appropriate to the circumstances.'[395]. And, as said above, under the PECL a contract may also be terminated and avoided in a very informal way: 'the

---

[390] See MARTIJN W. HESSELINK, *De redelijkheid en billijkheid in het Europese privaatrecht*, p. 15.

[391] See UGO MATTEI, 'The Issue of Civil Codification and Legal Scholarship: Biases, Strategies and Developments', 21 *Hastings Int'l & Comp. L. Rev.* (1998), p. 883 ff.; J.M BARENDRECHT, 'What kind of European Liability Law?; About the optimal level of detail in rules regarding (tort) liability in a European civil code', and, for France, CHRISTIAN ATIAS, 'Le code civil nouveau', *D.* 1999.

[392] The Commission on European Contract Law speaks of 'progressive' (p. xxii.), 'a more satisfactory answer' (p. xxii.), and 'a workable system' (p. xxvi) as if they were unproblematic concepts, as if they could be established objectively. However, American realism and the CLS movement have shown us that they are clearly not: law is politics. See further *supra*.

[393] See further *supra*, Section IV.

[394] But this is only the 'general part' of contract law. Specific rules on consumer contracts or on sureties (guarantees) may contain form requirements.

[395] See also Section (6): 'In this Article, "notice" includes the communication of a promise, statement, offer, acceptance, demand, request or other declaration.' See for avoidance art. 4:112 (Notice of Avoidance).

Principles endeavour to encourage "self-help" by minimising the need for formal steps.'

4. Favor contractus. - Under the PECL there will be fewer cases of the complete invalidity of a contract than under most European legal systems. The *favor contractus* seems to have been a basic guideline for the drafters of the PECL. This also reflects a modern trend[396]. Examples include: initial impossibility of performance does not render the contract void (avoidance for mistake is possible) (art. 4:102)[397]; if a party is entitled to avoid a contract for mistake the other party can prevent avoidance by proposing to perform the contract as the mistaken party understood it (adaptation of contract) (4:105)[398]; if a ground for avoidance affects only particular terms of a contract, in principle the contract may only be partially avoided (partial avoidance) (4:116)[399]. Arts. 6:104-6:108 provide solutions for gaps in contracts which help to avoid the contract becoming invalid (void) for uncertainty. Penalty clauses are not void, but can be reduced by the courts when they are 'grossly excessive' (9:509).

5. Not 'all or nothing'.- Remedies are not available in an 'all or nothing' manner. The PECL rather allow for intermediate solutions. This also seems to reflect a modern trend[400]. Examples include the possibility of partial avoidance, mentioned above, and adaptation of the contract when performance becomes excessively onerous because of a change of circumstances (article 6:111). See also art. 8:101 (Remedies available): 'A party may not resort to any of the remedies set out in Chapter 9 *to the extent that* its own act caused the other party's non-performance.'[401]

6. Flexible time-limits. - Under the PECL time-limits are flexible. See for example art. 2:206 (2), on time-limits for acceptance: 'a reasonable time', and art. 4:113, on time-limits for avoidance: 'Notice of avoidance must be given within a reasonable time'.

7. Other examples. - Termination does not have retroactive effect. This solution also seems to be in line with the modern trend[402]. The reverse solution, adopted by the legal systems of the French tradition, may lead to many restitutionary problems in case of partially performed contracts. Moreover, in the definition of 'writing' explicit reference is made to e-mails:

---

[396] Compare the 1992 Dutch civil code (see A.S. HARTKAMP, *Aard en opzet van het nieuwe vermogensrecht*, in: *Monografieën Nieuw BW*, A1, Deventer 1990, no. 21; J.B.M. VRANKEN, 'Themis en het vermogensrecht nieuw BW; Naar een inhoudelijke beoordeling van de boeken 3, 5, 6 Nieuw BW', *NJB* 1988, p. 682 ff.) and the UP (see MICHAEL JOACHIM BONELL, *An International Restatement of Contract Law*, p. 117).

[397] Contrast e.g. 306 *BGB*, 1346 Italian c.c., 290 Portuguese *Código civil*.

[398] A similar rule is known in Italy (art. 1432 *c.c.*), the Netherlands (art. 6:230 *BW*), and the UP (art. 3.13 UP).

[399] Such a provision is new to many codes (see, however, art. 139 BGB and art. 3:41 Dutch BW).

[400] Compare W.H. VAN BOOM & C.E.C. JANSEN & J.G.A. LINSSEN (eds.), *Tussen 'Alles' en 'Niets'; Van toedeling naar verdeling van nadeel*, Zwolle 1997.

[401] Emphasis added.

[402] See art. 6:269 BW and art. 7.3.5 UP.

'"written" statements include communications made by telegram, telex, fax and e-mail and other means of communication capable of providing a readable record of the statement on both sides'(art. 1:301 (6))[403]. Finally, the Comments contain many examples of modern contracts (e.g. franchise, software design), and of modern contracting situations.

B. *Innovations*

Compared to many legal systems, especially to their codes, the Principles contain several innovations: some solutions have not been adopted in any of the systems as yet, as the Lando Commission explicitly states[404]. New to all or most legal systems (or their codes) are the following rules: Art. 2:107 declares that promises are binding without acceptance. Under art. 2:201 (3) a public advertisement is presumed to be an offer. Unlike most codes, the PECL take into account that in practice agreement is frequently reached although there is no distinguishable succession of offer and acceptance (art. 2:211). Art 2:209 (conflicting general conditions) introduces a creative solution to the problem of conflicting general conditions: the knock-out rule[405]. The rule in art. 2:210 (a professional's written confirmation) is new to most legal systems[406]. Many systems contain a rule on breach of confidentiality during negotiations (2:301), but not in their codes[407]. Art. 4:106 (incorrect information): no European code has a specific rule on this[408]. Art. 6:109 (Contract for an Indefinite Period) contains a rule which is accepted in most European legal systems, either on the basis of the principle of non-perpetuity or on the basis of good faith[409], but is not explicitly provided for in any code. Art. 6:111 (2) says that in case of an unanticipated change of circumstances the parties must first try to sort out the consequences amongst themselves. This rule is new to all European systems. Unlike most European codes, art. 9:304 gives the innocent party the right to terminate when there is anticipatory non-

[403] Compare art. 1.10 UP (Definitions): 'In these Principles (...) "writing" means any mode of communication that preserves a record of the information contained therein and is capable of being reproduced in tangible form', and Article 13 CISG (1980): 'For the purposes of this Convention "writing" includes telegram and telex.'
[404] P. xxvi.
[405] Not many codes contain a rule on the battle of forms (see, however, art. 6:225 (3) Dutch BW). Most systems do have such a rule, however. There are various options: first shot, last shot, and knock-out. The knock-out rule seems to be a good solution. See further CHANTAL MAHÉ, 'Conflit de conditions générales: quelle tactique adopter?' in: F.W. Grosheide, K. Boele-Woelki (eds.), *Molengrafica Europees privaatrecht*, Lelystad 1997.
[406] See further *supra*.
[407] See MARTIJN W. HESSELINK, 'Precontractual Good Faith', in: Hugh Beale et. al. (eds.) *Cases, Materials and Text on Contract Law, Oxford and Portland*, Oregon 2002, Chapter 2, Section 2 (pp. 237-293), and MARTIJN W. HESSELINK, *De redelijkheid en billijkheid in het Europese privaatrecht*, pp. 90 ff., with further references
[408] In most civil law systems this is dealt with by tort law. Here a party may be liable even in the absence of fraud or fundamental mistake under 4:103.
[409] See MARTIJN W. HESSELINK, *De redelijkheid en billijkheid in het Europese privaatrecht*, p. 365, with further references.

performance[410]. The remedy of price reduction (art. 9:401) is known to many systems with regard to sales contracts (*actio quanti minoris*) [411], but not as a general remedy for all contracts. Art. 9:501(2)(a) provides for the general recovery of non-pecuniary loss[412]. In many systems, recovery is (in practice) much more limited[413].

X. Final remarks

Making law means making choices. The Lando Commission had to make choices of many kinds. Some of the most important ones have been highlighted in this paper.

When the Restatement (First) of Contracts was published it met with the following sharp criticism from Charles E. Clark, the then Dean of the Yale School of Law[414]: 'Actually the resulting statement is the law nowhere and in its unreality only deludes and misleads. It is either a generality so obvious as immediately to be accepted, or so vague as not to offend, or of such antiquity as to be unchallenged as a statement of past history. (...) There are a large number of purely bromidic sections (...). No one would wish to dissent from them. They cannot be used in deciding cases; nor are they now useful in initiating students into contract law (...). They may afford convenient citations to a court, but that is all. (...) The other sections cover up rather than disclose the problems they face. (...) Such citations, limited as they are to non-controversial points, will have no appreciable effect in unifying and clarifying our common law.' Does the same criticism also apply to the PECL? One would expect that it does, since the differences between the various European legal systems are presumably much greater than in the United States. However, I do not think that it does. I think that the Lando Commission has attained an astonishingly good result. Of course, the rules are very abstract. But they are no more abstract than most European civil codes, in many cases rather less so. And, contrary to these codes, the PECL also provide a very useful Commentary with Illustrations and Notes. In addition, they are drafted in a more elegant and plain style than most, if not all, European codes. Moreover, they are more social than many civil codes, though admittedly not enough to be a model code for all types of contracts. Finally, they contain some very interesting new, creative solutions. On the whole, I think that the Lando Commission has provided us with a highly inspiring starting point for a truly European debate on contract law and with an elegant and useful common language for that debate.

---

[410] See, however, art. 6:80 BW. A similar rule has been accepted by the courts in England and many other countries. See art. 9:304, Notes. See also art. 7.3.3 UP and 71 CISG.

[411] See *supra*. Compare art. 50 CISG (sales). Also in the directive on consumer guarantees (sales law).

[412] Compare art. 7.4.2(2) UP.

[413] See e.g. in the Netherlands art. 6:106 BW.

[414] See CHARLES E. CLARK, 'The Restatement Of The Law Of Contracts', p. 654.

MODELS

4
The New Dutch Civil Code: An Example For A European Civil Code?

I. Introduction

DURING THE last few years there has been an ongoing discussion in Europe on the desirability and the feasibility of a European Civil Code. Within this context the Dutch experience could be of some relevance since the new civil code of the Netherlands is the most recently enacted civil code in the European Union. Indeed, the central part of the *Burgerlijk Wetboek* (*BW*) entered into force in 1992. In this Chapter I will briefly examine to what extent the recent codification experience in the Netherlands could represent an example which is of some relevance for Europe. I will do so by addressing five aspects of codification. First, the actors: who made the new code? (II). Secondly, I will discuss the style of the new code, especially its degree of abstraction (III). Then, I will turn to the political choices which the codifiers have made, in particular the ideological choices in terms of left (solidarity) and right (autonomy) (IV). Subsequently, I will address the aspect of legal culture: to which legal family does the new Dutch system belong? (V). Finally, I will devote some attention to the innovations which the new *BW* has brought, i.e. the new rules, doctrines and concepts (VI). I will conclude with some more general observations regarding codification today (VII).

The first Dutch Civil Code was adopted in 1838. It was a - frequently literal - copy of the French *Code civil* of 1804. In 1938, on the centenary of the civil code, Professor Meijers, a famous Leiden professor, launched an appeal for a new code[1]. The main reason for his appeal was the scattered state of the law. In his view, too large a part of private law was by then located outside the code, notably in specific legislation (e.g. the regulation of labour contracts) and in case law (e.g. the 'general clause' of delictual liability[2]). Hence, there was a need to 'recodify'. However, Paul Scholten, an Amsterdam professor of equally high standing, proclaimed himself to be

---

[1] E.M. MEIJERS, 'Wijzigingen en aanvullingen van het Burgerlijk wetboek na 1838', in: Paul Scholten & E.M. Meijers (eds.), *'Gedenkboek Burgerlijk Wetboek 1838-1938*, Zwolle 1938, p. 33 ff.

[2] HR, 31 January 1919, *NJ* 1919, 161, *W* 10365, note Molengraaff (Lindenbaum/Cohen).

against this idea. In his view there was no political interest whatsoever in such an operation, the existing interest being limited entirely to the academic world[3]. Nevertheless, in 1947, in the wake of the Second World War (during which Meijers, who was Jewish, had been deported to a concentration camp and had survived), the Minister of Justice appointed Meijers as the drafter of a new civil code. He took up this task very swiftly and presented his first draft in 1954. However, shortly afterwards he suddenly died. Three professors were appointed as his successors. However, unfortunately the collaboration among this triumvirate was not very harmonious. After them various other jurists were in charge of parts of the drafting work. Most were academics, although some judges were involved as well. After Meijers' death the preparatory work proceeded rather slowly, partly because of the number of people involved, and the sometimes difficult collaboration between them, and partly because of the scant interest which the legislator demonstrated for this project. The first part of the new code (Book 1: 'The law of persons and the family') was not enacted until 1970, and was followed by the second part (Book 2: 'Legal persons') in 1976. More than 20 years later, after the introduction of the new Book 8 (on transport) in 1991 had passed virtually unnoticed, the central part of the code came into force in 1992: Book 3 ('Patrimonial law in general'), Book 5 ('Real rights'), Book 6 ('General part of the law of obligations') and a part of Book 7 ('Specific contracts', especially Title 1, on 'Sales'). During the 1980s strong doubts had been expressed by both academics and practitioners as to the need for a new patrimonial law. The fact that the core part of private law was eventually recodified was largely the result of the efforts by Wouter Snijders, the then president of the Civil Division of the *Hoge Raad* (Supreme Court)[4], and his collaborators[5]. Since 1992, various other parts of Book 7 have entered into force, for example Title 10 on 'Labour Contracts'. Book 4 ('The Law of succession') has recently been enacted and will soon enter into force. Book 9 ('intellectual property') and Book 10 ('Private international law') are still being prepared, whereas some of the last remaining parts of Book 7 (especially insurance and rental contracts) are currently being debated in Parliament[6].

---

[3] PAUL SCHOLTEN, 'De codificatie-gedachte vóór honderd jaar en thans', in: Paul Scholten & E.M. Meijers (eds.), *Gedenkboek Burgerlijk Wetboek 1838-1938*, Zwolle 1938, 1 ff.

[4] See T.J. VEEN, *''En voor berisping is hier ruime stof''. Over codificatie van het burgerlijk recht, legistische rechtsbeschouwing en herziening van het Nederlands privaatrecht in de 19de en 20ste eeuw*, Amsterdam 2001.

[5] A prominent collaborator was Arthur S. Hartkamp, who is at present *Procureur-generaal* at the *Hoge Raad*, Professor of private law at the *Universiteit van Amsterdam* and the author of the main commentary on the law of obligations in the Netherlands: A.S. HARTKAMP, *Mr. C. Asser's handleiding tot de beoefening van het Nederlands burgerlijk recht; Verbintenissenrecht* (3 volumes), 11th ed., Deventer 2000-2002.

[6] On the history of the new code see E.O.H.P. FLORIJN, *Ontstaan en ontwikkeling van het nieuwe Burgerlijk Wetboek*, Maastricht 1995, and VEEN, *En voor berisping is hier ruime stof.*

II. Legal Actors

The first aspect of codification that I will address is the aspect of the legal actors: who makes the law? Or, in the words of the great Italian comparatist Rodolfo Sacco, what is the relative importance of the various legal formants?[7] More specifically, I am interested in the question to what extent the codification has influenced the relative importance of the various legal actors (*empowerment*). One important characteristic of the new Dutch Civil Code, and indeed of any codification, is the confirmation of the legislator's primacy. Indeed, the principal purpose of the recodification has been to return all private law into the civil code with a view to reaffirming the status of the civil code as the principal source of private law which emanates from the democratically elected legislator.

The new code has repealed some rules and doctrines which had been accepted by the courts. The most striking example is the ban on the *fiducia cum creditore* which is proclaimed by art. 3:84 (2) *BW*. On the other hand, the new code has also introduced many rules and doctrines which were absent both in the previous code and in case law. Some examples include: the doctrine of unjustified enrichment (6:212 *BW*)[8], the possibility to adapt the contract (in order to avoid annulment) in the case of abuse of circumstances or mistake (arts. 3:54 and 6:230 *BW*), and the category of 'qualitative obligations' (art. 6:252 *BW*) (which have characteristics both of relative and absolute rights). Moreover, the legislator has introduced new concepts, sometimes in order to replace very ancient ones, for example *redelijkheid en billijkheid* ('reasonableness and equity') instead of *goede trouw* for objective good faith and *goederenrecht* instead of *zakenrecht* for property law (*droit des biens, diritto dei beni, Sachenrecht*). Moreover, the new code has deliberately made private law much more systematic and less casuistic.

However, upon closer inspection, the legislator's role has been a rather formal one. As a matter of fact, the government and Parliament have only made very few major contributions to the structure and the content of the new code. In reality, it has rather been academics (legal doctrine) who have played a key role. Not only was the general structure of the new *BW* already present in the proposals which Meijers (and subsequently his successors) had made[9], but the same was also true concerning most of the changes with regard to the previous code. To refer to only some of the examples mentioned above: the abolition of the *fiducia cum creditore* and the adoption of new terminology 'good faith' and for 'property law' were explicitly envisaged by Meijers.

Moreover, one of the main characteristics of the new code is the omnipresence of so-called 'general clauses', especially good faith (see in

[7] See especially RODOLFO SACCO, 'Legal Formants: A Dynamic Approach To Comparative Law', 39 *AJCL* (1991), pp. 1-34, pp. 343-401 and, in Italian, RODOLFO SACCO, *Introduzione al diritto comparato*, 5th ed. Torino 1997.

[8] In the past the *Hoge Raad* had explicitly refused to introduce such a doctrine (HR, 30 January 1959, *NJ* 1959, 548 (Quint/Te Poel)).

[9] On the political importance of the structure of a code see *infra*, Section IV.

particular arts. 6:2, 6:248 *BW*, while dozens of more specific provisions also refer to good faith). The presence of such general clauses does not reinforce the power of the legislator (or only in a very formal sense). On the contrary, their main function is to effectively delegate a considerable amount of law making power to the courts[10]. In other words, the new code has rather reinforced (and legitimised) the extensive role which the courts already played in the development of private law.

On a European level things would probably develop in a similar fashion. In principle, a European Civil Code would affirm the legislator's primacy also in the field of private law and would emphasise the democratic foundation of the law. Nevertheless, in reality it would probably be mainly academics who would exercise power, since, in all likelihood, they will be the ones who will be asked to draft the code[11]. In this scenario legal doctrine would succeed in reoccupying, at least in part, the initiative which it had lost to the European Commission when the latter started to enact directives which interfered increasingly with the core areas of private law. On the other hand, an abstract code (for example a code which would be limited to general contract law, after the example of the Lando Commission's *Principles of European Contract Law*) would leave the courts with a great deal of room and they would effectively be in charge of developing more specific rules which are suitable for application in specific cases. Moreover, a general good faith clause, like the one contained in art. 1:201 of the PECL, would in fact confer extensive law making powers on the courts.

III. Style

The new Dutch Civil Code is characterised by a distinctly dogmatic style (*Professorenrecht*). In particular, the new *BW* is a rather conceptual and abstract code[12]. The most dogmatic part of all is probably the law relating to contracts. There, the most abstract concept is the *rechtshandeling* ('juristic act', *Rechtsgeschäft*, *negozio giuridico*) which is regulated in the general part of patrimonial law (Title 3.2). However, the 'juristic act' is only the first of the many layers of abstraction which relate to contracts. This does not make the code very accessible and user-friendly[13]. For example, if a consumer who

[10] See M.W. HESSELINK, *De redelijkheid en billijkheid in het Europese privaatrecht*, Deventer 1999, and *infra*, Chapter 7.

[11] See also the traditions in other countries. In France, many private law reforms have been prepared by professors, for example the reforms of family law (Carbonnier), of traffic liability (Tunc), and of product liability (Ghestin). In Germany the recent reform of the law of obligations was prepared by a commission which included many professors (including Hein Kötz, Dieter Medicus, and Peter Schlechtriem) as its members. And also in England many law reforms have been prepared by the Law Commission, which partly consist of academics. Indeed, Hugh Beale, who has been a central member of both the Lando Commission and the Study Group for a European Civil Code (Von Bar group), is currently a Law Commissioner.

[12] OLE LANDO, 'Is codification needed in Europe? Principles of European Contract Law and the relationship to Dutch law', 1 *ERPL*, (1993), p. 157.

[13] Depending on the particular circumstances of the case he will have to look in Book 3 (Title 3.2

has just bought a new computer which does not work, wants to know whether he is entitled to obtain a new one, he has to search 6 different levels of abstraction in order to discover the answer. On the other hand, the new code also contains some extremely detailed rules. A striking example is the regulation of *mora debitoris* (art. 6:81ff *BW*). The system is extremely nuanced, composed of so may rules and exceptions that in practice most lawyers advise their clients to always send a letter which contains a final warning to the debtor in order to be absolutely certain that he will be effectively 'in delay'.

In my view the style of the new Dutch Civil Code is an example which should definitely not be followed. Its modernity has by now become old-fashioned. It would probably have been a very modern code in the early 1950s when Meijers designed its main structure, but today the glory days of hyper-rationalism seem to have come to an end. For example, both the UNIDROIT and the Lando Principles consist of only one layer of abstraction. Moreover, the more abstract a code, the more difficult it will be to implement the usually very pragmatic and instrumental EC Directives. Even if a European Civil Code or a European Code of Contracts were to be enacted there would probably still be a regular stream of new legislative initiatives by the Union which would in all likelihood continue to have the same pragmatic and instrumental characteristics as the present directives and which would therefore raise the same systematic problems as the directives currently do in those systems which have highly abstract codes. Finally, such an abstract code would be completely unacceptable, not only to lawyers from the common law tradition but also to French lawyers, who are usually not very fond of general parts[14].

IV. Politics

The Dutch Civil Code assigns a central role to the private autonomy of legal subjects and, as said, to the most typical expression of party autonomy, the 'juristic act' (*rechtshandeling*) (art. 3:33 *BW*). Admittedly, the new *BW* has also codified the reliance principle as an exceptional source of 'juristic acts' (3:35 *BW*). However, upon closer inspection, this only confirms the basic structure of the code: the new private law is in principle based on party autonomy, which is only limited in exceptional cases. Three typical

on juristic acts), which contains the rules on formation and validity; Book 6 (on obligations in general), which contains general rules on the performance and non-performance of obligations; more specifically Title 6.5 (contracts in general), where the rules on standard terms, interpretation and third-party rights are located; and even more specifically Section 6.5.5 (on synallagmatic contracts), where he will find the rules concerning a change of circumstances, the right to withhold performance and to terminate; Book 7, where Title 7.1 (on sales) contains some specific rules e.g. relating to conformity and transfer of risk; and, finally, in the same Section some specific (and mandatory) rules relating to the protection of consumer buyers.

[14] See also Tallon's criticism of the new Dutch Civil Code: DENIS TALLON, 'The new Dutch Civil Code in a comparative perspective - French view-point', 1 *ERPL* 1993, p. 189 ff.

exceptions include (i) cases where the autonomy of one party is itself considered to be vitiated, (ii) cases where a party belongs to a group which is deemed to be structurally in need of protection, and (iii) cases where the unlimited respect of private autonomy would lead to 'excessive results'. For contract law this means, for example, that many rules and doctrines are aimed at restoring defects of consent (typically by introducing pre-contractual duties to inform) instead of more openly policing the content of contracts; that most protective rules are regarded as special and limited to certain categories of weak parties (employees, tenants, consumers) instead of extending the underlying ideas to broader or even all categories; and that many altruistic duties (duties of care, duties to co-operate, duties to inform and to warn during performance) are not codified but are recognised at best in a casuistic way in view of the exceptional circumstances of a specific case (6:248 *BW*). For tort law this means that fault liability is the norm whereas strict liability continues to be regarded as exceptional. And for property law this means that instead of adopting a social concept of property[15] it is now still defined as an essentially exclusive right (art. 5:1(2) *BW*), subject only to the prohibition of abuse (art. 3:13 *BW*). In sum, from an ideological perspective the basic structure of the new Dutch Civil Code is rather classical. Too classical, I would say. In the 21st century a civil code should express the fact that private law is based not on one but on two basic (and conflicting) principles: autonomy and solidarity[16].

In recent times, various European scholars have argued in favour of a European private law which should be sufficiently 'social'[17]. I share this view completely. In concrete terms, this means that a European civil code should be based not only on the principle of private autonomy but also (and not only exceptionally) on the principle of social solidarity, i.e. on the obligation to take the interests of others into account. The structure of the code should reflect this double characteristic, also in those parts which deal with 'general

[15] See for example art. 14 (2) German *Grundgesetz* ('Eigentum verpflichtet. Sein Gebrauch soll zugleich dem Wohle der Allgemeinheit dienen.') and art. 42 (2) Italian *Costituzione* ('La proprietà privata è riconosciuta e garantita dalla legge, che ne determina i modi di acquisto, di godimento e i limiti allo scopo di assicurarne la funzione sociale e di renderla accessibile a tutti.').

[16] These two ideas correspond to the two dominant ideologies which have dominated the political arena in most European countries during the 20th century: liberal-conservative (right) and social-democrat-progressive (left). See further *supra*, Chapter 3, Section VI, and *infra*, Chapter 7. On the future of the political distinction between the right and the left, see NORBERTO BOBBIO, *Destra e sinistra; Ragioni e significati di una distinzione politica*, Roma 1999.

[17] THOMAS WILHELMSSON, *Social Contract Law and European Integration*, Aldershot 1995; BRIGITTA LURGER, *Vertragliche Solidarität, Entwicklungschancen für das allgemeine Vertragsrecht in Österreich und in der Europäischen Union*, Baden-Baden 1998; JAN B.M. VRANKEN, 'Over partijautonomie, contractsvrijheid en de grondslag van gebondenheid in het verbintenissenrecht' in: J.M. Barendrecht, M.A.B. Chao-Duivis and H.A.W. Vermeulen (eds.), *Beginselen van contractenrecht: Opstellen aangeboden aan B.W.M. Nieskens-Isphording*, Deventer 2000; CHRISTOPHE JAMIN, 'Plaidoyer pour le solidarisme contractuel', in: Gilles Goubeaux et al. (eds.), *Études offertes à Jacques Ghestin; Le contrat au début du XXIe siècle*, Paris 2001; GUIDO ALPA, *Trattato di diritto civile, I Storia, fonti, interpretazione*, Milano 2000, p. 604 ff. See further *infra*, Chapter 5.

private law'. In this respect the Lando principles are somewhat disappointing[18]. In particular, the exaltation of the freedom of contract in article 1:102 *PECL* seems neither to be in accordance with today's practice of regulating contracts in many European countries, where freedom of contract is limited in many cases, nor with the aspirations of many European citizens[19]. As far as 'special private law' rules are concerned, which are meant to provide a further going protection to certain categories of parties which are considered to be particularly vulnerable, like employees, tenants, consumers and small businesses, these rules should be included in the code itself (as indeed they are in the new Dutch code) and not be retained outside in order to maintain the 'pure' and 'neutral' character of private law (as the German legislator had done when it enacted the separate protective statute on standard terms (*AGBG*) which has only very recently been admitted to the *BGB*)[20]. Finally, in my view the 'general part' of contract law, as contained in the PECL for example, should not be enacted without the contemporary enactment of at least some 'special contract rules', like the rules on labour contracts, rental contracts and consumer contracts. Otherwise, a European Code of Contracts would seem either rather irrelevant (freedom of contract needs no code), or hopelessly old-fashioned (19th century) or singularly one-sided (neo-liberal)[21].

V. Legal Culture

The drafters of the new Dutch Civil Code were inspired by various legal systems. In the *travaux préparatoires* one can find references to virtually all civil codes in the world. Nevertheless, according to foreign observers, with the entry into force of the new *BW*, the Dutch legal system has passed from the French (or 'Latin') legal family to the German (or 'Germanic') family[22]. Indeed, the structure, concepts and many of the specific rules and doctrines (to give merely one example: the rules on the right to withhold performance) in the new Dutch code share many similarities with the German *BGB*.

This development only confirms the increasing dominance of German legal culture in Europe. Today, apart from Germany and the Netherlands, also Austria, Greece and Portugal are part of the same legal tradition[23]. According to some scholars, this dominant position carries a risk of German cultural

[18] In the same sense THOMAS WILHELMSSON, 'Private Law in the EU: Harmonised or Fragmented Europeanisation?', 10 *ERPL* (2002), p. 77-94.

[19] For an ideological analysis of the PECL, see *supra*, Chapter 3, Section IV.

[20] In the same sense GUIDO ALPA, *I contratti in generale; introduzione alla nuova giurisprudenza*, Torino 1990, n. 19 ff.

[21] See further *infra*, Chapter 5.

[22] See DENIS TALLON, 'The new Dutch Civil Code in a comparative perspective - French viewpoint'. More moderate: ULRICH DROBNIG, 'Das neue niederländische bürgerliche Gesetzbuch aus vergleichender und deutscher Sicht' 1 *ERPL* 1993, p. 171 ff.

[23] See also my 'Review' (3 *The Edinburgh Law Review* (1999), p. 412 ff.) of B.S. MARKESINIS, W. LORENZ, G. DANNEMANN, *The German Law of Obligations, Volume I The Law of Contracts and Restitution: A Comparative Introduction*, Oxford 1997.

imperialism[24], although this concern is not shared by all observers[25]. However, the Northern European bias within the various principles projects and within the European private law movement at large is undeniable[26]. Inevitably, this raises a serious legitimacy issue from a Southern European perspective.

VI. Innovations

The new *Burgerlijk Wetboek* introduces a number of changes which constitute innovations with regard to both the previous code and, in many instances, case law. Probably the largest structural innovation has been the abolition of the distinction between civil law and commercial law: the *Burgerlijk Wetboek* is a code of *private law* (never mind its title). A second fundamental structural innovation has been the acceptance of a general action in case of unjustified enrichment (6:212 *BW*). Some of the other prominent novelties include the introduction of a fourth type of 'defect of consent' (i.e. 'abuse of circumstances' and art. 3:44 (4) *BW*), a rule on change of circumstances (6:258 *BW*) and the possibility of adaptation (instead of annulment) in cases of abuse of circumstances and mistake (6:230 *BW*). Maybe the most significant innovation has been the omnipresence of the concept of good faith throughout the new code.

However, from an international perspective, these 'innovations' are not really all that new. In fact, most were already present in the Italian Civil Code of 1942. In the meantime they have all been adopted by the Lando Commission in its *Principles of European Contract Law* and by Von Bar's Study Group on a European Civil Code respectively[27]. In this sense, the Dutch Civil Code is not (at least no longer) the best example of modernity. Indeed,

---

[24] UGO MATTEI, 'The Issue of Civil Codification and Legal Scholarship: Biases, Strategies and Developments', 21 *Hastings Int'l & Comp. L. Rev.* 883; P.G. MONATERI, 'Black Gaius; A Quest for the Multicultural Origins of the "Western Legal Tradition"', 51 *Hastings Law Journal* (2000), 479-555.

[25] CARLO CASTRONOVO, 'Recensione a Reinhard Zimmermann, Roman Law, Contemporary Law, European Law. The civilian tradition today', 3 *Europa e diritto privato* (2001), p. 737 ff. Moreover, from a broader (i.e. global) perspective the German hegemony seems to be relative. In the words of Ugo Mattei, 'the wind has changed': from a continent which was used to exporting its ideas Europe has now turned into a continent which imports legal ideas from the United States of America. Not only are many rules and doctrines which are very successful in practice (which itself is more and more dominated by law firms of American origin or which are modelled upon them) of American origin (product liability, franchising, leasing and other 'transplants'), but also the idea of principles (UP and *PECL*) and other types of 'soft law' are inspired by the American Restatements. See UGO MATTEI, 'Why The Wind Changed: Intellectual Leadership In Western Law', 42 *AJCL* (1994) 195.

[26] The Gandolfi Group's project seems to be more inspired by the Latin tradition. It is not without significance that they have published their draft code of contracts in French. See GIUSEPPE GANDOLFI (ed.), *Code Européen des contrats - Avant-projet*, Milano 2001. Another important project is also based in Italy, the Trento Common Core Project. However, that project seems to be mostly inspired by the common law tradition, especially by American legal culture.

[27] On the work in progress see the website: www.sgecc.net.

in many respects the Lando principles are without any doubt more modern[28]. The same applies to Von Bar's drafts on tort law[29].

VII. Final Remarks

Although the new Dutch civil code may certainly be regarded as a respectable codification, and although the *BW* is definitely quite a modern code if compared with most other Western European civil codes[30], it nevertheless does not, in my view, provide an ideal model which should be followed by the drafters of a European Civil Code[31]. With regard to most of the aspects discussed above (authors, style, politics, legal culture, innovations) both the PECL and the ECC seem to be more appropriate and more modern.

This final consideration brings me to a concluding observation with regard to codification today. In the 1950s, when it was originally designed by Meijers, the Dutch Civil Code was indeed very modern. However, when its most important part finally entered into force in 1992, it had already lost much of its modern novelty and avant-garde splendour. On a European scale, the adoption of a new comprehensive code will probably not be possible in a much shorter period of time. Therefore, in Europe today it may be advisable to be less ambitious and to approach the unification of European private law on a step by step basis, starting with those subjects (especially functional fields) which are considered to be in most urgent need of uniform regulation. Frankly, in determining which those fields are, the common market should not be the only (not even the primary) consideration. There are many other highly relevant political, economic and social concerns[32].

---

[28] See especially GERARD J.P. DE VRIES, 'Are The Principles Of European Contract Law Better Than Dutch Contract Law?' in: M.W. Hesselink, G.J.P. De Vries, *Principles of European Contract Law; Preadviezen uitgebracht voor de Vereniging voor Burgerlijk Recht*, Deventer 2001, p. 107 ff. See also DANNY BUSCH & EWOUD H. HONDIUS & HUGO J. VAN KOOTEN & HARRIET N. SCHELHAAS (GENERAL EDITOR) & WENDY M. SCHRAMA (eds.), *The Principles of European Contract Law and Dutch Law: A Commentary*, Nijmegen and The Hague, London, New York 2002.

[29] See www.sgecc.net.

[30] Compare BRIGITTA LURGER, *Grundfragen der Vereinheitlichung des Vertragsrechts in der Europäischen Union*, Wien, New York 2002, p. 16, 'Das niederländische Gesetzbuch ist am stärksten von allen europäischen Zivilgesetzbüchern von den neueren gesellschaftlichen Entwicklungen der letzten Jahrzehnte geprägt'.

[31] If, indeed, a national code can ever serve as a model for a European Civil Code. Explicitly in favour of a European Code of Contracts inspired by Book 4 of the Italian *codice civile* is GIUSEPPE GANDOLFI, 'Pour un code européen des contrats', *RTD Civ.* 1991, p. 707 ff.; GIUSEPPE GANDOLFI (eds.), *Code Européen des contrats - Avant-projet*, Milano 2001. However, the idea is explicitly rejected, and on good grounds, by BRIGITTA LURGER, *Grundfragen der Vereinheitlichung des Vertragsrechts in der Europäischen Union*, p. 16: 'Ein europäisches Zivilgesetzbuch sollte von vornherein aus europäischen und nicht aus nationalen Entstehungsbedingungen zehren können.'

[32] See further Chapter 5.

POLITICS

5

The Politics Of European Contract Law: Who Has An Interest In What Kind Of Contract Law For Europe?

I. Introduction

I COME to the debate on the future of European contract law as a Dutch scholar with (moderate) left-wing ideological sympathies. With many of my compatriots I share a, admittedly sometimes somewhat naïve, faith in international and European ideals and organisations. Like most legal scholars I have a particular interest in the structure of the law. And like most social-democrats I have limited faith in markets and a belief in the need to regulate them in order to achieve social aims. I am telling you this not because I think these facts could in themselves be of any interest to you, but because they may be relevant when appreciating what I am going to say.

The subject of this Chapter is: the political stakes in the European contract law debate[1]. In particular, I will focus on the question: who has an interest in what kind of European contract law? I will discuss three political dimensions

[1] On the politics of contract law see generally: DUNCAN KENNEDY, 'Form and Substance in Private Law Adjudication', 89 *Harv. L. Rev.* 1685, 1713-24 and DUNCAN KENNEDY, *A Critique of Adjudication {fin de siècle}*, Cambridge Massachusetts 1997. With a focus on European contract law see UGO MATTEI, 'The Issue of Civil Codification and Legal Scholarship: Biases, Strategies and Developments', 21 *Hastings Int'l & Comp. L. Rev.* (1998) 883; DANIELA CARUSO, 'The Missing View of the Cathedral: The Private Law Paradigm of European Legal Integration', 3 *European Law Journal* (1997), pp. 3-32; *supra* Chapter 3, Section VI; and the contributions to the special issue of the *European Review of Private Law* (2002:1) dedicated to the Amsterdam seminar on 'Critical Legal Theory and European Private Law': MARTIJN W. HESSELINK, 'Editorial - Special Issue on Critical Legal Theory and European Private Law', pp. 3-5; DUNCAN KENNEDY, 'The Political Stakes in "Merely Technical" Issues of Contract Law', pp. 7-28; UGO MATTEI & ANNA DI ROBILANT, 'The Art and Science of Critical Scholarship; Post Modernism and International Style in the Legal Architecture of Europe', pp. 29-59; PIERRE LEGRAND, 'On the Unbearable Localness of the Law: Academic Fallacies and Unseasonable Observations', pp. 61-76; THOMAS WILHELMSSON, 'Private Law in the EU: Harmonised or Fragmented Europeanisation?', pp. 77-94; ; EWAN MCKENDRICK, 'Traditional Concepts and Contemporary Values', pp. 95-109; C.W. MARIS VAN SANDELINGENAMBACHT, 'Legal Postism and the End of European Private Law', pp. 111-132.

of the European contract law debate: empowerment (II), national interests (III) and ideology (IV). At the end I will express my own preference (V).

II. Empowerment

The various possible outcomes of the present debate would have different consequences for the power which different (groups of) actors exercise with regard to contract law. This may frequently explain their position in the debate.

A. Academics

Academics specialise in rationality, objectivity, abstraction and system. They are therefore often critical of the present state European contract law is in[2]. Especially, many scholars lament the patchwork approach which the European Union has adopted with its directives, and many of them would be even prepared to abandon their national civil code in favour of a European code so as to restore order and system into private law. One of the alternative solutions suggested by the European Commission (further: EC) in its Communication (the second one), is the promotion of principles[3]: The European Commission could promote comparative law research aimed at finding common principles. This option has received a warm welcome from the academic world. Not only from those who would immediately benefit from such a course of action, i.e. the Lando Commission and the Von Bar Group[4], which have actually been drafting such principles[5], but also from other academics[6]. This is not surprising since with that option the future of European contract law would be largely in the hands of academics[7].

---

[2] See e.g. OLE LANDO & HUGH BEALE (eds.), *Principles of European Contract Law, Parts I and II*, The Hague 2000, p. xxii, and HEIN KÖTZ, 'Comparative Law in Germany Today', *RIDC* 1999, p. 753 ff. Compare PETER CHRISTIAN MÜLLER-GRAFF, 'EC Directives as a Means of Private Law Unification', in : A.S. Hartkamp et al. (eds.), *Towards a European Civil Code*, 2nd ed., pp. 71 ff., at p. 82, CHRISTIAN JOERGES, 'The Impact of European Integration on Private Law: Reductionist Perceptions, True Conflicts and a New Constitutional Perspective', *ELJ* 1997, pp. 378-406, DANIELA CARUSO, DANIELA CARUSO, 'The Missing View of the Cathedral', p. 14, OLIVIER REMIEN, 'Einheit, Mehrstufigheit und Flexibilität im europäischen Privat- und Wirtschaftsrecht', 62 *RabelsZ* (1998), p. 627 ff., p. 639, VINCENZO ZENO-ZENCOVICH, 'The "European Civil Code", European Legal Traditions and Neo-positivism', in: Guido Alpa, Emilio Nicola Buccico (eds.), *Il codice civile europeo; Materiali dei seminari 1999-2000*, Milano 2001, pp. 375 ff., at. p. 378, MARTIJN W. HESSELINK, *De redelijkheid en billijkheid in het Europese privaatrecht*, Deventer 1999, p 20, all with further references.

[3] Communication from the Commission to the Council and the European Parliament, COM(2001) 398 final (11.07.2001), No. 52.

[4] See for example the *Joint Response* that the Commission on European Contract Law and the Study Group on a European Civil Code sent to the European Commission in reply to its Communication (published in 10 *ERPL* 2002, pp. 183-248).

[5] See OLE LANDO & HUGH BEALE (eds.), *Principles of European Contract Law, Parts I and II.*

[6] Of course there is no unity among academics. This became very clear at the 1997 Scheveningen conference where every scholar promoted his own project. See the contributions published in *ERPL* 1997, especially MICHAEL JOACHIM BONELL, 'The Need and Possibilities of a Codified

Academics may also welcome the more further-reaching fourth suggested solution, i.e. some kind of formal enactment, possibly within a European Code of Contracts or even a European Civil Code. However, the prospect of handing the project over to politicians also worries them. Politicians are not experts in contract law, at least not to the extent that academics are, and politicians tend to compromise and enter into political deals which may seriously endanger the quality of the end-product[8].

B. Legislators

The legislator's claim to have a say in the future of European contract law is obviously based on its democratic authority, although in the case of the European legislator the democratic basis is rather slim. The European Parliament has called for a European civil code on several occasions, most recently in November 2001[9]. However, as everybody knows, the power of the European Parliament is still rather limited. The real political power in the European Union lies with the Council of Ministers and with the European Commission. The Council of Ministers tends to mainly follow national interests which I will come back to in a moment. What stake does the Commission have in the debate? From which option would the Commission gain most in terms of empowerment?

Clearly, for the Commission things only become interesting in the options which involve some kind of formal enactment (Options 3 and 4)[10]. Therefore,

---

European Contract Law', *ERPL* 1997, p. 505 ff., ULRICH DROBNIG, 'Scope and General Rules of a European Civil Code', *ERPL* 1997, p. 489 ff., WALTER VAN GERVEN, 'Coherence and National Laws; Is There a Legal Basis for a European Civil Code?', *ERPL* 1997, p. 465 ff., OLE LANDO, 'Why Codify the European Law of Contract?', *ERPL* 1997, p. 525 ff., BASIL S. MARKESINIS, 'Why a Code is Not the Best Way to Advance the Cause of European Legal Unity', *ERPL* 1997, p. 519 ff., UGO MATTEI, 'A Transaction Costs Approach to the European Code', *ERPL* 1997, p. 537 ff.

[7] This would restore the tradition in many European countries. Especially in Germany there is such a long-standing tradition from the drafting of the *BGB* through to the recent *Schuldrechtreform* (among the members of the *Kommission zur Überarbeitung des Schuldrechts* which presented its proposals in 1992 were Hein Kötz, Dieter Medicus, and Peter Schlechtriem). And in the Netherlands Meijers and most of his successors who drafted the 1992 Civil Code were academics. Also in Great Britain many statutes and law reforms are prepared by the Law Commissions, which also (but not exclusively) include academics (e.g. at this moment Hugh Beale, a prominent member of the Lando Commission and the Von Bar group). And in France many private law legislation in many areas, like family law (Carbonnier), traffic liability (Tunc) and product liability (Ghestin) has been prepared by academics. This tradition has been disturbed by recent activism in the field of contract law by the European Union, especially by its many directives.

[8] An example that is frequently referred to is the Vienna Sales Convention (United Nations Convention on Contracts for the International Sale of Goods) which contains many compromises, some of which even contradict each other. Compare EWOUD HONDIUS, 'Weens koop- en verdragenrecht', *WPNR* 6233 (1996), p. 567 f.

[9] Resolution of May 26th, 1989, OJEC No. C 158/401, Resolution of May 6th, 1994, OJEC No. C 205 (519), and Resolution of November 15th, 2001, COM(2001) 398 - C5-0471/2001 - 2001/2187 (COS).

[10] However, option 2 may be strategically preferable as far as the Commission is concerned. The

from the perspective of the EC the first option it mentions (leave everything to market forces) would not be any good. And clearly, for the EC the more extensive the field of action, the better. This may explain the broad definition which the EC gives in its Communication to contract law[11].

However, there may be a problem: why should the European Union be allowed to take action in the field of contract law? Do any of the European treaties give the European Commission the necessary power to interfere with contract law? The strategy which the EC has adopted is to focus on the internal market, which has always been the EC's trump card for empowerment. Contract law is a central institution of the market and the differences between the contract laws of the various member states amount to obstacles to the proper functioning of the common market. Therefore, if the European systems of contract law differ, and if this obstructs the market, then the EC should take action in order to remove these obstacles[12]. Another obstacle which the EC will have to deal with are existing doubts as to whether the EC is capable of carrying out this task. Especially the specific competence of civil servants with regard to (comparative) contract law has been doubted[13]. Are the best contract lawyers to be found in Brussels? This may explain the suggestion by the EC that academic 'experts' could carry out the preparatory work of establishing common principles which could provide a legitimate basis for the EC's actions.

Until now I have spoken of the EC as one monolithic player in the overall power game. However, within the EC internal struggles for power have been going on. Therefore, the Directorate-General for Health and Consumer Protection may be better off with a Consumer Code. A first step in that direction would be the enactment, for example by regulation, of a consolidated version of the *acquis communautaire* in the field of consumer law. This approach is indeed suggested by the EC as the third option in its communication. On the other hand, the option of integrating European

---

Commission would thus give a good impression of its faithfulness to the subsidiarity principle. And at a later stage they could propose to formally enact what will then in substance have become a common European contract law.

[11] In the view of the EC 'contract law' includes large parts of what is regarded in most European countries as the general law of obligations, tort law and property law (securities in movables). See Communication, No. 13.

[12] In a moment I will come back to the question whether the only imaginable function of contract law is to facilitate the smooth functioning of the Internal Market.

[13] VINCENZO ZENO-ZENCOVICH, 'The "European Civil Code", European Legal Traditions and Neo-positivism', p. 377-378: 'Legrand's doubts, expressed in a manner that could be even more forthright, as to the legal skills of the EU bureaucracy should be entirely supported. (...) with obvious exceptions, this group does not have at its disposal great legal skills. This is because of its background, its methods of recruitment, the cultural differences amongst its members, and the lack of a profound knowledge of the legal traditions of member states. (...) It is therefore perfectly justifiable to be severely critical of the EU legislation, both as regards its content and the mentality it expresses.'; PIERRE LEGRAND, PIERRE LEGRAND, 'On the Unbearable Localness of the Law', OLIVER REMIEN, 'Einheit, Mehrstufigheit und Flexibilität im europäischen Privat- und Wirtschaftsrecht', p. 646.

consumer law into a European code of contracts, risks jeopardising the strong grip on European contract law which this DG has had to date[14].

C. Courts

Courts are active in the business of resolving conflicts. That is, they apply the law. However, it has long been recognised in all European countries that in practice courts also play an important role in further developing the law. European law is ultimately developed by the European Court of Justice. The power which the ECJ currently yields would be immensely enhanced if it were also to be the final instance in all contract or even all private law cases in Europe, as a result of the enactment of either a Contracts Code or a Consumer Code or regulation (options 3 and 4)[15]. This would especially be the case if the code were to be as abstract, general and open-textured as the Principles of European Contract Law are[16]. These principles only provide starting points for decision making and give rise to many specific questions that courts would have to resolve. Therefore, if some degree of uniform application is aspired to, then the ECJ will have to play a very active role right from the very beginning. If, however, the interpretation of the Code were to be left entirely to national courts, as is the case for CISG, the uniforming effect would be much smaller. Therefore, it seems likely that the strongest empowerment effect of enacting a European Code of Contract Law would be very much in favour of the ECJ. It would not only become the ultimate authority in Europe in cases concerning contract law, but it would also be its task to further develop it[17].

D. Local Actors

Obviously, national academics, practitioners, courts and legislators are the ones who share a clear common interest in the first option mentioned in the EC's Communication: no EC action. In all the other options they would only lose power: they will either have to share or even completely have to give up the power which they have invested in. Today, scholars are the exclusive specialists with regard to their respective national laws. They do not have to fear any competition from foreigners. Even the opinion of the most eminent foreign scholar will not be regarded as a higher authority on Dutch law than a Dutch commentary. Similarly, Dutch practitioners share a monopoly in

[14] Consumer law is frequently referred to as the driving force of European contract law. However, there are also examples of directives in the field of contract law which do not apply to consumers. See e.g. Council Directive 86/653/EEC of 18 December 1986 on self-employed commercial agents (OJ L 31.12.1986, p. 17) and Directive 2000/35/EC of the European Parliament and the Council of 29 June 2000 on combating late payment in commercial transactions (OJ L 210, 8.8.2000, p. 35).

[15] The drawback of course would be the resulting tremendous workload.

[16] See *supra*, Chapter 3, Section V, A.

[17] In the case of preliminary rulings (art. 234 (former 177) EC) the ECJ's power is shared with the national courts.

advising their clients on Dutch law and in representing them in Dutch courts. If Dutch contract law were to be replaced by European contract law, this would be different. Dutch scholars and practitioners would have to compete with their colleagues from other member states. Of course, competition in itself would not necessarily render them worse off. On the contrary, they might even be able to increase their market share. However, that would require a significant new investment whereas the investment they have made so far in specific expertise in Dutch national law would become largely worthless. National courts of last instance would undergo a decline in status since in private (or contract) law cases they would no longer be the highest authority. Moreover, if the EU were to adopt a similar judiciary system to the US, then 'federal' cases would be administered by a network of European federal courts spread all over the Union which would also reduce the power of the lower national (i.e. non-'federal') courts. As to national legislators, they have never been very active in general contract law. Nevertheless, it is (at least formally) the national legislator who enacts civil codes[18] and law reforms[19]. In the case of the adoption of one of the courses of action suggested by the EC as the fourth option they would partially or completely lose that power with regard to contract law.

III. National Traditions

Of course, there are also important national interests at stake. All European countries are proud of their own national legal tradition. Austria has one of the oldest codes, the Netherlands has the newest. The French with their *Code civil* and the Germans with their *BGB* are each the godfather of powerful legal families. And England and Wales and Ireland share a tradition of their own which is characterised by a case to case approach instead of general solutions like a code. Therefore, if the European Commission were to enact a European contracts code it would find itself before *l'embarras du choix*. Which national system should be the model? The Italian code, says the Gandolfi Group[20]. None of them reposts the Lando Commission: we should adopt new concepts and new terminology[21]. However, it is of course neither possible nor indeed desirable to create a new European contract law that bares no similarity at all to the contract law of any of the member states (that would be somewhat similar to the buildings which figure on the Euro banknotes). Of course, it would be rather odd to leave a possible solution unused merely because is has been successfully adopted in one or more member states. Therefore, it seems much more appropriate to borrow from all the European systems[22]. However,

[18] See e.g. the global or partial recodifications in Italy (1942), Greece (1946), Portugal (1967), the Netherlands (1992) and Germany (2001).

[19] See, as a recent example, in England the Contracts (Rights of Third Parties) Act 1999.

[20] See GIUSEPPE GANDOLFI, 'Pour un code européen des contrats', *RTD Civ.* 1991, p. 707 ff.; GIUSEPPE GANDOLFI (ed.), *Code Européen des contrats - Avant-projet*, Milano 2001.

[21] PECL, Introduction, p. xxv.

[22] That is what the Lando Commission claims to have done. See for a cultural analysis of the

that raises the question of how much and what should be borrowed from which country. Any proposal for a European code of contracts is likely to be scrutinised for its cultural ingredients: is my national tradition sufficiently represented?

Some concerns have already been expressed[23]. Some scholars warn against German cultural imperialism[24]. Others point out that enacting a European code would effectively mean replacing in England and Wales and Ireland a minority tradition (common law[25]) with the tradition shared by the majority of EU member states (civil law)[26]. And still others see the risks of a north/south divide[27]. Clearly, this debate is merely a specific contract law variant of a general debate that European politicians have been only too familiar with.

IV. Ideology

I will address three ideological questions raised by the Commission's Communication: a) the functions of contract law; b) the ideological basis of contract law; c) the ideological implications of the structure of contract law. I will thereby mainly concentrate on the political distinction between the left (social-democrat) and the right (liberal, conservative) which for more than a century has been the main ideological opposition in most European countries[28].

A. Functions of Contract Law

What functions does contract law perform in our society? When reading the Commission's communication one would think that contract law has only one role to fulfil: to facilitate the proper functioning of the Internal Market. Contracts and contract law are crucial market institutions which should ensure efficient exchange. The ideology underlying the Communication is clearly a market ideology. The only reason which it suggests for possible EC activity is

---

PECL *supra*, Chapter 3, Section VII.

[23] See generally HUGH COLLINS, 'European Private Law and Cultural Identity of States', *European Review of Private Law*, 1995, pp. 353-365, and TONY WEIR, 'Die Sprachen des europäischen Rechts; Eine skeptische Betrachtung', *ZeuP* 1995, p. 368 ff.

[24] UGO MATTEI, 'The Issue of Civil Codification and Legal Scholarship: Biases, Strategies and Developments', 21 *Hastings Int'l & Comp. L. Rev.* 883; P.G. MONATERI, 'Black Gaius; A Quest for the Multicultural Origins of the "Western Legal Tradition"', 51 *Hastings Law Journal* (2000), 479-555.

[25] In Europe; outside Europe many countries share the common law tradition including the U.S., Canada, Australia and New Zealand.

[26] See especially PIERRE LEGRAND, 'Against a European Civil Code', 60 *MLR* (1997), pp. 44-62.

[27] See *supra*, Chapter 2 Section IV, H, 4, and Chapter 4, V.

[28] The idea of a third way merely begs the question: where does the third way exactly lie between the path of autonomy and the route of solidarity? There is no right answer; choices (including choices for compromises) have to be made. See the scholars mentioned in footnote 1. On the future of the political distinction between the left and the right see NORBERTO BOBBIO, *Destra e sinistra; Ragioni e significati di una distinzione politica*, Rome 1999; contrast RONALD DWORKIN, *Sovereign Virtue; The Theory and Practice of Equality*, Cambridge Massachusetts and London 2000.

the possible market impediments stemming from differences between the contact laws of the member states and from transaction costs resulting from a lack of information with regard to the presence of such differences. The underlying assumption seems to be, on the one hand, that if there are no important divergences or if the market can function with such divergences, then the EC should not interfere, whereas, on the other hand, the mere fact that divergent national rules impede the Internal Market may be a sufficient reason for an intervention of some kind by the EC. Such action would obviously consist of removing the impediment.

However, obstructing the proper functioning of the common market is not the only role these diverging rules of contract law (especially the mandatory ones) play. Most rules other than the general principles of freedom of contract and the binding force of promises protect one party against the other in order to avoid what is perceived as injustice. Therefore, unless EC action would categorically consist of adopting the highest standard of protection, replacing national laws by European law would not only lead to a gain (enhancing the functioning of the market), but would also entail a loss (at least in the perception of those who benefit from the diverging national rule): a loss of protection for those groups of citizens who are currently protected by this diverging rule.

B. *The Ideological Basis of Contract Law: Autonomy and Solidarity*

Clearly, such a market-oriented approach to contract law which is based on an ideological choice which is closely related to classical liberal *laissez-faire* ideology, also has important consequences for the question of what the uniform law should look like. If the only or the main function of contract law is to facilitate efficient exchange, then the best contract law is clearly a contract law that is based on freedom of contract[29] and which places as few limits as possible on the enforceability of contracts. At best, we would need some uniform mandatory rules in order to remedy market deficiencies (especially information deficiencies), and some default rules in order to reduce transaction costs.

However, if it is accepted that contract law also performs other functions, e.g. distributionist and other social functions, then the picture becomes completely different. The history of contract law in the 20th century shows that there is no reason to have such excessive confidence in the market. If the case law on contracts has demonstrated one thing, then it is that many contracting parties (not only consumers) are not 'rational agents' as most market models assume. Abundant European case law shows that players on the market frequently make decisions that do not best serve their interests, even if they have been given all the relevant information they need in order to make a 'rational' decision. Therefore, since the beginning of the last century,

[29] See explicitly the Communication, no. 27.

the courts have in many cases protected such parties. In most European countries the courts have felt the need to impose all kinds of duties and to place innumerable limits on (the exercise of) all kinds of rights. They did so frequently in the guise of mystifying doctrines like good faith and abuse of right which formally uphold the principle of freedom of contract[30]. The courts in particular have imposed many altruistic duties to take the interests of the other party into account (duties of care, duties to co-operate, duties to inform, duties of loyalty) which do not fit well in a market model which is based on self-reliance. It is important to note that most of these protective interventions were not limited to consumers and other categories of presumed weaker parties. On the contrary, in many countries they were developed in highly commercial settings, where, however, one party had ended up in serious trouble and where the courts thought it to be inappropriate under the circumstances to stick to the principles of the freedom and the binding force of contract. These court interventions are usually inspired by social interventionist and other paternalistic concerns. Thus, the protection of parties that have taken wrong decisions, even while having all the relevant information, is a fully legitimate concern of contract law which is inspired by social-democrat and christian-democrat ideology.

A 19th century-like code, exclusively or primarily based on the principle of party autonomy, would be wholly unacceptable from a social-democrat political perspective. It would bring us back to a *laissez-faire* conception of the economy which the courts and the legislators in all European countries successfully overcame during the course of the 20th century. For the 21st century we need a Code which contains these important social achievements[31]. Today, one can no longer claim that private law is essentially based on autonomy and tuck all the so-called exceptions away in a correction device like good faith or abuse of right. A European code of general contract law should be based on both (conflicting) principles which underlie contemporary politics and private law: autonomy and solidarity.

---

[30] See *supra*, Chapter 7, and (in Dutch) my *De redelijkheid en billijkheid in het Europese privaatrecht*, Deventer 1999, where I examine nearly a thousand cases from various European jurisdictions in which the courts 'apply the doctrine of good faith'.

[31] In the same sense THOMAS WILHELMSSON, *Social Contract Law and European Integration*, Dartmouth 1995; THOMAS WILHELMSSON, 'Private Law in the EU: Harmonised or Fragmented Europeanisation?'; BRIGITTA LURGER, *Vertragliche Solidarität, Entwicklungschancen für das allgemeine Vertragsrecht in Österreich und in der Europäischen Union*, Baden-Baden 1998; BRIGITTA LURGER, *Grundfragen der Vereinheitlichung des Vertragsrechts in der Europäischen Union*, Wien, New York 2002; JAN B.M. VRANKEN, 'Over partijautonomie, contractsvrijheid en de grondslag van gebondenheid in het verbintenissenrecht' in: J.M. Barendrecht, M.A.B. Chao-Duivis and H.A.W. Vermeulen (eds.), *Beginselen van contractenrecht: Opstellen aangeboden aan B.W.M. Nieskens-Isphording*, Deventer 2000; CHRISTOPHE JAMIN, 'Plaidoyer pour le solidarisme contractuel', in: Gilles Goubeaux et al. (eds.), *Études offertes à Jacques Ghestin; Le contrat au début du XXIe siècle*, Paris 2001; GUIDO ALPA, *Trattato di diritto civile, I Storia, fonti, interpretazione*, Milano 2000, p. 604 ff.

C. *'General Contract Law' and Regulation*

For the same reason a European code which would merely contain non-mandatory general contract law would (at least from a (moderate) left-wing perspective) itself be politically unacceptable. A European code of contracts should not merely contain rules that parties can freely deviate from (party autonomy) but also those rules which protect consumers, tenants, workers, small businesses et cetera, which mandatorily apply to their transactions. A code which only contains general contract law without including protective regulation would seem excessively liberal and would really be of little use to most European citizens. Or, to put it in more explicitly political terms: from a left-wing perspective most of the important law (most of the political achievements in the 20th century) would be missing. As far as protective rules of an EU origin are concerned, the third option mentioned by the EC would be a logical first step. Annex III to the Communication provides an interesting starting point. A next step might be the extension of the field of application of some of these rules.

V. Final Remarks

When discussing the political agendas of the participants to the debate on the future of European contract law, I do not mean to accuse anybody of doing anything indecent. There is nothing indecent (at least in my view) in standing up for one's own interests, values and ideologies, especially if one does so with transparency. I only want to point out that these interests, values and ideologies do not necessarily coincide. Rather, they are frequently diametrically opposed. In other words, the questions which are on the table are far from being politically neutral, and there are many stakeholders in the debate. Moreover, there is no 'right answer' to these questions: the future of European contract law will depend on political choices.

What choice would I make? From what I have said at the beginning you will probably have guessed. As an European idealist I believe in some benefits from European unity, although I fully appreciate the value of plurality which, if anything, has been the main characteristic of Europe. Therefore, I would favour a European code or restatement with a sufficiently open and flexible structure in order to take all these varying interests and ideologies into account. It should provide a framework for debate, a common European language. Moreover, I would only favour European action if it would mean social progress.

Therefore, in terms of the communication, today I would favour a combination of the second, third and fourth approaches: on the one hand, a consolidated version of European regulation ('mandatory law'), especially in the field of consumer law, as a firm basis for the further development of harmonised protective regulation in other fields (protection of small businesses, patients, employees et cetera), combined with, or followed by, a set of principles of European contract law, on the other hand, provided that the latter are truly based on both (contradicting) ideas underlying contemporary contract law in Europe, i.e. autonomy and solidarity[32].

This could lead to a comprehensive European regulation of consumer law[33], and later also, for example, the law of distribution or labour law. The most appropriate form would probably be regulations rather than directives. Those common regulations should be brought together, as far as possible, in a frequently updated consolidated version in order to promote normative coherence. Where policies can be generalised, a general part of European contract law could be developed (compare Annex III to the Commission's Communication on European Contract Law), which could also be inspired by the efforts undertaken by scholars (especially the Principles of European Contract Law). Such a piecemeal approach would be in line with the subsidiarity principle, with the policy which the European Commission has adopted so far (although admittedly the approach should be more coherent than it has been so far; in this respect the recent suggestion for a framework directive is a step in the right direction[34]), and with the tradition of European integration in general. Admittedly, for that purpose the new European Constitution should provide a much larger range of policies in which the Union can be active, rather than the current limited focus on the common market which is also wholly inappropriate for private law, which serves many other purposes than facilitating an efficient common market[35].

[32] The PECL provide a good starting point. They are more social than most European codes (although case law in many countries is more social). However, adding the principle of solidarity to the principle of freedom of contract in art. 1:102 PECL would be indispensable. See further *supra*, Chapter 3, Section VI.

[33] See also the Commission's Green Paper on European Union Consumer Protection COM (2001) 531, October 2001.

[34] See the Commission's Green Paper on Consumer Protection.

[35] On another constitutional dimension (fundamental rights), see *infra*, Chapter 6.

Rights

6

The Horizontal Effect of Social Rights in European Contract Law

I. Introduction

THE SUBJECT of this Chapter is the horizontal effect of 'social rights' in European contract law. I will address this subject in the following way. First, I will make a few general remarks on European contract law (II). Then, I will briefly discuss the general question whether and how fundamental rights may have a horizontal effect (III). Subsequently, I will address horizontal effects specifically in contract cases (IV), after which I will come to my main topic: the role that social rights may play in contract cases (V). Finally, I will conclude with some remarks on the politics of rights (VI).

II. European Contract Law

Today, many European legal scholars are involved in a debate on the future of contract law in Europe. This debate has been ongoing for some ten years, but it has gained specific momentum since last summer when the European Commission published a Communication on the future of European Contract Law[1]. In that Communication the Commission considers four possible courses of action: 1) to take no action, 2) to promote comparative law research aimed at finding common principles, 3) to enact a consolidated version of the *acquis communautaire*, especially in the area of consumer law[2], 4) to enact a European code of contracts, either as a an optional or as a mandatory code.

In each of these options fundamental rights can be of great relevance. They can be especially so in two ways. First, during the stage of drafting either a formally binding (classical) code or 'soft law' device like 'principles' they may prove to be an important source of normative inspiration. Indeed, in the European context which shows an overwhelming cultural diversity both between the various Member States and within them (multi-cultural societies), and in an age which is characterised in many Member States by ongoing

[1] Communication from the Commission to the Council and the European Parliament, COM(2001) 398 final (11.07.2001), No. 52. See *supra*, Chapter 5.

[2] See also the Green Paper on European Union Consumer Protection COM (2001) 531, October 2001.

individualisation and fragmentation of society (secularisation, post-ideology after the end of the Cold War, post-modernism), it seems to make sense to base a common European private law on those common values which are generally recognised throughout the European Union[3].

Of special interest in this respect is the recent Charter of Fundamental Rights of the European Union which was adopted in Nice in December 2000[4]. The values contained in that Charter may be regarded as an interesting statement of common values of the European Union which could be used as a basis for a European Civil Code[5]. The Preamble to the Charter states[6]: 'Conscious of its spiritual and moral heritage, the Union is founded on the indivisible, universal values of human dignity, freedom, equality and solidarity.' The Charter itself dedicates a Chapter - containing rights, freedoms and principles - to each of these values[7].

However, European fundamental rights cannot only serve as a source of inspiration for the drafters of a European Civil Code or of Principles of European Contract Law[8]. Once such a code is formally enacted fundamental rights will probably continue to be highly relevant to private law. That brings

---

[3] Thus the adoption of a common set of European human rights would lead to unity on a community level. However, they may also have a disruptive effect on a national level where a European right (or its level of protection, or - in the case of horizontal effect - its balancing against a conflicting right of another citizen) would happen to conflict with national constitutional arrangements within a Member State, which that particular Member State may regard as a fundamental societal choice and as an important part of its national identity. See on this problem J.H.H. WEILER, *The Constitution of Europe; "Do the New Clothes Have an Emperor?" and Other Essays on European Integration*, Cambridge 1999, p. 102 ff.

[4] See for the full text with comments http://ue.eu.int/df/default.asp. See also LUIGI FERRARI BRAVO & FRANCESCO M. DI MAJO & ALFREDO RIZZO, *Carta dei diritti fondamentali dell'Unione europea commentata con la giurisprudenza della Corte di giustizia CE e della Corte europea dei diritti dell'uomo e con i documenti rilevanti*, Milano 2001. The Charter is generally regarded as being non-binding because it has not been formally enacted as such. However, see *Corte d'appello di Roma*, 11 April 2002, which applied (among other provisions) art. 47 of the Charter (Right to an Effective Remedy and to a Fair Trial) in order to declare an Act of Parliament inapplicable, after having considered that 'la Carta dei diritti, anche se non ancora inserita nei trattati, è ormai considerata pienamente operante come punto di riferimento essenziale non solo per l'attività delle istituzioni comunitarie, ma anche per l'attività interpretativa dei giudici europei, tanto che è costantemente richiamata negli atti degli organi europei, ma anche invocata più volte nelle conclusioni dell'avvocato generale nei giudizi dinanzi alla Corte di giustizia europea'. The Court of First Instance has referred to the Charter (arts. 41(1) and 47) in its judgements of 30 January 2002 (Case T-54/99, max.mobil Telekommunikation Service GmbH) and of 3 May 2002 (Case T-177/01, Jégo-Quéré et Cie SA).

[5] See VINCENZO ZENO-ZENCOVICH, 'Le basi costituzionali di un diritto privato europeo' (forthcoming; presented at the conference *Diritti fondamentali e formazione del diritto privato europeo* in Rome on June 28th, 2002).

[6] P. 11.

[7] Dignity (Chapter 1), Freedom (Chapter 2), Equality (Chapter 3), Solidarity (Chapter 4), Citizens' Rights (Chapter 5), and Justice (Chapter 6).

[8] The Lando Commission does not explicitly state that it has been inspired by European or national fundamental rights, like e.g. the ECHR or the ESC. However, it should be noted that it could not have taken the Nice Charter into account since the PECL were published before the enactment of the Charter. See OLE LANDO, HUGH BEALE (eds.), *Principles of European Contract Law, Parts I and II, Prepared by The Commission on European Contract Law*, The Hague 2000.

us to the second way in which fundamental right can be of relevance for European contract law: they may have a horizontal effect.

III. The Horizontal Effect of Fundamental Rights

The issue of horizontal effect (*Drittwirkung*) is controversial. Initially, fundamental rights were perceived as a way to protect individual citizens against the State (vertical relationship). However, in recent decades it has become increasingly clear that not only the State but also private parties may endanger the peaceful enjoyment of fundamental rights. Sometimes, for example in the case of powerful private companies, the risk is even greater. An Italian example may illustrate this.

> In this case, a private person, Mr. Pedrazzoli, had a contract for life insurance with an insurance company called Mediolanum Vita. When the owner of that company, Mr. Silvio Berlusconi, decided to enter politics he founded his own political party Forza Italia. The process of founding this party, which took only two months, was so efficient partly because it was organised with the help of the acquisition network of the insurance company Mediolanum Vita.
>
> Mr. Pedrazzoli, who did not share Mr. Berlusconi's political views, wanted to withdraw from the contract but the company indicated that according to the contract he would then lose all the premiums he had already paid.
>
> Then he invoked his freedom of association which is protected by article 18 of the Italian Constitution. He argued that as a result of Mediolanum's policy he was now effectively contributing to the foundation of a political party that he did not want to be a part of and that, as a result of the contested clause, he was effectively barred from withdrawing from the contract. The case was decided in 1994 by the *Tribunale di Milano* which ruled in his favour. The court held that upholding the clause would lead to a violation of his freedom of association and that therefore invoking the clause against him would be contrary to good faith[9].

This case clearly shows that not only the State but also private parties may endanger the enjoyment of fundamental rights. Cases like this have raised the question in many European countries whether some or even all fundamental rights should not also have a horizontal effect, i.e. an effect between the citizens themselves[10].

---

[9] *Trib. Milano*, 30 March 1994, *Foro it.* 1994, I, 1572.

[10] For the ECHR see P. VAN DIJK & G.J.H. VAN HOOF, *Theory and Practice of the European Convention on Human Rights*, 3rd ed., The Hague, London and Boston 1998, p. 24: 'Precisely on account of the fundamental character of these rights it is difficult to appreciate why they should deserve protection in relation to the public authorities, but not in relation to private parties.' See

In many European countries such a horizontal effect has indeed been accepted[11], both as regards constitutional rights[12] and rights which derive from international treaties, especially the European Convention on Human Rights and the International Covenant on Civil and Political Rights[13]. However, it is still controversial in many countries exactly how this effect should operate, directly or indirectly. In the former case a citizen has, in his action against another citizen, a claim or a defence which is directly based on the Constitution. In the latter situation, the claim or defence is based on a provision in the Civil Code, e.g. on a provision for liability in tort cases or on a general good faith clause in contract cases, which is interpreted (*Konkretisierung*) in the light of the Constitution.

The main arguments in favour of direct horizontal effect are: that it would provide the most effective protection of fundamental rights, and that if a right is fundamental, it should not make any difference, in principle, whether it has been violated by the State or by a private party.

However, many arguments have been raised against direct horizontal effect. First, it has been argued that, whereas in vertical relationships only one

---

also JEAN-PIERRE MARGUÉNAUD, *CEDH et droit privé; L'influence de la jurisprudence de la Cour des droits de l'homme sur le droit privé français*, Paris 2001, p. 75 ff.

[11] It is generally recognised that if the State operates 'in private law' or 'as a private party' this still remains a case of vertical (and therefore direct) effect. See e.g. L. Prakke & J.L. de Reede & G.J.M. van Wissen, *Van der Pot Donner Handboek van het Nederlandse staatsrecht*, 14th ed., Deventer 2001, p. 247; HELMUT HEINRICHS, in: *Palandt Bürgerliches Gesetzbuch*, 61st ed., München 2002, § 242, no. 11.

[12] The way in which constitutional review is organised differs considerably among the various European jurisdictions. For example, in France only the *Conseil constitutionnel* is allowed to review the constitutionality of Acts of Parliament and only before their enactment and in an abstract way (no right of complaint for individual citizens; see MARC FRANGI, *Constitution et droit privé; les droits individuels et les droits économiques*, Aix-en-Provence and Paris 1992) whereas in Great Britain and the Netherlands no court is allowed to declare a statute unconstitutional. See for an overview CHRISTIAN VON BAR, *Gemeineuropäisches Deliktsrecht*, München 1996, Vol. I, nos. 562-564.

[13] In the Netherlands the courts are prohibited from reviewing the constitutionality of Acts of Parliament (art. 120 Constitution). Since the Netherlands does not have a Constitutional Court either, the legislature itself is the sole 'judge' of the constitutionality of its own legislation. As a result, the Dutch litigants and courts have taken a particular interest in international treaties, especially the ECHR, since, as a consequence of the monistic system (art. 93 Constitution), self-executing provisions in such treaties have direct effect. See further ARTHUR S. HARTKAMP, 'On European Freedoms and National Mandatory Rules: The Dutch Judiciary and the European Convention on Human Rights', 8 *ERPL* (2000), p. 111-124. See also France where the direct horizontal effect of the ECHR is uncontroversial (see ANNE DEBET, *L'influence de la Convention européenne des droits de l'homme sur le droit civil*, Paris 2002, p. 79: 'En France, l'application horizontale de a Convention n'a pas suscité de controverse'); admittedly the number of applications is still rather limited (see ANNE DEBET, *L'influence de la Convention européenne des droits de l'homme sur le droit civil*, p. 117: 'une source de droit civil négligée', who counts 105 cases until 2001 (p. 126)), but the ECHR is expected to play an important role in the future development of French private law (see ANNE DEBET, *L'influence de la Convention européenne des droits de l'homme sur le droit civil*, p. 156). A similar development may take place in Great Britain now that the Human Rights Act 1998 has entered into force. See HUGH BEALE & NICOLA PITTAM, 'The Impact of the Human Rights Act 1998 on English Tort and Contract Law', in Daniel Friedmann, Daphne Barak-Erez, *Human Rights in Private Law*, Oxford 2001, pp. 131-159.

party may have a fundamental right (since the State has no rights against citizens), in horizontal situations both parties frequently have conflicting rights, and that these rights must be balanced, which would make any direct effect impracticable. Secondly, it is argued that if constitutional rights would have direct effect in private law cases, this would raise much of private law to a constitutional level because not only the norm but also the remedies would gain a constitutional status, which is considered to be undesirable. Finally, it is argued that private law is an autonomous branch of the law which has its own internal logic and is based on its own considerations of fairness.

The question has been much debated in many countries, especially in Germany. There, it has now been established that fundamental rights may have a horizontal effect, but only an indirect one, by way of the general clauses[14]. It is held that, although fundamental rights have a direct effect on private law, they only bind the legislator and the courts; individual citizens are not addressed by them. This means that the legislator and the courts are not allowed to make or develop private law rules that violate constitutional rights. However, a citizen cannot invoke a constitutional right directly against another citizen. In particular, it cannot invoke a fundamental right as a defence against a claim which is based on a rule of private law, e.g. a contractual claim or a claim in tort. The only thing a private citizen can do is to invoke one of the general clauses, especially good faith (*Treu und Glauben* (242 *BGB*) *bona fides*) and good morals (*gute Sitten* (138 *BGB*, 826 *BGB*), *boni mores*).

The same or similar solutions have been adopted in many other European countries[15], including Italy. Indeed, in the a example I gave a moment ago we saw that the freedom of association was protected by way of the general good faith clause[16].

---

[14] See BVerfG 7, 198 (*Lüth Urteil*) (15 January 1958); CLAUS-WILHELM CANARIS, *Grundrechte und Privatrecht*, Berlin, New York 1999; MANFRED WOLF, in: *Soergel Bürgerliches Gesetzbuch mit Einführungsgesetz und Nebengesetzen* (1999), Vor § 145, 47.

[15] Since horizontal effect is a relatively new issue most Constitutions and international treaties are themselves silent on the matter. In the parliamentary debate before the reform of the Constitution in the Netherlands in 1983 the issue was indeed addressed, but it was explicitly left to the courts to be further developed. For the ECHR see P. VAN DIJK & G.J.H. VAN HOOF, *Theory and Practice of the European Convention on Human Rights*, p. 24.

[16] See further for Italy STEFANO RODOTÀ, *Le fonti di integrazione del contratto*, Milano 1969, pp. 167 ff.; GUIDO ALPA, *L'arte di giudicare*, Roma 1996, p. 89 ff.; ADOLFO DI MAJO, *Delle Obbligazioni in Generale, artt. 1173-1176*, in: *Commentario del codice civile Scialoja-Branca*, Bologna/Roma 1988, pp. 65, 289 (however, see also p. 342); GIORGIO CIAN & ALBERTO TRABUCCHI, *Commentario breve al codice civile*, 5th ed., Padova, 1997, art. 1175, II, 2; MICHELE CANTILLO, *Le Obbligazioni*, in: *Giurisprudenza sistematica di diritto civile e commerciale*, Torino 1992, I, pp. 203-282. See also PIETRO RESCIGNO, *Manuale di diritto privato*, 2000, p. 36. Sceptical RODOLFO SACCO & GIORGIO DE NOVA, *Il contratto*, in: *Trattato di diritto civile*, Torino 1993, I, p. 416. However, in other cases outside contract law (e.g. the law of persons), direct horizontal effect is accepted. See especially the abundant case law on personality rights. Compare GUIDO ALPA, *Trattato di diritto civile, I Storia, fonti, interpretazione*, p. 521 ff. Similarly, neither the Dutch constitutional legislator (upon the occasion of the Constitutional reform in 1983) nor the Dutch courts are very dogmatic with regard to the issue of direct or indirect effect; they adopt a more

IV. Horizontal Effects in Contract Cases

If a European Code of Contracts were to be enacted what would its relationship be to fundamental rights? A variety of sets of rights would be of relevance including the ones contained in the national Constitutions, the European Convention on Human Rights, the European Social Charter, the EC Treaty which contains a few fundamental rights (e.g. property, equality), the UN Conventions and, probably at that time, the European Constitution which will undoubtedly contain a chapter on fundamental rights[17], probably quite similar to the Nice Charter[18].

The Nice Charter contains a large number of provisions which may be of direct relevance for relationships between citizens. A hint as to its horizontal effect is to be found in the preamble[19]: 'Enjoyment of these rights entails *responsibilities and duties with regard to other persons* (...)'. However, it remains unclear whether 'entails' is meant to refer to a direct or an indirect effect.

There are many examples of the horizontal effect of fundamental rights in contract law from various European jurisdictions[20]. The horizontal effects which are recognised are usually indirect, by way of one of the general clauses[21]. The general clauses which are most frequently used in contract law are the ones on good morals[22] and on good faith[23].

---

pragmatic (and inconsistent) approach. See TK 1975-1976 13872 no. 3, p. 16-17. Compare ARTHUR S. HARTKAMP, 'On European Freedoms and National Mandatory Rules', p. 119 and MARTIJN VAN EMPEL & MARIANNE DE JONG, 'Constitution, International Treaties, Contracts and Torts', in: EWOUD HONDIUS & CARLA JOUSTRA (eds.), *Netherlands Reports to the Sixteenth International Congress of Comparative Law*, Antwerp, Oxford, New York, 2002, pp. 283-304, on p. 294: 'No coherent conclusions be drawn so far'.

[17] See on its progress http://european-convention.eu.int.

[18] This brings us to the issue of multi-level governance. I will not develop this any further here. See *infra*, Chapter 8, Section V. See on European private law and multi-level governance and on the constitutionalisation of European private law especially CHRISTIAN JOERGES, 'The Impact of European Integration on Private Law: Reductionist Perceptions, True Conflicts and a New Constitutional Perspective', *ELJ* 1997, pp. 378-406.

[19] P. 12 (emphasis added).

[20] For a recent overview in the Netherlands see ARTHUR S. HARTKAMP, 'On European Freedoms and National Mandatory Rules', and MARTIJN VAN EMPEL & MARIANNE DE JONG, 'Constitution, International Treaties, Contracts and Torts'. It is not easy today to predict the likely impact of the Human Rights Act 998 on the law of contract in England and Wales. HUGH BEALE & NICOLA PITTAM, 'The Impact of the Human Rights Act 1998 on English Tort and Contract Law', p. 159, conclude that it seems likely that there will be some "weak horizontal" effect, in that the courts will be influenced by human rights thinking in developing the common law. See also the Lord Chancellor, HL Debs., 3 Nov. 1997, vol. 582, cols. 1231-2 (quoted by HUGH BEALE & NICOLA PITTAM on p. 136): '[the courts] may have regard to the Convention in developing the common law'.

[21] However, there are also examples of direct horizontal effect. For example, in France the *Cour de Cassation* has accepted that art. 8 ECHR (family life) may have a direct horizontal effect on the enforceability of a contractual clause in a lease which limited the tenants right to take his relatives into his house: 'les clauses d'un bail d'habitation ne peuvent, en vertu de l'article 8-1 de la Convention de sauvegarde des droits de l'homme et des libertés fondamentales, avoir pour effet de priver le preneur de la possibilité d'héberger ses proches' (*Civ. III*, 6 March 1996, *JCP* 1997,

> A clear example is the German case where a landlord refused his tenant the right to install a satellite t.v. dish on the roof. The tenant and his family, who had Turkish nationality, wanted to receive Turkish television programmes, which could not be received by using the antenna which was available in the building as this could only receive five German channels. The German Constitutional Court held that article 5 of the German Constitution, which protects the freedom of speech including the freedom to receive information, has a horizontal effect on the contractual relationship between a landlord and a tenant, by way of the general obligation of the landlord (§ 536 *BGB*) and the good faith clause (§ 242 *BGB*)[24]. Therefore, since the tenant was dependant on a satellite t.v. dish for receiving the information he wished, the landlord was under an obligation to provide permission to install one[25].

Other rights which have been granted horizontal effect in contract cases include the right to human dignity[26], the general personality right[27], the right to equality[28] and the freedom of conscience[29]. It is frequently said by

II, 22764, note Nguyen Van Tong ; *JCP* 1996, I, 3958, no. 1, obs. Jamin ; *D.* 1997, 167, note Lamy ; *RTD civ.* 1996, 580, obs. Hauser ; RTD civ. 1996, 897, obs. Mestre).

[22] E.g. § 138 *BGB*. See VINCENT VAN DEN BRINK, *De rechtshandeling in strijd met de goede zeden*, The Hague 2002, pp. 38 ff.

[23] In Germany e.g. §§ 137 *BGB*, 242 *BGB*, 9 *AGBG*. See e.g. HELMUT HEINRICHS, in: *Palandt Bürgerliches Gesetzbuch*, § 242, no. 7; MANFRED WOLF, in: Manfred Wolf & Norbert Horn & Walter F. Lindacher, *AGB-Gesetz Kommentar*, München 1999, § 9, 113 ('Eingangstor für die mittelbare Drittwirkung der Grundrechte im Privatrecht'). In the Netherlands e.g. arts. 3:40; 6:2, 6:162, 6:248. Compare ARTHUR S. HARTKAMP, 'On European Freedoms and National Mandatory Rules', p. 117; VINCENT VAN DEN BRINK, *De rechtshandeling in strijd met de goede zeden*, pp. 38 ff.; MARTIJN VAN EMPEL & MARIANNE DE JONG, 'Constitution, International Treaties, Contracts and Torts'.

[24] BVerfGE 90, 27 (9 February 1994).

[25] As said above, in horizontal relationships there is frequently a clash of rights. The same happened in this case, where the landlord invoked his property right (art. 14, Section 1 *GG*) which allowed him to maintain the aesthetic integrity of the building. However, in the view of the *BVerfG*, in the specific circumstances of the present case the tenant's right to be informed had to prevail.

[26] Art. 1 *GG*. See HERBERT ROTH, in: *Münchener Kommentar zum Bürgerlichen Gesetzbuch*, 4th ed., München 2001, § 242, no. 54.

[27] See generally GIORGIO RESTA, 'Diritti della personalità e limiti dea libertà contrattuale nell'evoluzione del diritto europeo' (forthcoming; presented at the conference *Diritti fondamentali e formazione del diritto privato europeo* in Rome on June 28th, 2002.) In Germany art. 2 *GG*. Compare HERBERT ROTH, in: *Münchener Kommentar*, § 242, no. 54. In the Netherlands a general personality right was originally unknown as such. Then it was developed by the civil courts, in HR, 15 April 1994, *NJ* 1994, 608 and HR, 1 July 1997, *NJ* 1997, 685. The latter was a contract case: [...]. See on this 'judge-made fundamental right' ARTHUR S. HARTKAMP, 'On European Freedoms and National Mandatory Rules', p. 123.

[28] Art. 3 *GG*. See HELMUT HEINRICHS, in: *Palandt Bürgerliches Gesetzbuch*, § 242, no. 10; HERBERT ROTH, in: *Münchener Kommentar*, § 242, no. 56.

[29] Art. 4 *GG*. See HELMUT HEINRICHS, in: *Palandt Bürgerliches Gesetzbuch*, § 242, no. 9;

commentators that, in principle, all constitutional rights could have an indirect horizontal effect by way of the general good faith clause[30]. They may thus provide the basis for a further 'constitutionalisation' of European contract law[31].

V. Social Rights in Contract Cases

Not only are the so-called freedom rights, which are frequently referred to as 'classical', given an indirect horizontal effect, but in many countries also the same is also true for social rights, which by now may frankly be regarded as equally classical.

In Italy, for example, article 2 of the Constitution guarantees social solidarity[32]. The article says: 'La Repubblica (...) richiede l'adempimento dei doveri inderogabili di solidarietà politica, economica e sociale.' It has been accepted by the Italian courts that this article has indirect horizontal effect. For example, in 1994 the *Corte di Cassazione* held that the obligation of solidarity determines the content, effects, interpretation and performance of contracts by way of the general good faith clauses[33].

In Germany it is generally accepted that the *Sozialstaatsklausel* (articles 20 and 28 *GG*)[34] is the normative basis for controlling the content of standard

---

HERBERT ROTH, in: *Münchener Kommentar*, § 242, no. 54.

[30] See e.g. HELMUT HEINRICHS, in: *Palandt Bürgerliches Gesetzbuch*, § 242, no. 12.

[31] On the 'constitutionalisation of private law' see BASIL MARKESINIS, 'Comparative Law - A Subject in Search of an Audience, 53 *MLR* (1990), pp. 1-21, on p. 10, on the constitutionalisation of European tort law see CHRISTIAN VON BAR, *Gemeineuropäisches Deliktsrecht*, nos. 553 ff. (see p. 551: 'Denn mehr und mehr wird das Deliktsrecht im heutigen Europa als eine Form der Konkretisierung der verfassungsrechtlich verbürgten Freiheitsrechte begriffen'), and GUIDO ALPA, *Trattato di diritto civile, I Storia, fonti, interpretazione*, who dedicates the first Section of the chapter on the sources of private law to 'La Costituzione e la costituzionalizzazione del diritto civile'.

[32] See on the history, the meaning and the importance (p. 604: 'Nella Còstituzione italiana del 1947-1948 la solidarietà è considerata un valore forte') of the concept of solidarity GUIDO ALPA, ALPA, *Trattato di diritto civile, I Storia, fonti, interpretazione*, p. 604 ff.

[33] *Cass.*, 20 April 1994, no. 3775, *Corr. giur.* 1994, p. 566, note Carbone: 'che l'ossequio alla legalità formale non si traduca in sacrificio della giustizia sostanziale e non risulti, quindi, disatteso quel dovere (inderogabile) di solidarietà, ormai costituzionalizzato (art. 2 Cost.), che, applicato ai contratti, ne determina integrativamente il contenuto o gli effetti (art. 1374 *c.c.*) e deve, ad un tempo, orientarne l'interpretazione (art. 1366 *c.c.*) e l'esecuzione (art. 1375).' See earlier *Trib. Bologna*, 21 July 1970, *Riv. dir. comm.* 1971, II, 277, note Alpa, *Giur. it.* 1971, I, 2, 211 (= *Trib. Bologna*, 5 November 1970, *Foro it.* 1971, I, 1030). See further for the obligation of solidarity, without explicit reference to art. 2 *Cost.*: *Cass.*, 5 January 1966, no. 89, *Corr. giur.* 1994, p. 566, note Carbone, *Foro Pad.* 1966, I, 524; *Cass.*, 18 July 1989, no. 3362, *Foro it.* 1989, I, 2750, notes Di Majo and Mariconda; *Cass.*, 20 July 1989, no. 3386, *Foro it.* 1989, I, 3100, note Mariconda; *Cass.*, 9 March 1991, no. 2503, *Foro it.* 1991, I, 2077, note Bellantuono. Compare GUIDO ALPA, *L'arte di giudicare*, p. 89f.

[34] Art. 20 (1): 'Die Bundesrepublik Deutschland ist ein demokratischer und sozialer Bundesstaat.'; Art. 28 (1): 'Die verfassungsmäßige Ordnung in den Ländern muß den Grundsätzen des republikanischen, demokratischen und sozialen Rechtsstaates im Sinne dieses Grundgesetzes entsprechen. (...)'.

terms (*Inhaltskontrolle*) (art. 9 *AGBG*)[35]. Moreover, that clause may, more generally, be the basis for the protection of weaker contracting parties, either through § 138 *BGB* (invalidity in case of immorality) or through § 242 *BGB* (the general good faith clause)[36].

A striking German example, which is based in part on the *Sozialstaatsklausel*, is the famous case which was decided in 1993 on the validity of a personal guarantee[37].

> In that case a bank had offered a businessman a loan of DM 100,000 on condition that his daughter would accept to provide a personal guarantee. The daughter, who was 21, uneducated, unemployed and without any property, accepted to act as a guarantor for the whole of her father's debt. Four years later the father's business got into financial difficulties and the bank claimed DM 100,000 plus interest from the daughter. After having been rejected by the court of appeal, the bank's claim was upheld by the highest civil court (*BGH*).
>
> However, the daughter appealed to the constitutional court (*BVerfG*). She claimed that the *BGH*, through its decision, had violated her rights to the protection of her dignity (art. 1, Section 1 *GG*) and her party autonomy (art. 2, Section 1 *GG*) in connection with the

[35] See HELMUT HEINRICHS, in: *Palandt Bürgerliches Gesetzbuch*, § 242, no. 12.

[36] See HELMUT HEINRICHS, in: *Palandt Bürgerliches Gesetzbuch*, §138 no. 6: 'Der in der Rechtsprechung seit langem anerkannte Grundsatz, dass mit Hilfe des § 138 dem Mißbrauch wirtschaftlicher Macht entgegenzuwirken ist, hat im Sozialstaatsprinzip seine Grundlage.' However, HERBERT ROTH, in: *Münchener Kommentar*, § 242, no. 53 argues that this role should be rather limited: 'dem Sozialstaatsprinzip kann wiederum nicht die Bedeutung beigemessen werden, daß es jedermann im Privatrechtsverkehr zu unbegrenzter Rücksichtnahme auf die Interessen des wirtschaftlich Schwächeren verpflichte (...) tendenziell [kommt] dem Sozialstaatsprinzip bei den im Rahmen des § 242 erforderlichen Abwägungen keine hervorragenden Bedeutung [zu].' See on political claims of this type further *infra*, Section VI.

[37] BverfGE 89, 214, *NJW* 1994, 36. Similar cases have occurred in other countries as well. However, there the solution was rather found in terms of precontractual obligations to inform. See for example Barclays Bank plc v. O'Brien [1994] 1AC 180. See on this case JOHN CARTWRIGHT, *Taking Stock of O'Brien* [1999] R.L.R. 1. See in the Netherlands *HR*, 1 June 1990, *NJ* 1991, 759, note Brunner, where the *Hoge Raad* held in a similar case (a lady had given a personal guarantee in order to enable her son to obtain additional credit for his business) that a bank, as a professional credit supplier, is under a duty to generally inform a non-professional party of the risk concerned with providing a personal guarantee. Cf. on this case R.P.J.L. TJITTES, *Bezwaarde verwanten* (inaugural lecture *VU*), Deventer 1996, p. 54 ff. Such solutions are clearly inspired by the classical idea of contract law as the agreement between two parties who are presumed to be equal and therefore responsible for their acts. This idea is linked to the idea of a market economy which in turn is based on the notion of rational agents. In that classical theory contract law only has the task of making promises enforceable and to correct market failures. In this theory most unbalanced contracts are explained as being a result of information asymmetry. As a result, the obvious legal remedy is a duty to inform. However, everyday experience in contract cases (and in life at large) shows that the notion of contracting parties as rational agents is highly unrealistic. A more realistic (and straightforward) approach to unbalanced contracts is therefore to directly control their content, as the German constitutional court does here, and to openly admit that contract law also has a re-distributionist function.

> *Sozialstaatsprinzip* (art. 20, Section 1, Art. 28, Section 1 *GG*). She was successful in her appeal.
>
> It is interesting to note that in its decision the court held, in very broad terms, that, although normally contracts must be upheld by the courts as an expression by both parties of their constitutionally protected autonomy, civil courts must nevertheless intervene, on the basis of the general clauses (§ 138 and 242 *BGB*), in cases where a structural imbalance of bargaining power has led to a contract which is exceptionally onerous for the weaker party. This obligation for the civil courts to intervene is based, according to the Constitutional Court, on their constitutional obligation to protect party autonomy in connection with the *Sozialstaatsprinzip*[38].

The Italian art. 2 and the German art. 20 are both post-WW II provisions. Many other European constitutions, especially the older ones, do not contain similar rules. However, many national Constitutions, and especially a number of international conventions - notably the European Social Charter -, contain other social rights, especially workers' rights. A typical example of a right which has gained constitutional protection in many European constitutions and also in the European Social Charter (art. 24) is the employee's right to protection against unjustified dismissal.

However, in some countries the courts have been reluctant to give such social rights any real effect, especially in horizontal relationships[39]. And in any case, their effect is usually limited to labour contracts and is generally not extended to other contracts.

---

[38] See pp. 231-234. The *BVerfG* held: 'Handelt es sich um eine typisierbare Fallgestaltung, die eine strukturelle Unterlegenheit des einen Vertragsteils erkennen läßt, und sind die Folgen des Vertrages für den unterlegenen Vertragsteil ungewöhnlich belastend, so muß die Zivilrechtsordnung darauf reagieren und Korrekturen ermöglichen. Das folgt aus der grundrechtlichen Gewährleistung der Privatautonomie (art. 2 Abs. 1 GG) und dem Sozialstaatsprinzip (art. 20 Abs. 1, Art. 28 Abs. 1 GG). (...) Heute besteht weitgehend Einigkeit darüber, daß die Vertragsfreiheit nur im Falle eines annähernd ausgewogenen Kräfteverhältnisses der Partner als Mittel eines angemessenen Interessenausgleichs taugt und daß der Ausgleich gestörter Vertragsparität zu den Hauptaufgaben des Zivilrechts gehört. (...) Für die Zivilgerichte folgt daraus die Pflicht, bei der Auslegung und Anwendung der Generalklauseln darauf zu achten, daß Verträge nicht als Mittel der Fremdbestimmung dienen. Haben die Vertragspartner eine an sich zulässige Regelung vereinbart, so wird sich regelmäßig eine weitergehende Inhaltskontrolle erübrigen. Ist aber der Inhalt des Vertrages für eine Seite ungewöhnlich belastend und als Interessenausgleich offensichtlich unangemessen, so dürfen sich die Gerichte nicht mit der Feststellung begnügen: "Vertrag ist Vertrag". Sie müssen vielmehr klären, ob die Regelung eine Folge strukturell ungleicher Verhandlungsstärke ist, und gegebenenfalls im Rahmen der Generalklauseln des geltende Zivilrechts korrigierend eingreifen.'

[39] Compare for the Netherlands MARTIJN VAN EMPEL & MARIANNE DE JONG, 'Constitution, International Treaties, Contracts and Torts', p. 290. However, see HR, 30 May 1986, *NJ* 196, 688, where art. 6(4) ESC, which grants a right to take industrial action, was held to be self-executing.

VI. The Politics of Rights

This brings me to the politics of rights. In his book *L'età dei diritti* (1990) the famous Italian legal and political philosopher Norberto Bobbio states the following:

> 'i diritti dell'uomo, per fondamentali che siano, sono diritti storici, cioè nati in certe circostanze, contrassegnate da lotte per la difesa di nuove libertà contro vecchi poteri, gradualmente, non tutti in una volta e non una volta per sempre.'[40]

In the case of the so-called first generation 'classical' freedom rights this is obvious: they were affirmed with the American Independence and the French Revolution. Similarly, the social rights are clearly the result of workers' emancipation and their organisation in trade unions[41]. In the same way, feminism and claims from ethnic minorities have now firmly established the right to equality. And consumer rights would not have been as strong as they currently are without the endeavours of consumer organisations and pressure groups.

Today, in Europe, the situation is even more obvious since the European Convention on the Future of the European Union, which is chaired by Valéry Giscard D'Estaing and which is currently preparing a European Constitution, is clearly and openly marked by political bargaining.

Therefore, Bobbio is right when be says that human rights, fundamental as they may be, are not 'natural' but the result of a political struggle. What then would be an acceptable outcome of that struggle for European contract law?

Today, it is quite broadly accepted that contract law is best understood as being based on two fundamental - and conflicting - ideas, i.e. autonomy and solidarity[42]. The idea of autonomy is politically linked to liberalism ('the right') and its typical dogmas in contract law are the 'freedom of contract' and the 'binding force of contract'. The idea of solidarity, on the other hand, is politically linked to socialism ('the left') and its main dogmas in contract law are the 'duty of good faith' and the 'need for specific mandatory rules for the protection of weaker parties'.

The most important practical function of fundamental rights, not only in vertical but also in horizontal situations, is their rhetorical strength[43]. Private law rules and the civil courts try to resolve conflicts between citizens by balancing their interests. The balance of interests is likely to tip in one party's

---

[40] NORBERTO BOBBIO, *L'età dei diritti*, Torino 1997, p. XIII. In the same sense Alberto Trabucchi, *Istituzioni di Diritto Civile*, 40th ed., Padova 2001, § 43 (p. 97).

[41] Similarly, the Italian post-War Constitution was clearly marked (in part) by the communist partisans.

[42] See *supra*, Chapter, 3, Section VI, B, and Chapter 5, with further references.

[43] Compare DUNCAN KENNEDY, *A Critique of Adjudication {fin de siècle}*, Cambridge Massachusetts 1997, p. 297 ff, esp. p. 311 and p. 331 ('Rights then function as no more than interests (perhaps with an exclamation point).')

favour if that party claims that its interest is constitutionally protected as a fundamental right[44].

Therefore, it is crucial that adequate constitutional protection is available for both types of rights which are fundamental to contract law: a general right of autonomy and other specific freedom rights on the one hand, and a general right to solidarity together with other specific social rights on the other[45].

Moreover, and even more importantly[46], both rights should be formulated in such a way that they can be made equally effective, also in private law cases, be it directly or indirectly (by way of general clauses)[47]. In particular, the right should not be formulated as an open-ended instruction to the legislator. In Germany scholars place fundamental rights in two distinct categories, 1) '*Eingriffsverbote*' which prohibit the State from interfering with personal freedom, and 2) '*Schutzgebote*' which merely impose an obligation on the State to realise a certain value. In the former case constitutional review is intense (*Übermaßverbot*), in the latter case control is only very marginal (*Untermaßverbot*). In this view classical freedom rights belong to the first category whereas the right to equality and, especially, social rights, belong to the second. For private law the effect of the adoption of this distinction would be that interventions in party autonomy are strictly scrutinised whereas the

---

[44] Compare again NORBERTO BOBBIO, *L'età dei diritti*, p. XX: 'Il linguaggio dei diritti ha indubbiamente una grande funzione pratica, che è quella di dar particolare forza alle rivendicazioni di quei movimenti che richiedono per sé e per gli altri soddisfazione di bisogni materiali e morali'.

[45] In the same sense BRIGITTA LURGER, *Grundfragen der Vereinheitlichung des Vertragsrechts in der Europäischen Union*, Wien, New York 2002, p. 242, who argues (on p. 294) for an even more specific right to contractual relationships which are at least 'somewhat fair': 'das "soziale" Grundrecht auf einigermaßen faire Vertragsbeziehungen, die eine einseitige schwerwiegende Verletzung der wirtschaftlichen Interessen einer der Parteien verhindern.' A very powerful plea for a set of European social rights, not only on re-distributionist but also on efficiency grounds, is made by MIGUEL POIARES MADURO, 'Striking the Elusive Balance Between Economic Freedom and Social Rights in the EU', in: PHILIP ALSTON (ed.), *The EU and Human Rights*, Oxford 1999, pp. 449-472.

[46] Of great practical importance is also that courts should have the power - and indeed the obligation - to declare the unconstitutionality of the contract *ex officio*.

[47] I would favour a direct horizontal effect. (In the same sense for the Netherlands EVERT VERHULP, *Vrijheid van meningsuiting van werknemers en ambtenaren*, The Hague 1996, p. 32.) In my view, the arguments against direct horizontal effect (see *supra*) are not very convincing. The argument that private law is autonomous and is based on its own considerations of fairness is a *petitio principii*. The argument that direct horizontal effect would raise much of private law to a constitutional level (e.g. the rules on delictual an contractual liability, the rules on the validity of contracts) is not convincing either since the same argument would apply to some provisions from the EC Treaty, like for example art. 85 on competition, which have a direct horizontal effect, which is generally accepted and does not seem to raise insurmountable problems. Ultimately, the choice is a political one (constitutional politics). BRIGITTA LURGER, *Grundfragen der Vereinheitlichung des Vertragsrechts in der Europäischen Union*, p. 228, quite rightly points out that the really important issue is not how fundamental rights operate in private relationships but how strong their impact is. Nevertheless, it should be kept in mind that this effect is most likely to be stronger when it is direct. Hence, the conservative strategy to limit horizontal effects to an indirect effect. Compare GUIDO ALPA, *Trattato di diritto civile, I Storia, fonti, interpretazione*, pp. 497 and 516.

realisation of social rights is limited to 'extreme cases'. This view is defended especially by Canaris[48]. However, it is strongly - and convincingly - rejected by Brigitta Lurger as a classical attempt to win a political battle by introducing a supposedly 'technical' dogmatic distinction[49]: 'auch die am staatlichen Eingriff orientierte Differenzierung nach Schutzgebots- und Eingriffsverbotsfunktion (*Canaris*) [läuft] nur auf den Versuch hinaus, der formellen Vertragsfreiheit gegenüber sie einschränkendem zwingendem Schutzrecht größeren Raum einzuräumen, eine inhaltliche Argumentation, die sich natürlich auch auf einfachgesetzlicher Ebene findet.'[50] Neither should such a general social right be subject to many qualifications, since those legislative techniques are frequently held to be an impediment to direct (vertical ànd horizontal) effect since they leave the legislator with a (supposedly broad) margin of appreciation[51].

In the absence of social rights which are sufficiently enforceable in horizontal relationships - i.e. between private parties -, the whole 20th century battle for the socialisation of contract law (good faith duties, workers', tenants' and consumer protection) would risk having to start all over again, but now on a higher - i.e. the constitutional - level where the stakes in the political debate are even higher[52]. (Note the parallel with the reinvention of crude capitalism in the guise of 'globalisation' where complete 'freedom of contract' is advocated as the central notion of a new global private law[53].)

The European Charter contains an article, in Chapter II on 'Freedoms', which could provide a basis for the constitutional protection of party autonomy in contract cases: art. 6 which is called the 'right to liberty and security'. However, a similar general provision is lacking in Chapter IV on 'Solidarity'. Therefore, it would be advisable for the drafters of a European Constitution to add a rule similar to the German *Sozialstaatsklausel* and the Italian rule on *solidarietà politica, economica e sociale*. The argument that such a rule would necessarily be too vague is unacceptable. The rule should simply be drafted in such a way that it can be made operational by the courts,

---

[48] CLAUS-WILHELM CANARIS, *Grundrechte und Privatrecht*, p. 41.

[49] See on the politics of 'technical' questions: DUNCAN KENNEDY, 'The Political Stakes in "Merely Technical" Issues of Contract Law', 10 *ERPL* (2002), pp. 7-28.

[50] BRIGITTA LURGER, *Grundfragen der Vereinheitlichung des Vertragsrechts in der Europäischen Union*, p. 238.

[51] Compare ARTHUR S. HARTKAMP, 'On European Freedoms and National Mandatory Rules', p. 117.

[52] Compare the United States where the Supreme Court in Lochner v. New York (1905) stroke down a maximum-hours law for bakers and thus, effectively, constitutionalised freedom of contract, without guaranteeing any social counterpart on the constitutional level.

[53] See for example KLAUS PETER BERGER, 'Transnational Commercial Law in the Age of Globalization', in: Centro di studi e ricerche di diritto comparato e straniero (directed by M.J. Bonell), *Saggi, conferenze e seminari*, no. 42, Rome 2001. On the social costs of globalisation compare NOAM CHOMSKY, *Profit over people; neoliberalism and global order*, New York 1999 and NAOMI KLEIN, *No Logo*, London 2000, especially pp. 195 ff. Strongly in favour of private law regulation of (European and global) markets is UGO MATTEI, 'Hard Code Now!', *Global Jurist Frontiers* (2002): Vol. 2: No. 1, Article 1.

especially in horizontal relationships. I will once again quote Norberto Bobbio:

> 'Si ricordi che il più forte argomento addotto dai reazionari di tutti i paesi contro (...) i diritti sociali, non è già la loro mancanza di fondamento, ma la loro inattuabilità. (...) Il problema di fondo relativo ai diritti dell'uomo è oggi non tanto quello di *giustificarli*, quanto quello di *proteggerli*. È un problema non filosofico ma politico.'[54]

[54] P. 15.

Social Rights in Contract Cases

CONCEPTS

7
The Concept Of Good Faith

I. Introduction

MOST EUROPEAN civil codes contain a general good faith provision[1]. In addition, some codes contain specific rules in which reference is also made to the concept of good faith. Moreover, many specific rules in the codes are said to be special applications of good faith.

Most systems make a distinction between subjective good faith and objective good faith. Subjective good faith is usually defined as a subjective state of mind: not knowing nor having to know of a certain fact or event (*bona fide* acquisition). It is of relevance particularly in property law. Objective good faith, the concept that the general good faith clauses refer to, is usually regarded as a norm for the conduct of contracting parties: 'acting in accordance with or contrary to good faith'. Some systems have even emphasised this distinction by introducing separate terminology for objective good faith (*Treu und Glauben, correttezza, redelijkheid en billijkheid*). In France, however, such a distinction is not usually made[2]. The English common law traditionally does not recognise a concept of objective good faith. However, the concept has recently been introduced into English law by statute[3].

In this Chapter I will discuss whether a European Civil Code or a Code of Contracts, if it were to be enacted[4], should contain a provision on objective good faith. Therefore I will examine first how the concept of objective good faith is understood in the various countries (II). Then I will give a brief account of how good faith is applied by the courts (III). Finally, I will raise the question whether the traditional view of good faith constitutes an adequate representation

---

[1] See Art. 1134, Section 3 French Civil Code; § 242 German Civil Code; Art. 2 Swiss Civil Code arts. 1175 and 1375 Italian Civil Code; Art. 288 Greek Civil Code; Art. 762, Section 2, Portuguese Civil Code; arts. 6:2 and 6:248 Dutch Civil Code. See also Art. 1.7 UP and Art. 1.201 PECL.

[2] The same holds true for observations which many English lawyers make on the concept of good faith. They often speak of 'acting in bad faith' when referring to the conduct of contracting parties where most continental European lawyers would speak of 'acting contrary to good faith'.

[3] Unfair Terms in Consumer Contracts Regulations 1994, *SI* 1994/3159 which implemented EC Council Directive 93/13/EEC. See GUNTHER TEUBNER, 'Legal Irritants: Good Faith in British Law or How Unifying Law Ends Up in New Divergences', *MLR* 1998, p. 11 ff.

[4] On the desirability of a European Civil Code or a European Code of Contracts see *supra*, Chapter 5, and *infra*, Chapter 8.

of the way in which good faith actually operates (IV). The answer to that question will determine my final conclusions (V).

II. Good Faith in Theory

A. Introduction

Objective good faith is usually regarded as a normative concept (B). However, a general good faith clause is not an ordinary rule like most others in the code. It contains an open norm (C), it is said, the content of which must be established through concretisation (D) into functions and groups of typical cases (E).

B. Normative Concept

In all systems objective good faith is usually regarded as a normative concept. Indeed good faith is often seen as the highest norm of contract law, or of the law of obligations or even of all private law. For that reason many provisions in the code which make no explicit reference to good faith are nevertheless said to be based on it.

Good faith is often said to be in some way connected with moral standards. On the one hand, it is said to be a moral standard itself, a legal-ethical principle[5]; good faith means honesty, candour, loyalty et cetera. It is often said that the standard of good faith basically means that a party should take the interest of the other party into account[6]. On the other hand, good faith is said to be the gateway through which moral values enter the law[7].

Reference is thereby sometimes made to the Aristotelian concept of equity[8]. Actually, some systems do not distinguish between equity and good faith; they regard them as the same objective standard[9]. It is then said that abstract rules may lead to an unjust result in a specific case, and that good faith may provide

---

[5] See e.g. JOACHIM GERNHUBER & BARBARA GRUNEWALD, *Bürgerliches Recht; Ein systematisches Repertorium*, 4th ed., München 1998, p. 106 (*grundlegendes rechtsethisches Prinzip*); GIORGIO CIAN & ALBERTO TRABUCCHI, *Commentario breve al codice civile*, 5th ed., Padova, 1997, Art. 1175, I, 1 (*principio etico-giuridico*).

[6] See e.g. ARNDT TEICHMANN, in: *Soergel Bürgerliches Gesetzbuch mit Einführungsgesetz und Nebengesetzen*, Vol. 2 *Schuldrecht I (§§ 241-610)*, 12th ed., Stuttgart, Berlin and Köln 1990, § 242, no. 4; C. MASSIMO BIANCA, *Diritto Civile*, III, *Il contratto*, Milano 1987 (reprinted in 1992), no. 224; A.S. HARTKAMP, *Verbintenissenrecht* (in: *Asser* series), Vol. II, *Algemene leer der overeenkomsten*, 11th ed., Deventer 2001, no. 300; MICHAEL P. STATHOPOULOS, *Contract law in Hellas*, The Hague, London and Boston, Athens 1995, no. 51.

[7] See e.g. HELMUT HEINRICHS, in: *Palandt Bürgerliches Gesetzbuch*, 61st ed., München 2002, § 242, no. 3; FRANÇOIS TERRE & PHILIPPE SIMLER & YVES LEQUETTE, *Droit civil, Les obligations*, 6th ed, Paris 1996, no. 414; Art. 1.106 PECL, Comment, A.

[8] ARISTOTLE, *Nicomachean Ethics*, V, x.

[9] In France, accessory duties like the duty to inform or the duty of care, are founded by the courts on Art. 1134, Section 3 (*bonne foi*) and Art. 1135 (*équité*) alternatively, and sometimes on both. In the Netherlands the new Civil Code merged the concepts of *goede trouw* (Art. 1374, Section 3 old BW) and *billijkheid* (Art. 1375 old BW) into the new concept of *redelijkheid en billijkheid* (objective good faith) (arts. 6:2; 6:248 BW).

the basis for an exception on the facts of that particular case. For that reason it is sometimes argued (as it was for early Equity in England)[10] that a decision based on good faith cannot serve as a precedent, as it is only meant to prevent injustice in a particular case, and that therefore no effort should be made to determine the content of the good faith norm in more general terms. However, this view is not generally accepted and the next Section will show that it does not correspond with the way in which good faith operates in practice.

Finally, in some systems good faith is regarded - and actually used by the courts - as a means through which the values of the Constitution enter into private law[11].

C. Open Norm

At first sight, the theoretical status of good faith may seem quite unclear to an outsider since the terminology used by legal authors is far from unitary. Good faith is said to be a norm[12], a (very important)[13] principle[14], a rule[15], a maxim[16], a duty[17], a rule or standard for conduct[18], a source of unwritten law[19], a general clause[20]. To an English lawyer - often accused by his continental European colleagues of making inconsistent use of terminology - this may seem rather confusing.

---

[10] See J.H. BAKER, *An Introduction to English Legal History*, London 1979 (reprinted in 1988), p. 89; S.F.C. MILSOM, *Historical Foundations of the Common Law*, 2nd ed., London 1981, p. 90.

[11] For Germany see e.g. HERBERT ROTH, in: *Münchener Kommentar zum Bürgerlichen Gesetzbuch*, 4th ed., München 2001, § 242, no. 52 ff.; for Italy see e.g. M. CANTILLO, *Le Obbligazioni*, in: *Giurisprudenza sistematica di diritto civile e commerciale* (founded by Walter Bigiavi), Vol. I, Torino 1992, p. 207. See further *infra*, Chapter 6.

[12] See e.g. KARL LARENZ, *Lehrbuch des Schuldrechts*, Vol. I *Allgemeiner Teil*, 14th ed., München 1987, p. 129 (*Norm*); JACQUES HERBOTS, *Contract Law in Belgium*, Deventer, Boston and Bruxelles 1995, no. 109 ('norm').

[13] See e.g. Art. 1.106 PECL, Comment, A ('a basic principle running throughout the Principles'); DIETER MEDICUS, *Schuldrecht I; Allgemeiner Teil*, 12th ed., München 2000, no. 125 ('ein den einzelnen Rechtsvorschriften übergeordnetes Prinzip'); C. MASSIMO BIANCA, *Il contratto*, no. 223 ('un principio di ordine pubblico che supera anche la legge').

[14] See e.g. A.S. HARTKAMP, *Verbintenissenrecht II* (in: *Asser* series), no. 300, 301, 304 (*beginsel*); MICHAEL P. STATHOPOULOS, *Contract law in Hellas*, no. 50 (*principle*).

[15] See e.g. A. MENEZES-CORDEIRO, 'Rapport portugais', *Travaux de l'association Henri Capitant, Tome XLIII, année 1992. Journées louisianaises de Baton-Rouge et La Nouvelle Orléans, 'La bonne foi'*, Paris 1994, p. 338 (*règle*); Art. 1.106 PECL, Comment, A (*rule*).

[16] See JEAN CARBONNIER, *Droit Civil*, Vol. IV *Les Obligations*, 22nd ed., Paris 2000, no. 113: *maxime*.

[17] See e.g. PHILIPPE MALAURIE & LAURENT AYNES, *Cours de droit civil*, part IV, *Les obligations*, 10th, Paris 1999, no. 622 (*devoir*); C. MASSIMO BIANCA, *Il contratto*, no. 223 (*obbligo giuridico*).

[18] See e.g. C. MASSIMO BIANCA, *Il contratto*, no. 223 (*precetto di condotta*); A. MENEZES-CORDEIRO, 'Rapport portugais', p. 337 (*règle de conduite*); MICHAEL P. STATHOPOULOS, *Contract law in Hellas*, no. 52 ('criterion of conduct').

[19] See e.g. A.S. HARTKAMP, *Verbintenissenrecht II* (in: *Asser* series), no. 305.

[20] See e.g. KONRAD ZWEIGERT &HEIN KÖTZ, *Einführung in die Rechtsvergleichung*, 3rd ed., Tübingen 1996, p. 149 (*Generalklausel*); MASSIMO BIANCA, *Il contratto*, no. 223 (*clausola generale*); MICHAEL P. STATHOPOULOS, *Contract law in Hellas*, no. 50 ('general clause').

However, on closer inspection, the picture is less confused than it seems. It is generally agreed that a general good faith clause does not contain a rule, at least not one like most other rules in the code. It is not, like other rules, susceptive to subsumption since neither the facts to which it applies nor the legal effect that it stipulates can be established *a priori*. Good faith is therefore usually said to be an open norm, a norm the content of which cannot be established in an abstract way but which depends on the circumstances of the case in which it must be applied, and which must be established through concretisation[21]. Most lawyers from a system where good faith plays an important role, will therefore agree that these differences in theoretical conception do not matter very much. Indeed, many authors are themselves not very consistent in their indication of the status of good faith. What really matters is the way in which good faith is applied by the courts: the character of good faith is best shown by the way in which it operates.

D. Concretisation

As said, the abstract standard of good faith must be concretised in order to be able to be applied. The court determines what good faith requires in the circumstances of the specific case (*Einzelfallgerechtigkeit*)[22]. However, the judge is not allowed to simply decide the way which seems most equitable to himself. He has to determine the requirements of good faith in such an objective way as possible[23]. In the Netherlands the code therefore provides in a specific provision what should be taken into account in determining what good faith requires in a particular case[24]. In addition to that, in most systems, particularly in Germany, scholars both in private law and in jurisprudence have developed methods for rationalising and objectivating the decisions of the court. The purpose of these *Methodenlehren* is to render the application of the law in general, and of general clauses like good faith in particular, as rational and objective (and thereby predictable) as possible, instead of leaving it to the subjective judgement of the individual judge. The generally agreed method for rationalising is that of distinguishing functions and developing groups of cases in which good faith has previously been applied (*Fallgruppen*). In doing so legal doctrine has developed an 'inner system' of good faith[25], which is regarded as the content of that norm.

---

[21] See e.g. HELMUT HEINRICHS, in: *Palandt Bürgerliches Gesetzbuch*, § 242, no. 3 and 13, and GIORGIO CIAN & ALBERTO TRABUCCHI, *Commentario breve al codice civile*, Art. 1175, II, 1.

[22] See e.g. ARNDT TEICHMANN, in: *Soergel Bürgerliches Gesetzbuch*, § 242, no. 6.

[23] See e.g. KARL LARENZ, *Lehrbuch des Schuldrechts I*, pp. 126 ff.

[24] Art. 3:12 BW: 'In determining what reasonableness and equity require, reference must be made to generally accepted principles of law, to current juridical views in the Netherlands, and to the particular societal and private interests involved'. (Translation P.P.C. HAANAPPEL & E. MACKAAY, *New Netherlands Civil Code Patrimonial Law*, Deventer and Boston 1990).

[25] The term inner system (*Binnensystem*) is taken from JÜRGEN SCHMIDT, in: *J. von Staudingers Kommentar zum Bürgerlichen Gesetzbuch mit Einführungsgesetz und Nebengesetzen; Zweites Buch Recht der Schuldverhältnisse; Einleitung zu §§ 241 ff.; §§ 241-243*, Berlin 1995, § 242, no. 87.

In Germany this operation has already been accomplished to a large extent. Compare Palandt/Heinrichs[26]: 'In einer jetzt fast 100jähriger Rechtsentwicklung ist der Inhalt des § 242 durch Herausarbeitung von Funktionskreisen und durch Bildung von Fallgruppen präzisiert und im wesentlichen abschließend konkretisiert worden.' The effort of concretisation has made the content of the good faith norm quite comprehensible. The result is a system of sometimes quite specific duties, prohibitions, (sub-)rules and doctrines which are all part of the content of good faith. It is said to have made decisions on the basis of § 242 BGB agreeably predictable (legal certainty) and rational[27].

It is often emphasised, however, that concretisation will not and indeed should not lead to the fossilisation of good faith. First of all, it would be an illusion to think that concretisation will ever lead to a limited set of clearly distinguishable rules[28]. But, it is said, more importantly good faith should remain an open norm in order to be able to continue to play its important role of making the law flexible. The inner system of good faith should not become a strait-jacket[29].

It should be added that the process of concretisation has not been totally identical in all countries. Whereas in Germany and in the Netherlands legal doctrine rather reacts to court decisions and tries to regroup them, and thus they build up a system (a rather more inductive approach), French and Italian legal doctrine seem to follow the more deductive approach of asking themselves what, in theory, the content of the duty of good faith, or the good faith standard could be, and thus they build up a system of sub-duties et cetera, in which the legal decisions are given their place at a later stage, the Italian authors thereby relying heavily on the achievements of German courts and legal doctrine.

E. Functions and Fallgruppen

Most systems distinguish between several functions of good faith. Here again French law takes a somewhat different position since there the approach seems to be rather one of distilling sub-duties from the general duty of good faith[30]. But, as said, in most other systems legal doctrine has distinguished several

[26] HELMUT HEINRICHS, in: *Palandt Bürgerliches Gesetzbuch*, § 242, no. 2.
[27] See ARNDT TEICHMANN, in: *Soergel Bürgerliches Gesetzbuch*, § 242, no. 7.
[28] See J. GERNHUBER, *Bürgerliches Recht; Ein systematisches Repertorium für Fortgeschrittene*, 3rd ed., München 1991, p. 167: 'Die Vorstellung einer totalen Vertypung ist eine reine Utopie'.
[29] See HERBERT ROTH, in: *Münchener Kommentar*, § 242, no. 32.
[30] The sub-duties most often mentioned are the duty of loyalty (*obligation de loyauté*) and the duty to co-operate (*obligation de coopération*). See e.g. Y. PICOD, *Le devoir de loyauté dans l'exécution du contrat*, Paris 1989, *passim*; FRANÇOIS TERRE & PHILIPPE SIMLER & YVES LEQUETTE, *Les obligations*, nos. 415-416; A. RIEG, 'Articles 1134 et 1135' in: *Jurisclasseur, Contrats et obligations* (1989), nos. 86-104; B. STARCK & H. ROLAND & L. BOYER, *Droit civil, Les obligations, 2. Le Contrat*, 3rd ed., Paris, 1989, nos. 1140-1146. The (important!) duty to inform (*obligation de renseignement*) is usually regarded as a sub-duty of the duty to co-operate. See e.g. FRANÇOIS TERRE & PHILIPPE SIMLER & YVES LEQUETTE, *Les obligations*, no. 430). See on these duties, *infra*, III, A, 4.

functions of good faith. It is interesting to see that the number of functions attributed is usually three.

In Germany a distinction made by Siebert has been *grundlegend.* He distinguished three functions of § 242 BGB[31]: 1) supplementation of duties; 2) limitation of rights; 3) *Wegfall der Geschäftsgrundlage.* In addition to these three functions there is good faith interpretation which is based on § 157 BGB. This distinction has essentially been followed by most scholars[32]. Some authors have defined one or more of the functions differently, while others have split the first function into two functions, thus arriving at a quadripartition.

In Italy scholars distinguish between a supplementing function (*funzione integrativa*) and an evaluating function (*funzione valutativa*) of good faith. However, not both are recognised by all scholars. As a matter of fact, a fierce debate has taken place between scholars who regarded a *funzione valutativa* as the exclusive role of good faith[33], and those who wished that a *funzione integrativa* be recognised[34]. However, today both functions seem to have been recognised by the courts[35]. In addition the code provides for good faith interpretation (Art. 1366).

In the Netherlands good faith has a supplementing function (or effect, as it is usually called: *aanvullende werking*)[36] and a limiting function (*beperkende werking*)[37]. In addition, good faith plays a role in interpretation[38]. Before the adoption of the 1992 Civil Code the limiting effect was the object of a lively debate amongst legal scholars, somewhat similar to the debate in Italy. Some authors favoured a broad concept of good faith interpretation and held the *beperkende werking* to be superfluous[39]; others upheld the necessity of a

---

[31] See W. KNOPP & W. SIEBERT, in: *Soergel Bürgerliches Gesetzbuch*, 10th ed., Stuttgart, Berlin, Köln and Mainz 1967, § 242, no. 34 ff.

[32] See explicitly F. WIEACKER, '*Zur Rechtstheoretischen Präzisierung des § 242,* in: *Recht und Staat in Geschichte und Gegenwart; Eine Sammlung von Vorträgen und Schriften aus dem Gebiet der gesamten Staatswissenschaft*, 193/194, Tübingen 1956, p. 22; JOACHIM GERNHUBER & BARBARA GRUNEWALD, *Bürgerliches Recht*, no. 4 ff.; DIETER MEDICUS, *Schuldrecht I*, no. 132.

[33] See in particular U. NATOLI, *L'attuazione del rapporto obbligatorio,* in: *Trattato di diritto civile e commerciale diretto dai professori Antonio Cicu e Francesco Messineo*, vol. XVI, t. 1, Milano 1974, pp. 14 ff. See also e.g. L. BIGLIAZZI GERI, 'Buona fede nel diritto civile', pp. 171-172; U. BRECCIA, *Le obbligazioni*; in: *Trattato di diritto Privato a cura di Giovanni Iudica e Paolo Zatti*, Milano 1992, p. 3.

[34] See in particular STEFANO RODOTÀ, *Le fonti di integrazione del contratto*, Milano 1969, *passim*, especially chapter 2 (pp. 111 ff.). See also, e.g. A. DI MAJO, *Delle Obbligazioni in Generale, arts. 1173-1176*, in: *Commentario del codice civile Scialoja-Branca*, Bologna, Roma 1988, p. 322; C. MASSIMO BIANCA, *Il contratto*, p. 223.

[35] See e.g. Cass., 18 July 1989, n. 3362, Foro it., 1989, I, 2750, notes Di Majo and Mariconda. See e.g. GIORGIO CIAN & ALBERTO TRABUCCHI, *Commentario breve al codice civile*, I, 2; M. CANTILLO, *Le Obbligazioni*, p. 210.

[36] See A.S. HARTKAMP, *Verbintenissenrecht II* (in: *Asser* series), no. 307 ff.

[37] See A.S. HARTKAMP, *Verbintenissenrecht II* (in: *Asser* series), no. 312 ff.

[38] See A.S. HARTKAMP, *Verbintenissenrecht II* (in: *Asser* series), no. 280 ff.

[39] J.M. VAN DUNNÉ, *Normatieve uitleg van rechtshandelingen; Een onderzoek naar de grondslagen van het geldende verbintenissenrecht*, Deventer 1971, *passim*; H.C.F. SCHOORDIJK, *Het algemeen gedeelte van het verbintenissenrecht naar het Nieuw Burgerlijk Wetboek*, Deventer 1979, pp. 21 ff.

separate limiting or correcting function[40]. The *Hoge Raad* took the latter view, just like the legislator who explicitly recognised the *beperkende werking* in the new code[41].

Also in Belgium good faith is usually said to have three functions[42]: an interpretative function (*fonction interprétative*), a supplementing function (*fonction complétive*) and a restricting or limiting or mitigating function (*fonction restrictive, limitative, modératrice*). Sometimes a fourth function is distinguished that would allow the courts in certain circumstances to change the content of the contract, but this function, just as the *imprévision* theory, has not been accepted by the majority of authors and the courts[43].

In a famous lecture published in 1956 Wieacker made an effort to specify the theoretical status of § 242 BGB[44]. That lecture is usually regarded as the theoretical foundation for Siebert's trichtonomy. What Wieacker did was to assimilate the functions of good faith to those which Papinian had attributed to the praetorian law[45]. In a well-known passage Papinian had said[46]: 'Ius praetorium est, quod praetores introduxerunt adiuvandi vel supplendi vel corrigendi iuris civilis gratia propter utilitatem publicam (...)'. Wieacker stated: 'Auch § 242 BGB wirkt *iuris civilis iuvandi, supplendi* oder *corrigendi gratia.*' Similar to the *ius praetorium*, Wieacker said, good faith has three functions: 1) 'die sinngemäße Verwirklichung des gesetzgeberischen Wertungsplanes durch den Richter' (*officium iudicis*); 2) 'alle Maximen richterlicher Anforderung an das persönliche rechtsethische Verhalten einer Prozeßpartei' ((*praeter legem*); 3) 'rechtsethische Durchbrüche durch das Gesetzesrecht' (*contra legem*). That trichtonomy looks very similar to the distinctions made in Italy, the Netherlands, and Belgium: interpretation, supplementation, correction. In Greece and in Portugal good faith does have an interpretative, a supplementing and a correcting role, although legal authors do not seem to think so explicitly in terms of three functions of good faith. Therefore, ignoring the subtleties, one could regard this trichtonomy as the European common core[47].

It should be remarked, however, that the way in which Wieacker elaborates the assimilation of the functions of good faith to the three functions distinguished by Papinian as he continues his lecture is somewhat surprising. He regards the supplementation of duties as *iuvare*, whereas under Roman law and

[40] See in particular P. ABAS, *Beperkende werking van de goede trouw*, Deventer 1972, *passim*.
[41] See Art. 6:2, Section 2, and Art. 6:248, Section 2 BW. See *Parl. Gesch. Boek 6*, pp. 43 ff.
[42] See e.g. JACQUES HERBOTS, *Contract Law in Belgium*, no. 272; JACQUES PÉRILLEUX, 'Rapport belge', in: *Travaux de l'association Henri Capitant, Tome XLIII, année 1992. Journées louisianaises de Baton-Rouge et La Nouvelle Orléans, "La bonne foi"*, Paris 1994, p. 250.
[43] See JACQUES PÉRILLEUX, 'Rapport belge', p. 248.
[44] F. WIEACKER, '*Zur Rechtstheoretischen Präzisierung des § 242*, especially p. 20 ff.
[45] Followed explicitly by DIETER MEDICUS, *Schuldrecht I*, no. 132. See, previously, *RG*, 26 May 1914, *RGZ* 85, 108.
[46] D. 1, 1, 7.
[47] P. SCHLECHTRIEM, *Good Faith in German Law and in International Uniform Law*, in: Centro di studi e ricerche di diritto comparato e straniero (directed by M.J. Bonell), *Saggi, conferenze e seminari*, 24, Roma 1997, p. 8, has suggested Wieacker's distinction of functions as a tentative understanding of how good faith might work under the UNIDROIT Principles or CISG.

under contemporary law in Italy, the Netherlands, Greece, and Belgium this is regarded as *supplere*. Accordingly, he regards the *exceptio doli* (abuse of right) as *supplere*, whereas under Roman law and under contemporary law in Italy, the Netherlands and Belgium this is seen as *corrigere*. Several explanations may be given for this choice, which is followed by most German scholars: one being that the *exceptio doli* actually supplements a norm ('you must not abuse your right'), another that a distinction should be made between abuse of right and correction, because in the latter case (e.g. unforeseen circumstances) no reproach is made to the conduct of the party who requests performance. However, the most likely reason seems to lie in the fact that Wieacker was determining the functions of § 242 BGB, and not those of good faith. Therefore he did not regard concretisation (interpretation), which is not based on § 242 but on § 157 BGB, as the first function (*iuvare*), thus making the others move down one place, and creating space for (and actually adding) another (fourth) function[48].

In most systems good faith is said to have three functions. Between the systems, and within each system, there is some difference of opinion about the exact definition of each of the functions. But it seems fair to say that in Europe usually three functions of good faith are distinguished, each of which correspond to one of the functions Papinian attributed to the *ius honorarium* with respect to the *ius civile*: 1) concretisation/interpretation (*adiuvare*); 2) supplementation (*supplere*) (mainly of duties, e.g. duties to be loyal, to protect, to co-operate, to inform); 3) correction/limitation (*corrigere*) (prohibition of abuse of right; *Fallgruppen* include: *venire contra factum proprium non valet*[49], *dolo agit qui petit quod statim redditurus est, tu quoque*, prohibition of excessive disproportion). In addition, sometimes (in Germany and by some Belgian authors) a fourth function is added[50] in order to distinguish between the correction/limitation of a right for one's own (present or past) improper behaviour (*exceptio doli generalis* (*praesentis*) and *exceptio doli specialis*

[48] Siebert actually regarded *Wegfall der Geschäftsgrundlage* merely as a sub-group of the cases on abuse of right (W. KNOPP & W. SIEBERT, in: *Soergel Bürgerliches Gesetzbuch*, no. 40).

[49] This *Fallgruppe* has been accepted in many jurisdictions. For Germany see e.g. HERBERT ROTH, in: *Münchener Kommentar*, § 242, no. 322 ff.; for the Netherlands ('*rechtsverwerking*') see e.g. A.S. HARTKAMP, *Verbintenissenrecht II* (in: *Asser* series), no. 320 ff.; for Italy see e.g. A. DI MAJO, *Delle Obbligazioni in Generale, artt. 1173-1176*, p. 341; for Spain ('*prohibición de ir contra los actos propios*') see e.g. L. DÍEZ-PICAZO & A. GULLÓN, *Sistema de Derecho Civil*, Vol. II, Madrid 1998, pp. 433 and 438 ff.; for Portugal see e.g. A. MENEZES-CORDEIRO, 'Rapport portugais', p. 341; for Switzerland see e.g. THEO MAYER-MALY, in: Heinrich Honsell, Nedim Peter Vogt and Thomas Geiser (eds.), *Kommentar zum Schweizerischen Zivilgesetzbuch I*), Basel and Frankfurt am Main 1996, art. 2, no. 48 ff. Compare for Greece MICHAEL P. STATHOPOULOS, *Contract law in Hellas*, no. 50. In France the principle has been recently discovered. See MARTINE BEHAR-TOUCHAIS (ed.), *L'interdiction de se contredire au détriment d'autrui*, Paris 2001.

[50] See the four functions distinguished by HELMUT HEINRICHS, in: *Palandt Bürgerliches Gesetzbuch*, § 242, no. 13 (who, however, in addition to these functions of § 242 *BGB*, distinguishes a separate role for § 157 *BGB*, regarding § 157 *BGB* as a provision dealing with *Wollen* and § 242 *BGB* as dealing with *Sollen* (see no. 18)): 1) *Konkretisierungsfunktion*; 2) *Ergänzungsfunktion*; 3) *Schrankenfunktion*; 4) *Korrekturfunktion*.

(praeteriti) respectively) and the correction/limitation of the right of an 'innocent' party (mainly when there is a change of circumstances or other *Unzumutbarkeit*).

III. Good Faith in Practice

Good faith has had great success in many European legal systems during the 20th century. In most countries the number of cases where the good faith clause has been applied has grown explosively over the last few decades. Also the field of application has been growing considerably in many systems. In the various systems good faith has been applied in virtually all fields of contract law (A), and sometimes even far outside it (B). In the following a few examples will be given of the way in which good faith has been applied. It is clear that this account will be nowhere near exhaustive[51].

A. Contract Law

1. Formation. - Many systems recognise a general duty of precontractual good faith[52]. Some codes contain a specific provision on precontractual good faith[53], in other systems the duty of precontractual good faith has been established by the courts[54]. On the basis of this general duty they usually recognise a precontractual duty to inform[55]. Moreover, they hold that a party may be liable if it breaks off negotiations in a manner contrary to precontractual good faith[56]. In some systems it is held to be contrary to good faith under certain

[51] The same is true for references. See for more details M.W. HESSELINK, *De redelijkheid en billijkheid in het Europese privaatrecht*, Deventer 1999, pp. 65-397, with references to many cases from various European jurisdictions.

[52] See M.W. HESSELINK, 'Precontractual Good Faith', in: Hugh Beale et. al. (eds.) *Cases, Materials and Text on Contract Law, Oxford and Portland*, Oregon 2002, Chapter 2, Section 2 (pp. 237-293).

[53] See Art. 1337 Italian Civil Code; Art. 197 Greek Civil Code; Art. 227 Portuguese Civil Code; Art. 2.15 UP; Art. 2:301 PECL. The German doctrine of *culpa in contrahendo*, which was frequently said to be based on good faith, has now been codified in § 311 (2) (*new*) BGB.

[54] See for France, e.g. Com., 20 March 1972, *Bull. civ.* IV, no. 93; *J.C.P.* 1973, 17534, note Schmidt; *R.T.D. civ.* 1972, p. 722, observation Durry; for the Netherlands, e.g. HR, 15 November 1957, *NJ* 1958, 67, note Rutten; for Spain L. DÍEZ-PICAZO & A. GULLÓN, *Sistema de Derecho Civil*, Vol. II, p. 68.

[55] For France, e.g., Cass. com., 8 November 1983, *Bull. civ.* IV, no. 298, p. 260; for the Netherlands e.g. HR, 30 November 1973, *NJ* 1974, 97, note GJS (under the new code good faith is no longer necessary as a basis; see now Art. 6:228(1)(b)); for Italy RODOLFO SACCO & G. DE NOVA, *Il contratto*, Vol. I, p. 434 ff.; for Greece MICHAEL P. STATHOPOULOS, *Contract law in Hellas*, no. 86; for Portugal J. DE MATOS ANTUNES VARELA, *Das Obrigações em geral*, Vol. I, 9th ed., Coimbra 1996, no. 67.

[56] See for France, e.g., Civ. I, 12 April 1976, *Bull. Civ.*, I, no. 122, *Def.*, 1976, a. 31434, no. 5, p. 389, note Aubert; for Italy, e.g., Cass., 17 June, 1974, 1781, *Foro padano* 1975, I, 80, note Prandi, Temi, 175, 408, note Fajella; for the Netherlands, e.g., HR 18 June 1982, *NJ* 1983, no. 723, note Brunner; *AA* 32 (1983), 758, note Van Schilfgaarde; for Spain L. DÍEZ-PICAZO & A. GULLÓN, *Sistema de Derecho Civil*, Vol. II, p. 69; for Greece, MICHAEL P. STATHOPOULOS, *Contract law in Hellas*, no. 86; for Portugal J. DE MATOS ANTUNES VARELA, *Das Obrigações em geral*, Vol. I, no. 67.

circumstances to invoke the non receipt of the acceptance of an offer (*exceptio doli specialis* (*praeteriti*))[57].

2. Validity. - A violation of the duty of good faith may lead to invalidity. For example, in many systems, before the introduction of statutory rules, standard terms could be held void on the basis of the general good faith clause[58], and today in these statutes the test for the unfairness of a term often lies in good faith[59]. Further, a violation of a precontractual duty to inform, based on good faith, may lead to invalidity for mistake or fraud (see above)[60]. On the other hand, good faith may limit invalidity. The right to offer an adaptation in order to avoid invalidity is often based on good faith[61]. In the Netherlands under the old code conversion was based on the general good faith clause[62].

3. Interpretation. - In most systems good faith plays a role in interpretation. Many systems contain a statutory provision on good faith interpretation[63]; in other systems the role of good faith in interpretation has been established by the courts[64]. Particularly the objective method of interpretation is often based on good faith. In addition to 'objective' interpretation in some systems there is a concept of supplementing interpretation (*ergänzende Vertragsauslegung*), also based on good faith[65]. It amounts to what could be called 'gap filling'. If a contract does not contain any specific provision for a question that arises, the gap in the contract is filled by way of supplementing interpretation. Some authors have suggested a doctrine of good faith interpretation that is even broader, operating not only in case of gaps[66].

4. Content. - English textbooks on contract law usually contain a chapter entitled 'Content' that deals with the express and implied terms of the contract[67]. The UP have followed this example[68]. Legal systems in the French

---

[57] See for Germany, *RG*, 13 July 1904, *RGZ* 58, 406; for the UP, Art. 1.7, Illustration 1.

[58] See for Germany e.g. *BGH*, 29 October 1956, *BGHZ* 22, 90 = *NJW* 1957, 17; for the Netherlands e.g. *HR*, 20 February 1976, *NJ* 1976, 486, note G.J. Scholten, *AA* 1976, p. 476, note Van der Grinten; for Greece, MICHAEL P. STATHOPOULOS, *Contract law in Hellas*, no. 34.

[59] See in Germany Art. 9 *AGBG*; in Portugal arts. 16 and 17 statute 1985 (see A. MENEZES-CORDEIRO, 'Rapport portugais', p. 349). For consumer contracts see also EC Council Directive 93/13/EEC, Art. 3, Section 1, which has been implemented in all EU jurisdictions.

[60] In Greece, the test for mistake is (partially) based on good faith (Art. 142 CC; MICHAEL P. STATHOPOULOS, *Contract law in Hellas*, no. 114 ff.).

[61] Art. 144 Greek Civil Code explicitly says so (see MICHAEL P. STATHOPOULOS, *Contract law in Hellas*, no. 121). See on Art. 1432 Italian Civil Code e.g. GUIDO ALPA & M. BESSONE, *I contratti in generale; Effetti, Invalidità e risoluzione del contratto*, Vol. II, Torino 1992, no. 36; on art. 6:230 Dutch Civil Code e.g. J.B.M. VRANKEN, 'Nietige overeenkomsten binden tot wat de goede trouw meebrengt', *NJB* 1990, p. 489.

[62] See e.g. *HR*, 8 July 1987, *NJ* 1981, 284. Art. 3:42 of the new code is said to be based on good faith. See *Parl. Gesch. Boek 3*, p. 199 (M.v.A. II).

[63] See § 157 German Civil Code; Art. 1366 Italian Civil Code; Art. 200 Greek Civil Code.

[64] See for the Netherlands e.g. *HR*, 20 May 1994, *NJ* 1995, 691, note Brunner.

[65] For Germany see e.g. *BGH*, 25 June 1980, *BGHZ* 277, 301; for Greece, see MICHAEL P. STATHOPOULOS, *Contract law in Hellas*, no. 154; for the UNIDROIT Principles see Art. 4.8 UP. The PECL do not contain a similar provision.

[66] See in the Netherlands J.M. VAN DUNNÉ, *Verbintenissenrecht I*, p. 137 ff.

[67] See e.g. G.H. TREITEL, *The Law of Contract*, 10th ed., London 1999, Chapter 6; M.P. FURMSTON, *Cheshire, Fifoot and Furmston's Law of Contract*, 14th ed., London, Edinburgh and

tradition speak of the effects of the contract[69]. Both for common law and civil law a distinction can be made between autonomous and heteronomous terms or effects of the contract. In Italian textbooks the determination of the heteronomous effects is usually called *integrazione* (supplementation or completion)[70], the term *interpretazione* being reserved for the determination of the autonomous effects.

In many systems good faith is regarded as one of the most important sources of heteronomous effects, or implied obligations as the Principles call them. The good faith duties most often incurred in the various legal systems are a duty of loyalty[71], a duty of care[72], a duty to co-operate[73] and a duty to inform[74]. The duty of loyalty protects the expectation interest. It obliges a party to secure performance or, more broadly, to ensure that the other party will have the use of the contract that he could reasonably expect from it. The contractual duty of care protects the negative interest. It obliges a party to take care that the person and the property of the other party do not suffer any damage during the performance. The adoption of a contractual duty of care is usually determined by the wish of the courts to provide victims (particularly when they are injured) with the protection tort liability (e.g. limited vicarious liability) or ordinary contractual liability (limited to impossible or late performance) does not provide or which is inaccessible (*non cumul*). In Germany there are even some who favour the adoption of a third track of liability (*dritte Spur*), which lies between

---

Dublin 2001, Chapter 6; EWAN MCKENDRICK, *Contract Law*, 4th ed., London 2000, Part II.

[68] Chapter 5 is called 'Content'.

[69] The PECL have not made a choice: see Chapter 6 which is entitled 'Content and Effects'.

[70] See C. MASSIMO BIANCA, *Il contratto*, Chapter 8; RODOLFO SACCO & G. DE NOVA, *Il contratto*, Vol. I, Part 5, II.

[71] See for Germany e.g. *BGH*, 28 April 1982, *NJW* 83, 998 (*Leistungstreuepflicht*); for France e.g. *Cass. soc.*, 30 April 1987, *Bull. civ.* V, no. 237, p. 152; *R.T.D. Civ.* 1988, 531, obs. Mestre (*devoir de loyauté*); for Italy e.g. *Cass.*, 18 July 1989, n. 3362, *Foro it.*, 1989, I, 2750, notes Di Majo and Mariconda (*obbligo di salvaguardia*); for Portugal A. MENEZES-CORDEIRO, 'Rapport portugais', p. 344; for Greece MICHAEL P. STATHOPOULOS, *Contract law in Hellas*, no. 155; for Denmark OLE LANDO, 'Each contracting party must act in accordance with good faith and fair dealing', in: *Festskrift till Jan Ramberg*, Stockholm 1996, p. 351.

[72] See for Germany e.g. *BGH*, 10 March 1983, *NJW* 83, 2813 = *MDR* 1982, 1000 = *LM* BGB § 242 (Be), no. 47 (*Schutzpflicht*) and since January, 2002, § 241(2) BGB (*new*) (*Pflichten aus dem Schuldverhältnis*): 'Das Schuldverhältnis kann nach seinem Inhalt jeden Teil zur Rücksicht auf die Rechte, Rechtsgüter und Interessen des anderen Teils verpflichten.' See for France e.g. *Civ. I*, 17 January 1995, *D.* 1995, 350, note Jourdain; *D.* 1996, *Somm.* 15, obs. Paisant; *R.T.D. civ.* 1995, 631, obs. Jourdain (*obligation de sécurité*). See for Greece MICHAEL P. STATHOPOULOS, *Contract law in Hellas*, no. 155; for Portugal, A. MENEZES-CORDEIRO, 'Rapport portugais', p. 344. In Italy the *obbligo di protezione* only plays a very limited role; see for an example where such a duty is said to have been adopted *Cass.*, 11 May 1973, n. 1269, *Giust. civ.*, 1973, I, 1306.

[73] See for Germany e.g. *BGH*, 25 June 1976, *BGHZ* 67, 35; for France e.g. Paris, 26 June 1985, *R.T.D. civ.* 1986, 100, n. 2, obs. J. Mestre; for Italy *Cass.*, 9 March 1991, n. 2503, *Foro it.*, 1991, I, 2077, note Bellantuono.

[74] See for France e.g. *Cass. I*, 18 December 1985, *Bull. civ.* I, no. 357; for Germany e.g. *BGH*, 7 December 1989, *LM* BGB § 242 (Be), no. 71 = *NJW* 1990, 1906 = *MDR* 1990, 690; for Italy e.g. *Cass.*, 8 August 1985, n. 4394, *Giur. it.* 1987, I, 1, 1136, note Romano; for Portugal see A. MENEZES-CORDEIRO, 'Rapport portugais', p. 344.

contractual liability and tort liability, for a violation of a *Schutzpflicht* which arises whenever there is a special relationship (*Sonderverbindung*) between two ore more persons[75]. The duty to co-operate was first proposed by Demogue, in a famous formula[76]: 'Les contractants forment une sorte de microcosme; c'est une petite société où chacun doit travailler pour un but commun qui est la somme des buts individuels poursuivis par chacun, absolument comme dans la société civile ou commerciale', and it was first 'codified' by the Principles[77]. It follows from the nature of this duty that it is more important in relational, long-term contracts, in particular long-term commercial contracts[78], than in simple exchange contracts. Finally, the duty to inform does not only operate during the pre-contractual stage, but also during performance[79].

5. *Privity.* - In Germany the doctrine of *Vertrag mit Schutzwirkung zugunsten Dritten*, which was adopted on the basis of good faith[80], considerably relaxed the privity of contract by broadening the possibility of a third party to profit from a contract between two other parties[81]. Under this doctrine certain third parties are included in the protection which a party to a contract has to provide for his partner and which makes full vicarious liability possible (*Schutzpflicht*; see above)[82]. In the Netherlands, under certain conditions a party may invoke a limitation clause against a third party[83].

---

[75] CLAUS-WILHELM CANARIS, 'Ansprüche wegen "positiver Vertragsverletzung" und "Schutzwirkung für Dritte" bei nichtigen Verträgen, Zugleich ein Beitrag zur Vereinheitlichung der Regeln über die Schutzpflichtverletzungen', *JZ* 1965, pp. 475-482, p. 479, proposed a theory of an *einheitliches gesetzliches Schutzverhältnis*, based on good faith: 'Alle Schutzpflichten finden ihre Grundlage in einem einheitlichen Schutzverhältnis, das mit der Aufnahme des geschäftlichen Kontaktes beginnt und sich über mehrere Stufen - Beginn der Vertragsverhandlungen, Vertragsschluß, Eintritt in das Erfüllungsstadium - verdichtet; es entsteht unabhängig vom Willen der Parteien, ist also "gesetzlicher" Natur, und findet seine Rechtfertigung im Vertrauensgedanken und seine positiv-rechtliche Grundlage in § 242 BGB'.

[76] R. DEMOGUE, *Traité des obligations en général, II Effets des obligations*, Part VI, Paris, 1931, no. 3 (p. 9). Compare however, the reaction by JEAN CARBONNIER, *Droit Civil*, Vol. IV *Les Obligations*, 22nd ed., Paris 2000, no. 114 (p. 227): 'L'outrance peut perdre une idée juste. On s'étonnera qu'à une époque où le mariage s'était peut-être trop transformé en contrat, d'aucuns aient rêvé de transformer tout contrat en mariage.'

[77] Arts. 5.3 UP and 1:202 PECL.

[78] See NAGLA NASSAR, *Sanctity of Contract Revisited: A Study in the Theory and Practice of Long-Term International Commercial Transactions*, Dordrecht, Boston and London 1995, pp. 156 ff. See, generally, IAN MACNEIL, 'Contract Adjustment of long-term economic relations under classical, neo-classical and relational contract law', (1978) 72 *Northwestern University LR*, p. 854.

[79] More precisely: in addition to a duty to give the other party information that may determine his consent, there may also be a duty to inform the other party in order to assure that a party obtains what he could expect from the performance. See M. FABRE-MAGNAN, *De l'obligation d'information dans les contrats; Essai d'une théorie*, Paris 1992, 281.

[80] The courts have based it on § 157 *BGB* (*ergänzende Vertragsauslegung*), but the majority of legal doctrine, maintaining that there cannot be said to be a gap in the contract, regards § 242 *BGB* as the real foundation (see e.g. KARL LARENZ, *Lehrbuch des Schuldrechts I*, p. 227).

[81] See, for Portugal, A. MENEZES-CORDEIRO, 'Rapport portugais', p. 337.

[82] A well-known example is the vegetable leaf case (*BGH*, 28 January 1976, *BGHZ* 66, 51), where the doctrines of *culpa in contrahendo* and *Vertrag mit Schutzwirkung für Dritte* were combined in order to find liability against a supermarket, where the child of a (potential) customer was injured

6. *Performance.* - In most systems if the parties have not made adequate provisions regarding the time and place of performance et cetera, and if the code does not provide for any specific regulations either, such rules are usually based on good faith or equity. However, one may ask whether a separate heading 'performance' is necessary in addition to 'content'. The (rules on) rights and duties which the code adds to what the parties have agreed upon may be spelled out under the heading 'content'.

In the UP the second section of the chapter on performance deals with hardship. However, since the effect of hardship may not only be that a party is no longer under a duty to perform a still existing obligation, but also that the obligations are changed or even the contract terminated, it seems more appropriate to distinguish hardship as a separate doctrine.

7. *Hardship.* - During the course of the 20th century a doctrine of hardship was adopted in most European systems. Often it was based on good faith, either because the courts based their doctrine on the general good faith clause[84] or because a specific code provision referred to the concept of good faith[85] and is regarded as a *lex specialis* of the general good faith clause[86]. Indeed, the problem of unforeseen circumstances is often cited as the paradigm example of the operation of the concept of good faith and of the need for such a concept.

8. *Remedies for Non-Performance.* - On the one hand, in many systems some of the remedies for non-performance are based on good faith. The right to withhold performance forms the most significant example. Most systems recognise an *exceptio non adimpleti contractus.* In some systems this remedy (which is actually a defence) is or was based on good faith[87]. In addition,

---

because it had slipped on a vegetable leaf that an employee of the supermarket had dropped.

[83] See e.g. *HR*, 12 January 1979, *NJ* 1979, 36, note Bloembergen; *AA* 1979, p. 556. Exceptions to the privity principle like this one are said to be based on good faith (see A.S. HARTKAMP, *Verbintenissenrecht II* (in: *Asser* series), no. 386).

[84] See for German law, e.g. *BGH*, 8 February 1984, *NJW* 1984, 1746 = *MDR* 1985, 47 = *LM* BGB § 242 (Bb), no. 108. See now § 313 *BGB* (*new*) (Störung der Geschäftsgrundlage): '(1) Haben sich Umstände, die zur Grundlage des Vertrags geworden sind, nach Vertragsschluss schwerwiegend verändert und hätten die Parteien den Vertrag nicht oder mit anderem Inhalt geschlossen, wenn sie diese Veränderung vorausgesehen hätten, so kann Anpassung des Vertrags verlangt werden, soweit einem Teil unter Berücksichtigung aller Umstände des Einzelfalls, insbesondere der vertraglichen oder gesetzlichen Risikoverteilung, das Festhalten am unveränderten Vertrag nicht zugemutet werden kann. (2) Einer Veränderung der Umstände steht es gleich, wenn wesentliche Vorstellungen, die zur Grundlage des Vertrags geworden sind, sich als falsch herausstellen. (3) Ist eine Anpassung des Vertrags nicht möglich oder einem Teil nicht zumutbar, so kann der benachteiligte Teil vom Vertrag zurücktreten. An die Stelle des Rücktrittsrechts tritt für Dauerschuldverhältnisse das Recht zur Kündigung.'

[85] See Art. 388 Greek Civil Code; Art. 437 Portuguese Civil Code; Art. 6:258 Dutch Civil Code.

[86] See for the Netherlands *Parl. Gesch. Boek 6*, p. 974 (M.v.A. II); for Greece MICHAEL P. STATHOPOULOS, *Contract law in Hellas*, no. 60, no. 292.

[87] For both German and Dutch law the reason for this lies in the fact that the relevant provisions (§ 320 *BGB* and Art. 6:262 *BW* respectively) are seen as *leges speciales* of the general right to withhold (§ 273 *BGB* and Art. 6:52 *BW* respectively), which in turn is regarded as a *lex specialis* of the general good faith clause (see *infra*). Under the old code the Dutch *Hoge Raad* based the *e.n.a.c.* on the general good faith clause (see *HR*, 30 June 1978, *NJ* 1978, 693, note G.J. Scholten). Also in France the *e.n.a.c.* is sometimes based on good faith (see PHILIPPE MALAURIE

Germany and the Netherlands recognise a more general right to withhold performance which is said to be a *lex specialis* of the general good faith clause[88]. Further, the German doctrine of *positive Vertragsverletzung* is often said to be (ultimately) based on good faith[89].

On the other hand, the exercise of a remedy may be limited by good faith. In many systems a party is not allowed to terminate the contract or withhold its own performance for a merely minor non-performance. In some systems this is conceived as an exception to the general right to terminate or to withhold, based on good faith[90]. Moreover, the right to request specific performance may be limited by good faith[91]. Furthermore, in France the invocation of a *clause résolutoire* is limited by good faith[92]. Finally, in some systems the right (and its modalities) to end a contract which was concluded for an indeterminate period - not a remedy for *non-performance*, of course - is based on good faith[93].

B. Outside Contract Law

It is often thought, particularly by common law lawyers, that good faith typically operates in contract law. Good faith is often seen, partly due to its collocation in codes of the French legal family, as a counterbalance to the rigour of the *pacta sunt servanda* rule. Although this may be an important role, in most systems the field of application of good faith is far from limited to contract law. First, many codes already themselves indicate that the obligor and obligee to *any* obligation have to meet the standard of good faith in their conduct[94]. This means that a person who is liable in tort towards another person (e.g. because he has injured him or damaged his property) or who has been unjustifiedly enriched at the expense of another person has to act in accordance with good faith. However, in addition to that, in some systems the field of application is

& LAURENT AYNÈS, *Les obligations*, no. 722).

[88] For Art. 273 German Civil Code, see HELMUT HEINRICHS, in: *Palandt Bürgerliches Gesetzbuch*, § 273, no. 1; for Art. 6:52 Dutch Civil Code, see *Parl. Gesch. Boek 6*, p. 205 (T.M.).

[89] See e.g. *BGH*, 13 November 1953, *BGHZ* 11, 80 = *NJW* 1954, 229; CLAUS-WILHELM CANARIS, 'Ansprüche wegen 'positiver Vertragsverletzung' und 'Schutzwirkung für Dritte' bei nichtigen Verträgen', pp. 475-482, p. 479; E. KRAMER, in: *Münchener Kommentar*, 'Einleitung Band 2', no. 73. See now § 280 (*new*) *BGB*. See for Portugal A. MENEZES-CORDEIRO, 'Rapport portugais', p. 340.

[90] See for the Netherlands e.g. *HR*, 10 August 1992, *NJ* 1992, 715; A.S. HARTKAMP, *Verbintenissenrecht II* (in: *Asser* series), no. 516. See for Germany e.g. HERBERT ROTH, in: *Münchener Kommentar*, § 242, no. 438 ff. See explicitly § 320 *BGB* (*e.n.a.c.*).

[91] See for the Netherlands *HR*, 5 January 2001, *NJ* 2001, 79 (Multi Vastgoed/Nethou); A.S. HARTKAMP, *Verbintenissenrecht I* (in: *Asser* series), no 639.

[92] See, e.g., *Cass. Civ. III*, 15 December 1976, *Bull. Civ.* III, no. 465, *R.T.D. Civ.* 1977, 340, obs. Cornu.

[93] For Germany see e.g. *BGH*, 15 June 1951, *LM*, § 242 (Bc) BGB, no. 1; for the Netherlands see e.g. *HR*, 21 April 1995, *NJ* 1995, 437.

[94] See § 242 German Civil Code, in the Section on the content of obligations in general; Art. 1175 Italian Civil Code, in the title on obligations in general; Art. 288 Greek Civil Code, in the Section on the law of obligations in general; Art. 762, Section 2, Portuguese Civil Code, in the Section on performance of obligations in general; Art. 6:2 Dutch Civil Code, in the title on obligations in general.

even broader[95]. In the Netherlands good faith has been applied in, for example[96], the law of succession, company law, bankruptcy law, property law and private international law. Hartkamp concludes that good faith must be held to be applicable in the whole of patrimonial law[97]. German law goes even further. There good faith operates not only in the whole of private law (e.g. family law, labour law, commercial law, copyright law)[98], but even outside it, in administrative law, tax law, procedural law (not only civil procedure) et cetera[99]. In other words: it is applicable in all fields of the law, except maybe in penal law[100].

In Germany an effort has been made to limit the field of application of good faith in a rational way. The solution was found in the *Sonderverbindung* (special relationship). It was said that only in the case of a 'special connection' between two or more persons, which is defined as a relationship of mutual trust similar to a contractual relationship, does their conduct have to meet the standard of good faith[101]. That standard being higher than the one generally prevailing in society (i.e. between 'strangers'), the *gute Sitten* (*boni mores*), the violation of which leads to tort liability. The *Sonderverbindung* concept was adopted by the courts. However, in their wish to apply the good faith standard (and all the duties, doctrines, and rules that come with it!) in many situations, they have broadened the concept considerably. As a result now not only neighbours, but also, e.g. plaintiff and defendant, competitors in a market, and a citizen and the State are

---

[95] See MARTIJN W. HESSELINK, *De redelijkheid en billijkheid in het Europese privaatrecht*, p. 382 ff, where I give examples from various European jurisdictions of applications of good faith in property law, family law, company law, procedural law, public law, international law.

[96] See, for more examples, A.S. HARTKAMP, *Verbintenissenrecht II* (in: *Asser* series), no. 304.

[97] A.S. HARTKAMP, *Verbintenissenrecht II* (in: *Asser* series), no. 304.

[98] See already *Reichsgericht*, 26 May 1914, *RGZ* 85, 108 (117): 'Das System des Bürgerlichen Gesetzbuchs wird durchdrungen von dem Grundsatze von Treu und Glauben mit Rücksicht auf die Verkehrssitte und von dem Grundsatze der Zurückweisung jeder Arglist im weitesten Sinne. Die §§ 157, 226, 242, 826 erscheinen nur als besondere Ausprägungen eines allgemeinen Prinzips. (...) das allgemeine Prinzip beherrscht alle Einzelbestimmungen und muß gerade in ihnen lebendige Wirkung üben, zur Klärung, Erweiterung, Ergänzung oder Beschränkung des vereinzelten Wortlauts'. Compare the Swiss Civil Code which has put the general good faith clause right at the beginning (Art. 2).

[99] See for examples, e.g. ARNDT TEICHMANN, in: *Soergel Bürgerliches Gesetzbuch*, § 242, nos. 65-106; HERBERT ROTH, in: *Münchener Kommentar*, § 242, no. 57 ff. Compare the *Travaux de l'association Henri Capitant, Tome XLIII, année 1992. Journées louisianaises de Baton-Rouge et La Nouvelle Orléans, 'La bonne foi'*, Paris 1994, that discuss good faith in contract law, penal law, fiscal law, administrative law, and international law, in several systems.

[100] See e.g. HELMUT HEINRICHS, in: *Palandt Bürgerliches Gesetzbuch*, § 242, no. 1 ('eine das gesamte Rechtsleben beherrschenden Grundsatz'). It is often said that only (substantive) penal law seems to be excluded from the application of good faith, as a result of the *nulla poena sine lege* principle. See e.g. JÜRGEN SCHMIDT, in: *J. von Staudingers Kommentar*, § 242, no. 237, and Y. LOUSSOUARN, 'Rapport de synthèse', in: *Travaux de l'association Henri Capitant, Tome XLIII, année 1992. Journées louisianaises de Baton-Rouge et La Nouvelle Orléans, 'La bonne foi'*, Paris 1994, p. 18.

[101] See e.g. HELMUT HEINRICHS, in: *Palandt Bürgerliches Gesetzbuch*, § 242, no. 6; KARL LARENZ, *Lehrbuch des Schuldrechts I*, p. 128.

said to have a special relationship[102]. It is therefore held that the concept of the *Sonderverbindung* has failed to limit the field of application of good faith and that its field of application must therefore be regarded as being unlimited[103].

IV. An Alternative View

A. Introduction

Section III shows that in all systems the courts have developed many - often very important - new rules and doctrines on the basis of the general good faith clause, in contract law and far outside it. These rules at first sight do not seem to have very much in common. In particular there seems to be nothing else that distinguishes them from other rules than the fact that the courts, when adopting them, have mentioned a general good faith clause as their basis. However, in the traditional view, as shown in Section II, all these rules are regarded as concretisations of good faith, as the content of the open good faith norm. Here I will argue that good faith as it has developed cannot be regarded as a norm and that it does not make sense to regard rules like those mentioned in Section III as the content of an open good faith norm. What are usually called the three functions of good faith are in reality the normal tasks of the judge. There is no inner coherence between so-called good faith rules and doctrines. Instead of trying to develop an inner system of good faith that is supposed to concretise the open norm, legal doctrine should try to give the rules and doctrines that the courts have developed while invoking good faith their proper place in the system of the code.

B. The Judge and the Code

Immediately after the enactment of the codes in Europe it was thought that the only thing the courts had to do was to apply the law, which they could find in the codes. This led to the traditional civil law view that the courts do not create the law, they merely apply it. Today, however, it is broadly accepted that this traditional view may be in conformity with the ideals of Enlightenment (separation of powers), but not with reality: also in civil law systems the courts do not only apply the law, they also create it.

As a matter of fact, in civil law as in common law systems, applying the law necessarily implies creating it. This follows from the simple fact that a court has to make a decision in every case that comes before it. In continental European legal systems the courts have to resolve cases by applying the rules from the code. This means that they have to apply abstract rules to concrete cases. A rule

---

[102] See for other examples e.g. JÜRGEN SCHMIDT, in: *J. von Staudingers Kommentar*, § 242, no. 159 ff.

[103] See e.g. JÜRGEN SCHMIDT, in: *J. von Staudingers Kommentar*, § 242, no. 163; DIETER MEDICUS, *Schuldrecht I*, no. 130. In *BGH*, 22 October 1987, *BGHZ*, 102, 95 (102), the *BGH* explicitly left open the question whether a *Sonderverbindung* is required for the application of § 242 *BGB*.

may be conceived as an abstract formula that links certain legal consequences to certain facts: if facts *a*, *b* and *c* occur the legal effect will be *x* (e.g.: 'a person who promises to do something but then breaks his promise must repair the damage'). In applying a rule to a certain factual situation the judge may have to face three major problems. First, it may occur that he has some doubts as to whether the facts presented before him correspond to the facts as defined in the rule (e.g.: does silence constitute a promise?), or whether the remedy which the plaintiff requests corresponds to the legal effect as defined in the rule (e.g.: is lost profit part of the damage that must be repaired?). Secondly, it may be that not all the facts mentioned in the rule have occurred, but some others have, which he regards as equivalent, so that he finds it suitable that the same legal effect should follow in this case (or he regards the remedy requested as equivalent to the remedy mentioned in the rule). Thirdly, it may occur that all the facts mentioned in the rule have indeed occurred, but also some other facts which, in the eyes of the judge, mean that the legal effect indicated in the rule should not follow. Therefore the court may find it necessary to interpret (concretise), to supplement and to correct the abstract rule in order to reach an acceptable result. This necessarily follows from the fact that it has to apply a system of abstract rules to a concrete case.

If a judge decides in a certain case to concretise, supplement or correct the law in a certain way, would he be doing justice if he refused to do so in a following similar case? The answer is no, in most systems it is thought that justice requires like cases to be treated alike[104]. Therefore a court in civil law countries is bound by *stare decisis* just as much as a common law court. But if a court should decide in the same way as it decided in a precedent similar case, this means nothing less than that the court with its earlier decision has established a new rule, a rule which is a concretisation, a supplementation or a correction of an existing rule[105]. Thus the concretisation, supplementation, and correction of the law has become part of the law. Therefore the conclusion must be that the application of the law necessarily implies the creation of law[106].

---

[104] In most systems the right to equal treatment is even constitutionally protected. See e.g. in the Netherlands art. 1 *GW*. For the EU see Chapter III (Equality) (arts. 20-26) Charter of Fundamental Rights of the European Union (Nice, 2000), especially art. 20 (Equality before the Law): 'everyone is equal before the law'. See also art. 14 ECHR.

[105] The rule is new in the sense that its existence was not known before. Unless one believes in natural law there seems to be no reason to take the view that the judge discovers a pre-existing concretisation, supplementation, or a correction to or of the rule. In that latter (rather fictitious) view all three problems could be regarded as questions of interpretation. For a debate on this issue (and on other related issues) see M.J. BORGERS & I. GIESEN & C.E.C. JANSEN & F.G.H. KRISTEN & F.W.J. MEIJER & T.H.D. STRUYCKEN & F.M.J. VERSTIJLEN & J.B.M. VRANKEN, 'Vragen aan Hesselink over zijn alternatieve visie op de functies van de redelijkheid en billijkheid en de taak van de rechter', *NJB* 2000, pp. 2029-2031 and M.W. HESSELINK, '"Wat is recht etc.?"; Antwoorden op vragen van Tilburgers over rechtsregels, rechtspraak en rechtsvorming', *NJB* 2000, pp. 2032-2040.

[106] For this reason it is important that the judge indicates the facts that were decisive in persuading him to adopt a certain interpretation, supplementation, or correction of the law. Legal certainty depends on the extent to which the judge makes it explicit which facts are decisive (i.e. which

The same wish to treat like cases alike and different cases differently in accordance with the differences, also means that the law - be it common law or civil law - has to be a system[107]: rules are related to each other, according to the similarities and differences of the cases to which they apply[108]. The difference between civil law and common law is that most civil law systems have (temporarily) fixed their system of rules in a code in which the system is made more explicit; in most codes, particularly the German BGB and the new Dutch BW, as a result of a higher degree of abstraction. The creation of new rules (concretisations, supplementations, and corrections of existing rules) leads to new ramifications of the system. What has been said with regard to rules applies accordingly to the system. Clearly, the need to treat like cases alike may mean that as a result of the concretisation, supplementation, and correction of a rule other rules, located in other places within the system, are also adapted accordingly. Moreover, just like rules, the system as such (which is, as said, nothing more than the formalisation of the wish to treat like cases alike) may be concretised, supplemented and corrected. Again, this is equally true for civil law as it is for common law. The fact that in civil law systems the legislator at a certain point in time has fixed the system does not mean that it will remain unchanged and closed. Just as the legislator cannot make rules that will remain unchanged in their application neither can it make a system that does not change when it is applied.

From the time when it was discovered that the courts (occasionally, it was thought) do create rules, civil lawyers have been trying, on the one hand, to determine why and when a judge is allowed to create law, and, on the other, to find a way by which to render the court's judgement as rational and as objective as possible, by developing - sometimes descriptive, but usually prescriptive - analyses of the decision-making by the judge. However, both these efforts presuppose that judge-made law is an anomaly. But, as we have just seen, that presumption is incorrect. Therefore there is no need for a justification that goes any further than the (constitutional) attribution to the judge of the power to resolve disputes at the basis of the law in the code. Also, there is no need to develop a prescriptive method for guaranteeing the objectivity and rationality of the court's judgement. We should merely recognise that we have confidence in the subjective judgement of our judges - in particular those in our Supreme Courts - with regard to the interpretation, supplementation and correction of the law, and in the way our judicial system is organised (e.g. the selection and

---

facts constitute elements of the new (sub-)rule) (and on consistency of course: *stare decisis*). A summary justification of a legal decision fits in with the idea that the courts merely apply the law, but is no longer justified when it is recognised that the courts create the law when applying it.

[107] This is not a factual but a normative statement, based on the (fundamental) idea of equality.

[108] In the same sense DAVID HOWARTH, 'The General Conditions of Unlawfulness', in: A.S. Hartkamp et al. (eds.) *Towards a European Civil Code*, 2nd ed., Nijmegen and The Hague, London, Boston 1998, pp. 397 ff. See also J.H. BAKER, *An Introduction to English Legal History*, p. 89, who says that in England the law has been regarded as a system since Tudor times.

training, the career system, the plurity of judges, the duty to provide the grounds for the decision in question, and the appeal system)[109].

C. *Functions of Good Faith or Tasks of the Court?*

It is interesting to see that these three activities with regard to the law - concretising (or interpreting), supplementing, and correcting - which follow from the normal task of the judge (i.e. to apply the law), correspond to the three tasks that Papinian attributed to the *praetor* with regard to the written law in Rome. The *praetor* (and other magistrates) had to help (concretise), supplement and correct the *ius civile*, and the results of these three operations were regarded as new law which was called *ius honorarium*.

As I said before, Wieacker transplanted the Papinian trichtonomy into modern German law. However, he did not do so in order to indicate the tasks of the judge with regard to the law in the code, or to show the relationship between German judge-made law and the law in the code, but rather in order to indicate the functions of modern good faith. Good faith, Wieacker said, concretises, supplements and corrects the law. And, as shown above, this view has not only been followed by most German legal scholars, it is also the common view in most European legal systems, albeit that there the contract (and not the law) is often regarded as the object of interpretation, supplementation and correction by good faith[110].

However, if the functions of good faith are the same as the tasks of the judge, i.e. interpreting, supplementing or correcting the law, does it then still make sense to regard good faith as a specific norm?

D. *Good Faith is not a Norm*

Good faith is usually said to be an open rule or open norm (see above, Section II)[111]. From the use of the term 'open norm' one could conclude that there must be a category of open norms which can be distinguished from other norms which are not open. However, such a conclusion would not be correct: all norms

---

[109] This latter point has been the subject of criticism. See especially M.J. BORGERS & I. GIESEN & C.E.C. JANSEN & F.G.H. KRISTEN & F.W.J. MEIJER & T.H.D. STRUYCKEN & F.M.J. VERSTIJLEN & J.B.M. VRANKEN, 'Vragen aan Hesselink over zijn alternatieve visie op de functies van de redelijkheid en billijkheid en de taak van de rechter' (see also OLIVER REMIEN, *ZEuP* 2001, p. 420). In reply to those critics I have further developed this point in my article '"Wat is recht etc.?"; Antwoorden op vragen van Tilburgers over rechtsregels, rechtspraak en rechtsvorming'. I will not pursue this point any further here since the questions of how a judge must operate when he creates new rules and whether in doing so he has discretion, are not specific to judge-made law 'on the basis of good faith' (they arise in all cases where judges make new rules), and since my main claims regarding the nature of good faith, which I will make in the remainder of this Section IV and in the Conclusions (V), do not depend on this point. One may very well accept these claims without accepting that courts, when creating new rules, have discretion and/or do actually decide according to their own subjective views.

[110] I will come back on this later.

[111] A norm is only part of a rule, the other part being the effect of non-compliance with the norm. The term 'general clause' reflects openness on both sides.

are more ore less open. Every norm could be placed on a scale which ranges from totally open to totally closed: a norm is more open when fewer situations are excluded from its applicability. The closer a rule gets to one of both extremes, the less it makes sense to speak of a rule: a totally closed rule (all cases but one are excluded) is an order, a totally open rule (no case excluded) is equivalent to the (potential) law. Although all norms are more or less open there are some norms which are usually explicitly called 'open', like *gute Sitten* in Germany, the *zorgvuldigheidsnorm* in the Netherlands, 'a reasonable time' in the Unidroit Principles, 'unfair term' in the European Directive. Often the legislator has deliberately formulated them in an open manner, usually because it was not yet able to determine which cases should be covered by the rule. The content of more open (or abstract) rules becomes clearer by their concretisation[112]. Through application, sub-rules are developed which are interconnected. Thus a sub-system of the rule is developed. Therefore, as a result of its application, every rule will become the top of a subsystem[113]. Thus through a process of concretisation it becomes more and more clear what the content of the norm is.

However, the particularity of the general good faith clause as it has developed in many European legal systems is that - unlike other 'general clauses' - it does not contain (or no longer contains) a rule, because it is completely open: with regard to the premises (the norm) as well as with regard to the effects it is totally open[114]. Section III has given an impression of the variety of norms and legal effects that have been based on good faith by the courts. Statements, which are sometimes uttered to the effect that a general good faith clause makes the whole of contract law superfluous, or that the concept of equity could replace the whole law, are correct to the extent that in its field of application (see *infra*) good faith may be applied in *any* factual situation to establish *any* legal effect. In other words: any rule could be based on it. There is no difference between saying 'good faith requires' and 'justice requires' or 'the law requires'[115].

---

[112] This is true for any rule (since all rules are more or less open) and accounts for the fact that after a certain period of time during which it is applied a code becomes unworkable: the system of the code has developed huge subsystems with ramifications that often reach a degree of abstraction that is so low that they nearly touch the ground of the facts. Hence the call for recodification.

[113] See as an illustration the commentaries on the various Civil Codes: the text of each article effectively serves as a heading for a very detailed account of a particular branch of the law, each of which may discuss hundreds of cases and cover dozens of pages of fine print.

[114] The fact that good faith is not a norm may explain why its formulation or its place in the code of the general good faith clause does not seem to have been of any importance for its 'application' in most systems.

[115] If, for example in a case of application of good faith in its corrective function, Parliament had allowed the same exception in the code, that would have been the result of a debate among MPs, who had all expressed their opinion about what would be most just, and then voted, whereas, if the need for this exception is 'discovered' by a judge in a concrete case lying before him, the judge has to state that the objective standard of good faith requires the exception instead of frankly admitting that in his view justice so requires.

The cause of good faith having become a completely open norm, and therefore having ceased to be a norm at all, probably lies in the fact that the content of good faith is said to consist of three functions which in reality are the tasks of the judge with regard to the law. Had the courts given real content to the good faith norm (e.g. leaving it a norm for the way in which an obligor has to perform), instead of calling the three main tasks of the judge its content, it would have been a real (open) norm. However, the assimilation of the functions of good faith with the tasks of the judge has resulted in good faith becoming a completely open norm. In every system where the content of good faith is said to consist of these three functions good faith is a completely open norm, i.e. no norm at all[116].

Therefore, it seems, because of the way in which good faith has developed in most European legal systems (see above), it can no longer be regarded as a norm. In reality, good faith is not a norm but a mouthpiece (a *porte parole*) for new rules (see for a few examples Section III) [117]. However, if the general good faith clause is not a rule, it does not make sense to say that a decision is based on it. In reality such a decision is based on the new rule. Therefore the court should mention the new rule, and formulate it as explicitly as possible.

E. Field of Application Unlimited

It is clear that good faith, as is the case with the judge, should fulfil these three tasks with regard to the whole of private law, not only with regard to contract

[116] The content of no other norm has been said to consist of functions which in reality are the tasks of the judge. This may explain why no other norm has become a totally open norm. Very broad concepts like *boni mores* and *zorgvuldigheidsnorm* are not completely open: not only is the norm not completely open, also their effect (in terms of remedies) is limited. As a result, the inner systems of provisions like § 826 BGB and art. 6:162 *BW* do not 'compete' (see *infra*, Section F) with the system of the code. See further my *op. cit.*, p. 423f.

[117] In the same sense JÜRGEN SCHMIDT, in: *J. von Staudingers Kommentar*, § 242, no. 176 ff.; CHRISTIAN E.C. JANSEN, 'Good Faith in Construction Law: the Inaugural King's College Construction Law Lecture' (1999) 15 *Const. L.J.*, pp. 347 ff, on p. 358; H.J. DE KLUIVER, 'Goede trouw en rechtspersonenrecht', in: *A-T-D; Opstellen aangeboden aan Prof.mr. van Schilfgaarde*, Deventer 2000, pp. 225 ff.; W. SNIJDERS, *WPNR* 6376 (1999), p. 792 ff, see on p. 793, who agrees in principle, but regards the present version as being too radical; DUNCAN KENNEDY, 'The Political Stakes in "Merely Technical" Issues of Contract Law', 10 *ERPL* (2002), pp. 7-28, on p. 19 ('the phrase good faith has no content at all'); SIMON WHITTAKER & REINHARD ZIMMERMANN, 'Good faith in European contract law: surveying the legal landscape', in: Reinhard Zimmermann & Simon Whittaker (eds.), *Good Faith in European Contract Law*, Cambridge 2000, pp. 7-62, p. 32: 'All in all, therefore, § 242 BGB is often needed merely for a transitory phase until a new rule is sufficiently well established to be able to stand on its own legs: so that "figuratively speaking, the statutory foundation of § 242 could be withdrawn without any risk of having the judge-made edifice collapse" [reference to HEIN KÖTZ]. All in all, therefore, § 242 BGB is neither 'queen of rules' nor 'baneful plague' but an invitation, or reminder, for courts to do what they do anyway and have always done [reference to the present essay]: to specify, supplement and modify the law, i.e. to develop it in accordance with the perceived needs of their time.' See also H. MERZ, *Berner Kommentar, Einleitungsband*, Bern 1966, Art. 2 *ZGB*, no. 42 (*Durchgangsfunktion*). Critical are P. VAN SCHILFGAARDE, 'Deel 4 van Hesselink', *WPNR* 6377 (1999), pp. 811 ff; J.H. DALHUISEN, *RM Themis* 1999, pp. 332 ff, OLIVER REMIEN, *ZEuP* 2001, pp. 418 ff.; M.J. VAN LAARHOVEN &.W.M. NIESKENS-ISPHORDING, *NTBR* 2001.

law. The assimilation of the functions of good faith with the normal tasks of the judge therefore explains why it has proved to be impossible in most countries to limit the field of application of good faith. The idea that the field of application of good faith should be limited follows from the conception of good faith as a standard for conduct which is higher than the one prevailing between strangers, and which should therefore be limited to contractual and similar situations. If, however, concretisation, supplementation, and correction of the law are regarded as the functions of good faith, there is no reason why good faith should only operate in a limited field of the law. Any rule is subject to interpretation, supplementation, correction, or, to put it in terms of rights and obligations: rights and obligations are never abstract, but always subject to concretisation, supplementation and limitation. To give an example, it is clear that not only a contractual right but any right should not be abused (i.e. any abstract right has certain limits)[118].

F. Rejection of an Inner System of Good Faith

Section III has shown that the courts have developed many new rules and doctrines on the basis of good faith, which for an outsider at first sight do not seem to have much in common. Section II has shown that all these rules are usually regarded as sub-rules of good faith, as part of the content of the good faith norm. However, if, as maintained here, good faith is not a norm, and if the functions of good faith in reality are the normal tasks of the judge, it does not make any sense to regard these new rules as the content of the good faith norm.

This also means that it does not make much sense to develop a sub-system of good faith either[119]. As said, the content of more open rules becomes clearer by their concretisation into a subsystem of rules et cetera[120]. However, the sub-system of a completely open rule inevitably turns out to be a parallel system of the law, which covers the whole field of law in which it applies, but in an alternative manner[121]. The result of the concretisation of good faith would be

[118] In some systems the prohibition of the abuse of a right is seen as one of the rules contained in good faith. In some others it is seen as a separate doctrine. It is clear, however, that it is simply equivalent to the third task of the judge: in certain circumstances he has to make an exception to the right. Of course, the question of in which circumstances a right should be limited ('the test for abuse') depends entirely on the right involved. Usually, a property right is thought to be more sovereign than a contractual right. But the mechanism is the same: an abstract right does not exist in certain concrete circumstances. It is sometimes said that an existing right may not be invoked in certain circumstances. That terminology, however, reflects the idea of a higher norm ('you should not abuse your right') setting aside the lower norm ('you have a right'). This difference in terminology reflects the debates in Germany (*Innentheorie/Außentheorie*) and in France (Planiol/Josserand). In Germany one approach won the debate, in France it was the other.

[119] For this reason the rules in Section III were not presented in the shape of a tentative three functions plus *Fallgruppen* subsystem of European good faith but according to the structure of a possible European contract law. This approach is not correct, of course, in the sense that these rules must be seen in their own system.

[120] JÜRGEN SCHMIDT, in: *J. von Staudingers Kommentar*, § 242, nos. 192 ff, uses the term 'inner system' (*Binnensystem*).

[121] See JÜRGEN SCHMIDT, in: *J. von Staudingers Kommentar*, § 242, nos. 194.

just another system of law, parallel to the system of the code, but not self-sufficient[122].

'Good faith rules' have nothing more in common that distinguishes them from other rules than that the courts, when adopting them, have mentioned the general good faith clause as their legal basis. In particular, good faith rules are not fairer or more equitable or more moral than other rules[123]. Therefore, the sum of good faith rules and doctrines has no inner coherence. It is frequently assumed that good faith rules are necessarily or normally altruistic rules which impose solidarity and counterbalance party autonomy[124]. However, this is not necessarily the case. Indeed, it is more a question of which is the rule and which is the exception[125]. Most civil codes, especially those which were enacted in the 19th century, were almost exclusively based on the idea of party autonomy. As a result, most concretisations, supplementations and corrections were inspired by concerns of solidarity. However, to the extent that contemporary private law is increasingly based on solidarity courts may well decide to concretise, supplement and correct those rules, on the basis of good faith, in a more autonomy-oriented way[126].

Good faith shows the perceived weak spots of a legal system which the courts felt they had to repair by supplementation and correction on the basis of good faith[127]. In this respect 'the content of good faith' is very similar to equity in old English law and *ius honorarium* in Roman law[128]. And it is striking to see how much of what has been said on equity and on the *ius honorarium* is equally true for good faith in many civil law systems today. See, for example, Maitland on equity[129]: 'we ought to think of equity as supplementary law, a sort of appendix added on to our code, or a sort of gloss written round our code. (...) Equity without common law would have been a castle in the air, an

[122] Compare for equity F.W. MAITLAND, *Equity; also The Forms of Action at Common Law; Two Courses of Lectures*, Cambridge 1920, pp. 18-19, and for *ius honorarium*, M. KASER, 'Ius honorarium' und 'ius civile', *SZRA* 101 (1984), pp. 1-114, p. 4.

[123] See JÜRGEN SCHMIDT, in: *J. von Staudingers Kommentar*, § 242, no. 195.

[124] See especially DUNCAN KENNEDY, 'Form and Substance in Private Law Adjudication', and more recently, MARIETTA AUER, 'Good Faith: A Semiotic Approach', 10 *ERPL* (2002), p. 279-301.

[125] SIMON WHITTAKER & REINHARD ZIMMERMANN, 'Coming to terms with good faith', in: Reinhard Zimmermann & Simon Whittaker (eds.), *Good Faith in European Contract Law*, Cambridge 2000, p. 699.

[126] See, as a recent Dutch example, *HR*, 1 October 1999, *NJ* 2000, 207 (Geurtzen/ Kampstaal) where the concept of good faith was used to limit the effect of a (protective) statutory rule, thus reinforcing party autonomy. See further *supra*, Chapter 3, Section VI, B, 3.

[127] Compare SIMON WHITTAKER & REINHARD ZIMMERMANN, 'Coming to terms with good faith', p. 677 (with a focus on contract law, the subject of their study): 'a legal system which is generally at ease with its own legal rules for the creation and regulation of contracts will have much less of a need to have a recourse to a general legal principle such as good faith; if the legal rules are seen as generally good (however this is conceived), there will be no need to correct or to supplement them.'

[128] In the same sense with regard to equity now also SIMON WHITTAKER & REINHARD ZIMMERMANN, 'Coming to terms with good faith', p. 675.

[129] F.W. MAITLAND, *Equity*, pp. 18-21.

impossibility. For this reason I do not think that any one has expounded equity as a single consistent system, an articulate body of law. It is a collection of appendixes between which there is no very close connection. (...) To have acknowledged the existence of equity as a system distinct from law would in my opinion have been a belated, a reactionary measure. (...) I think, for example, that you ought to learn the many equitable modifications of the law of contract, not as part of equity, but as part, and a very important part, of our modern English law of contract', and Kaser on *ius honorarium*[130]: 'Das *ius honorarium* ist stofflich kein geschlossenes Ganzes, kein System. (...) Während man dem *ius civile* zwar das Merkmal einer gewissen Kohärenz, wenn auch, wie der notwendig gewordene Hinzutritt des *ius honorarium* beweist, nicht das der Vollständigkeit zuerkennen darf, bleibt das *ius honorarium* eine bloße Summe von miteinander nicht, jedenfalls zumeist nicht notwendig, zusammenhängenden Einzelerscheinungen.' The 'content' of present-day good faith could be regarded as a new *ius honorarium* or as civil law's equity[131]. It shows the perceived weak spots of a legal system which the courts felt had to be repaired by supplementation and correction on the basis of good faith[132].

Legal doctrine, instead of bringing the new rules developed on the basis of good faith in connection with each other, and becoming involved in discussions on whether a decision may be based on good faith and, if yes, on which good faith article or on which function et cetera, should relate them to the rules or doctrines that are concretised, supplemented or corrected by them[133]. In Germany, the present commentator to § 242 *BGB* in the prestigious Staudinger commentary has come to the same conclusion[134]. The 11th edition (1961) of that commentary, by Weber, counted 1553 pages. J. Schmidt, the present commentator, rightly says that ideally the commentary to § 242 *BGB* should be limited to a few phrases explaining that good faith is not a norm, and should then refer, for a discussion of rules which the courts have adopted mentioning § 242 *BGB*, to the commentary to the rules that were changed by them[135].

---

[130] M. KASER, '"Ius honorarium' und "ius civile"', pp. 4, 72.

[131] Of course, it is hardly surprising that the *ius honorarium* should be comparable to the good faith rules, since 'the functions of good faith' are parallel to those of the *ius honorarium* (see *supra*, Section C). However, there are differences as well. The most important one seems to be that the *ius honorarium* in principle contained all the rules created by the magistrates, whereas today the courts do not base all their new rules on good faith (see *infra*, Section G).

[132] Compare SIMON WHITTAKER & REINHARD ZIMMERMANN, 'Coming to terms with good faith', p. 677 (with a focus on contract law, the subject of their study): 'a legal system which is generally at ease with its own legal rules for the creation and regulation of contracts will have much less of a need to have a recourse to a general legal principle such as good faith; if the legal rules are seen as generally good (however this is conceived), there will be no need to correct or to supplement them.'

[133] On this approach see SIMON WHITTAKER & REINHARD ZIMMERMANN, 'Good faith in European contract law: surveying the legal landscape', p. 32: 'Whilst a radical adoption of this approach would probably go too far, and might also be impractical, the development is heading, in some respects, in this direction.'

[134] JÜRGEN SCHMIDT, in: *J. von Staudingers Kommentar*, § 242, no. 236.

[135] No. 241.

In addition to these theoretical objections, in many countries there will soon be a practical need for abolishing the inner system of good faith. As a result of the enormous number of cases 'based on good faith' it will no longer be manageable. However, this number will inevitably continue to rise in all systems where the tasks of the judge with regard to the law are regarded as the functions of good faith. More and more lawyers will question the sense of a distinction between the rules of the code and the rules that are said to be the content of the good faith norm[136]. Therefore it seems likely (and indeed desirable) that the same will happen to good faith as happened to equity and *ius honorarium*: when the distinction is no longer held to be justified and in addition will prove to be impractical, it will be abolished[137]. German law may already have reached that point.

However, the rejection of an inner system of good faith does not mean that the efforts made by legal doctrine over the last century have been useless. First of all, it has been of great importance that scholars have formulated the rules or even doctrines which were adopted in cases where the general good faith clause was 'applied'. Secondly, many parts of the inner system of good faith may be directly transferred into the system of the code, particularly to its general provisions (e.g. the *Fallgruppe* of *venire contra factum proprium*)[138], and, for contract law, into the chapter on content (e.g. the obligations to be loyal, to protect, to co-operate, to inform). That is not only true for rules, but also for entire doctrines. This is shown where countries have adopted a new code: many doctrines that were adopted on the basis of good faith under the old code have been given their proper place in the new code, e.g. *culpa in contrahendo*[139], *e.n.a.c*[140], hardship[141], *Schutzpflicht*[142], the duty to co-operate[143], *Vertrag mit Schutzwirkung für Dritte*[144]. Incidentally, if good faith really were a norm it would have been much more logical for these legal systems to have placed all the good faith sub-rules in one section under a heading like 'Good faith concretisations'.

G. Good Faith is a Cover

Good faith is not the highest norm of contract law or even of private law, but no norm at all, and is merely the mouthpiece through which new rules speak, or the cradle where new rules are born. What the judge really does when he applies

[136] Compare once again, on equity, F.W. MAITLAND, *Equity*, p. 20.
[137] It should be submitted, however, that in this respect good faith is closer to the *ius honorarium* than to equity, since the practical need for the abolition of the distinction is less urgent because good faith rules are not, like equity was until the Judicature Acts of 1873 and 1875, administered by a separate jurisdiction.
[138] Compare DIETER MEDICUS, *Schuldrecht I*, no. 135.
[139] See § 311 (2) (*new*) *BGB*.
[140] See Art. 6:262 Dutch Civil Code.
[141] See Art. 6:258 Dutch Civil Code, § 313 (*new*) *BGB*, Art. 6:111 PECL, Art. 6.2.1 UP.
[142] See § 241(2) (*new*) *BGB*.
[143] See Art. 5.3 UP and Art. 1.202 PECL.
[144] See § 311 (3) (*new*) *BGB*.

good faith is to create new rules. These new rules are concretisations, supplementations and corrections to the rules and system of the code. One may ask why the courts mention the good faith clause when they develop these new rules and doctrines. Why did the courts say - and are still saying - that they apply good faith instead of openly saying that they are interpreting, supplementing and correcting the law? Several reasons can be given. They all show that good faith has not only been a mouthpiece but also a cover[145]. Judges in continental European systems have felt uncomfortable with their role as creators of law. First, there is the traditional civil law view with regard to the role of the judge: the judge's task is to apply the law (*trias politica*). Therefore, the courts may have felt uncomfortable in creating law instead of merely applying it, and they were encouraged to feel this way by legal doctrine[146]. Secondly, civil law judges may have felt somewhat at fault when they changed or created new rules because the law created by them was not democratically legitimised. Therefore, it was much easier for them, instead of openly declaring that they changed the law, to state that they merely applied it, invoking the general good faith clause in the code which had been adopted by the democratically elected legislator, and attributing to it the functions of concretising, supplementing and correcting the law. A third reason why the judge felt uncomfortable, and probably the most significant one, lies in the sanctity of contract. In many of the cases where the courts have 'applied' good faith (particularly those in the first period) they have more or less radically interfered with the binding force of what parties had freely agreed to (the most typical example: unforeseen circumstances)[147]. They therefore preferred to say that the highest norm of contract law required that in the given case the contractual right could not be exercised rather than to bluntly state that in their view it would be just to accept an exception to the abstract rule *pacta sunt servanda*. Then there is the argument of convenience. It is much easier for a judge to just mention the general good faith clause as the rule he applies than to formulate the new rule (*Die Flucht in die Generalklauseln*)[148]. Finally, it should not be forgotten that many judges actually believed that good faith is a truly existing supreme norm, a belief that fitted perfectly in a European tradition of Aristotelian and Christian belief in natural law.

---

[145] See HERBERT ROTH, in: *Münchener Kommentar*, § 242, no. 26: 'Deckmantel richterlicher Rechtsfortbildung'. In the same sense BRIGITTA LURGER, *Grundfragen der Vereinheitlichung des Vertragsrechts in der Europäischen Union*, Wien, New York, 2002, p. 383: 'Deckmantel für einen immensen Bestand an richterlicher heteronomer Rechtsetzung'.

[146] The same ideals of the Enlightenment also explain why the *Methodenlehre* has been developed. It was clearly aimed at rendering the judgement as objective as possible, as close as possible to the mere application of the law. See e.g. the efforts made by KARL LARENZ, *Lehrbuch des Schuldrechts I*, p. 126 ff.

[147] In all systems the emancipation of good faith occurred together with the decline of party autonomy.

[148] J.W. HEDEMANN, *Die Flucht in die Generalklauseln; Eine Gefahr für Recht und Staat*, Tübingen 1933, pp. 60, 66.

On the other hand, the question arises why the courts did not invoke the general good faith clause in all the cases where they interpreted, supplemented and corrected the law. Firstly, the courts only invoked good faith when they thought that the new rule could not realistically be based on another provision in the code[149]. That is why good faith interpretation of the law is fairly rare. The courts usually only invoke good faith when they want to supplement or correct it. Secondly, if one looks at the (often explosive) expansion of the field of application and the number of applications of the general good faith clause over the last few decades it seems that the courts themselves have been asking the same question: why not also use good faith as a foundation for change in fields of law other than contracts?

The discussion as to whether good faith has a supplementing and correcting function has served as a facade for the question whether the judge may supplement and correct the law (first: the contract). In other words, the emancipation of the judge has taken place under the cover of the emancipation of good faith and equity. The judge as a creator of new rules which supplement or correct the law has entered the scene behind the mask of good faith. Today all European code systems have accepted a supplementative and a corrective function of good faith[150]; the pretensions of the Enlightenment have been overcome. It seems that in this post-modern age the time has come to recognise that what the judge is doing is nothing to be ashamed of and that he can remove his good faith mask.

Rightly, in some systems it has been pointed out that if there had been no general good faith clause the courts would have adopted the same new rules[151]. Indeed, most of these new rules have been adopted in other systems without the use of the doctrine of good faith[152]. On the other hand, still other systems with a

---

[149] See HERBERT ROTH, in: *Münchener Kommentar*, § 242, no. 20; JAN SMITS, *Het vertrouwensbeginsel en de contractuele gebondenheid*, Arnhem 1995, p. 101.

[150] Including France. See e.g. the cases on *clauses résolutoires* mentioned *supra* which date from the 1970s. Since then the increase in the application of art. 1134 (3) *Cc*, which had been dormant for almost two centuries, has been explosive. See CHRISTOPHE JAMIN, 'Une brève histoire politique des interprétations de l'art. 1134 du CC', *D.* 2002, pp. 901-907, and M.W. HESSELINK, 'De opmars van de goede trouw in het Franse contractenrecht', *WPNR.* 6154 (1994), pp. 694-698. In addition French law recognises the concept of *abus de droit.*

[151] MICHAEL P. STATHOPOULOS, *Contract law in Hellas*, no. 50; JÜRGEN SCHMIDT, in: *J. von Staudingers Kommentar*, § 242, no. 181.

[152] To give only a few examples among the 'good faith applications' discussed *supra*, in Section III: in some systems including present Dutch law the precontractual duty to inform is based directly on the mistake provision; in several countries including Germany liability for breaking off negotiations is based on a specific doctrine (*culpa in contrahendo*) or on tort; in many systems objective interpretation is not based on good faith; English law has developed the doctrine of implied terms without the concept of good faith; in some countries statutory provisions on unfair terms were adopted without making any reference to good faith; in most systems the relaxations of privity are not based on good faith; in various countries including Italy a rule on hardship was adopted by the legislator or the courts without basing it on good faith; in several countries including England the availability of remedies (for English law particularly: specific performance) may be limited but on a different basis than good faith (for English law: the discretionary character of an equitable remedy).

general good faith clause did not adopt the same rule[153]. This shows that the real question is whether the new rule should be adopted. In resolving this question the general good faith clause is of no assistance[154].

V. Some Conclusions

The main conclusion must be that if the role of the judge as a creator of rules is fully recognised, there is no need for a general good faith clause in a code or restatement of European private law[155]. It may even do harm because it gives the courts an excuse for not formulating the rule which they apply. If, however, there is still some doubt as to the power of the courts, a good faith clause could be useful in order to assure that the judge may create new rules. This may be of particular importance for a new code for Europe where the European Court of Justice and the other courts may need extensive powers right from the beginning. It would then be logical not to put the article in the chapter on contract law, but right at the beginning as one of the first preliminary provisions of the code, just like in Switzerland. The wording would not matter much; experience shows that any phrase containing the words 'good faith' will suffice. However, if good faith were to have only such an *Ermächtigungsfunktion*[156], it could be argued that it would be more straightforward instead of using good faith terminology to provide expressly that the courts may interpret, supplement and correct the code where necessary. It may be argued that for the sake of tradition the term 'good faith' should be used. However, since this term may

[153] These observations, which as said are based on comparative research (see my *op. cit. supra*), have now also been confirmed by the results of the Trento project. See especially SIMON WHITTAKER & REINHARD ZIMMERMANN, 'Coming to terms with good faith', especially p. 653 ff.

[154] Neither is a provision like Art. 3:12 *BW*: 'In determining what reasonableness and equity require, reference must be made to generally accepted principles of law, to current juridical views in the Netherlands, and to the particular societal and private interests involved'. (Translation P.P.C. HAANAPPEL & E. MACKAAY, *New Netherlands Civil Code Patrimonial Law*; 'reasonableness and equity' is the term which the new code uses for 'objective good faith'). Quite apart from whether these factors are specific for law making 'on the basis of good faith'(should they not always play a role when courts create new rules?), these factors can hardly be said to provide any guidance. 'Principles of law' (e.g. in the sense in which Ronald Dworkin understands them) either do not exist or cannot be known or are usually in conflict with each other (e.g. the principles of autonomy and solidarity). 'Current juridical views in the Netherlands' are manifold: we have quite a broad spectrum of political parties and we live in a strongly individualised and multicultural society. And 'private interests involved' (i.e. especially the interest of the parties) are usually diametrically opposed (that is why they have gone to court in the first place). And even if all these factors could be determined and weighed objectively, does a judge really have enough time to study the programmes of the political parties, hold opinion polls, visit various communities et cetera?

[155] However, it may be worthwhile to anchor a general principle of solidarity in the most general part of the code next to the principle of autonomy. In the same sense see BRIGITTA LURGER, *Grundfragen der Vereinheitlichung des Vertragsrechts in der Europäischen Union*, p. 385. Such a principle, although admittedly quite broad and open, would nevertheless retain some distinct normative coherence especially if conceived in opposition to party autonomy. See further *supra*, Chapter 3, Section VI, B, 2.

[156] The term is taken from H. MERZ, *Berner Kommentar, Einleitungsband*, Art. 2 *ZGB*, no. 22.

lead to hostile reactions from common law lawyers (however unjustified) 'equity' may be an acceptable compromise, since it is part of both the civil law and the common law traditions. It is submitted, however, that this term has the disadvantage of having a strong natural law connotation.

Secondly, this Chapter shows that the concept of good faith in itself should not keep common law and civil law lawyers divided. On the one hand, common law lawyers should not fear the concept of good faith. The adoption of a general good faith clause in itself does not say anything about which rules will speak through its mouth[157]. Good faith does not differ much from what the English lawyers have experienced with equity. The real question is whether the rules adopted by the courts mentioning good faith should be included in a European code or restatement. It does not make any more sense for a common law lawyer to fight the concept of good faith than it would have been to fight the whole of equity. Rather, good faith serves as a guarantee against the rigidity that the English fear from a code. On the other hand, civil law lawyers should not insist too much on including a good faith provision in a code or restatement of European private law. If they fully recognise what the courts do when they 'apply' good faith they should acknowledge that it should not be necessary that a court mentions the words 'good faith' when it creates a new rule which supplements or corrects the law[158]. Common law lawyers do not believe that the law should be exclusively made by the legislator, nor do they consider it necessary that all the law should be democratically legitimated. This may largely explain why English law has not needed the concept of good faith.

Finally, it has become clear that it is not possible to say anything on the 'content' of European good faith without knowing the system that it will be operating in[159]. Ideally it should be empty. All the rules mentioned in Section III, for example, if accepted, could (and indeed should) be given their proper place in a code or restatement of European private law[160].

[157] In the same sense now WHITTAKER & REINHARD ZIMMERMANN, 'Coming to terms with good faith'., p. 687 : 'the recognition of a principle of good faith does not require a particular result in the circumstances, it merely allows the possibility of a particular result, leaving the court to decide whether or not it should be brought about. From this perspective, it could indeed be argued there would be no *substantive* legal change were English or Scots law to accept a general principle of contractual good faith (...).'

[158] The same is true for a (separate) doctrine of abuse of right: if the courts are only prepared to limit a right if they can say that the right is set aside by a higher norm (the prohibition of abuse), such a doctrine should be maintained. If, however, a court is prepared to say that the right given in abstract terms by the code is limited in certain situations, then such a doctrine is not necessary.

[159] On the question whether the 'content' of good faith necessarily consists of altruistic rules which impose solidarity and counterbalance party autonomy see *supra*, Chapter 3, Section VI, B, 3.

[160] In the same sense see BRIGITTA LURGER, *Grundfragen der Vereinheitlichung des Vertragsrechts in der Europäischen Union*, p. 384.

STRUCTURE

8

The Structure Of The New European Private Law

I. Introduction

IT IS now time to bring a few of the ideas which I have developed in the previous chapters together. Assuming that at least part of private law could and should be common in the future[1], the question arises what structure this future common European private law should take[2]. For most participants in the debate on the future of European private law, both partisans and adversaries, the default model for such a structure would be a European civil code[3]. In this Chapter I will address the question whether a classical code in the sense of the French *Code civil* of 1804, the German *Bürgerliches Gesetzbuch* of 1900 or indeed the Dutch *Burgerlijk Wetboek* of 1992 would be the most appropriate form for the new European private law. I will discuss eight aspects of the structure of European private law which cast some doubt on the desirability today of a civil code (or a code of contracts) in the classical sense. Some of these considerations are very practical, others are more theoretical[4].

II. A Classical Civil Code

The two main characteristics of a classical civil code are its (presumably) comprehensive and coherent character[5]. Comprehensive in the sense that, as a result of abstraction, it deals in principle with all matters of private law (as opposed to public law), not in the sense of exclusivity: the legislator (or the courts) may come up with specific rules outside the code (e.g. in separate statutes). The code is presumed to be coherent in the sense that there is no contradiction between the rules contained in it, that each rule has one true

---

[1] I have addressed this question *supra*, in Chapter 5. Briefly stated, my position is that it may be worthwhile to substitute national private law by European private law where the latter is 'better' in substance. For me, that means, among other things, that it should be sufficiently social.

[2] On the structure of the present European (i.e. EU) contract law see STEFAN GRUNDMANN, 'The Structure of European Contract Law', *ERPL* 2001, pp. 505-528.

[3] See e.g. ARTHUR HARTKAMP, MARTIJN W. HESSELINK, EWOUD HONDIUS, CARLA JOUSTRA, EDGAR DU PERRON, *Towards a European civil code*, 2nd ed., Nijmegen and The Hague, London, Boston 1998; PIERRE LEGRAND, 'Against a European Civil Code', 60 *MLR* (1997), pp. 44-62.

[4] I will pay special attention to Dutch law since this Chapter was originally conceived as a Dutch national report.

[5] See *supra*, Chapter 2, Section I, C, with further references.

meaning, and that it provides only one right answer to each legal question. Other characteristics of a classical code include its systematic character and its use of abstract rules and concepts[6].

III. The Private / Public Divide

The assumption that a civil code deals with all matters of private law and is applicable to all conflicts between private parties is based on another assumption, i.e. that it is possible (and indeed useful) to distinguish between private law and public law. Private law is usually defined as the law which governs relationships between citizens as opposed to public law, which is the law which deals with the relationships between citizens and the state, or among state institutions. However, this clear-cut distinction does give rise to some doubt. Not only as a result of the development of administrative law and, especially, of functional fields of the law which do not seem to fit in very well with this distinction; there is also a more fundamental *critique*.

First, in many countries the cases where the state 'acts as a private person' are problematic. Classical examples include the case where a municipality buys new office equipment. In many countries private law (the civil code) applies directly or by way of analogy to such cases. However, if a European Civil Code were to be enacted, should that code then also apply to (some) national (and European) public authorities? Moreover, in some countries national administrative law and private law are increasingly intertwined. For example, the recent Dutch *Algemene Wet Bestuursrecht* (1994), which codifies the 'general part' of administrative law, contains many structural and conceptual aspects which resemble the general part of private law (patrimonial law) contained in Books 3, 5, and 6 of the Civil Code which were enacted in 1992. With the enactment of a European Civil Code this strong link between national private law and national administrative law would be broken. Unless, of course, national administrative law was to be adapted to this new European Civil Code. This would mean, however, that administrative law in Europe would also indirectly undergo further harmonisation[7].

Even more problematic in this respect are the so-called functional fields of the law. In many European countries private law is rapidly disintegrating into functional fields of law. Usually, these functional fields are the most dynamic branches of the law: labour law, medical law, environmental law, information law, construction law, to name but a few. Their main characteristic, apart from their functional, pragmatic and non-dogmatic approach, is that they usually contain a mix of private and public law aspects. Some nostalgic civil law scholars will say that all these fields are in essence private law. However, they essentially miss the point. First, because these fields are mixes of private and public law (the relative quantity depending on the politico-economic climate

---

[6] The new Dutch Civil Code of 1992 has the characteristics of a classical civil code.

[7] See generally on the Europeanisation of administrative law J.H. JANS, R. DE LANGE, S. PRECHAL, R.J.G.M. WIDDERSHOVEN, *Inleiding tot het Europees bestuursrecht*, Nijmegen 1999.

of the day: regulation/deregulation). Secondly, because the approach to the law in those functional fields is much more pragmatic and less dogmatic. They have, as it were, abandoned the 'general part' of private law. It would be anachronistic to dissect these fields into a private part, to be regulated on the European level in a European Civil Code, and a public part, to be regulated on the national (and maybe sometimes the European or another international) level. In addition, such an approach would also be un-European: the European legislator has not demonstrated any great sensitivity to the public/private divide. On the contrary, the EU has consistently adopted a functional approach to the law, in which private law as much as public law is instrumental to the political aims which the EU means to achieve by way of its directives and regulations[8]. The difference between the various Directorates-General of the European Commission seems to have been more determinant of the structure of European private law than a dogmatic, esthetical or political dedication to the private/public divide.

As said, private law is usually defined as the law which governs relationships between citizens as opposed to public law, which is the law that deals with the relationships between citizens and the state, or among state institutions. This definition is quite descriptive. However, there is another recurrent definition of private law which is much more political. In this definition private law is the law relating to the private area which is free from State intervention. In the latter view the only function of private law is allocation: *suum cuique tribuere*. In that view private law has an internal logic of its own which is politically neutral and is only concerned with giving every person what she or he is entitled to[9]. In particular, private law in that view has no distributionist nor any other paternalistic function: rather it is held that private law should not be instrumentalised for political aims. In that view the main pillars of private law are absolute property, freedom of contract and fault liability. This view has been forcefully attacked, especially in the United States, by the Sociological, Realist and Critical Legal Studies movements[10]. They challenged the idea that absolute property, freedom of contract, fault liability and party autonomy were the natural, apolitical foundations of private law, and they showed that this view of private law was instead closely linked to a *laissez-faire* Liberal (Conservative) view of the economy and society at large. Instead, they argued that there is no pre-legal entitlement and that all law is public law[11]. This second definition of private law does indeed seem to be untenable in Europe today. There is no reason to accept any pre-legal right

[8] See further *supra*, Chapter 2, Section IV.

[9] Compare DANIELA CARUSO, 'The Missing View of the Cathedral: The Private Law Paradigm of European Legal Integration', 3 *European Law Journal* (1997), pp. 3-32.

[10] See M.D.A. FREEMAN, *Lloyd's Introduction to Jurisprudence*, 6th ed., London 1994, p. 669, and DUNCAN KENNEDY, *A Critique of Adjudication {fin de siècle}*, Cambridge Massachusetts 1997, both with further references.

[11] See MORTON J HORWITZ, *The Transformation of American Law 1870-1960; The Crisis of Legal Orthodoxy*, New York/Oxford 1992.

to property or binding force of contract or limitation of liability to fault, which should be protected by the courts. Even if one accepts, in one variant of natural law or another, that people have pre-legal rights to property, that promises (or agreements) should be binding or that no one should be liable except when she or he has caused damage by her or his fault, as soon as one is of the opinion that the State should protect and enforce such a right, the State shall do so only to the extent and in the way agreed upon democratically (including the democratically accepted rigid constitutions and international treaties which protect fundamental rights including private property). Therefore, property is protected, promises (agreements) are binding and people are liable for their torts only when and to the extent that the law says so (Constitutional law and private law). In that sense all law, including private law, is indeed public law: there is no area of the law which is free from paternalistic, distributionist and other functional and instrumental intervention by the State. Also in practice it has become obvious in the course of the 20th century that large parts of private law are subject to State intervention, which is driven by political concerns many of which are distributionist (strict liability, workers', tenants' and consumer protection in the special part, whereas objective causation rules, the doctrines of abuse of right and of good faith have similar effects in the general part). Moreover, as said, the whole *acquis communautaire* is instrumental, also in the case of private law.

These developments raise the question whether it still makes sense to uphold a sharp distinction between private and public law. Moreover, within the English legal system there has never been a strong tradition of distinguishing between private law and public law, although some scholars - who incidentally share an interest in civil law - have recently made use of this terminology[12]. Therefore, it may be worthwhile to go ahead with the functional and piecemeal approach which the European legislator has adopted and to address functional fields of the law rather than to embrace the grand idea of including all private law within a civil code[13], and thus reviving a distinction which does not seem desirable neither from a political nor from a practical perspective. Instead, it may be advisable to enact one or more functional European codes, for example in the area of distribution law, company law, or labour law.

IV. Civil Law, Commercial Law, Consumer Law

Another instance of the fragmentation of private law is not new at all. Indeed, it has been present from the first codifications: the division of private law according to the status of the persons involved. In many European countries different (or additional) rules apply depending on whether the parties are

---

[12] See e.g. PETER BIRKS (ed.), *English Private Law*, Oxford 2000. Moreover, Professor Ewan McKendrick holds a Chair in 'English Private Law' at Oxford.

[13] Compare PIERRE LEGRAND, 'Against a European Civil Code', *MLR* [Vol. 60] 1997 44-62.

ordinary citizens or merchants. In addition, more recently a new category has developed: the consumer.

In the first wave of codifications most continental European legal systems adopted both a civil code and a commercial code. However, since the first half of the 20th century the significance of this distinction has gradually decreased. And some countries, notably Italy (1942) and the Netherlands (1992), officially abolished the distinction on the occasion of the implementation of their new civil codes[14]. Interestingly, however, during the last decades of the 20th century a counter-development started to arise as a result of the birth of 'consumer law'. Thus a new distinction arose, between general civil law, which was thought to be largely based on party autonomy, and specific consumer law, which exceptionally was more protective[15]. In the course of the 1980s and '90s in many European countries consumer law developed into an important branch of the law (not least as a result of the many European directives), with a great deal of autonomy *vis-à-vis* general private law. In France, all consumer regulations have even been brought together in the *Code de la Consommation* (1997). This development was enhanced by the way in which European Union bureaucracy is organised in Brussels. Different Directorates-General are responsible for the Common Market and for Consumer Protection, a factor which has significantly increased the tendency to enact separate rules for consumers and commercial parties. However, there are also counter-developments: many countries have tried to integrate consumer law into their civil codes as far as possible, thus trying to maintain the integrity of civil law. A clear example is the 1992 Dutch Civil Code. Another recent example is the Principles of European Contract Law which were drafted by the Lando Commission and which are meant to apply to all contracts independent of the status of the parties involved[16].

There are some strong arguments against schizophrenic European private law, as Ugo Mattei has called it[17]. First, the distinction between consumer contracts and commercial contracts is very problematic. Compare Mattei[18]: 'Since there is no such thing as a separate market for consumers (demand) and a separate market for producers (supply), contract law has to face the problem of how to merge supply and demand into a single market. The creation of two different bodies of law at odds with each other would ignore this reality, and, as a result, reduce the chance of building efficient private law institutions for modern Europe.' Secondly, by (re)introducing 'schizophrenic contract law'

[14] In the Netherlands the distinctions between *kooplieden* and other persons, and between *daden van koophandel* and other acts was abolished as early as in 1934. See R.J.Q. KLOMP, *Opkomst en ondergang van het handelsrecht*, Nijmegen 1998, p. 165.

[15] See for the Netherlands R.P.J.L. TJITTES, *De hoedanigheid van contractspartijen*, Deventer 1994.

[16] OLE LANDO, HUGH BEALE (EDS.), *Principles of European Contract Law, Parts I and II, Prepared by The Commission on European Contract Law*, The Hague 2000.

[17] UGO MATTEI, 'Efficiency and Equal Protection In The New European Contract Law: Mandatory, Default and Enforcement Rules', 39 *Va. J. Int'l L.*, p. 537.

[18] UGO MATTEI, 'Efficiency and Equal Protection In The New European Contract Law', p. 538.

the definition and proof of status (consumer or professional) becomes all-important, whereas it seems much more efficient to concentrate on contract rather than on status.

However, adopting uniform European contract law, as proposed, for example, by the Lando Commission in its *Principles of European Contract Law*, carries its own risks as well. That is, if one is concerned that European contract law should be sufficiently 'social'[19]. If contract law is dealt with on a general, abstract level there is a serious risk that those rules will not be sufficiently social and protective as far as weaker parties are concerned, as a result of the argument that such rules would otherwise not fit in with major international commercial contracts. The end result may then be that general contract law will be mainly autonomy-based and hardly protective at all. Indeed, it seems worrying that the PECL are very similar to the UNIDROIT Principles of International Commercial Contracts, which are exclusively intended for commercial contracts. Does this mean that the PECL have applied business logic to consumers?[20]

Alternatively, should general contract law be 'neutral', and should the protective rules (protecting categories which are presumed to be weaker, like consumers, employees, tenants) be regarded as special private law, as opposed to general private law, which should be placed elsewhere (maybe even outside the code)? However, this latter approach also has certain risks. In the first place, there is no such thing as neutral general contract law. Autonomy-based contract law is not neutral but Liberal (in the European sense), that is Conservative, or 'right wing', and it is highly questionable whether today's general contract law should be based exclusively or mainly on party autonomy[21]. Secondly, a system where all the protective rules are moved into (the) special part(s) makes the autonomy-based general contract law of little relevance since, on the one hand, the multinationals and other strong commercial parties will make their own contractual arrangements in long and detailed contracts for every imaginable contingency and will therefore probably find the default rules contained in the code of general contract law of

[19] See in favour of social European private law THOMAS WILHELMSSON, *Social Contract Law and European Integration*, Dartmouth 1995; BRIGITTA LURGER, *Vertragliche Solidarität, Entwicklungschancen für das allgemeine Vertragsrecht in Österreich und in der Europäischen Union*, Baden-Baden 1998; BRIGITTA LURGER, *Grundfragen der Vereinheitlichung des Vertragsrechts in der Europäischen Union*, Wien, New York 2002. See also JAN B.M. VRANKEN, 'Over partijautonomie, contractsvrijheid en de grondslag van gebondenheid in het verbintenissenrecht' in: J.M. Barendrecht, M.A.B. Chao-Duivis and H.A.W. Vermeulen (eds.), *Beginselen van contractenrecht: Opstellen aangeboden aan B.W.M. Nieskens-Isphording*, Deventer 2000; CHRISTOPHE JAMIN, 'Plaidoyer pour le solidarisme contractuel', in: Gilles Goubeaux et al. (ed.), *Études offertes à Jacques Ghestin; Le contrat au début du XXIe siècle*, Paris 2001, GUIDO ALPA, *Trattato di diritto civile, I Storia, fonti, interpretazione*, Milano 2000, p. 604 ff, and *supra*, Chapter 5.

[20] In their Preface and Introduction the PECL frequently refer to business. See e.g. p. xxv ('international business community').

[21] See DUNCAN KENNEDY, 'The Political Stakes in "Merely Technical" Issues of Contract Law', 10 *ERPL* (2002), pp. 7-28. See further *infra*, Section VIII.

little use for their purposes, whereas, on the other hand, for consumers, employees, tenants and other weaker parties many (or even most) of these rules would not be applicable whereas the important rules would be found in the Consumer, Labour or Housing (part of the) Code.

In conclusion, from both a practical and a political perspective it is not all that obvious whether European private law should be unitary as far as the status of parties is concerned. In any case, a classical civil code which contains only general private law - especially if that is based on party autonomy - does not seem to be the obvious structure for framing the needs of European citizens and business.

V. A Multi-Level System

A third fragmentation trend is what has been referred to as the development of European law into a multi-level system of governance where several institutions are responsible for the development of certain aspects of the law but no institution is in charge of private law in its entirety[22]. Christian Joerges suggests that: 'the much criticised patchwork character of European private law initiatives reflects the lack of a hierarchical order, and that Europe's legal pluralism will inevitably result in disintegrative effects within formerly national systems.' Accordingly, he argues that 'legal scholarship should try to imagine and conceptualise a "law of Europeanisation" rather than some pan-European system that might be codified or compiled out of Europe's common legal heritage.' Rather than creating new static coherent structures or rigid institutional arrangements we should find a dynamic solution for the interplay between EU law and 15 national legal systems of private law. In the process we will inevitably have to give up some of our hopes for national normative coherence.

The problems would not disappear (they would not even become significantly minor) in this respect if the EU decided to enact a European code of general contract law or even a European Civil Code[23]. The presence of such a code would inevitably give rise to many questions with regard to its connection with the rest of the law. First, some parts of private law would presumably remain national: the general law of obligations, the law of specific contracts (especially protective regulation), the law of contracts concluded by the State (administrative law), (real) property law (transfer of property), the law of persons, the law of succession, the law of evidence, the law of civil procedure. This would presumably also be the case for national public law, parts of which may be closely connected to private law (administrative law,

[22] See especially CHRISTIAN JOERGES, 'Interactive Adjudication in the Europeanisation Process? A Demanding Perspective and a Modest Example', *ERPL* 2000, p. 1-16. See also OLIVER REMIEN, 'Einheit, Mehrstufigheit und Flexibilität im europäischen Privat- und Wirtschaftsrecht', 62 *RabelsZ* (1998), p. 627 ff.

[23] As said, the Commission recently instigated the debate by publishing its *Communication on European Contract Law* (see *supra*, footnote 1).

criminal law, constitutional law). Secondly, a part of private law (in the sense of the law applicable to conflicts between private persons) would indeed be administered on a European level, but presumably not in the civil code.

A first example is provided by European competition law. This branch of the law frequently has a decisive influence on the contractual relationship between private parties (distribution and franchise contracts are among the most typical examples). Indeed, the block exemptions which are based on art. 81 (3) EC Treaty, especially the recent Commission Regulation (EC) 2790/1999 on vertical agreements[24], contain many rules which would normally be regarded as rules of contract law[25]. However, it is very unlikely that distribution competition law would be transferred from art. 81 EC Treaty and the block exemptions into a European Civil Code[26]. Moreover, EC competition law and general contract law have distinctly different logics and, as a result, they approach the subject from different perspectives: contract clauses that may be fair from the perspective of contract law may be doubtful from a competition perspective. For example, it may be completely acceptable in terms of contractual fairness between the parties (and indeed desirable) for a major supplier to grant his small distributor absolute territorial exclusivity in a certain geographical area, and a European Civil Code could even consider adopting a default rule in that sense[27], whereas it is obvious that such a clause would severely limit (intra-brand) competition. Of course, contract policy and competition policy may converge[28], but this is not necessarily the case,

---

[24] EC Regulation 2790/99 on Vertical Agreements and Guidelines on Vertical Restraints (2000/C 291/01).

[25] Article 81 (1) (ex Article 85 (1)) declares invalid, in short, all agreements and concerted practices which may affect trade between Member States and which have as their object or effect the prevention, restriction or distortion of competition within the common market. The European Commission and the European Court of Justice have long held that not only horizontal agreements but also vertical ones may fall within the scope of application of art. 81 EC Treaty. As a result, they may be invalid for restraint of trade. However, on the basis of Section 3 the European Commission may provide exemptions, both individual ones and for whole categories of contracts (block exemptions). The European Commission has indeed enacted a whole series of regulations. Recently, it has thoroughly revised its policy. It has now adopted a more general approach in Commission Regulation (EC) 2790/1999 on the application of Article 81(3) of the Treaty to categories of vertical agreements and concerted practices. In addition to this general approach the EC has adopted specific rules for certain specific sectors, e.g. the recent Draft Regulation on Vertical Agreements and Concerted Practices in the Motor Vehicle Industry (O.J. C 67/2, 16.3.2002). Therefore, as a result of EC competition law (and national competition law) a distribution contract may be invalid. The general consequences of invalidity (e.g. the doctrine of partial invalidity, which may be relevant e.g. in the case of partial exemption which may lead to partial validity (see art. 5 EC Regulation 2790/1999)) are left by the EC Treaty to national laws.

[26] That would endanger normative integrity within EC competition law.

[27] E.g. a default rule which presumes geographical areas mentioned in distribution contracts to be exclusive, or a default rule which grants legal exclusivity in case a party has *de facto* enjoyed exclusivity for some time because it has been the only one on the market in a certain geographical area (implied exclusivity).

[28] As said, the Commission has thoroughly reviewed the application of art. 81 to distribution agreements, which has resulted in EC Regulation 2790/99 on Vertical Agreements. See also the Guidelines on Vertical Restraints (2000/C 291/01). Compare MICHEL WAELBROECK & JULES

especially not if different authorities, on (horizontally or vertically) different levels of governance, are responsible for different branches of the law (e.g. if a new European Court of Civil Justice, or a separate Civil Chamber of the ECJ, were to become responsible for the application of the European Civil Code and the further development of European private law)[29].

Another important example is provided by human rights. In some European countries an important source of private law is the Constitution. In those countries human rights do not only have a vertical effect (they may be invoked by citizens *vis-à-vis* the State) but also a horizontal one (they may be invoked by citizens *vis-à-vis* other citizens). This horizontal effect may be either direct or indirect. In the former case, in her or his suit against another citizen, a citizen has a claim and a remedy which are directly based on the Constitution. In the latter situation, the claim and remedy are based on a provision in the civil code, e.g. on a provision for liability in tort or on a general good faith clause in contract cases. A typical example is the German cases where the *Bundesverfassungsgericht* has declared that extensive personal securities provided for the debts of close relatives are invalid due to a violation of the fundamental rights to dignity (art. 1, Section 1 *GG*) and party autonomy (art. 2, Section 1 *GG*) in connection with the *Sozialstaatsprinzip* (art. 20, Section 1, Art. 28, Section 1 *GG*) which is protected in relationships between private persons by art. 138 *BGB* on immorality (*Sittenwidrigkeit*)[30].

Within the European context fundamental rights are not only protected by national law but also by international law, notably the Convention for the Protection of Human Rights and Fundamental Freedoms (Rome, 1950)[31]. This Convention gives citizens an individual right of complaint in Strasbourg (when all national remedies/instances have been exhausted), and in some countries also in their own national courts[32]. This means that yet another authority is involved in the administration of 'private law'[33]. Moreover, the

STUYCK, 'Competition law in the European Community', in: Floris O.W. Vogelaar, *Competition Law in the EU and the Netherlands*, Deventer 2000, pp. 11-150, on p. 38.

[29] Compare CHRISTIAN JOERGES, 'The Impact of European Integration on Private Law: Reductionist Perceptions, True Conflicts and a New Constitutional Perspective', *ELJ* 1997, pp. 378-406, p. 398, referring to Case 161/84 (Pronuptia de Paris GmbH *v* Pronuptia de Paris Irmgard Schillgallis): 'How does the competition policy driven approach to franchising as a means of efficiently organising distribution interact with a private legal logic which seeks to assess the fairness of such arrangements under contract law? From the perspective of antitrust's new economic rationale, any protection of the franchisee's interest through mandatory rules of contract law will seem to be misguided in principle. All legal orders must deal with substantive conflicts of this kind. Within the European system, however, these tensions have an additional 'constitutional' dimension. European competition law claims 'supremacy' over national law.'

[30] Decision of 19 October 1993, *BVerfGE* 89, 214, *NJW* 1994, 36. See HELMUT HEINRICHS, in: *Palandt Bürgerliches Gesetzbuch*, 61st ed., München 2002, § 138 no. 37 ff. See further *supra*, Chapter 6.

[31] But see also e.g. the European Social Charter.

[32] See in the Netherlands art. 93 *Grondwet* (Constitution), which gives such provisions direct effect.

[33] Admittedly, the interference of the ECHR in Strasbourg with (European) private law is rather indirect, since complaints can only be made against States. However, States can violate

European Convention on the Future of the European Union chaired by Valéry Giscard D'Estaing is currently preparing a European constitution which will undoubtedly contain a chapter on fundamental rights[34], similar to the Charter of Fundamental Rights of the European Union (Nice, 2000)[35]. This raises the question of the relationship between that Charter or the Constitution and a possible European Civil Code (or, for the time being, national civil codes). The Charter contains a large number of provisions which may be of direct relevance for private law (i.e. for relationships between citizens). Moreover, the values contained in it may be regarded as the common values of the European Union which could be the basis of a European Civil Code. The Preamble states[36]: 'Conscious of its spiritual and moral heritage, the Union is founded on the indivisible, universal values of human dignity, freedom, equality and solidarity.' The Charter contains rights, freedoms and principles relating to Dignity (Chapter 1), Freedom (Chapter 2), Equality (Chapter 3), Solidarity (Chapter 4), Citizens' Rights (Chapter 5), and Justice (Chapter 6). A hint as to its horizontal effect is to be found in the same preamble[37]: 'Enjoyment of these rights entails responsibilities and duties with regard to other persons, to the human community and to future generations.'

There is yet another level. Some parts of the private law which is applicable in the Member States of the European Union are dealt with on a global level. For example, the most important contract is dealt with, as regards international cases, on a world-wide scale in the United Nations Convention on Contracts for the International Sale of Goods (CISG) (Vienna, 1980). This convention has now been ratified by 61 countries all over the world[38].

Therefore, it is very unlikely, also from the perspective of the hierarchy of sources of law, that all (or even most) of the private law applicable in Europe will be dealt with on the same level of governance, let alone in one single European civil code. Private law (like public law) will rather continue to be dealt with on various levels including (as a result of globalisation) increasingly on a world-wide level. This means that control over the development of private law will increasingly be in the hands of various institutions. This will inevitably have some consequences for our hopes of normative integrity (within and among each of the levels).

VI. Integrity Today

The use of codes is based on the assumption that it is possible to derive right answers to questions of law relating to specific cases from the words and the system of the code. This assumption also underlies the use of statutory rules

---

fundamental rights by their legislators' statutes (or codes) and by their courts' decisions.

[34] See on its progress http://european-convention.eu.int.

[35] See for the full text with comments http://ue.eu.int/df/default.asp.

[36] P. 11.

[37] P. 12.

[38] See UNCITRAL Status of Conventions and Model Laws, update 14 March 2002 (see www.uncitral.org).

generally. However, what is typical of a code is that it is more comprehensive (it deals with a greater part of the law) and it is usually more systematic: not merely a set of articles, but a system which itself has a normative meaning. However, today, *n'en déplaise* Ronald Dworkin[39], there is increasing scepticism with regard to the possibility to deduce right answers for concrete cases from abstract rules and general principles (rule scepticism), also in Europe. According to some observers this is the majority view today[40]. The most radical sceptical view concerning a European Civil Code would therefore be that it would be completely useless to enact any code at all.

Of course, (normative) integrity is a highly important characteristic of any legal order, because it is ultimately based on the fundamental value of equality. That value is deeply embedded in the European tradition. See for example art. 14 ECHR and, more recently, Chapter III of the European Charter. Therefore, an argument in favour of a code could be that it would express the aspirations of a legal order to attain normative integrity, without necessarily believing that the mere enactment of such a code would in itself lead to (or even enhance) normative integrity. It would have the (rhetorical) function of a symbol which shows that the legal community does still believe in this great idea and does not surrender, in a post-modern sceptical way, to the infinite fragmentation of the law.

A less radical sceptic would therefore advise the drafting and enactment of a code which does not pretend to contain all the right answers but which in its style and its structure would openly recognise that in any dispute resolution important choices will inevitably have to be made no matter how accurately the abstract rules of the code and its system are drafted. A contemporary code should therefore be open and discursive[41]. It should provide an efficient language and terminology (categories) for the debate and it should indicate which interests are at stake and which policy choices the legislator has made. An interesting example is provided by the American Restatements (Second). In this second wave of restatements strong criticism of the first Restatements, from Realists and others[42], was taken into account. In the Restatements (Second) there was a clear shift in emphasis from the black-letter rule to the

---

39 See especially his *Law's Empire*, London 1986.

40 See in the Netherlands J.M. BARENDRECHT, 'Door muren kijken; suggesties voor hervorming van de civiele cassatierechtspraak', *NJB* 2002, p. 297.

41 This is not the same as 'soft'. See *infra*, Section VII.

42 See CHARLES E. CLARK, 'The Restatement Of The Law Of Contracts', 42 Yale L J 643-667, HESSEL E. YNTEMA, 'What Should The American Law Institute Do?', 34 Michigan Law Review (1936) 461-473, ALBERT A. EHRENZWEIG, 'Das Desperanto des zweiten "Restatement of Conflict of Laws', in: ERNST VAN CAEMMERER c.s. (eds.), *Ius Privatum Gentium (Festschrift Max Rheinstein)*, Vol. I, pp. 343 ff, p. 344. Compare LAWRENCE M. FRIEDMAN, *A History of American Law*, 2nd ed., Touchstone, New York 1985, p. 676f, G. EDWARD WHITE, 'The American Law Institute and the Triumph of Modernist Jurisprudence', *Law and History Review* (1997) Vol. 16, p. 1, and RICHARD HYLAND, 'The American Restatements and the Uniform Commercial Code', A.S. HARTKAMP ET AL. (EDS.), *Towards a European Civil Code*, 2nd ed., Nijmegen and The Hague/London/Boston 1998, pp. 55.

comments, which were much more extensive than before[43]. The Restatements (Second) did not attempt to bring an end to the debate, but rather tried to state which positions had been taken and to leave it to the courts to decide. As a result there was also a shift in interest from the black-letter rule to the comment. The new restatements were also much less rigidly formulated. The black-letter rules frequently confined themselves to listing a number of aspects that should be taken into account when resolving the conflict. Similarly, also the PECL contain a number of rules which are rather discursive. Sometimes they do little more than provide the relevant elements for debate. Often they merely mention a set of factors which should be taken into account[44].

VII. Default Rules or Mandatory Rules?

There is a tendency in the European private law debate to mainly focus on default rules. The best example is provided by the *Principles of European Contract Law*[45]. This focus is explained in part by the fact that those parts of private law which are mainly mandatory are usually regarded as being 'too political'. The academics who draft these sets of principles, it is argued, are 'legal scientists' and not politicians. Therefore, they should leave those issues to politicians and should only concentrate on the 'general part' of private law which is supposed to be politically fairly neutral. However, there is something of a paradox here: if sets of principles like the PECL are not law themselves but merely an academic exercise which establishes the common core or which may at most be regarded as a draft or proposal made by some academics and containing what in their view would be good law for Europe, there is no reason why these committees should limit themselves to the so-called non-political branches of the law. They could also draft restatements of labour law and the like. Similarly, the European Civil Code project (Von Bar group) could also address the more 'political' subjects. Or, rather, they should indeed include these branches of the law. Because, if these principles are also meant to be used as models, sources of inspiration et cetera for national and European legislators and courts, they now seem inadequate because they too much resemble the Liberal 19th century Civil Codes, which were completely bare of any protective regulation. Or, to put it differently, they do not properly restate our private law because many relevant branches of private law are missing[46].

---

[43] See RICHARD HYLAND, 'The American Restatements and the Uniform Commercial Code'.

[44] See, for example, art. 4:107 (3) (Fraud): 'In determining whether good faith and fair dealing required that a party disclose particular information, regard should be had to all the circumstances, including: (a) whether the party had special expertise; (b) the cost to it of acquiring the relevant information; (c) whether the other party could reasonably acquire the information for itself; and (d) the apparent importance of the information to the other party.'

[45] See on the PECL *supra*, Chapter 2.

[46] The Study Group on a European Civil Code (Von Bar group) is currently drafting rules for the protection of consumers in certain specific contracts. On its progress see www.sgecc.net.

Another explanation which is frequently given for the focus on default rules, is that the Common Market mainly needs rules on general contract law and that the basic rule of contract law (and indeed the basic prerequisite of a well functioning market) is freedom of contract[47]. However, this neo-liberal reinvention of crude capitalism is severely contested by others. The market must be regulated, they argue[48], and therefore we need a hard code now![49] Moreover, the differences in mandatory rules are the real obstacles to the proper functioning of the common market. Those are the rules that the parties cannot contract around. This leads to the suggestion that if the functioning of the Common Market must be enhanced it is not the general rules of non-mandatory contract law that should be harmonised or unified but rather regulation, i.e. the mandatory rules of general contract law and especially those of special contract law. Those seem to be the true impediments to the Common Market, not the non-mandatory rules of general contract law. With regard to the latter, from an economic perspective, at best transparency is needed.

Therefore, there is a strong case for a European Civil Code which mainly or even only contains mandatory rules. Such a code would look very different - for one thing, much more empty - from a traditional civil code. It would hardly contain any rules of general contract law (no rules on performance, non-performance et cetera; to provide an indication, in the PECL only 6 rules are said to be mandatory[50]). However, if a European Civil Code should only contain mandatory regulation, would it still make sense to keep these rules separate from other regulation, i.e. regulation by public law?[51]

VIII. Ideological Pillars

Most civil codes in Europe were conceived in the 19th century when the Liberal *laissez-faire* ideology was dominant in Europe. It is not surprising that this ideology has determined the structure of private law[52]. The pillars of the civil codes in Europe were absolute property, binding force and freedom of

---

[47] In this sense, for example, KLAUS PETER BERGER, 'Auf dem Wege zu einem europäischen Gemeinrecht der Methode', *ZEuP* 2001, p. 4 ff.

[48] See e.g. THOMAS WILHELMSSON, 'Private Law in the EU: Harmonised or Fragmented Europeanisation?', 10 *ERPL* (2002), p. 77-94.

[49] See especially UGO MATTEI, 'Hard Code Now!', *Global Jurist Frontiers* (2002): Vol. 2: No. 1, Article 1.

[50] See PECL, Introduction, pp. xxix.

[51] This brings us back to the relevance today of the private/public divide which was discussed *supra*, Section III.

[52] Compare JACQUES DERRIDA, *Force de loi*, Paris, 1994, p. 32: '[l]es superstructures du droit qui cachent et reflètent à la fois les intérêts économiques et politiques des forces dominantes de la société.' See more generally on the fact that structures, classifications and codes are not 'objective' or 'neutral' or 'rational' MICHEL FOUCAULT, *Les mots et les choses*, Paris 1966, p. 11: 'Les codes fondamentaux d'une culture - ceux qui régissent son langage, ses schémas perceptifs, ses échanges, ses techniques, ses valeurs, la hiérarchie de ses pratiques - fixent d'entrée de jeu pour chaque homme les ordres empiriques auxquels il aura affaire et dans lesquels il se retrouvera.', and *passim*.

contract and fault-based liability in tort. Towards the end of the 19th and during the course of the 20th century these dogmas came under increasing pressure. However, the main institutions of the 19th century private law construction were never undermined as such. Rather, the desire for change was internalised within the system. New institutions were added in order to moderate their effect. Abuse of right, good faith, strict liability, and unjust enrichment operated as safety valves that removed the pressure on the system. Moreover, specific rules were enacted, first in special statutes outside the code, while were later in some countries they were admitted into the (new) code. This led to the invention of the distinction of general private law and special private law, the former being applicable to 'normal' cases where the parties are on an equal footing and special private law which is exceptionally protective of weaker parties. As a result, the structure of most civil codes is still primarily based on the assumption of equal bargaining power where party autonomy reigns. The general law is autonomy-based, protective law is an exception.

It is doubtful, to say the least, whether this 19th century structure which is so obviously linked to the *laissez-faire* concept of the State should be the model for the 21st century's private law in Europe. Rather a 19th century-like code, exclusively or primarily based on the principle of party autonomy, seems wholly unacceptable from a present-day political perspective. It would bring us back to a *laissez-faire* concept of the economy which the courts and the legislators in all European countries successfully overcame during the course of the 20th century. For the 21st century we need a Code which contains these important social achievements[53]. Today, one can no longer claim that private law is essentially based on autonomy and thereby tuck all the so-called exceptions away in a correction device like good faith or abuse of right. A European code of general contract law should be based on both (conflicting) principles which underlie contemporary politics and private law: autonomy and solidarity.

However, the present-day social and political situation in Europe is even more complex. Both individualisation and migration have led to a situation which can best be understood as pluralist, including large amounts of values emanating from sources other than the Western tradition as well (e.g. Islam). This raises the question of which values we have in common. In this respect the Charter of Fundamental Rights of the European Union may provide an

---

[53] In the same sense THOMAS WILHELMSSON, *Social Contract Law and European Integration*, Dartmouth 1995; BRIGITTA LURGER, *Vertragliche Solidarität, Entwicklungschancen für das allgemeine Vertragsrecht in Österreich und in der Europäischen Union*, Baden-Baden 1998; JAN B.M. VRANKEN, 'Over partijautonomie, contractsvrijheid en de grondslag van gebondenheid in het verbintenissenrecht' in: J.M. Barendrecht, M.A.B. Chao-Duivis and H.A.W. Vermeulen (eds.), *Beginselen van contractenrecht: Opstellen aangeboden aan B.W.M. Nieskens-Isphording*, Deventer 2000; CHRISTOPHE JAMIN, 'Plaidoyer pour le solidarisme contractuel', in: Gilles Goubeaux et al. (ed.), *Études offertes à Jacques Ghestin; Le contrat au début du XXIe siècle*, Paris 2001 ; GUIDO ALPA, *Trattato di diritto civile, I Storia, fonti, interpretazione*, Milano 2000, p. 604 ff.

interesting starting point. As said, according to the Preamble the Union is founded on the values of human dignity, freedom, equality and solidarity. It may be worthwhile to attempt to build the edifice of European private law on these four elegant pillars rather than on the monolith of party autonomy.

IX. The Power of Abstraction

The law relating to contracts could be stated, and indeed is stated in the various European legal systems, on various levels and in various modes of abstraction. For example, in the Dutch Civil Code, the law relating to a consumer sales contract is dealt with in 6 different degrees and types of abstraction whereas the Portuguese code contains even further layers. However, in our post-modern age many scholars have become sceptical about the use of abstractions and even suspicious of some of their implications. What are the advantages and the drawbacks of abstraction today?

The main practical function of the law's structure is of course that it should allow for efficient communication[54]. Abstraction may contribute to efficient communication. Between specialists that is, because abstraction (in the sense of stripping off those elements which are considered to be irrelevant) may also lead to the exclusion of non-experts (because without these concrete elements the category is no longer immediately recognisable to them), which is an important social cost especially since the law is meant to be equally relevant to all citizens. Another area where a code plays an important role in communication is education. A well structured, general code can easily communicate to a law student what the main policies are and in which categories one is supposed to express oneself if one wishes to sound like a lawyer[55]. However, teaching law with the code as a starting point also carries some risks. First, after graduation a law student may think that the categories she or he has learned actually exist 'out there' and (worse) that they are the only correct way of framing reality. This may lead to problems when communicating, in interdisciplinary collaborations, with members of other professions (economists, social scientists to name but a few) who have learned to conceive the world in different categories, or, in international collaborations, with lawyers from other jurisdictions with a different taxonomy (common law v civil law, Hindu law et cetera). Secondly, teaching the law from a code leads to a conception of the law and legal problems as something which starts from general principles and leads logically (by way of deduction) and smoothly to the resolution of concrete problems. In this model of teaching, which is the dominant method on the Continent, a student is hardly ever confronted with the problematic match between the harmony of the abstract system of categories and the chaotic character of concrete reality. In other words, a neat, logical and harmonious system communicates the

---

[54] See JACQUES VANDERLINDEN, *Comparer les droits*, Brussels, 1995, pp. 227-304.

[55] See DUNCAN KENNEDY, *Legal Education and the Reproduction of Hierarchy; A Polemic Against the System*, Cambridge, Massachusetts, 1983.

wrong messages with regard to the real character of the law and dispute resolution which is much more chaotic, illogical, unpredictable, unfair, and complex than the system of the code might suggest. Therefore, the drafters of a code should not make too much of an effort in making their edifice as rational and logical as possible. Exactly because such harmony and clarity can be most easily attained on a abstract level, the most logical, harmonious and abstract code is likely to be the most useless one in practice.

Even if abstract categories are used it may make sense to use categories which are more recognisable to practitioners and even for ordinary citizens. Categories that fit better with the way in which they conceive the law. For example, when one looks at the way in which practitioners organise their law firms and their specialities one rarely finds a lawyer or a section in a firm which specialises in the law of obligations, or the law of restitution, or juristic acts. No, more likely one will find merger & acquisition, litigation, company law, medical law, environmental law, labour law. These are functional categories which seem to fit the needs of practice. What would be convincing new, less abstract categories? For contract law, the Tilburg team within the European Civil Code project has proposed new categories to deal with the law of services[56]. Most legal systems deal with most services in a combination of general contract law and the general law of services (*mandat, Dienstvertrag, opdracht*). The Tilburg team now proposes 10 new categories in addition to general contract law[57]. Thus they divide the broad category of service provision into 10 activities. This means tremendous progress, although, admittedly, some of the proposed categories still seem rather abstract and therefore not very recognisable. However, the two obvious alternatives for the activity approach (contract and status) would have their own drawbacks. Partly as a result of freedom of contract, partly as a result of the gradual fading away of differences between traditional professions, it would be very difficult to sum up the 10 (or 20) most frequently concluded types of contracts or economically most important professions. Clearly, an even more functional approach to categories would go hand in hand (in the sense that they would mutually facilitate each other) with a structure of the law which no longer makes a division between private and public law, but rather divides the law into functional fields which are mixed (private and public)[58].

Another aspect of abstraction in a traditional code (and indeed in all statutes) is that it is contained in articles. Such articles are impersonal and stripped of all 'irrelevant facts'[59]. Moreover, the law may look very inhuman when it is formulated in a very abstract way. The 1992 Dutch code provides

[56] MARCO B.M. LOOS, 'Towards a European Law of Service Contracts', *ERPL* 4(2001), p.565-574.

[57] They propose the following categories: advice, agency, construction, design, information, intermediation, processing, storage, transportation and treatment.

[58] See on the private/public divide *supra*, Section III.

[59] Compare MICHEL FOUCAULT, *Les mots et les choses*, Paris 1966, p. 147: 'La structure, en limitant et en filtrant le visible, lui permet de se transcrire dans le langage.'

some startling examples[60]. After all, the law is meant to organise human behaviour. Therefore, it would make sense for the law to address its actors as recognisable categories and with recognisable labels: 'buyer', 'seller', 'landlord', 'doctor' are more convincing labels than 'debtor' or 'creditor' from the general law of obligations, which hardly convince us that they are meant to indicate flesh and blood people. Moreover, a very deliberate use of certain terms by the legislator (or the courts), which raises them to the status of concepts and categories, leads to an excessive focus by legal actors and observers on the language of the law. What really matters in the law are the relationships between people and the policy choices by lawmakers with regard to the resolution of conflicts between people. The function of language is nothing more than to communicate these policy choices. However, legal practice and legal science today are still far too preoccupied with the language of the law[61]. There is a widespread belief that for a lawyer a good command of language is essential because language plays a crucial role in the law[62]. Although there are many parallels between the common law and civil law traditions in Europe[63], here we find a major difference between them. English judges, and as a result their observers, have traditionally paid less attention to the uniformity of their terminology than their colleagues on the Continent. Whereas many (appellate) courts on the Continent tend to exactly follow the terminology provided by the code, to phrase their *attendus de principe* as if they were a new article in the code, and to literally repeat their considerations in previous decisions[64], English judges are generally much less strict in their use of terminology. What one judge calls 'rescission' is referred to as 'termination' by another[65] . Foreign observers (and some systematically-

[60] See e.g. art. 3:32, the article which determines e.g. whether two people have concluded a binding contract: 'A juridical act requires an intention to produce juridical effects, which intention has manifested itself by a declaration', or art. 6:1: 'Obligations can only arise if such results from the law.' As if the law lived a life of its own which has nothing to do with people and their behaviour!

[61] In the same sense HORATIA MUIR WATT, 'La fonction subversive du droit comparé', *RIDC* 3-2000, p. 503 ff.

[62] There are also number fetishists. Some professors give students a lower grade if they do not know what number the legislator has given to a certain legal rule. Critical of learning the law by numbers is PETER BIRKS, lecture at the Opening session, 8th General Meeting, The Common Core of European Private Law, Trento, July 4th, 2002 (video on the Internet: www.jus.unitn.it/services/arc/2002/0704/home.html (1:14:45 ff.)).

[63] See *supra*, Chapter 2, Section I, G.

[64] See e.g. *BGH,* 11 October 1994, *NJW* 1995, 47, *LM* § 242 *BGB* (Bb), no. 151: 'Nicht jede einschneidende Veränderung der bei Vertragsabschluß bestehenden oder gemeinsam erwarteten Verhältnisse rechtfertigt jedoch eine Vertragsanpassung nach den Grundsätzen des Wegfalls der Geschäftsgrundlage. Weitere Voraussetzung eines solchen Eingriffs ist vielmehr, daß ein Festhalten an der vereinbarten Regelung zu einem untragbaren, mit recht und Gerechtigkeit schlechthin unvereinbaren Ergebnis führen würde und der betroffenen Partei nicht zuzumuten ist.', a standard phrase which the *BGH* has used many times previously (e.g. *BGH,* 13 November 1975, *NJW* 1976, 565, *MDR* 1976, 382, *LM* § 242 *BGB* (Bb), no. 80) and after that decision.

[65] See Lord Wilberforce and Lord Diplock in *Photo Production Ltd.* v *Securicor Transport Ltd.* [1980] AC 827 (p. 844 and p. 851 respectively). Compare G.H. TREITEL, *The Law of Contract*, 10th ed., London 1999, p. 702 ff.

oriented British academics) find this very disturbing. However, a loose use of terminology is of course only confusing for those who expect the same label to be consistently used when referring to a certain situation or policy. For those who are interested in the policy itself it may even be very enlightening when a court rephrases its policy on every occasion. It may help us to understand what they really mean. For example, for nearly twenty years the Dutch *Hoge Raad* has continually repeated, since the Plas/Valburg case, that negotiations may reach a stage where breaking off leads to liability to the extent of the expectation interest (the so-called 'third stage'), always in nearly exactly the same terms[66]. The advantage is of course that we now know that the judges of our Supreme Court have still not changed their minds: the policy is still the same. However, because of its abstract formula, we still have no clue what the policy is: when may a party be liable for the expectation interest because it breaks off negotiations before a contract has actually been concluded?

X. Final Remarks

There are other developments which should be taken into account. An important one is the fact that today no one now considers the code to be the only (maybe not even the main) source of private law. First, of course, one of the main characteristics of the development of private law on the European Continent in the 20th century is the central role which the courts have gained as the creators and developers of private law. Moreover, there are other legal actors and formants[67]. A code is merely one of them: apart from the courts, legal scholarship, legal education, legal practitioners (professionals), and other institutions are other actors which make important contributions to the development of the law. A contemporary European code should take this into account. To say the least, a modern code (or the Constitution) should explicitly deal with the relationship between the various legal formants. It is not at all obvious that the code should today be the starting point and the focal point of all legal reasoning. Another aspect is the dynamic character of the law which is probably one of its most important characteristics. The structure of private law should explicitly take into account the fact that the law develops, which means that the structure should not be static and immobilising. It should rather provide a framework for the process of developing private law. An aspect which should be taken into account when conceiving the structure of European private law is that we are living in an electronic age. Therefore, if a code is going to be drafted it should be conceived as an electronic code right from the beginning, with all the

---

[66] HR, 18 June 1982 (Plas/Valburg), *NJ* 1983, 723, note Brunner, *AA* 32 (1983), 758, note Van Schilfgaarde.

[67] See RODOLFO SACCO, *Introduzione al diritto comparato*, 5th ed. Torino 1997, p. 43 ff; RODOLFO SACCO, 'Legal Formants: A Dynamic Approach To Comparative Law', 39 *AJCL* (1991), pp. 1-34, pp. 343-401.

technical features which are possible today (hyperlinks et cetera). In such a code, for example, there is no need for general parts, abstractions et cetera since (unlike in the paper age) repetition has no cost. Moreover, an electronic code can be updated much more easily. It could even be a democratic project on the Web: a program which organises referendums of the Web and asks citizens whether the code should be changed (direct democracy).

Most of these developments which have been taken into account in this Chapter had not yet taken place when most of our classical codes were first conceived, in the 19th century, and not even when most of the recodification projects started in Europe, half way through the 20th Century. However, today we are familiar with them and it does not seem likely that they will go away. Therefore, before embarking upon the preparation of a European Civil Code (an endeavour which, as the Dutch experience shows, may take a considerable amount of time and energy[68]), or of a Code of Contracts in the broad sense in which the European Commission understands it, it seems advisable to thoroughly rethink the structure of private law in Europe today[69]. The relationship between private law and public law, and between commercial law, civil law and consumer law, the developments towards a multi-level system of governance, today's scepticism with regard to the law's integrity, the appropriate mix of mandatory and default rules, the ideological pillars of the new European private law, and the power of abstraction, are merely some of the factors which should be taken into account. Such reflection and debate may very well lead to the conclusion that a comprehensive Civil Code in a classical sense is not the appropriate way to deal with private law today. The challenge is to develop better alternatives. In this Chapter, and indeed throughout this book, I have made some preliminary suggestions to this end.

[68] It has taken the legislator of a small European country like the Netherlands more than 50 years to enact its new civil code, and the work has still not been completed. See E.O.H.P. FLORIJN, *Ontstaan en ontwikkeling van het nieuwe Burgerlijk Wetboek*, Maastricht 1995, T.J. VEEN, *''En voor berisping is hier ruime stof''. Over codificatie van het burgerlijk recht, legistische rechtsbeschouwing en herziening van het Nederlands privaatrecht in de 19de en 20ste eeuw*, Amsterdam 2001, and *supra*, Chapter 4.

[69] On the structure of European contract law see STEFAN GRUNDMANN, 'The Structure of European Contract Law', *ERPL* 2001, pp. 505-528

STRUCTURE

Bibliography

Abas, P., *Beperkende werking van de goede trouw*, Deventer 1972

Abschlußbericht der Kommission zur Überarbeitung des Schuldrechts, herausgegeben vom Bundesminister der Justiz, Bundesanzeiger, Köln 1992

Alpa, Guido, *I contratti in generale; introduzione alla nuova giurisprudenza*, Torino 1990

Alpa, Guido, *L'arte di giudicare*, Roma 1996

Alpa, Guido, *Trattato di diritto civile, I Storia, fonti, interpretazione*, Milano 2000

Alpa, G., Bessone, M. *I contratti in generale; Effetti, Invalidità e risoluzione del contratto*, Vol. II, Torino 1992

Ankum, J.A., 'Stenen voor brood', *AA* 42 (1993), p. 459 ff

Antoniolli Deflorian, Luisa, *La struttura istituzionale del nuovo diritto comune europeo: competizione e circolazione dei modelli giuridici*, Trento 1996

Aristotle, *The Nicomachean Ethics*, in: *The Loeb Classical Library*, Cambridge, Massachusetts and London 1994

Arnaud, André-Jean, *Pour une pensée juridique européenne*, Paris 1991

Asser, W.D.H., *Fair, redelijk en billijk; Over deformalisering in het burgerlijk procesrecht*, 2000

Atias, Christian, 'Le code civil nouveau', *D.* 1999

Atiyah, P.S., Summers, R.S., *Form And Substance in Anglo-American Law; A Comparative Study of Legal Reasoning, Legal Theory, and Legal Institutions*, London 1987

Auer, Marietta, 'Good Faith: A Semiotic Approach', 10 *ERPL* (2002), p. 279-301

Ayres, Ian, Gertner, Robert, 'Filling Gaps in Incomplete Contracts: An Economic Theory of Default Rules', 99 Yale L.J. (1989) 87-130

Bakels, F.B., *Ontbinding van wederkerige overeenkomsten*, Deventer 1993

Baker, J.H., *An Introduction to English Legal History*, London 1979 (reprinted in 1988)

Bar, Christian von, *Gemeineuropäisches Deliktsrecht*, München 1996

Bar, Christian von, Lando, Ole, 'Communication on European Contract Law: Joint Response of the Commission on European Contract Law and the Study Group on a European Civil Code', 10 *ERPL* 2002, pp. 183-248

Barendrecht, J.M., 'What kind of European Liability Law?; About the optimal level of detail in rules regarding (tort) liability in a European civil code', published on Internet (http://dlo.kub.nl:8080/courses/650062/index.html).

Barendrecht, J.M., 'Contractuele gebondenheid en het beginsel van belangenmaximalisatie', in: J.M. Barendrecht, M.A.B. Chao-Duivis and H.A.W. Vermeulen (eds.), *Beginselen van contractenrecht: Opstellen aangeboden aan B.W.M. Nieskens-Isphording*, Deventer 2000

Barendrecht, J.M., 'Naar een echte visie op het onderwijs', *NJB* 2001, pp. 164-165

Barendrecht, J.M., 'Door muren kijken; suggesties voor hervorming van de civiele cassatierechtspraak', *NJB* 2002, p. 297.

Basedow, Jürgen 'Rechtskultur - zwischen nationalem Mythos und europäischem Ideal', 4 *ZEuP* 1996, pp. 379 ff

Basedow, Jürgen 'Un Droit Commun des contrats pour le marché commun', *R.I.D.C.* 1998, pp. 7-28

Basedow, Jürgen 'Europäische Vertragsvereinheitlichung und deutsches Recht - Einführung', in: Jürgen Basedow (ed.), *Europäische Vertragsvereinheitlichung und deutsches Recht*, Tübingen 2000

Beale, H.G., Bishop, W.D., Furmston, M.P., *Contract Cases and Materials*, 4th ed., London, Dublin, Edinburgh 2001

Beale, Hugh, Paper presented at the 4th Ius Commune Conference, Corsendonk, December 1999 (not yet published)

Beale, Hugh, Paper presented in Rome at the European Civil Code conference, June 2000 (not yet published)

Beale, Hugh et. al. (eds.) *Cases, Materials and Text on Contract Law (Casebooks on the common law of Europe: Contracts)*, Oxford and Portland, Oregon 2002

Beale, Hugh, Pittam, Nicola, 'The Impact of the Human Rights Act 1998 on English Tort and Contract Law', in Daniel Friedmann, Daphne Barak-Erez, *Human Rights in Private Law*, Oxford 2001, pp. 131-159.

Behar-Touchais, Martine (ed.), *L'interdiction de se contredire au détriment d'autrui*, Paris 2001

Berger, Klaus-Peter, *Formalisierte oder "schleichende" Kodifizierung des transnationalen Wirtschaftsrechts*, Berlin, New York 1996

Berger, Klaus-Peter, *The Creeping Codification of the Lex Mercatoria*, Kluwer Law International 1997

Berger, Klaus Peter, 'Auf dem Wege zu einem europäischen Gemeinrecht der Methode', *ZEuP* 2001, p. 4 ff

Berger, Klaus Peter, 'Transnational Commercial Law in the Age of Globalization', in: Centro di studi e ricerche di diritto comparato e straniero (directed by M.J. Bonell), *Saggi, conferenze e seminari*, no. 42, Rome 2001

Bergh, G.G.J.J. van den, *Geleerd recht; Een geschiedenis van de Europese rechtswetenschap in vogelvlucht*, 2nd ed., Deventer 1985

Bergh, G.G.J.J. van den, *Geleerd recht; Een geschiedenis van de Europese rechtswetenschap in vogelvlucht*, 4th ed., Deventer 2000

Betlem, Gerrit, 'Een vierde type van rechtsvinding; Richtlijnconforme interpretatie van de onrechtmatige daad', *NJB* 1991, p. 1363

Bianca, C. Massimo, 'La nozione di buona fede quale regola di comportamento contrattuale', *Riv. dir .civ.* XXIX (1983), I, pp. 205-216

Bianca, C. Massimo, Diritto Civile, III, *Il contratto*, Milano 1987 (reprinted in 1992)

Bigliazzi Geri, L., 'Buona fede nel diritto civile', in: *Digesto delle Discipline Privatistiche*; Sezione Civile II, Torino 1988

Birks, Peter (ed.), *English Private Law*, Oxford 2000

Birks, Peter, Lecture at Opening session, 8th General Meeting, The Common Core of European Private Law, Trento, July 4th, 2002 (video on the Internet: www.jus.unitn.it/services/arc/2002/0704/home.html (1:14:45 ff))

Blom, J.C.H., Leupen, P.H.D., Rooy, P. de, Veen, T.J., Kooijmans, L., (eds.), *Een brandpunt van geleerdheid in de hoofdstad; De Universiteit van Amsterdam rond 1900 in vijftien portretten*, Hilversum/Amsterdam 1992

Bobbio, Norberto, *Il positivismo giuridico*, Torino 1996

Bobbio, Norberto, *L'età dei diritti*, Torino 1997

Bobbio, Norberto, *Destra e sinistra; Ragioni e significati di una distinzione politica*, Roma 1999

Boele-Woelki, Katharina, *Principles en IPR; Enkele beschouwingen over de toepassing van de UNIDROIT Principles of International Commercial Contracts en de Principles of European Contract Law op internationale overeenkomsten*, Lelystad 1995

Boele-Woelki, Katharina, 'Principles and Private International Law', *Uniform Law Review* 1996, 652 ff.

Boer, Th.M. de, et al. (eds.), *De werkelijkheid van I. Henri Hijmans; symposium gehouden op 23 oktober 1987*, Deventer 1988

Bonell, Michael Joachim, *An International Restatement of Contract Law; The UNIDROIT Principles of International Commercial Contracts*, 2nd ed., New York 1997

Bonell, Michael Joachim, 'The Need and Possibilities of a Codified European Contract Law', *ERPL* 1997, p. 505 ff

Boom, W.H. van, Jansen C.E.C., and Linssen, J.G.A. (eds.), *Tussen 'Alles' en 'Niets'; Van toedeling naar verdeling van nadeel*, Zwolle 1997

Borgers, M.J., Giesen, I., Jansen, C.E.C., Kristen, F.G.H., Meijer, F.W.J., Struycken, T.H.D. Verstijlen, F.M.J., and Vranken, J.B.M., 'Een alternatieve visie op de functies van de redelijkheid en billijkheid en de taak van de rechter; Vragen aan Hesselink', *NJB* 2000, pp. 2029-2031

Braudel, Fernand, *Écrits sur l'histoire*, Paris 1969

Breccia, U., *Le obbligazioni; Trattato di diritto Privato a cura di Giovanni Iudica e Paolo Zatti*, Milano 1992

Brink, Vincent Van den, *De rechtshandeling in strijd met de goede zeden*, The Hague 2002

Bruinsma, F., 'De ondraaglijke lichtheid van de rechtenstudie', *NJB* 2000, p. 1371 ff

Brunner, C.J.H., 'De billijkheid in het nieuwe BW', in: *Rechtsvinding onder het NBW. Een Groningse kijk op het nieuwe vermogensrecht*, 1992, p. 87 ff.

Burrows, Andrew, *Understanding the Law of Obligations; Essays on Contract, Tort and Restitution*, Oxford 2000

Busch, Danny, 'Indirect Representation and the Lando Principles', vol 2.3 EJCL (December 1998), <http://law.kub.nl/ejcl/23/art23-1.html>

Busch, Danny, Hondius, Ewoud, Kooten, Hugo J. van, Schelhaas, Harriet N. (general editor), Schrama, Wendy M. (eds.), *The Principles of European Contract Law and Dutch Law: A Commentary*, Nijmegen and The Hague, London, New York 2002.

Bussani, Mauro, Mattei, Ugo, 'The Common Core Approach to European Private Law', 3 *The Columbia Journal of European Law* (1997/1998), 339

Bussani, Mauro, Mattei, Ugo, (eds.), *Making European Private Law; Essays on the 'Common Core' Project'*, Trento 2000

Calabresi, Guido, 'Two Functions of Formalism', 67 *U Chi L Rev* (2000), 479

Canaris, Claus-Wilhelm, 'Ansprüche wegen 'positiver Vertragsverletzung' und "Schutzwirkung für Dritte" bei nichtigen Verträgen, Zugleich ein Beitrag zur Vereinheitlichung der Regeln über die Schutzpflichtverletzungen, *JZ* 1965, pp. 475-482

Canaris, Claus-Wilhelm, *Handelsrecht*, 22nd ed., München 1995

Canaris, Claus-Wilhelm, *Grundrechte und Privatrecht*, Berlin, New York 1999

Cantillo, M., *Le Obbligazioni, Giurisprudenza sistematica di diritto civile e commerciale, fondata da Walter Bigiavi*, Vol. I, Torino 1992

Carbonnier, Jean, *Droit Civil*, Vol. IV *Les Obligations*, 22nd ed., Paris 2000

Carbonnier, Jean, *Droit Civil; Introduction*, 25th ed., Paris 1997

Cardozo, Benjamin N., *The Nature of the Judicial Process*, New Haven and London 1921

Caroni, Pio, 'Der Schiffbruch der Geschichtlichkeit; Anmerkungen zum Neo-Pandektismus', *Zeitschrift für Neuere Rechtsgeschichte* (1994), pp. 85-100

Cartwright, John, *Taking Stock of O'Brien* [1999] *R.L.R.* 1

Caruso, Daniela, 'The Missing View of the Cathedral: The Private Law Paradigm of European Legal Integration', 3 *European Law Journal* (1997), pp. 3-32

Castronovo, Carlo, 'Recensione a Reinhard Zimmermann, Roman Law, Contemporary Law, European Law. The civilian tradition today', 3 *Europa e diritto privato* (2001), p. 737 ff

Center for Transnational Law (ed.), *Transnational Law in Commercial Legal Practice*, Vol. 1, Münster 1999

Chomsky, Noam, *Profit over people; neoliberalism and global order*, New York 1999

Cian, G., Trabucchi, A., *Commentario breve al codice civile*, 5th ed., Padova, 1997

Clark, Charles E., 'The Restatement Of The Law Of Contracts', 42 Yale L J 643-667

Collins, Hugh, 'European Private Law and Cultural Identity of States', *ERPL*, 1995, pp. 353-365

Collins, Hugh, 'Formalism and Efficiency: Designing European Commercial Contract Law', *ERPL* 2000, p. 211 ff

Cooter, Robert, Ulen, Thomas, *Law & Economics*, 3rd ed., Adison-Wesley, Reading etc. 2000

Craig, Paul, Búrca, Gráinne de, *EU Law; Text, Cases, and Materials*, 2nd ed., Oxford 1998

Craswell, Richard, 'Contract Law, Default Rules, And The Philosophy Of Promising', 88 *Mich. L. Rev.* 489-529 (1989)

Dalhuisen, J.H., *RM Themis* 1999, pp. 332 ff

David, René, Jauffret-Spinosi, Camille, Les *grands systèmes de droit contemporain*, 19th ed. Paris 1988

Debet, Anne, *L'influence de la Convention européenne des droits de l'homme sur le droit civil*, Paris 2002

De Ly, Filip *De lex mercatoria: inleiding op de studie van het transnationaal handelsrecht*, Antwerpen 1989

De Matos Antunes Varela, J., *Das Obrigações em geral*, Vol. I, 9th edition, Coimbra 1996

Demogue, R., *Traité des obligations en général, II Effets des obligations*, Part VI, Paris, 1931

Derrida, Jacques, *Force de loi*, Paris, 1994

Derrida, Jacques, *L'Université sans condition*, Paris 2001

Dewey, John, 'Logical Method and Law', 10 *Cornell Law Quarterly* (1924), 17

De Witte, Bruno, Forder, Caroline (eds.), *The common law of Europe and the future of legal education*, Deventer 1992

Díez-Picazo, L., Gullón, A., *Sistema de Derecho Civil*, Vol. II, Madrid 1998

Dijk P. van, Hoof, G.J.H. van, *Theory and Practice of the European Convention on Human Rights*, 3rd ed., The Hague, London and Boston 1998

Di Majo, A. *Delle Obligazioni in Generale, arts. 1173-1176, Commentario del codice civile Scialoja-Branca*, Bologna/Roma 1988

Di Robilant, Anna 'The Aesthetics of Law', *Global Jurist Advances*: Vol. 1: No. 2, Article 1 (www.bepress.com/gj/advances/vol/iss2/art1) (2001)

Drobnig, Ulrich, 'Das neue niederländische bürgerliche Gesetzbuch aus vergleichender und deutscher Sicht', 1 *ERPL* 1993, p. 171 ff.

Drobnig, Ulrich, 'Private Law in the European Union', *Forum Internationale*, no. 22, September 1996

Drobnig, Ulrich, 'Scope and general rules of a European civil code', *ERPL* 1997, p. 489 ff

Dunné, J.M. van, *Normatieve uitleg van rechtshandelingen; Een onderzoek naar de grondslagen van het geldende verbintenissenrecht*, Deventer 1971

Dunné, J.M. van, *Verbintenissenrecht, Deel I, Contractenrecht*, Deventer 1997

Duxbury, Neil, *Patterns of American Jurisprudence*, Oxford 1995

Dworkin, Ronald, 'Is Wealth A Value?' (1980) 9 *Journal of Legal Studies* 191

Dworkin, Ronald, *Law's Empire*, London 1986

Dworkin, Ronald, *Sovereign Virtue; The Theory and Practice of Equality*, Cambridge Massachusetts, London 2000

Ehrenzweig, Albert A., 'Das Desperanto des zweiten "Restatement of Conflict of Laws', in: Ernst van Caemmerer e.a. (eds.), *Ius Privatum Gentium (Festschrift Max Rheinstein)*, Vol. I, pp. 343ff, p. 344.

Eisenberg, Melvin A., 'The Unification of Law', in: Mauro Bussani, Ugo Mattei (eds.), *Making European Private Law; Essays on the 'Common Core' Project*, Trento 2000, p. 15 ff.

Empel, Martijn van & Jong, Marianne de, 'Constitution, International Treaties, Contracts and Torts', in: Ewoud Hondius & Carla Joustra (eds.), *Netherlands Reports to the Sixteenth International Congress of Comparative Law*, Antwerp, Oxford, New York, 2002, pp. 283-304

Fabre-Magnan, M., *De l' obligation d' information dans les contrats. Essai d'une théorie*, Paris 1992

Farnsworth, E. Allan, 'Precontractual liability and preliminary agreements: fair dealing and failed negotiations', *Columbia Law Review*, vol. 87, 1987, pp. 217-294

Farnsworth, E. Allan, 'The American Provenance of the UNIDROIT Principles', *RDU* 1997, p. 397 ff

Faure, Michael, 'Economic aspects of environmental liability: an introduction', 4 *ERPL* (1996), p. 85 ff

Faure, Michael, 'Economic Analysis', in: Bernard Koch, Helmut Koziol (eds.) *Unification of Tort Law: Strict Liability*, The Hague 2001

Fénet, P.A., *Recueil complet des travaux préparatoires du Code civil, discussions, motifs, rapports et discours, livre troisième, titre troisième*, Paris 1836

Ferrari Bravo, Luigi, Di Majo, Francesco, M. Rizzo, Alfredo, *Carta dei diritti fondamentali dell'Unione europea commentata con la giurisprudenza della Corte di giustizia CE e della Corte europea dei diritti dell'uomo e con i documenti rilevanti*, Milano 2001

Fikentscher, Wolfgang, *Methoden des Rechts in vergleichender Darstellung*, Band III *Mitteleuropäischer Rechtskreis*, Tübingen 1976

Fletcher, George P., 'Comparative Law as a Subversive Discipline', 46 *AJCL* (1998), p. 683 ff

Florijn, E.O.H.P., *Ontstaan en ontwikkeling van het nieuwe Burgerlijk Wetboek*, Maastricht 1995

Flour, Jacques, Aubert, Jean-Luc, *Les obligations; 1. L'acte juridique*, 6th ed., Paris 1994

Flume, Werner, *Allgemeiner Teil des Bürgerlichen Rechts; Zweiter Band. Das Rechtsgeschäft*, 4th ed. Berlin/Heidelberg/New York 1992

Foucault, Michel, *Les mots et les choses ; une archéologie des sciences humaines*, Paris 1966

Frangi, Marc, *Constitution et droit privé; les droits individuels et les droits économiques*, Aix-en-Provence and Paris 1992

Frank, J., *Law and the Modern Mind*, 1930

Frank, J., *Law and the Modern Mind*, English edition, 1949

Frank, J., *Courts on Trial*, 1949

Freeman, M.D.A., *Lloyd's Introduction to Jurisprudence*, 6th ed., London 1994

Frenk, N., 'Ambtshalve toetsing van dwingend Europees consumentenrecht: gevolgen van het arrest van het Europese Hof van Justitie van 27 juni 2000 voor het Burgerlijk Wetboek', *WPNR* 6431 (2001), p. 73 ff

Friedman, Lawrence M., *A History of American Law*, 2nd ed., New York 1985

Furmston, M.P., *Cheshire, Fifoot and Furmston's Law of Contract*, 14th ed., London/Edinburgh/Dublin 2001

Galvão Telles, I., *Dereito das Obrigações*, 7th ed., Coimbra 1997

Gambino, Antonio, *Inventario italiano; Costumi e mentalità di un Paese materno*, Torino 1998

Gandolfi, Giuseppe, 'Pour un code européen des contrats', *RTD Civ.* 1991, p. 707 ff

Gandolfi, Giuseppe (ed.), *Code Européen des contrats - Avant-projet*, Milano 2001

Gény, François, *Méthode d'interprétation et sources en droit privé positif: Essai critique*, 1899

Gernhuber, J., *Bürgerliches Recht; Ein systematisches Repertorium für Fortgeschrittene*, 3rd ed., München 1991

Gernhuber, Joachim, Grunewald, Barbara, *Bürgerliches Recht; Ein systematisches Repertorium*, 4th ed., München 1998

Ghestin, Jacques, *La formation du contrat*, in: *Traité de droit civil*, 3rd ed., Paris 1993

Ghestin, Jacques, 'Le nouveau titre IV bis du Livre III du Code civil "De la responsabilité du fait des produits défectueux"; L'application en France de la directive dur la responsabilité du fait des produits défectueux après l'adoption de la loi n° 98-389 du 19 mai 1998', *JCP*, 1998, no. 27, pp. 1201 ff.

Ghestin, Jacques, Goubeaux, Gilles, *Traité de droit civil, Introduction générale*, 3rd ed., Paris 1990

Gilmore, Grant, *The Death of Contract*, Columbus, Ohio 1997

Glendon, Mary Ann, 'Comment', in: Amy Gutman (ed.), *A Matter Of Interpretation: Federal Courts And The Law*, New Jersey 1998

Gordley, James, 'Common law und civil law: eine überholte Unterscheidung', *ZeuP* 1993, p. 498 ff.

Gordley, James, 'An American Perspective on UNIDROIT Principles', in: Centro di studi e ricerche di diritto comparato e straniero (lead by M.J. Bonell), *Saggi, conferenze e seminari*, no. 23, Roma 1996

Gordley, James, 'The Common Law in the Twentieth Century: Some Unfinished Business', *California Law Review* 2000

Gordley, James (ed.), *The Enforceability of Promises in European Contract Law*, Cambridge 2001

Groenewegen, John, 'Blind volgen economische school kan ongezond zijn', *NRC Handelsblad*, 20 July 2000

Grundmann, Stefan, 'European sales law - reform and adoption of international models in German sales law', 9 *ERPL* 2001, p. 85 ff

Grundmann, Stefan, 'The Structure of European Contract Law', *ERPL* 2001, pp. 505-528

Haanappel, P.P.C., Mackaay, E., *New Netherlands Civil Code Patrimonial Law*, Deventer/Boston 1990

Haazen, O.A., *Algemeen deel van het rechterlijk overgangsrecht; Een verhandeling over de terugwerkende kracht van rechtspraak, de rechtsdwaling en de democratische rechtsvindingsleer*, 2001

Hartkamp, A.S., *Aard en opzet van het nieuwe vermogensrecht, Monografieën Nieuw BW*, A1, Deventer 1990

Hartkamp, A.S., *Wetsuitleg en rechtstoepassing na de invoering van het nieuwe Burgerlijk Wetboek*, Deventer 1992

Hartkamp, Arthur, 'The UNIDROIT Principles for International Commercial Contracts and the Principles of European Contract Law', *ERPL* 1994, 2, pp. 341-357

Hartkamp, Arthur, 'The Use of the UNIDROIT Principles of International Commercial Contracts by National and Supranational Courts', in *UNIDROIT Principles for International Commercial Contracts: A New Lex Mercatoria, ICC/Dossier of the Institute of International Business Law and Practice* 1995, p. 253ff

Hartkamp, A.S., 'Indirect Representation According to the Principles of European Contract Law, the Unidroit Agency Convention and the Dutch Civil Code', in Jürgen Basedow, Klaus J. Hopt and Hein Kötz (eds.), *Festschrift für Ulrich Drobnig zum siebzigsten Geburtstag*, Tübingen 1998, pp. 45 ff.

Hartkamp, A.S., *Mr. C. Asser's handleiding tot de beoefening van het Nederlands burgerlijk recht; Verbintenissenrecht; Deel I De verbintenis in het algemeen*, 11th ed., Deventer 2000

Hartkamp, Arthur S., 'On European Freedoms and National Mandatory Rules: The Dutch Judiciary and the European Convention on Human Rights', 8 *ERPL* (2000), p. 111-124

Hartkamp, A.S., *Mr. C. Asser's handleiding tot de beoefening van het Nederlands burgerlijk recht; Verbintenissenrecht; Deel II Algemene leer der overeenkomsten*, 11th ed., Deventer 2001

Hartkamp, Arthur, Hesselink, Martijn, Hondius, Ewoud, Joustra, Carla, Perron, Edgar du, *Towards a European civil code*, 2nd ed., Nijmegen and The Hague, London, Boston 1998

Hartlief, T., *Ontbinding: over ongedaanmaking, bevrijding en rechterlijke bevoegdheden bij ontbinding wegens wanprestatie*, Deventer 1994

Hartlief, Ton, *De vrijheid beschermd*, Deventer 1999

Hayton, D.J., Kortmann, S.C.J.J., Verhagen, H.L.E. (eds.), *Principles of European Trust Law*, The Hague/Deventer 1999

Hedemann, J.W., *Die Flucht in die Generalklauseln; Eine Gefahr für Recht und Staat*, Tübingen 1933

Herbots, Jacques, *Contract Law in Belgium*, Deventer, Boston, Bruxelles 1995

Hesselink, M.W., 'De opmars van de goede trouw in het Franse contractenrecht', *WPNR* 6154 (1994), pp. 694-698

Hesselink, M.W., 'Vragen bij de toepassing van art. 6:230 BW', *WPNR* 6191-6192 (1995), pp. 541-545, 563-567

Hesselink, M.W., 'De schadevergoedingsplicht bij afgebroken onderhandelingen in het licht van het Europese privaatrecht', *WPNR* 6248 (pp. 879-883), 6249 (pp. 906-910)

Hesselink, M.W., *De redelijkheid en billijkheid in het Europese privaatrecht*, Deventer 1999

Hesselink, M.W., *Review*, 3 *The Edinburgh Law Review* (1999), p. 412 ff

Hesselink, M.W., 'De redelijkheid en billijkheid in het Europese privaatrecht', *AA* 1999, p. 687 ff

Hesselink, M.W., '"Wat is recht etc.?"; Antwoorden op vragen van Tilburgers over rechtsregels, rechtspraak en rechtsvorming', *NJB* 2000, p. 2032 ff

Hesselink, Martijn W., 'Special Issue on Critical Legal Theory and European Private Law- Editorial', 10 *ERPL* 2002, pp. 3-5

Hesselink, Martijn W., 'Precontractual Good Faith', in: Hugh Beale et. al. (eds.) *Cases, Materials and Text on Contract Law, Oxford and Portland*, Oregon 2002, Chapter 2, Section 2 (pp. 237-293)

Hesselink, Martijn W., 'Il codice civile olandese del 1992 - un esempio per un codice civile Europeo?', in Guido Alpa and Emilio Nicola Buccico (eds.), *La riforma dei codici in Europa e il progetto di codice civile europeo; Materiali dei seminari 2001*, Milan 2002, pp. 71-82

Hesselink, Martijn, Oosting, Bert, Perron, Edgar du, 'Verandering van omstandigheden en de uitleg van overeenkomsten, naar aanleiding van "Rebus sic stantibus" door prof. mr. P. Abas,' *AA* 39 (1990) 9, 563-570

Hijmans, I. Henri, *Het recht der werkelijkheid*, Haarlem 1910

Hijmans, I. Henri, *De tweesprong der rechtswetenschap*, Zwolle 1933

Hoefer-Van Dongen, Pauline, 'Meesters en Masters; De NJB-Salon op 16 februari 2001', *NJB* 2001, p. 528 ff

Hol, Ton, 'Recht als ervaring; Over academische vorming in de juridische opleiding', *NJB* 2001, p. 158 ff

Holmes Jr., Oliver Wendell, *The Common Law*, Boston 1881

Holmes Jr., Oliver Wendell, 'The Path of the Law', in: Sheldon M. Novick (ed.) *The Collected Works of Justice Holmes; Complete Writings and Selected Judicial opinions of Oliver Wendell Holmes*, Vol. III, Chicago and London 1995, pp. 391 ff (originally published in 1897 in 10 *Harvard Law Review*, 457)

Hondius, Ewoud H., 'General Report', in: *Precontractual Liability; Reports to the XIIIth Congress International Academy of Comparative Law; Montreal, Canada 18-24 August 1990*, Deventer/Boston 1991

Hondius, Ewoud, *Consumer Guarantees: Towards a European Sale of Goods Act*, in: Centro di studi e ricerche di diritto comparato e straniero (directed by M.J. Bonell), *Saggi, conferenze e seminari*, no. 18, Rome 1996

Hondius, Ewoud, 'Weens koop- en verdragenrecht', *WPNR* 6233 (1996), p. 567f

Hondius, E.H., 'Ambtshalve toepassing van algemene voorwaarden: het Europese Hof van Justitie spreekt zich uit', *WPNR* 6417 (2000), p. 651-652

Hondius, E.H., 'De betekenis van de Principles of European Contract Law voor het Nederlandse recht / inleiding', *NTBR* 2000, p. 428 ff.

Hondius, Ewoud H., 'The Genesis of the Principles of European Contract Law and of Modern Dutch Private Law', in: Danny Busch & Ewoud H. Hondius & Hugo J. Van Kooten & Harriet N. Schelhaas (General Editor) & Wendy M. Schrama (eds.), *The Principles of European Contract Law and Dutch Law: A Commentary*, Nijmegen and The Hague, London, New York 2002, pp. 13-27

Hondius, Ewoud, Jeloschek, Christoph, 'Towards a European Sales Law - Legal Challenges posed by the Directive on the Sale of Consumer Goods and Associated Guarantees, 9 *ERPL* 2001, p. 3 ff

Horwitz, Morton J., *The Transformation of American Law 1780-1860*, Cambridge Massachusetts 1977

Horwitz, Morton J., *The Transformation of American Law 1870-1960; The Crisis of Legal Orthodoxy*, New York/Oxford 1992

Howarth, David, 'The General Conditions of Unlawfulness', in: A.S. Hartkamp et al. (eds.) *Towards a European Civil Code*, 2nd ed., Nijmegen and The Hague/London/Boston 1998, pp. 397 ff.

Hultmark, Christina, 'Obligations, Contracts and Sales', in: Michael Bogdan (ed.) *Swedish Law in the New Millennium*, Stockholm 2000

Hyland, Richard, 'The American Restatements and the Uniform Commercial Code', A.S. Hartkamp et al. (eds.) *Towards a European Civil Code*, 2nd ed., Nijmegen and The Hague/London/Boston 1998, pp. 55

Jacobs, W.A., *ADR en consument: Een rechtsvergelijkende studie naar de mogelijkheden van alternatieve geschillenoplossing*, Deventer 1998

Jamin, Christophe, 'Henri Capitant et René Demogue: notation sur l'actualité d'un dialogue doctrinal', in: *Mélanges François Terré*, Paris, 1999, p. 125 ff

Jamin, Christophe, 'Plaidoyer pour le solidarisme contractuel', in: Gilles Goubeaux et al. (ed.), *Études offertes à Jacques Ghestin; Le contrat au début du XXIe siècle*, Paris 2001

Jamin, Christophe, 'Une brève histoire politique des interprétations de l'art. 1134 du CC', *D.* 2002, pp. 901-907

Jans, J.H., Lange, R. de, Prechal, S., Widdershoven, R.J.G.M., *Inleiding tot het Europees bestuursrecht*, Nijmegen 1999

Jansen, Christian E.C., 'Good Faith in Construction Law: the Inaugural King's College Construction Law Lecture' (1999) 15 *Const. L.J.*, pp. 347 ff

Jestaz, Philippe, Jamin, Christoph, 'L'entité doctrinale française', *D.* 1997, p. 167 ff

Jhering, Rudolph von, *DerKampf ums Recht*, Darmstadt 1874

Jhering, Rudolph von, *Scherz und Ernst in der Jurisprudenz; Eine Weihnachtsgabe für das juristische Publikum*, 12th ed., Leipzig 1921 (first published in 1884)

Jhering, Rudolph von, *Geist des Römischen Rechts auf den verschiedenen Stufen seiner Entwicklung*, Part III, 3rd ed., Leipzig 1877

Jhering, Rudolph von, *Geist des Römischen Rechts auf den verschiedenen Stufen seiner Entwicklung*, Part I, 6th ed, Leipzig 1907

Jhering, Rudolph von, *Geist des römischen Rechts auf den verschiedenen Stufen seiner Entwicklung*, 8th ed. Part I, p. 15

Joerges, Christian, 'The Impact of European Integration on Private Law: Reductionist Perceptions, True Conflicts and a New Constitutional Perspective', *ELJ* 1997, pp. 378-406

Joerges, Christian, 'Editorial and Acknowledgements', *ERPL* 2000, p. vii

Joerges, Christian, 'Interactive Adjudication in the Europeanisation Process? A Demanding Perspective and a Modest Example', *ERPL* 2000, p. 1-16

Kantorowicz, Hermann (Gnaeus Flavius), 'Der Kampf um die Rechtswissenschaft', Heidelberg 1906, reprinted in: Würtenberger 1962, pp. 13-39

Kaser, M., 'Ius honorarium' und 'ius civile', *SZRA* 101 (1984), pp. 1-114

Kaser, M., *Römisches Privatrecht*, 15th ed., München 1989

Kennedy, Duncan, 'Form and Substance in Private Law Adjudication', 89 Harv. L. Rev. (1976) 1685 ff

Kennedy, Duncan, *Legal Education and the Reproduction of Hierarchy; A Polemic Against the System*, Cambridge, Massachusetts, 1983

Kennedy, Duncan, *A Critique of Adjudication {fin de siècle}*, Cambridge Massachusetts 1997

Kennedy, Duncan, 'The Political Stakes in "Merely Technical" Issues of Contract Law', 10 *ERPL* 2002, pp. 7-28

Kennedy, Duncan, Michelman, 'Are Property and Contract Efficient?' (1980) 8 Hofstra L.Rev. 711

Kessedjian, Cathérine, 'Une exercise de rénovation des sources du droit des contrats du commerce international: les Principes proposées par l'Unidroit', *Rev. crit. dr. internat. privé.*, 84 (4) October-December 1995, pp. 641-670

Keus, L.A.D., 'Europees privaatrecht - Een bonte lappendeken', in: *Preadviezen, uitgebracht voor de Vereniging voor Burgerlijk Recht en de Nederlandse Vereniging voor Europees Recht*, Lelystad 1993

Klein, Naomi, *No Logo*, London 2000

Klomp, R.J.Q., *Opkomst en ondergang van het handelsrecht : over de aard en de positie van het handelsrecht, in het bijzonder in verhouding tot het burgerlijk recht, in Nederland in de negentiende en twintigste eeuw*, Nijmegen 1998

Klomp, R.J.Q., 'Geschiedenis, bij wijze van inleiding', in: *Preadvies van de Vereniging Handelsrecht 2000; Het eigen gezicht van het handelsrecht*, Deventer 2000

Kluiver, H.J. de, 'Goede trouw en rechtspersonenrecht', in: *A-T-D; Opstellen aangeboden aan Prof.mr. van Schilfgaarde*, Deventer 2000, pp. 225 ff.

Knopp, W. (auf Grund der Erläuterungen von Prof. Dr. W. Siebert in der neunten Auflage), §242, Bürgerliches Gesetzbuch mit Einführungsgesetz und Nebengesetzen, *Band 2 Schuldrecht I* (§§ 241-610), 10th ed., Stuttgart/Berlin/Köln/Mainz 1967

Kop, P.C., *Legisme en Privaatrechtswetenschap*, Deventer 1982

Kötz, Hein, 'A common private law for Europe: perspectives for the reform of European legal education', in: Bruno De Witte, Caroline Forder (eds.), *The common law of Europe and the future of legal education*, Deventer 1992

Kötz, Hein, *Europäisches Vertragsrecht*, Part I, Tübingen, 1996

Kötz, Hein, *European Contract Law*, Part I (translated by Tony Weir), Oxford 1997

Kötz, Hein, 'Vertragliche Aufklärungspflichten; Eine rechtsökonomische Studie', in: Jürgen Basedow, Klaus J. Hopt, Hein Kötz (eds.), *Festschrift für Ulrich Drobnig zum siebzigsten Geburtstag*, Tübingen 1998, p. 563 ff

Kötz, Hein, 'How to Achieve A Common European Private Law', in: Franz Werro (ed.), *New Perspectives on European Private Law, Forum Europarecht*, no. 4, Fribourg 1998

Kötz, Hein, 'Comparative Law in Germany Today', *RIDC* 1999, p. 753 ff

Kötz, Hein, 'The Trento Project and Its Contribution to the Europeanization of Private Law', in: *Making European Law; Essays on the 'Common Core Project'* (Mauro Bussani, Ugo Mattei eds.), Trento 2000

Kramer, E., *Einleitung Band 2, Münchener Kommentar zum Bürgerlichen Gesetzbuch*, München 1994

Kronman, Anthony, Posner, Richard A., *The Economics of Contract Law*, Little, Brown and Company, Boston and Toronto 1979

Laarhoven, M.J. van, Nieskens-Isphording, W.M., Recensie *NTBR* 2001

Lando, O., 'Denmark', in: *Precontractual Liability; Reports to the XIIIth Congress International Academy of Comparative Law*; Montreal, Canada 18-24 August 1990, Deventer/Boston 1990

Lando, Ole, 'Is codification needed in Europe? Principles of European Contract Law and the relationship to Dutch law', 1 *ERPL*, (1993), p. 157

Lando, O., Performance and Remedies in the Law of Contract, in: *Towards a European Civil Code*, Nijmegen and Dordrecht/Boston/London 1994

Lando, O., *Each contracting party must act in accordance with good faith and fair dealing*, Festskrift till Jan Ramberg, Stockholm 1996

Lando, Ole, 'Some Issues Relating to the Law Applicable to Contractual Obligations', (1996-97) 7 *King's College Law Journal* 55 ff.

Lando, Ole, 'Why Codify the European Law of Contract?', *ERPL* 1997, p. 525 ff

Lando, Ole, 'The Principles of European Contract Law after Year 2000', in: Franz Werro (ed.), *New Perspectives on European Private Law, Forum Europarecht*, no. 4, Fribourg 1998

Lando, Ole, Beale, Hugh (eds.), *The Principles of European Contract Law, Part I: Performance, Non-Performance and Remedies, Prepared by the Commission on European Contract Law*, Dordrecht/Boston/ London 1995

Lando, Ole, Beale, Hugh (eds.), *Principles of European Contract Law, Parts I and II, Prepared by The Commission on European Contract Law*, The Hague 2000

Larenz, Karl, *Lehrbuch des Schuldrechts, I Band Allgemeiner Teil*, 14th ed., München 1987

Larenz, Karl, *Methodenlehre der Rechtswissenschaft*, 5th ed., Berlin, Heidelberg, New York, Tokyo 1991

Lasser, Mitchel de S.-O.-I'E., 'Judicial (Self-) Portraits: Judicial Discourse in the French Legal System', 104 *Yale L.J.* (1995), p. 1325 ff

Leff, Arthur, 'Economic Analysis of Law: Some Realism About Nominalism' (1974) 60 Virginia L. Rev. 451

Legrand, Pierre, 'European legal systems are not converging', 45 *International and Comparative Law Quarterly* (1996), pp. 52-81

Legrand, Pierre, 'Against a European Civil Code', 60 *MLR* (1997), pp. 44-62

Legrand, Pierre, *Fragments on Law-as-Culture*, Deventer 1999

Legrand, Pierre, *Que sais-je? Le droit comparé*, Paris 1999

Legrand, Pierre, 'On the Unbearable Localness of the Law: Academic Fallacies and Unseasonable Observations', 10 *ERPL* 2002, pp. 61-76

Leible, Stefan, 'Die Rolle der Rechtsprechung des Europäischen Gerichtshofes bei der europäischen Privatrechtsentwicklung', in Dieter Martiny, Normann Witzleb (eds.), *Auf dem Wege zu einem Europäischen Zivilgesetzbuch*, Berlin, Heidelberg, New York 1999

Le Tourneau, Philippe, Cadiet, Loïc, *Droit de la responsabilité*, Paris 1996

Lewis, W.D., 'Introduction', in: *Restatement of the Law of Contracts, as adopted and promulgated by the American Law Institute at Washington D.C. May 6, 1932*, Vol. I

Llewellyn, Karl N., 'Some Realism about Realism', (1931) 44 *Harv. L. Rev.* 1222 (reprinted, with adaptations, in Llewellyn, Karl N., *Jurisprudence; Realism in Theory and Practice*, Chicago and London 1962, pp. 42, where quotes are take from).

Llewellyn, Karl N., 'The Normative, The Legal and The Law-Jobs: The Problem of Juristic Method', 49 *Yale L.J.* 1355

Llewellyn, Karl N., *The Bramble Bush; On Our Law and its Study*, New York 1951

Llewellyn, Karl N., *Jurisprudence; Realism in Theory and Practice*, Chicago and London 1962

Loos, Marco B.M., 'Naar een Europees dienstverleningsrecht', *NJB* 2000, p. 452 ff

Loos, Marco B.M., 'Towards a European Law of Service Contracts', *ERPL* 4(2001), p.565-574

Loos, Marco B.M., 'Europese toetsing van algemene voorwaarden', *NTBR* 2001, p. 98 ff

Loussouarn, Y., Rapport de synthèse, Travaux de l'association Henri Capitant, Tome XLIII, année 1992. *Journées louisianaises de Baton-Rouge et La Nouvelle Orléans*, 'La bonne foi', Paris 1994

Lurger, Brigitta, *Vertragliche Solidarität, Entwicklungschancen für das allgemeine Vertragsrecht in Österreich und in der Europäischen Union*, Baden-Baden 1998

Lurger, Brigitta, *Grundfragen der Vereinheitlichung des Vertragsrechts in der Europäischen Union*, Wien, New York 2002

Macaulay, Stewart, 'Non-Contractual Relations in Business: A Preliminary Study', 28 American Sociological Review 55 (1963)

Macneil, Ian, 'Restatement (Second) of Contracts and Presentiation' (1974) 60 Virginia LR 589

Macneil, Ian, 'Contract Adjustment of long-term economic relations under classical, neo-classical and relational contract law', (1978) 72 Northwestern University LR 854

Macneil, Ian 'Relational Contract Theory as Sociology', 1987 (143 Journal of Institutional and Theoretical Economics 272

MacQueen, Hector L., 'Good Faith in the Scots Law of Contract: An Undisclosed Principle?', in: *Good Faith in Contract and Property*, Oxford 1999, p. 5 ff

MacQueen, Hector, 'Scots Law and the Road to the New Ius Commune', *Ius Commune Lectures on European Private Law*, 1, Maastricht 2000

MacQueen, Hector L., Thomson, J., *Contract Law in Scotland*, Edinburgh 2000

Magnus, U., (ed.), *Unification of Tort Law: Damages*, in: Helmut Koziol, Jaap Spier (eds), *Principles of European Tort Law*, Volume 5), The Hague, London, Boston 2001

Mahé, Chantal, 'Conflit de conditions générales: quelle tactique adopter?' in: F.W. Grosheide, K. Boele-Woelki (eds.), *Molengrafica Europees privaatrecht*, Lelystad 1997

Maitland, F.W., *Equity; also The Forms of Action at Common Law; Two Courses of Lectures*, Cambridge 1920

Malaurie, Philippe, Aynès, Laurent, *Cours de droit civil*, part IV, *Les obligations*, 10th ed., Paris 1999

Marguénaud, Jean-Pierre, *CEDH et droit privé; L'influence de la jurisprudence de la Cour des droits de l'homme sur le droit privé français*, Paris 2001

Maris van Sandelingenambacht, C.W., 'Legal Postism and the End of European Private Law', *ERPL* 2001, pp. 111-132

Markesinis, Basil, 'Comparative Law - A Subject in Search of an Audience, 53 *MLR* (1990), pp. 1-21

Markesinis, Basil (ed.), *The gradual convergence; Foreign Ideas, Foreign Influences, and English Law On the Eve of 21st Century*, Oxford 1994

Markesinis, Basil, *Five Days in the House of Lords: Some Comparative Reflections on White v. Jones*, in: Centro di studi e ricerche di diritto comparato e straniero (directed by M.J. Bonell), *Saggi, conferenze e seminari*, no. 16, Roma 1995

Markesinis, Basil S., 'Why a Code is Not the Best Way to Advance the Cause of European Legal Unity', *ERPL* 1997, p. 519 ff

Markesinis, Basil.S., Lorenz, W., Dannemann, G. *The German Law of Obligations, Volume I The Law of Contracts and Restitution: A Comparative Introduction*, Oxford 1997

Mattei, Ugo, 'Efficiency in Legal Transplants: An Essay in Comparative Law and Economics', *International Review of Law and Economics*, 14 (1994), p. 3 ff.

Mattei, Ugo, 'Why The Wind Changed: Intellectual Leadership In Western Law', 42 *AJCL* (1994) 195

Mattei, Ugo, 'Three Patterns of Law: Taxonomy and Change in the World's Legal Systems', 45 *AJCL* (1997), p. 5 ff

Mattei, Ugo, 'A Transaction Costs Approach to the European Code', *ERPL* 1997, p. 537 ff.

Mattei, Ugo, *Comparative Law and Economics*, 1998

Mattei, Ugo, 'The Issue of Civil Codification and Legal Scholarship: Biases, Strategies and Developments', 21 *Hastings Int'l & Comp. L. Rev.* 883

Mattei, Ugo, 'Efficiency and Equal Protection In The New European Contract Law: Mandatory, Default and Enforcement Rules', 39 Va. J. Int'l L. 537

Mattei, Ugo, 'Hard Code Now!', *Global Jurist Frontiers* (2002): Vol. 2: No. 1, Article 1

Mattei, Ugo, Di Robilant, Anna, 'The Art and Science of Critical Scholarship; Postmodernism and International Style in the Legal Architecture of Europe', 10 *ERPL* 2002, pp. 29-59

Mayer-Maly, Theo, *Art. 2 ZGB*, in: Heinrich Honsell, Nedim Peter Vogt, Thomas Geiser (eds.), *Kommentar zum Schweizerischen Zivilgesetzbuch I*), Basel and Frankfurt am Main 1996

McKendrick, Ewan, *Contract Law*, 4th ed., London 2000

McKendrick, Ewan, 'Traditional Concepts and Contemporary Values', 10 *ERPL* 2001, pp. 95-109

McKendrick, Ewan, 'Codification: the Current State of Play in the United Kingdom' in: Guido Alpa and Emilio Nicola Buccico (eds.), *La riforma dei codici in Europa e il progetto di codice civile europeo; Materiali dei seminari 2001*, Milan 2002, pp. 71-82

Medicus, Dieter, *Schuldrecht I; Allgemeiner Teil*, 12th ed., München 2000

Medicus, Dieter, *Bürgerliches Recht*, 18th ed., Köln/Berlin/Bonn/München 1999

Meijers, E.M., *Dogmatische rechtswetenschap*, Amsterdam 1903

Meijers, E.M., *De taak der rechtswetenschap ten aanzien der vrije rechtspraak*, Haarlem 1910

Meijers, E.M., 'Wijzigingen en aanvullingen van het Burgerlijk wetboek na 1838', in: Paul Scholten, E.M. Meijers (eds.), *Gedenkboek Burgerlijk Wetboek 1838-1938*, Zwolle 1938, p. 33 ff

Meijers, E.M., *Ontwerp voor een Nieuw Burgerlijk Wetboek (Groene Boeken), Tekst eerste gedeelte (Boek 1-4)*, The Hague 1954

Mendel, M.M., 'Welke rol spelen in het handelsrecht de redelijkheid en billijkheid - met name in hun beperkende werking - in rechtsverhoudingen tussen ondernemers en wat behoort die rol te zijn?', in: *Preadvies van de Vereniging Handelsrecht 2000; Het eigen gezicht van het handelsrecht*, Deventer 2000

Menezes-Cordeiro, A., 'Rapport portugais', *Travaux de l'association Henri Capitant, Tome XLIII, année 1992. Journées louisianaises de Baton-Rouge et La Nouvelle Orléans, 'La bonne foi'*, Paris 1994

Merz, H., Article 2 ZGB, *Berner Kommentar*, Einleitungsband, Bern 1966

Milsom, S.F.C., *Historical Foundations of the Common Law*, 2nd ed., London 1981

Monateri, P.G., 'Black Gaius; A Quest for the Multicultural Origins of the "Western Legal Tradition"', 51 *Hastings Law Journal* (2000), 479-555

Montesquieu, *De l'esprit des lois*, Paris 1979 (first edition 1748)

Müller-Graff, Peter Christian, 'EC Directives as a Means of Private Law Unification', in : A.S. Hartkamp et al. (eds.), *Towards a European Civil Code*, 2nd ed., pp. 71ff

Muir Watt, Horatia, 'La fonction subversive du droit comparé', *RIDC* 3-2000, p. 503 ff

Münchener Kommentar zum Bürgerlichen Gesetzbuch, 4th ed., München 2001

Musy, Alberto M., *Il dovere di informazione; Saggio di diritto comparato*, Trento 1999

Nassar, Nagla, *Sanctity of Contract Revisited: A Study in the Theory and Practice of Long-Term International Commercial Transactions*, Dordrecht/Boston/London 1995

Natoli, U., *L'attuazione del rapporto obbligatorio, Trattato di diritto civile e commerciale diretto dai professori Antonio Cicu e Francesco Messineo*, vol. XVI, t. 1, Milano 1974

Nielsen, Ruth, *Contract Law in Denmark*, The Hague/London/Boston 1997

Nieuwenhuis, H., *Confrontatie en compromis; Recht, retoriek en burgerlijke moraal*, Deventer 1992

Nieuwenhuis, J.H., 'Vernietigen, ontbinden of aanpassen; Wat is het lot van teleurstellende overeenkomsten?', *WPNR* (1995), nos. 6164 (pp. 23-26) and 6165 (pp. 37-41)

Nieuwenhuis, J.H, 'Principles of European Contract Law; Vooraankondiging Preadviezen voor de Vereniging voor Burgerlijk Recht', *NTBR* 2001, p. 132 ff

Oderkerk, A.E., *De preliminaire fase van het rechtsvergelijkend onderzoek*, Nijmegen 1999

Ogus, Anthony, 'Competition between National Legal Systems: A Contribution of Economic Analysis to Comparative Law', 48 *International and Comparative Law Quarterly* (1999), 405-418

Ogus, Anthony, 'Comparative Regulatory Techniques and Cultures: First Steps for Lex Commune', keynote lecture delivered at the Ius Commune Congress, Priorij Corsendonk, 26 November 1999 (unpublished)

Osman, Filali, *Les principes généraux de la lex mercatoria; contribution à l'étude d'un ordre juridique anational*, Paris 1992

Palandt Bürgerliches Gesetzbuch (Beck'sche Kurz-Kommentare, Part 7), 60th ed., München 2001

Périlleux, Jacques, 'Rapport belge', in: *Travaux de l'association Henri Capitant, Tome XLIII, année 1992. Journées louisianaises de Baton-Rouge et La Nouvelle Orléans, "La bonne foi"*, Paris 1994

Perron, Edgar du, 'Contract and Third Parties', in: *Towards a European Civil Code*, 2nd ed., Nijmegen and The Hague, London, Boston 1998, pp. 211ff.

Picod, Y., *Le devoir de loyauté dans l'exécution du contat*, Paris 1989

Plateringen, Annemieke van, *Imprévision in Latijns-Amerika; Een rechtsvergelijkend onderzoek naar de toepassingseisen van wettelijke imprévision-regelingen in Latijns-Amerika* (forthcoming)

Poiares Maduro, Miguel, 'Striking the Elusive Balance Between Economic Freedom and Social Rights in the EU', in: Philip Alston (ed.), *The EU and Human Rights*, Oxford 1999, pp. 449-472

Portalis, 'Discours préliminaire', in: P.A. Fénet, *Recueil complet des travaux préparatoires du Code civil, discussions, motifs, rapports et discours*, livre troisième, titre troisième, Paris 1836, Part I, p. 463 ff

Posner, Richard A., *The Economics of Justice*, Cambridge Massachusetts 1983

Posner, Richard A., 'Foreword', in: Michael Faure and Roger Van den Bergh (eds.), *Essays in Law and Economics*, Antwerpen/Apeldoorn 1989

Posner, Richard A. (ed.), *The Essential Holmes; Selections from the Letters, Speeches, Judicial Opinions, and Other Writings of Oliver Wendell Holmes, Jr*, Chicago and London 1992

Posner, Richard A., *Overcoming Law*, Cambridge (Massachusetts) and London 1995

Posner, Richard A., *Economic Analysis of Law*, 5th ed., Aspen Law & Business, New York 1998

Pound, Roscoe, 'The Call for a Realist Jurisprudence', (1931) 44 *Harv. L. Rev*, 697

Pound, Roscoe, 'Law in Books and Law in Action' (1910) 44 *Am. L. Rev.*, 12

Prakke, L, de Reede, J.L., Wissen, G.J.M. van, *Van der Pot Donner Handboek van het Nederlandse staatsrecht*, 14th ed., Deventer 2001

Prechal, Sacha, *Directives in European Community Law; A Study on EC Directives and their Enforcement by National Courts*, Ph. D. thesis Amsterdam 1995

Ramberg, Christina H., 'The E-Commerce Directive and Formation of Contract in a Comparative Perspective', *Global Jurist Advances*: Vol. 1: No. 2, Article 3 (www.bepress.com/gj/advances/vol1/iss2/art3)

Ranieri, Filippo, *Europäisches Obligationenrecht; Lehr- und Textbuch*, Wien, New York 1999

Reimann, Mathias, *Einführung in das US-amerikanische Privatrecht*, München 1997

Remien, Olivier, 'Über den Stil des europäischen Privatrechts', *RabelsZ* 60 (1996), pp. 1-39

Remien, Oliver, 'Einheit, Mehrstufigheit und Flexibilität im europäischen Privat- und Wirtschaftsrecht', 62 *RabelsZ* (1998), p. 627 ff

Remien, Oliver, *ZeuP* 2001, p. 420

Rescigno, Pietro *Manuale di diritto privato*, 2000

Resta, Giorgio, 'Diritti della personalità e limiti dea libertà contrattuale nell'evoluzione del diritto europeo' (forthcoming; presented at the conference *Diritti fondamentali e formazione del diritto privato europeo* in Rome on June 28th, 2002

Rieg, A., *Jurisclasseur*, Contrats et obligations, Effet obligatoire des conventions, Exécution de bonne foi des conventions, Articles 1134 et 1135, 1989

Rodotà, Stefano, *Le fonti di integrazione del contratto*, Milano 1969

Rodotà, Stefano, 'Ma l'Europa già applica la nuova Carta dei diritti', *la Repubblica*, 3 January 2001

Rodríguez Iglesias, Carlos Gil, 'Gedanken zum Entstehen einer Europäischen Rechtsordnung', *NJW* 1999, 1, 8ff

Rorty, Richard, *Philosophy and Social Hope*, London 1999

Roth, H., *§ 242, Münchener Kommentar zum Bürgerlichen Gesetzbuch*, München 1994

Rutgers, Jacobien W., *International Reservation of Title Clauses; A study of Dutch, French and German Private International Law in the Light of European Law*, The Hague 1999

Sacco, Rodolfo, 'Legal Formants: A Dynamic Approach To Comparative Law', 39 *AJCL* (1991), pp. 1-34, pp. 343-401

Sacco, R., De Nova, G., *Trattato di diritto civile*, diretto da Rodolfo Sacco, *Il contratto*, Vol. I, Torino 1993

Sacco, Rodolfo, *Introduzione al diritto comparato*, 5th ed. Torino 1997

Sacco, Rodolfo, 'Formation of Contracts', in: A.S. Hartkamp et al. (eds.) *Towards a European Civil Code*, 2nd ed., Nijmegen and The Hague, London, Boston 1998, pp. 191 ff

Salomons, A.F., 'Inpassen of aanpassen? Vermogensrecht voor het digitale tijdperk', *WPNR* 6427 (2000), p. 901 ff

Samuel, Geoffrey, Rinkes, Jac, *The English law of obligations in comparative context*, Nijmegen 1992

Scalia, Antonin, *A Matter of Interpretation; Federal Courts and the Law*, Princeton 1997

Schellen, J. van, 'Het recht der Werkelijkheid', in: Th.M. de Boer et al., *De werkelijkheid van I. Henri Hijmans; symposium gehouden op 23 oktober 1988*, Deventer 1988, p. 57 ff

Schilfgaarde, P. van, 'Deel 4 van Hesselink', *WPNR* 6377 (1999), pp. 811 ff

Schlechtriem, P., *Good Faith in German Law and in International Uniform Law*, Saggi, conferenze e seminari 24; Centro di studi e ricerche di diritto comparato e straniero, diretto da M.J. Bonell, Roma 1997

Schlesinger, Rudolf B. (ed.), *Formation of contracts, a study of the common core of legal systems*, New York 1968

Schilfgaarde, P. van, 'Uitleg van rechtshandelingen', *WPNR* 6282-6283 (1997), pp. 587-592, pp. 611-615

Schmidt, Jürgen, § 242, *J. von Staudingers Kommentar zum Bürgerlichen Gesetzbuch mit Einführungsgesetz und Nebengesetzen; Zweites Buch Recht der Schuldverhältnisse; Einleitung zu §§ 241ff; §§ 241-243*, Berlin 1995

Scholten, Paul, *Mr. C. Asser's handleiding tot de beoefening van het Nederlands burgerlijk recht; Algemeen Deel*, Zwolle 1974 (first edition 1931)

Scholten, Paul, 'De codificatie-gedachte vóór honderd jaar en thans', in: Paul Scholten & E.M. Meijers (eds.), *Gedenkboek Burgerlijk Wetboek 1838-1938*, Zwolle 1938, 1 ff.

Schoordijk, H.C.F., *Het algemeen gedeelte van het verbintenissenrecht naar het Nieuw Burgerlijk Wetboek*, Deventer 1979

Schoordijk, H.C.F., *De Nederlandse rechtscultuur vergeleken met de Anglo-Amerikaanse; Rede uitgesproken bij de aanvaarding van de buitenlandse Fransquileerstoel 1987-1988 in de aula van de Universitaire Instellingen Antwerpen (Wilrijk) op 11 maart 1988*, Antwerpen, Zwolle 1989

Schoordijk, H.C.F., *Redelijkheid en billijkheid aan de vooravond van een nieuw millennium*, Zwolle 1996

Schoordijk, H.C.F., 'Een en ander over dogmatiek, constructie en (hun betekenis voor het) onderwijs', in: *J.L.P. Cahen bundel*, Deventer 1997

Schoordijk, H.C.F., 'Het einde van het recht der werkelijkheid?', *WPNR* 6444 (2001), p. 449

Schulze, Reiner, 'Gemeineuropäisches Privatrecht und Rechtsgeschichte', in Peter-Christian Müller-Graff (ed.), *Gemeinsames Privatrecht in der Europäischen Gemeinschaft*, Baden-Baden 1993.

Scotton, Manola, 'Directive 99/44/EC on certain aspects of the sale consumer goods and associated guarantees', 9 *ERPL* 2001, pp 143-153

Sefton-Green, Ruth, *La notion d'obligation fondamentale: comparaison franco-anglaise*, Paris 2000

Sefton-Green, Ruth, '*Compare and contrast*: monstre à deux têtes', *Global Jurist Advances*: Vol: No. 3, Article 1 (www.bepress.com/gj/advances/vol1/iss3/art1)

Sefton-Green, Ruth (ed.), *Mistake, fraud and duties to inform in European contract law*, Cambridge (forthcoming)

Shapiro, Martin, 'The Common Core: Some Outside Comments', in: Mauro Bussani, Ugo Mattei (eds.), *Making European Private Law; Essays on the "Common Core' Project"*, Trento 2000

Smits, J., *Het vertrouwensbeginsel en de contractuele gebondenheid*, Arnhem 1995

Smits, Jan, 'Privaatrecht en postmodernisme; Over recht en tijdsgeest, toegelicht aan de hand van enige civielrechtelijke fenomenen', *R&K* 1997, p. 155 ff.

Smits, Jan, 'Eenheid en verscheidenheid in het contractenrecht; Over het gedetermineerde verleden en de postmoderne toekomst van het privaatrecht', *R&R* 1998, p. 10 ff

Smits, J.M., 'Een Europees privaatrecht als gemengd rechtsstelsel', *NJB* 1998, p. 61

Smits, J.M., *Europees Privaatrecht in wording: naar een Ius Commune Europaeum als gemengd rechtsstelsel*, Antwerpen/Groningen 1999

Smits, Jan M., *The Good Samaritan in European Private Law; On the Perils of Principles without a Programme and a Programme for the Future*, Deventer 2000

Smits, J.M., 'Naar een nieuw Europees consumentenkooprecht; Over de Europese richtlijn verkoop van en garanties voor consumentengoederen in het Nederlandse recht', *NJB* 2000, p. 1825f

Smits, J.M., 'De Principles of European Contract Law en Common Law en Civil Law', *WPNR* 6436 (2001), p. 235 ff

Smits, Jan, *The Making of European Private Law; Towards a Ius Commune Europaeum as a Mixed Legal System*, Antwerp, Oxford, New York 2002

Snijders, W., 'The organisation of the drafting of a European Civil Code: a walk in imaginary gardens', *ERPL* 1997, p. 483 ff.

Snijders, W., 'Boekbespreking', *WPNR* 6376 (1999), p. 792 ff

Soergel Bürgerliches Gesetzbuch mit Einführungsgesetz und Nebengesetzen, 13th ed., Berlin, Köln, Mainz 1999)

Spier, Jaap (ed.), *The Limits of Expanding Liability; Eight Fundamental Cases in a Comparative Perspective* (in: Jaap Spier, Helmut Koziol (eds.) *Principles of European Tort Law Series*), Dordrecht 1998

Spier, Jaap (ed.), *Unification of Tort Law: Causation* (in: Jaap Spier, Helmut Koziol (eds.) *Principles of European Tort Law,* Volume IV), Dordrecht 2000

Starck, B., *Droit civil, Les obligations*, 2. contrat, 3rd ed. by H. Roland and L. Boyer, Paris, 1989

Stathopoulos, Michael P., *Contract law in Hellas*, The Hague-London-Boston/ Athens 1995

Stein, Peter (ed.), *Incontro di studio su: Il futoro codice europeo dei contratti*, Milano 1993

Stolp, M.M., 'De bevoegdheid tot ontbinding ex art. 6:265 lid 1 BW in het licht van subsidiariteit en proportionaliteit', *NTBR* 2000, p. 352 ff

Summers, Robert S., 'How Law is Formal and Why it Matters', in: Robert S. Summers, *The Jurisprudence of Law's Form and Substance*, Hampshire 2000

Tallon, Denis, 'Redazione del Codice europeo e necessità di rifarsi alle più valide esperienze normative', in: Peter Stein (ed.), *Incontro di studio su: Il futoro codice europeo dei contratti*, Milano 1993, p. 148 ff

Tallon, Denis, 'The new Dutch Civil Code in a comparative perspective - French view-point', 1 *ERPL* 1993, p. 189 ff

Teichmann, A., §242, Bürgerliches Gesetzbuch mit Einführungsgesetz und Nebengesetzen, *Band 2 Schuldrecht I* (§§ 241-610), 12th ed., Stuttgart/Berlin/Köln 1990

Terré, François, Simler, Philippe, Lequette, Yves, *Droit civil, Les obligations*, 6th ed, Paris 1996

Teubner, Gunther, *Global Law Without a State*, Dartmouth, Ardershot etc. 1997

Teubner, Gunther, 'Legal Irritants: Good Faith in British Law or How Unifying Law Ends Up in New Divergences', *MLR* 1998, p. 11 ff.

Tjittes, R.P.J.L., *De hoedanigheid van contractspartijen; Een rechtsvergelijkend onderzoek naar de betekenis van de (onderlinge) hoedanigheid van partijen voor de totstandkoming en de vaststelling van de inhoud van rechtshandelingen*, Deventer 1994

Tjittes, R.P.J.L., *Bezwaarde verwanten* (inaugural lecture *VU*), Deventer 1996

Tjittes, R.P.J.L., 'Naar een bijzonder contractenrecht voor ondernemers', in Onderneming en 5 jaar Nieuw Burgerlijk Recht, Deventer 1997, p. 375 ff.
Tjittes, Rieme-Jan, 'Zaken zijn zaken', RM Themis 2000, p. 321-322
Touffait, Adolphe, Tunc, André, 'Pour une motivation plus explicite des décisions de justice notamment de celles de la Cour de cassation', *R.T.D. civ.*1974, p. 487 ff
Trabucchi, Alberto, *Istituzioni di Diritto Civile*, 40th ed., Padova 2001
Treitel, G.H., *Remedies for Breach of Contract*, Oxford 1988
Treitel, G.H., *The Law of Contract*, 10th ed., London 1999
Twining, William, *Karl Llewellyn and the Realist Movement*, London 1973
Twining, William, *Law in Context; Enlarging a Discipline*, Oxford 1997
Twining, William, *Globalisation & Legal Theory*, Butterworths, London, Edinburgh, Dublin 2000

Vanderlinden, Jacques, *Comparer les droits*, Brussels, 1995, pp. 227-304
Van Gerven, Walter, 'Coherence and National Laws; Is There a Legal Basis for a European Civil Code?', *ERPL* 1997, p. 465 ff
Van Gerven, Walter, 'The ECJ Case-law as a Means of Unification of Private Law?', in: *Towards a European Civil Code*, 2nd ed., Nijmegen and The Hague/London/Boston 1998, pp. 91 ff
Van Gerven, W., 'L'harmonisation du droit des contrats en Europe; Rapport introductif', in : Christophe Jamin, Denis Mazeaud (eds.), *L'harmonisation du droit des contrats en Europe*, Paris 2001
Van Gerven, Walter, Lever, Jeremy, Larouche, Pierre, Bar, Christian von, Viney, Geneviève, *Cases, Materials and Text on National, Supranational Tort Law; Scope of Protection (Ius Commune Casebooks for the Common Law of Europe)*, Oxford 1998
Veen, T.J., Kop, P.C., (eds.), *Zestig juristen ; Bijdragen tot een beeld van de geschiedenis der Nederlandse rechtswetenschap*, Zwolle 1987
Veen, T.J., *'En voor berisping is hier ruime stof''. Over codificatie van het burgerlijk recht, legistische rechtsbeschouwing en herziening van het Nederlands privaatrecht in de 19de en 20ste eeuw*, Amsterdam 2001
Veldman, Muriel, 'Grenzen aan het recht op nakoming', *WPNR* 6455 (2001), pp. 727-738
Verhulp, Evert, *Vrijheid van meningsuiting van werknemers en ambtenaren*, The Hague 1996
Viney, Geneviève, *Traité de droit civil; Les obligations; Introduction à la responsabilité*, 2nd ed., Paris 1995
Vranken, J.B.M., 'Themis en het vermogensrecht nieuw BW; Naar een inhoudelijke beoordeling van de boeken 3, 5, 6 Nieuw BW', *NJB* 1988, p. 682 ff
Vranken, J.B.M., Nietige overeenkomsten binden tot wat de goede trouw meebrengt, *NJB* 1990, p. 489
Vranken, J.B.M., 'Vertrouwen en rechtszekerheid in het overeenkomstenrecht', in: *Vertrouwensbeginsel en rechtszekerheid,*

Preadviezen Vereniging voor de vergelijkende studie van het recht van België en Nederland, Deventer 1997

Vranken, J.B.M., 'De radicale vernieuwing van het civiele procesrecht in Engeland en Wales', *NJB* 1999, p. 1879 ff

Vranken, J.B.M. 'Over partijautonomie, contractsvrijheid en de grondslag van gebondenheid in het verbintenissenrecht' in: J.M. Barendrecht, M.A.B. Chao-Duivis and H.A.W. Vermeulen (eds.), *Beginselen van contractenrecht: Opstellen aangeboden aan B.W.M. Nieskens-Isphording*, Deventer 2000

Vries, Gerard J.P. de, 'Are The Principles Of European Contract Law Better Than Dutch Contract Law?' in: M.W. Hesselink, G.J.P. De Vries, *Principles of European Contract Law; Preadviezen uitgebracht voor de Vereniging voor Burgerlijk Recht*, Deventer 2001, p. 107 ff.

Waelbroeck, Michel, Stuyck, Jules, 'Competition law in the European Community', in: Floris O.W. Vogelaar, *Competition Law in the EU and the Netherlands*, Deventer 2000, pp. 11-150

Watson, Alan 'Legal Transplants and European Private Law', in: Hesselink, Hondius, Smits, Stijns eds., *Ius Commune Lectures on European Private Law*, no. 2, Maastricht 2000

Weiler, J.H.H., *The Constitution of Europe; "Do the New Clothes Have an Emperor?" and Other Essays on European Integration*, Cambridge 1999

Weir, Tony, 'Die Sprachen des europäischen Rechts; Eine skeptische Betrachtung', *ZeuP* 1995, p. 368 ff.

White, G. Edward, 'The American Law Institute and the Triumph of Modernist Jurisprudence', *Law and History Review* (1997) Vol. 16, p. 1

White, Morton, *Social Thought in America: the Revolt Against Formalism*, Boston 1957

Whittaker, Simon, Zimmermann, Reinhard, 'Good faith in European contract law: surveying the legal landscape', in: Reinhard Zimmermann & Simon Whittaker (eds.), *Good Faith in European Contract Law*, Cambridge 2000, pp. 7-62

Whittaker, Simon, Zimmermann, Reinhard, 'Coming to terms with good faith', in: Reinhard Zimmermann & Simon Whittaker (eds.), *Good Faith in European Contract Law*, Cambridge 2000, p. 699

Wiarda, G.J., *Drie typen van rechtsvinding*, 3rd ed. 1988

Wieacker, F., *Zur Rechtstheoretischen Präzisierung des § 242*, in: *Recht und Staat in Geschichte und Gegenwart; Eine Sammlung von Vorträgen und Schriften aus dem Gebiet der gesamten Staatswissenschaft 193/194*, Tübingen 1956

Wilhelmsson, Thomas, *Social Contract Law and European Integration*, Dartmouth, Aldershot 1995

Wilhelmsson, Thomas, 'Standard Form Conditions', in: A.S. Hartkamp et al. (eds.) *Towards a European Civil Code*, 2nd ed., Nijmegen and The Hague/London/Boston 1998, pp. 255 ff

Wilhelmsson, Thomas, 'Private Law in the EU: Harmonised or Fragmented Europeanisation?', 10 *ERPL* 2002, pp. 77-94

Wissink, M.W., *Richtlijnconforme interpretatie van burgerlijk recht*, Deventer 2001

Wolf, Manfred, Horn, Norbert, Lindacher, Walter F., *AGB-Gesetz Kommentar*, München 1999

Würtenberger, Thomas (ed.), *Rechtswissenschaft und Soziologie; Ausgewählte Schriften zur Wissenschaftslehre von Hermann Kantorowicz*, Karlsruhe 1962

Yntema, Hessel E., 'What Should The American Law Institute Do?', 34 Michigan Law Review (1936) 461-473.

Zeno-Zencovich, Vincenzo, 'The "European Civil Code", European Legal Traditions and Neo-positivism', in Guido Alpa, Emilio Nicola Buccico (eds.), *Il codice civile europeo; Materiali dei seminari 1999-2000*, Milano 2001, pp. 375 ff

Zeno-Zencovich, Vincenzo, 'Le basi constituzionali di un diritto privato europeo' (forthcoming; presented at the conference *Diritti fondamentali e formazione del diritto privato europeo* in Rome on June 28th, 2002)

Zimmermann, Reinhard, 'Civil Code and Civil Law- The "Europeanization" sof Private Law within the European Community and the Re-Emergency of a European Legal Science', *The Columbia Journal of European Law*, 1995, pp. 63ff

Zimmermann, Reinhard, '"Common law" und "civil law", Amerika und Europa', in Reinhard Zimmermann (ed.), *Amerikanische Rechtskultur und europäisches Privatrecht*, Tübingen 1995

Zimmermann, Reinhard, *The Law of Obligations*, Oxford 1996

Zimmermann, Reinhard, 'Roman Law and European Legal Unity', in: A.S. Hartkamp et al. (eds.) *Towards a European Civil Code*, 2nd ed., Nijmegen and The Hague/London/Boston 1998, pp. 21 ff

Zimmermann, Reinhard, *Roman Law, Contemporary Law, European Law; The Civilian Tradition Today*, Oxford 2001

Zimmermann, Reinhard, Visser, Daniel (eds.), *Southern Cross; Civil Law and Common Law in South Africa*, Oxford 1996

Zimmermann, Reinhard, Whittaker, Simon, *Good Faith in European Contract Law*, Cambridge 2000

Zweigert, K., Kötz, H., *Einführung in die Rechtsvergleichung*, 3rd ed., Tübingen 1996.

Zweigert, Konrad, Kötz, Hein, *Introduction to Comparative Law*, 3rd ed., Oxford 1998

Zwemmer, J.W., 'De bachelor-masterstructuur', 50 *AA* (2001), p. 240 ff

Index

www.ingramcontent.com/pod-product-compliance
Lightning Source LLC
LaVergne TN
LVHW020642300926
849161LV00004B/780
9789041119629